The al-Qaeda Franchise

The al-Qaeda Franchise

The Expansion of al-Qaeda and Its Consequences

BARAK MENDELSOHN

OXFORD
UNIVERSITY PRESS

OXFORD
UNIVERSITY PRESS

Oxford University Press is a department of the University of
Oxford. It furthers the University's objective of excellence in research,
scholarship, and education by publishing worldwide.
Oxford is a registered trade mark of Oxford University Press
in the UK and in certain other countries

Published in the United States of America by Oxford University Press
198 Madison Avenue, New York, NY 10016, United States of America

Cataloging-in-Publication data is on file at the Library of Congress
ISBN 978–0–19–020560–7 (hbk.); 978–0–19–020561–4 (pbk.)

1 3 5 7 9 8 6 4 2
Printed in the United States of America
on acid-free paper

*In loving memory of Ilan Mendelsohn
and Catherine Marie Stringer*

Contents

Acknowledgements

GRADUATE SCHOOL WAS a place for many remarkable revelations, but perhaps the most important one came from my mentor and friend Peter Katzenstein, who encouraged us to ask why and to challenge and problematize what appears self-evident at first look. This book is the result of his advice. Rather than simply accept al-Qaeda's branching-out as an obvious move, I was eager to identify what drives the specific form of the group's organizational expansion. In the process I learned new and important things about terrorist groups in general and al-Qaeda in particular.

While this book was in my head for years, the bulk of it was written during a particularly fruitful sabbatical at Harvard's Kennedy School. I wish to thank Steve Walt, Steve Miller, and Sean Lynn-Jones, as well as the fellows in the Belfer Center's International Security Program (ISP) for their valuable feedback and for creating an environment so conducive to research and intellectual exchange.

I count myself blessed to work in a community of brilliant scholars who are dedicated to the study of the jihadi movement. I have gained tremendously from the work of many colleagues. I am especially grateful to Will McCants, Thomas Hegghammer, Aaron Zelin, Clint Watts, Nelly Lahoud, J. M. Berger, and Leah Farrall for their assistance, responding to queries I sent them as I was struggling to fill information gaps. My friend and colleague Assaf Moghadam contributed important feedback on the book's theoretical chapters, and Ronit Berger enriched the work with her own expertise.

This book would not have been possible without the support of Haverford College and my colleagues there, as well as Haverford's library staff, particularly the wonderful Margaret Schaus. I would like to express my immense gratitude to my students, particularly those who took my course on the evolution of the jihadi movement. Through their queries and comments they forced me to think hard about the question of al-Qaeda's expansion, refine my arguments, and clarify my analysis. I am also grateful to my research assistants who constructed the Al-Qaeda Statement Index over the past few years: Matthew Cebul, Carrie Clowney, Rupinder Garcha, Katie Drooyan, Hannah Jaenicke, Rose Kautz, Harry Levin, Nick Lotito, Ryan Rubio, Nick Sher, and Rob Williams. I am particularly indebted to Jack Hasler, Gabrielle LoGaglio, and Rachel Miller for providing research for this book.

My dear friend Matthew Budman did a remarkable job editing this book and making it readable without losing my voice in the process. Ashly Bennett offered much needed support, while my mother Varda Mendelsohn, brother Amit, and sister Inbal rooted for me from afar. The writing of this book would not have been possible without all of them.

This book is dedicated to my father Ilan Mendelsohn and my wife Catherine Stringer who passed too soon as I was just starting my work. I wish they were here to watch the book completed. Cambridge MA. 2015

Abbreviations

AQAP	al-Qaeda in the Arabian Peninsula
AQC	al-Qaeda Central
AQI	al-Qaeda in Iraq
AQIM	al-Qaeda in the Islamic Maghreb
AQIS	al-Qaeda in the Indian Subcontinent
EIJ	Egyptian Islamic Jihad
GI	Gama'a Islamiya
GIA	Groupe Islamique Armé, or Armed Islamic Group
GSPC	Groupe Salafiste Pour la Prédication et le Combat, or Salafist Group for Preaching and Combat
ICU	Islamic Courts Union
IS	The Islamic State
ISI	Islamic State of Iraq
ISIS	Islamic State of Iraq and al-Sham (also ISIL)
JAA	Jund Ansar Allah
JI	Jema'a Islamiya
JN	Jabhat al-Nusra
LIFG	Libyan Islamic Fighting Group
MSC	Mujahideen Shura Council
TFG	Transnational Federal Government
TWJ	al-Tawhid wal-Jihad

I

Introduction

IN AUGUST 2013, growing chatter in al-Qaeda communication channels—echoing the talk preceding the 9/11 attacks—led the United States to close about two dozen embassies and consulates, predominantly in the Middle East and North Africa.[1] After a week in which the terrorist threat dominated the news, the United States reopened nearly all its diplomatic posts. It is unclear whether the attack failed to materialize because the intelligence was wrong, a blitz of drone attacks in Yemen thwarted it, or the official warning led al-Qaeda to change its plans. Regardless, the revelations suggested that the organization still constituted an ongoing threat to the West, years after American leaders had assured the public that the threat has significantly declined.

Since taking office, but especially after the May 2011 killing of al-Qaeda leader Osama bin Laden, the Obama administration sought to promote a message that the terrorist organization was essentially defunct; this message helped justify the winding down of the still-unresolved military campaigns in Iraq and Afghanistan. Although the continuing (and even expanding) use of drones and National Security Agency (NSA) surveillance apparatus indicated that the United States was hardly relaxing its anti-terrorism efforts, downplaying the threat would allow a shift to counterterrorism with a much lighter footprint. The administration's message also resonated with President Obama's political needs: with much of the American public unimpressed with his stewardship of the economy, the president could at least present achievements in the security realm. Against this background, the embassies scare put the administration's previous claims under close scrutiny and reignited the debate about al-Qaeda's true status, the magnitude of the threat, and the measures required to effectively confront it.

A shadowy organization, al-Qaeda is not easy to decipher. Despite the investment of enormous resources, information gaps regularly hinder

American experts' attempts to fully understand the group. Particularly confounding is al-Qaeda's formal expansion, the subject at the heart of this book. Since 2003, the group has introduced branches throughout the Muslim world, beginning in Saudi Arabia, Osama bin Laden's homeland. Al-Qaeda moved on to establish branches in Iraq (2004), Algeria (2006), Yemen (2009), Somalia (circa 2010), Syria (2012), and the Indian subcontinent (2014).

Understanding al-Qaeda's franchising is a precondition to comprehending the threat it constitutes and formulating an effective confrontation strategy. The organization's continuing expansion may create the impression that, 14 years after the 9/11 attack and despite the relentless US campaign to destroy the group, al-Qaeda is as strong as ever and poses an even graver threat. Indeed, this is the image that al-Qaeda's leadership hopes to nurture.[2] But the real picture is more complicated.

This book explores al-Qaeda's franchising strategy and its particular expansion choices. I propose that the organization's weakening position was a central factor driving its leaders to expand via franchising. I also aim to debunk the notion that having franchises necessarily indicates that al-Qaeda poses a greater level of threat to the international community than it did pre–9/11, or even before its expansion efforts. To some extent, franchising neither increased the threat nor enhanced al-Qaeda's political objectives—the strategy actually incurred heavy costs.

Accurately understanding the threat is important for shaping US and Western foreign policy. First, if al-Qaeda poses a lesser threat and its central leadership is in disarray, the importance of deploying US and NATO forces in Afghanistan declines. Second, the tendency of franchises to become entangled in local conflicts distracts from the organization's general objectives and the threat to US interests, making confronting those franchises a lower priority. Third, the friction between the group's central command and some of its affiliates opens new avenues for counterterrorism, relying less on the use of force and thus reducing collateral damage among locals in areas where al-Qaeda is embedded. Finally, as al-Qaeda is just one of several terrorist threats facing the United States, the government must contemplate how its actions against the group might affect other interests, particularly the fight against the Islamic State of Iraq and al-Sham (ISIS). Al-Qaeda's stubborn persistence hinders the quest of the self-styled caliphate to dominate the jihadi scene, inadvertently serving American interests. But al-Qaeda's position as a bulwark against ISIS is fragile and largely dependent on the mechanisms of the oath of allegiance (*bay'a*) between branch leaders and al-Qaeda chief Ayman al-Zawahiri. Thus, the United States must consider how its preferred counterterrorism tool—assassination by drone—might affect the surging ISIS threat, given that killing al-Zawahiri or the heads of franchises could push these affiliates into the arms of ISIS.

With this book, I seek to elevate the discussion about the al-Qaeda threat through problematizing the group's expansion. A first step is to acknowledge that the organization's branching out is a puzzling development—neither a trivial course of action for the organization nor an inevitable outgrowth of its ideology. For many years, al-Qaeda declared its primary mission to be inciting the Muslim public to action, making formal organizational expansion merely one possible strategy in a large set of available options geared toward broad recruitment and mobilization. Moreover, expansion diverged from al-Qaeda's earlier efforts to enhance its standing within the jihadi camp, including the 1998 establishment of a front—the World Islamic Front for Jihad Against Jews and Crusaders—that brought several jihadi organizations under one umbrella. The efforts to create local franchises are also bewildering because they have undermined one of al-Qaeda's signal achievements: the creation of a transnational entity based on religious, not national, affiliation. Although the group's ideology remains transnational and franchising could spread it, segmenting the effort risks reverting to the era of national-based Islamist resistance that al-Qaeda has always decried.

One may also question the timing of al-Qaeda's franchising strategy. The small group of Arab jihadis who founded the organization in 1988 were determined to preserve the spirit of jihad, or holy war, that Afghanistan's Soviet occupation had rekindled, and to utilize the human resources, infra-structure, and knowledge acquired through a decade of war. But al-Qaeda waited 15 years to introduce its first branch. It could have launched franchises immediately after 9/11—its biggest operational success—but instead waited until 2003.

Thus, this book asks why al-Qaeda adopted a branching-out strategy for its formal expansion rather than one of the alternative arrangements available: absorption, unification, and umbrella group. I also examine al-Qaeda's particular expansion choices. Why did it form branches in some arenas but not others? And why did its expansion in some locations, such as Yemen, take the form of in-house franchising—with branches run by al-Qaeda's own fighters—whereas in locations such as Iraq and Somalia, it merged with groups already operating in the target arena? Finally, the book aims to highlight the various ways in which al-Qaeda's expansion seriously harmed, rather than strengthened, the organization.

Why Study al-Qaeda's Branching-Out Strategy?

I emphasize the question of formal affiliation because it bears unique qualities that studies of al-Qaeda have so far largely neglected. When al-Qaeda announces the establishment of a new franchise, it is not simply making an operational choice—it is making a political statement. After all, the organization has various ways to make known its presence in an arena, including the most basic way: by carrying out terrorist attacks. Moreover, al-Qaeda can operate in an arena without designating a formal name for its operatives in the arena. Even when organizational considerations lead a terrorist group to organize its assets based on territorial division, the group need not announce the internal shift; al-Qaeda could keep its territory-based reorganizations quiet. Indeed, maintaining secrecy seems reasonable, given terrorists' constant need to evade state counterterrorism efforts. In fact, one would be hard pressed to recall occasions in which a terrorist organization felt compelled to release information about its structure to its enemies and to the general public. In addition, the record shows that al-Qaeda has operated in numerous locations—for example, Europe and Turkey—without publicly presenting a franchise.

The availability of alternatives suggests that publicly naming and announcing a branch is meaningful. To some extent, one may see it as a statement of advancement, perhaps a substitution for the higher bar of controlling territory; announcing a new franchise can also substitute, at least for some time, for carrying out terrorist attacks. In advancing a narrative of progress, it signals to the international community that the parent organization is on the march. Moreover, by gradually declaring its franchises, al-Qaeda has strengthened its ability to remain in the headlines, even at times when its operational capabilities have not matched its public profile.

Where al-Qaeda has sited its branches is also meaningful. When the organization declares that it has a branch in a certain location, it signals greater interest and a stronger commitment to that arena. Additionally, since not all jihad arenas are equally significant in a religious or strategic sense, the presence or absence of an official al-Qaeda franchise can be particularly important. Once the United States invaded Iraq in 2003, al-Qaeda's ability to present a local franchise became important for signaling to both the organization's foes and friends that it was serious about meeting its archenemy on the battlefield. Similarly, launching a branch in Saudi Arabia reflected the country's unique importance as the cradle of Islam and the host of its two holiest sites; it was also compatible with the country's place atop al-Qaeda's list of anti-American grievances.

Investigating al-Qaeda's franchising strategy is also important for international-relations theory. This case represents a useful starting point for exploring formal organizational expansion among transnational terrorist organizations. After all, although al-Qaeda has captured headlines for nearly two decades, there were other radical groups, such as the pan-Central Asian group Islamic Movement of Uzbekistan,[3] the South Asian Lashkar e-Taibe,[4] and the largely defunct Southeast Asian Jema'a Islamiya,[5] that expanded their political goals beyond one national arena and had to contemplate an organizational strategy. Perhaps the most vivid illustration of the expansion of transnational terrorist groups is the Islamic State (also known as ISIS, or ISIL), a group controlling vast territory in Iraq and Syria and spreading tentacles to additional countries in the Middle East, North Africa, and Central Asia. These examples and the context of growing challenges to the Westphalian state in an age of globalization and unprecedented interdependence, as well as the growing appeal of non-nationalist—including trans-boundary—identification markers, strongly suggest that the al-Qaeda case likely signals a prevalent trend in terrorism.

Framed more broadly, we should ask why a terrorist organization would seek to expand through the introduction of formal branches when alternatives exist. After all, an organization can maintain or increase its power through operational measures such as increasing its operational tempo, expanding its logistical infrastructure to new locations, and carrying out attacks beyond its original zone of activity. It need not present its forces as constituting formal branches. Moreover, even given that an organization has chosen to expand via formal organizational extension rather than operational growth, we need to explain why it would elect to introduce franchises when other organizational strategies are available. For instance, ISIS has expanded through the absorption of other groups, forcing their disbanding and the erasure of their independent identities as it incorporated them into its structure, and in 2013, several Syrian opposition groups established a looser framework of an umbrella group that they named the Islamic Front. Al-Qaeda itself is no stranger to different operational arrangements: a few months before 9/11, the Egyptian Islamic Jihad struck an agreement with the group that, at least rhetorically, implied integration between two equal partners.

As the al-Qaeda case reveals, the adoption of a branching-out strategy is only part of the puzzle. Scholars of terrorism should explore subsequent choices as well, including the arenas that terrorists target for franchising, the conditions under which they enter particular arenas, the pace of branching out, and the organizational form that franchises take (mergers or in-house creations). By studying organizational expansion, scholars can observe the consequences of each path to expansion, better understand terrorist leaders' decision-making, and gain insights into their ability to innovate and learn.

Formal Expansion

How do we define *formal organizational expansion*? The term refers to the reorganization of a terrorist group through publicly announced structural changes, involving formal relationships with other groups (or with organization-like factions within the group). Although any such strategic reorientation has operational ramifications—that is, it affects the ability of the organization to carry out attacks—these consequences are byproducts of a primarily political move.

Indeed, what makes formal expansion—whether through forging a relationship between organizations or through founding official franchises in new areas—distinct from solely operational measures is its political nature. Terrorist organizations seeking to enhance their capabilities can adopt mutually beneficial cooperative measures short of organizational affiliation: they can rely on each other's logistical cells to move around arms, funds, and operatives; they can even launch joint attacks. But they need not take the dramatic step of establishing, and announcing, a formal relationship. To understand the reasons that a group would opt to formally expand, we must look beyond simple operational considerations and unlock the move's political purpose. Formal expansion sends a political message to distinct audiences, including state enemies, rival and competing violent and nonviolent non-state organizations, sympathizers, and uncommitted publics.

Formal expansion should be seen as an effort to shape an organization's strategic environment, not only through terrorist acts, but also through shaping perceptions of power, intent, and resolve; in a way, it is part of a broader propaganda effort. Terrorism has always taken place in the context of asymmetric conflict: whether primarily expressive, as in the "propaganda of the deed," or, as is often the case, an attempt to gain political concessions through fear, terrorism is an exercise in overcoming power disparity through coercive communication. The revolution in communication technology has only increased the importance of shaping public perceptions through propaganda; it enables reaching a much larger audience more quickly. Moreover, in contrast to the past, when terrorists needed to rely on traditional media to broadcast their message, twenty-first-century terrorist organizations can communicate directly with targeted audiences. These changes have led terrorist groups to put greater emphasis on propaganda: al-Qaeda and other groups focus as much on their media products as on terrorist operations; they establish media production and distribution arms, and they invest immense energies in sharpening their use as political tools. Publicly expanding therefore represents more than a new policy announcement with tangible operational manifestation—it is a political message.

This book does not assume that branching out is the obvious move for a transnational terrorist organization seeking expansion. By problematizing the introduction of branches, I underscore the fact that franchising is a choice, a strategy that an organization selects instead of alternatives. Only when conceiving of branching out as one of several strategies for formal organizational expansion can we gain a comprehensive understanding of the reasons al-Qaeda has been introducing franchises, the specific message accompanying its expansion efforts, and the consequences of these expansions.

In addition to variations in the political statements associated with each expansion, formal organizational arrangements have different structural manifestations. Dissimilar arrangements exhibit different levels of hierarchy and institutionalization: hierarchy concerns the authority relations between the different actors participating in the organizational arrangement; institutionalization refers to the depth of actors' commitment to an arrangement and its permanency.

Hierarchy, institutionalization, and political signaling can each take a range of values. Hierarchy is manifested in the level of equality (or inequality) between the participators in the organizational arrangement. The institutionalization factor ranges from a very elaborate arrangement that fully suppresses actors' prior organizational structures and identities until their rejuvenation becomes impossible to a loose relationship that preserves the organizations' independence and could be severed with relative ease. Similarly, inter-organizational association can send a minimal message of political solidarity in the face of a shared enemy, but it can also signal an actor's exuberant self-confidence, power and dominance over other organizations, commitment to certain political order, interest in a particular arena, and declaration that change is imminent.

The combination of different political signals and levels of hierarchy and institutionalization create multiple types of inter-organizational arrangements. I identify four main configurations, or ideal types: the absorption model, the branching-out model, the integration model, and the umbrella group (or front) model.

In the absorption model, an organization expands across borders without dividing arenas politically. Its association with other actors is based on its complete dominance, and the organizations that join it get swallowed, losing their corporal structure and identity. Such an arrangement signals the expanding organization's great political ambition, as well as its preponderance of power and/or wide ideological appeal. This is the mode of expansion that the Islamic State has chosen.

Branching out, the strategy that al-Qaeda adopted in 2003, is based on creating a two-tier structure with a central command and, below it, branches, each responsible for a particular geographical area. While the center sets ideological orientation and concomitant broad political goals and the strategy to realize them, the affiliates have considerable organizational and operational autonomy. By introducing franchises, a transnational terrorist organization strongly communicates its intentions as well as confidence in its ability to bring change to the selected arenas. The group's leaders hope to encourage other groups and potential supporters to join, while signaling to enemy states the urgency of compliance or the risk of escalation or public backlash. Branching out reflects a more flexible approach to other groups. In contrast to the absorption model's one-size-fits-all rigidity, franchising allows flexibility by recognizing the unique context of dissimilar arenas, the appeal of local autonomy, and affiliate groups' reluctance to disband.

In the unification model, terrorist organizations enter into a power-sharing agreement, emphasizing equality rather than hierarchy. At the same time, the contracting groups aim at high level of institutionalization by creating a leadership structure in which members of both groups assume leadership positions and meaningful roles in decision-making. In entering such an agreement, the merging organizations signal the compatibility of their ideology and objectives, and their willingness to forgo primacy for the sake of promoting a political agenda.

Finally, the umbrella-group model, also referred to in this book as the front model, refers to a loose organizational arrangement between two or more independent terrorist groups. Although they come together, thus highlighting a shared cause, each retains its identity, internal structure, and a broad set of political objectives, some of which other groups may not share. As I will discuss in Chapter 4, in 1998 al-Qaeda initiated the establishment of the World Islamic Front for Jihad Against Jews and Crusaders as an umbrella group.

While this book presents a typology of arrangements for formal organizational expansion among transnational terrorist groups, it is also important to clarify what it does not aim to do: introduce a general theory of organizational expansion. I elected to adopt this limited approach for three reasons. The first concerns the underdeveloped state of scholarly research on the relationship between terrorist organizations. The academic enterprise normally advances piecemeal—a theory is introduced and then refined, based on examination of its internal logics and how well it matches the empirical record. Unfortunately, with scholars of terrorism only beginning to explore the dynamics of inter-organizational relations, it is necessary to begin by introducing building blocks for a theory.

Furthermore, the complexity of disentangling an organization's strategic logic from the ideological and organizational considerations that may guide its choices magnifies the problem of theory building. The literature on terrorism has been plagued by debates about the logic guiding terrorist actors' operations. As I discuss in Chapter 3, I do not find this debate particularly fruitful. Although in some exceptional cases we may be able to identify a dominant logic guiding an actor's behavior, terrorists often follow strategic, organizational, and ideological interests simultaneously. Moreover, many times the different logics are indistinguishable—for example, policies that advance a group's strategic objectives will almost always enhance its organizational interests as well. Actions that serve an organization's survival needs but that at first sight do not appear to strictly follow its ideological convictions may still serve ideological objectives by allowing the group to pursue its ideology at a more opportune time. Thus, instead of pitting the strategic, ideological, and organizational logics against each other, I aim to show how different factors interact and to articulate the conditions under which a transnational organization may adopt a particular expansion strategy and not another.

Second, the distinction between transnational terrorist organizations and state-focused terrorist groups introduces additional complexity. Ideally, a single theoretical framework would encompass the choices of organizations in both transnational and local contexts. However, it is unclear that such a unified theory is viable or even desirable, since the different contexts are likely to generate considerable variance in actors' considerations and, consequently, their actions. Terrorists operating within a national context may feel little pressure to unite until they are close to victory or need a united front to increase their bargaining position in negotiations.[6] Actors in a struggle that is limited to one state will likely have fewer and more limited objectives, and as a result, the range of subjects they contest will be smaller and the prospects for inter-organizational association higher. In an international context, on the other hand, whether groups should pursue a national, transnational, or even post-national agenda could be a major obstacle to formal relationships. The considerations of actors in a transnational context also differ from those of national terrorist organizations because operating across borders increases the number of state enemies and could lead to coordinated international military response. When the global community designates certain terrorist organizations as a threat to international peace and security, they may even generate a systemwide response.[7] Transnational groups are also likely to find that states' border-security measures constrain their ability to forge meaningful relationships. No doubt a comparison of the considerations shaping formal expansion in each context is important, but we must wait until completing a thorough study of each context in turn.

The demanding nature of the empirical question that this book sets out to solve is a third reason that I settle for relatively modest theoretical ambitions. A comprehensive study of formal expansion by transnational terrorist organizations would require a comparison between groups and their strategies. But space constraints do not allow both an in-depth analysis of al-Qaeda's organizational expansion and an exhaustive comparison with other organizations that followed alternative strategies. In problematizing al-Qaeda's decision to adopt a strategy of formal expansion and looking at nine specific expansion decisions it made, I accept a trade-off in which the explanation of the group's pursuit of the branching-out model, its choices of arenas for expansion, and the particular form its branches have taken inevitably require neglecting other organizations and conducting a less comprehensive discussion of the absorption, unification, and umbrella-group models.

Terminology and Definitions

The empirical part of this book focuses on a jihadi group, al-Qaeda. What do I mean by *jihadi*? In Arabic, the root of the word *jihad* refers to striving and exerting effort in the service of Allah. The Quran uses it primarily in the sense of fighting a holy war,[8] though it is important to recognize that throughout the ages many Muslims have interpreted jihad in other, nonviolent, ways—for example, one's efforts to better oneself. Jihadis, as referred to in this book, are Muslims who not only understand jihad as fighting but also view it as a central tenet of Islam that most members of the *umma*, the Muslim community, have neglected. It is a duty that these activists labor to revive. By using the term *jihadi*, I do not intend to lend legitimacy to their enterprise—it is merely a way to describe their shared commitment, with the added benefit of distinguishing them from most other Muslim and Islamist groups. In jihadis' eyes, they are "the *mujahideen*," holy warriors seeking to realize God's commands. While I am in no position to judge the legitimacy of their adoption of the term—which would imply judgment regarding what constitutes true Islam—I generally avoid the term in favor of the less charged *jihadi(s)*.

Scholars often refer to jihadis and jihadi groups as *Salafi-jihadis*. This term locates jihadis in the broader Salafi strand of Islam. Salafis aspire to return Islam to its pure form as exercised in the days of the Prophet Muhammad and the first three generations of Muslims, referred to as *salaf*, the pious predecessors. Salafis attribute the decline of the umma to Muslims' departure from the example of the Prophet and the *salaf* and thus believe that strict adherence to the Quran and the *sunna* (oral traditions attributed to Muhammad) would restore the umma to a time of prosperity and glory. Salafis are therefore associated with a puritanical form of Islam based on a literalist reading of its primary sources and the strict implementation of its commands. Their influence is most notable in Saudi Arabia, the cradle of Islam, and its neighboring Gulf countries.

While all jihadis are supposedly adherents of Salafism, not all Salafis are jihadis. Most Salafis are actually "quietist": they reject involvement in politics as a way to bring about change, instead focusing on bottom-up social change brought about by personal piety. Over the years, most notably when Egyptian and Syrian members of the Muslim Brotherhood relocated to Saudi Arabia, a branch of Salafism that incorporated political elements emerged. While largely peaceful, this faction—which Quintan Wiktorowicz dubbed "politicos"—nonetheless sought to affect society's morality in a more top-down manner and to use political means, such as petitions to the Saudi king, to shape how the state promotes Islamic values and behavior.[9]

For our purposes, we can distinguish jihadis from other Salafi strands by their willingness to use violent means and to subvert rulers' authority when their policies are deemed in conflict with Islamic imperatives (as jihadis understand them). Jihadis believe that it is their duty to appropriate the right to use violence when Muslim rulers abandon this obligation in the face of occupation of Muslim lands at the hands of non-Muslims. Jihadis' much more lax approach to *takfir*, excommunication, which puts its targets beyond the pale of Islam and makes shedding their blood permissible, is another significant difference between jihadis and other Salafis. Jihadi groups do not hesitate to denounce rulers of Muslim countries as un-Islamic and advocate violence to remove them. Some jihadis take *takfir* even further, branding states' security forces as apostates and infidels. The most radical elements within the jihadi movement may deem an entire citizenry infidels whose killing is not only legitimate but desirable.

There are also Islamist organizations that use violent means for political objectives but are not considered jihadis. The most notable of these groups are the Palestinian Hamas and the Lebanese Hezbollah. Similar to the jihadi groups at the center of this study, Hamas is a Sunni Muslim group. However, it traces its ideological and historical origins to the Muslim Brotherhood movement, not to Salafism. Most groups associated with the Muslim Brotherhood prioritize nonviolent means. Facing Israel—seen as a foreign occupier and oppressor—Hamas is more receptive than its sister groups to using violence, but it views the tactic principally as a means to serve an end. Violent jihad, though venerated, is understood as only one of several tools to promote political objectives. Unlike al-Qaeda and other jihadi groups, Hamas is open to using democratic means to achieve its objectives, although its Islamist ideology restricts its willingness to accept democratic principles. Hezbollah, on the other hand, is a Shia Muslim organization and therefore, despite the importance it assigns to Islam, ideologically distant from the Sunni jihadi groups. Many jihadi groups even consider the Shia and Hezbollah to be non-Muslims.

Notwithstanding the impression one may get from Western press coverage following the 9/11 attacks, the jihadi movement comprises many groups and individuals, not just al-Qaeda. Indeed, in its early years, al-Qaeda, with only a few dozen members, was one of the smaller jihadi groups. Nevertheless, bin Laden's ambitions were outsized, and he established al-Qaeda as a multinational organization, unlike nearly all other jihadi groups, whose membership is not based on one particular nationality. Others emphasized change in their home countries and prioritized fights against local regimes—the "near enemy"—but al-Qaeda called for systemic change and set its sight on a much bigger target than any one Muslim state. According to its stated ideology, the United States and, more broadly, the West—the "Jewish-Crusader" alliance—are the main obstacle to the umma's return to glory and divinely ordained supremacy. Al-Qaeda maintained that a domineering American empire, the "far enemy," is enslaving the Muslim world with the assistance of corrupt Arab regimes. Because these regimes serve its interests, the United States does not allow the righteous Muslims to topple its lackeys. Consequently, instead of fighting local regimes, jihadis should focus on "cutting the head of the snake." Only by bringing down the United States will Muslims be able to implement God's rule, *sharia*, re-establish the caliphate, and spread the Islamic faith unhindered throughout the world.

In this book, I use the name "al-Qaeda" to refer to the organization at large and to its central leadership, located mostly in the border regions in Afghanistan and Pakistan. It is this leadership that determines the organization's interests and the strategy to promote these interests. Until al-Qaeda began to branch out, its structure was relatively simple: although operatives had considerable freedom in executing terrorist attacks, the organization was fundamentally hierarchical. With the establishment of its franchises, al-Qaeda moved to a two-tier structure with a central command above and branches below. I refer to the central command as al-Qaeda Central (AQC); when I discuss al-Qaeda's interests, I refer to interests as conceived by AQC. To avoid confusion, when I discuss the particular interests of al-Qaeda's branches or their leaders (which in some cases conflict with the interests of the overall organization), I specifically note that.

Over the years, defining al-Qaeda itself has become increasingly problematic. Distortions regularly muddied analysis of the organization, including aspects concerning its expansion. Self-interested actors invoked the name "al-Qaeda" to characterize almost any plot or attack by Islamist groups, or any actor that at some point showed sympathy or had links to al-Qaeda and bin Laden. States and regimes invoked the al-Qaeda threat to attract American support for actions suppressing what would have otherwise been viewed as legitimate dissent or, at worst, localized threats. Irresponsible politicians exaggerated the organization's power to promote radical objectives, justify damaging and immoral policies, and violate democratic procedures. And sensationalist media joined a security industry dependent on expanding defense budgets to further inflate the threat.[10]

The misrepresentations of al-Qaeda's membership have led, naturally, to a mischaracterization of the threat it poses and to hyping the importance and capabilities of groups associated with it, confusing policymakers' efforts. Overall, the looser the conception of the group, the more alarming and less differentiated the portrayal of the threat it poses, and the less likely tailoring a nuanced and effective policy becomes. It is self-defeating in another way: assisting al-Qaeda propagandists in constructing and perpetuating their desired image and mobilizing support[11]—a boost al-Qaeda desperately needed after the overwhelming American response to 9/11 chased the group's remaining leadership into hiding.

It should surprise no one that officeholders and sound-bite pundits have often mischaracterized the al-Qaeda threat. But even among scholars—including people who similarly classify al-Qaeda as an organization—views have varied widely. In some cases, dissimilar definitions of affiliation have led observers to present differing tallies of al-Qaeda's affiliates and, consequently, of the magnitude of the threat.[12]

That even a leading scholar such as Bruce Hoffman, with a justified reputation for accuracy and nuanced reading, used a very broad definition of affiliation[13] indicates that, at least for a period of time, that definition had merit. It allowed scholars and practitioners to understand the greater jihadi universe, the myriad of connections within it, and the multiple roles al-Qaeda played in the jihadi movement as an organization offering resources and strategic guidance, as well as an ideological lighthouse from which groups and individuals drew inspiration.

However, such an expansive conception of affiliation and franchises elides important distinctions between types of relationships. In order to understand formal expansion, a restrictive view of affiliation is essential, viewing as franchising only formal association, rather than any kind of cooperation between al-Qaeda and other terrorist groups. Indeed, al-Qaeda's internal communications support such an approach: documents captured in the raid to kill bin Laden, as well as other material written by important group members, indicate that despite leaders' plans to expand, they were displeased to be automatically linked to other jihadi organizations, especially with groups whose actions deviated from the "correct" path. In fact, leaders worried about observers attributing unsanctioned acts—particularly the indiscriminate use of violence against civilians—to the organization.[14]

Therefore, in this book, "al-Qaeda" refers to the organization's central command (and accompanying apparatus) and to its formal branches. Franchises created through a merger must fulfill three conditions to be recognized as such: first, a pledge of allegiance, bay'a, to al-Qaeda's leader; second, the organization's acceptance of that oath; third, a public announcement of the affiliation. When franchising takes the form of in-house creation—spearheaded by al-Qaeda's own loyal personnel—it is manifested in the introduction of a group of operatives as a distinctive unit, operating in a specific geographic unit and using a distinct name (for example, al-Qaeda in the Arabian Peninsula), while clearly subordinated to the parent organization.

While franchises often use the word "al-Qaeda" in their name—even renaming themselves to include its name (for example, the GSPC became al-Qaeda in the Islamic Maghreb)—this is neither sufficient nor necessary. Al-Qaeda's branch in Somalia retained the name al-Shabab, and former Jema'a Islamiya bomb-maker Noordin Top named his group al-Qaeda for the Malay Archipelago even though al-Qaeda never considered it an affiliate.

In contrast, a public announcement of the relationship by both branch and central command is important because, as emphasized earlier, the act of franchising goes beyond reorganization for operational purposes. It is primarily a political measure designed to shape the strategic environment and communicate political messages to diverse audiences.

Al-Qaeda's Arena Selection

Exploring the reasons that a terrorist organization might adopt a branching-out strategy provides only part of the story. A strategic orientation toward the branching-out model informs the specific affiliation measures al-Qaeda has taken, but the distinct characteristics of these measures must be explored separately. The strategy suggests that al-Qaeda would seek to introduce branches, but it is insufficient as a guide for its choices of arenas, the timing of its entry into particular locations, and the form each franchise has taken. I therefore discuss each of the organization's franchising choices separately. Notwithstanding incomplete and fragmented information, I use process tracing to reconstruct nine franchising decisions, in order to identify the factors shaping leaders' decision-making concerning affiliation.

I examine al-Qaeda's formal expansion into six arenas. In three—Iraq, Algeria, and Somalia—it relied on mergers, while in two—Saudi Arabia and Yemen—it used its own members. Al-Qaeda's expansion into Syria is a sixth case, though characterizing the move is more complicated because the franchise emerged from al-Qaeda's Iraqi branch, making it somewhat of a hybrid creation. The concluding chapter will briefly discuss al-Qaeda's recently established franchise in the Indian subcontinent.

To strengthen our understanding of al-Qaeda's franchising decisions, I turn to three additional case studies: Egypt, Libya, and Palestine/Israel. "Positive" cases, in which a certain action—in this book, the introduction of an al-Qaeda branch—can be observed, shed important light on the considerations behind al-Qaeda's specific franchising choices. Yet complementing these cases with "negative" ones, arenas that al-Qaeda ultimately avoided, is invaluable. Despite Palestine's immense symbolic importance and al-Qaeda's repeated invocation of the plight of the Palestinian people, the group has shied away from entering that arena. Although al-Qaeda announced mergers with the Egyptian group Gama'a Islamiya and the Libyan Islamic Fighting Group, these relationships did not translate to actual franchises in Egypt or Libya—they were restricted to small factions of these organizations, manned by fighters who resided alongside AQC in Pakistan's tribal regions and in Iran. Meanwhile, these organizations' leaders, backed by most of their members, denied the affiliation claims and renounced al-Qaeda.

Notwithstanding the value of using multiple case studies, it is necessary to acknowledge the limits of this analysis. Even with nine case studies, it is impossible to present a conclusive claim about the conditions that lead a transnational terrorist organization to choose a particular target for its expansion or the form of affiliation—merger or in-house expansion—that it would take. The case studies are all taken from the experience of a single group and are insufficient as a guide for understanding the decisions of others.

Furthermore, they may not even suffice for a general claim regarding al-Qaeda itself. Because the group has spaced out its franchising decisions over more than a decade, the value of synthesizing and analyzing those decisions—notwithstanding the organization's stable ideology and leadership—is limited. Certain considerations have remained constant, but the conditions under which each affiliation decision was made have varied, sometimes dramatically. Moreover, al-Qaeda made each decision against the background of its prior experience and franchising choices. One may question the quality of its leaders' ability to learn from experience, but there is no doubt that learning took place. If a decision to enter one arena was influenced by the results of previous decisions, then these decisions cannot be understood as perfectly comparable. Shifting conditions can also affect franchising choices—early in the process, there are more potential targets for expansion. Later, with franchising established as a mode of expansion, pressure may mount to continue branching out, even though at that point there are fewer targets, and those available are likely to be less attractive—after all, they were not chosen earlier. In addition, decisions made when the organization is experiencing success may emphasize different factors from those made under pressure.

Recapitulation and the Structure of the Book

The book introduces a theoretical framework for understanding formal organizational expansion by a transnational terrorist organization while telling the story of al-Qaeda's expansion, its causes, and its consequences. I argue that the organization was pushed to adopt a branching-out strategy as a response to its decline. A poor strategist, bin Laden dragged his organization into a battle for which it was unprepared. To some extent, the 9/11 attacks were *too* successful, leading the United States to react with much more force than bin Laden expected. At the same time, he overestimated his ability to attract Muslim support and mobilize the umma in sufficient numbers to compensate for al-Qaeda's weak capabilities. The attack on American soil put jihadi groups worldwide on the defensive; most were resentful that al-Qaeda had dragged them into a conflict for which they were likewise unready, and they refused to join the fight against the West, let alone accept bin Laden's leadership.

Al-Qaeda's view of itself as the vanguard of the umma and the jihadi movement—destined to lead—exacerbated the pressure it felt to change the situation. But a recovery remained out of reach, because al-Qaeda's diagnosis of the problems of the umma and the way to resolve them required maintaining the focus on the United States—a position that, notwithstanding anti-American sentiment, particularly after the 2003 Iraq invasion, was simply not popular enough to rally the Muslim street to its cause. Leaders' blindness to their faults, particularly bin Laden's inability to admit that he made strategic mistakes, hindered al-Qaeda's ability to take corrective moves and led it to double down.

The organization's inflated self-image required it to stay in the news and prove its relevance; when aggressive counterterrorism measures hindered its ability to operate, organizational expansion became an attractive alternative. Thus, al-Qaeda elected to form franchises as a way to create the impression of expansion, hoping that the strategy would arrest the organization's decline and increase its power, not only by adding the resources of acquired groups but by swaying additional jihadi groups and ordinary Muslims to join.

While branching out injected new life into the organization and probably prolonged its life, in many ways it has proven self-defeating. Overall, in-house branches—harder to form given al-Qaeda's material weakness—have nevertheless been more reliable affiliates than those created through mergers. Indeed, leaders found that they had little control over groups brought under the organization's wing. Their excesses tainted al-Qaeda's reputation and made it appear either complicit in their extremism or impotent because it was unable to prevent these actions. Additionally, some branches undermined the coherence of al-Qaeda's ideology by strengthening *takfiri* and anti-Shia tendencies within al-Qaeda. Even affiliates more deferential to AQC ended up diluting its ideology by mixing national-based focus with al-Qaeda's original anti-American agenda.

A decade after it began franchising, al-Qaeda found that the turmoil created by the Arab revolutions presented a priceless opportunity to reverse past losses; despite the Muslim masses' clear rejection of its message, leaders saw new chances for making operational advances throughout the region.

Then, to its dismay, al-Qaeda's past affiliation decisions came back to haunt it when its Iraqi branch openly challenged and even overshadowed it.

I lay out these arguments throughout 10 chapters. Chapter 2 discusses the puzzle of formal organizational expansion among transnational terrorist groups. I argue that branching out is just one strategy of organizational expansion, and I discuss three alternative models. I also identify hierarchy, institutionalization, and political messaging as the underpinnings of formal organizational expansion and link the different ideal types of organizational arrangements with different values on these three dimensions.

In Chapter 3, I zoom in on the branching-out strategy, arguing that it brings four main risks: higher reputational costs in case of failure; the strengthening and internationalization of counterterrorism efforts; damage to the transnational parent organization's image and the coherence of its ideology due to preference divergence with the originally more narrowly focused affiliate; and increased threat to the organization's cohesion and its leaders' authority. I then use strategic, organizational, and ideological considerations to articulate the conditions under which a transnational terrorist actor is more likely to pursue a strategy of franchising, followed by a discussion of the differences between branching out through mergers and in-house affiliates.

In Chapter 4, I explain why al-Qaeda adopted a branching-out strategy instead of one of the alternative organizational arrangements and, then, discuss the timing of this move. Rather than highlighting al-Qaeda's prowess, branching out reflected an escalation of its commitments in response to earlier strategic mistakes, leaders' hubris, and its diminished capabilities.

Chapter 5 presents two perspectives for explaining particular branching-out expansion choices of transnational terrorist organizations. The first approach looks at the characteristics of target arenas, addressing the value of specific locations, particularly religious significance and historic symbolism, as well as strategic value and arenas' place in an organization's overarching strategic plan. I also examine how an opposition camp's terrain, state power, composition, and strength shape franchising. The second approach I propose emphasizes the quality of the expanding group's decision-making as a function of the psychological pressure its leaders experience.

The next four chapters comprise the book's main empirical section. In Chapter 6, I examine al-Qaeda's first expansion decisions, the creation of an in-house branch in Saudi Arabia and the merger with al-Zarqawi's group in Iraq. Chapter 7 looks at al-Qaeda's entry into the Algerian, Yemeni, and Somali arenas. Then, in Chapter 8, I examine three negative cases—arenas where al-Qaeda failed to introduce a branch despite claiming to do so (Egypt and Libya), and the Palestinian arena, where al-Qaeda has never tried to enter despite the Gaza Strip being home to a number of groups publicly identified with al-Qaeda's ideology. Al-Qaeda's expansion into Syria, through the establishment of Jabhat al-Nusra, and the challenge it faced when the Islamic State of Iraq decided to expand into Syria and subsume the Syrian branch, demonstrating in this way the ultimate price of al-Qaeda's branching-out strategy, stand at the heart of Chapter 9.

I conclude, in Chapter 10, with an assessment of al-Qaeda's branching-out strategy and the group's future following the Arab Awakening, the rise of the Islamic State, and American foreign policy.

2

Formal Organizational Expansion

A THEORETICAL FRAMEWORK

IN ESTABLISHING AL-QAEDA in 1988, Osama bin Laden viewed it as a vanguard that would carry the torch of jihad beyond the Afghan arena, even after Muslims had reclaimed the land. Although the war against the Soviets demonstrated the willingness of numerous Muslims to fight for a religious cause outside their home countries, the formation of a multinational terrorist organization, setting its sights on helping Muslim struggles worldwide, was a new development. Al-Qaeda's founders envisioned it as a systematic answer to the multiplicity of Muslim grievances around the world; it would serve as a standing force for the Muslim umma. The group's existence would help overcome the inefficiencies involved in mobilizing mujahideen afresh for each new cause. With al-Qaeda, the umma would bear minimal start-up costs; it would have the infrastructure and core force to allow an efficient and quick reaction.

Over the years, al-Qaeda's ranks swelled, but it remained a single, centralized organization (albeit one that provided services, particularly training, to many other jihadi terrorist organizations) with operational tentacles worldwide. But a couple of years after the 9/11 attack, its organizational model changed radically, as leaders announced the establishment of franchises in Saudi Arabia, Iraq, Algeria, Yemen, Somalia, Syria, and the Indian subcontinent.

Despite the immense interest in al-Qaeda, observers paid surprisingly little attention to the reasons for this organizational transformation. Many saw the shift as a natural response to the relentless US-led international campaign to eradicate al-Qaeda and, specifically, to the operational pressure on its cadre in Afghanistan and Pakistan. According to the common narrative, al-Qaeda's response to the dragnet was decentralization, manifested in franchising.

But decentralization does not require franchising. The organization could have adopted a model of "leaderless jihad" in which small cells and lone wolves operate independently from al-Qaeda.[1] Alternatively, decentralization could mean the flattening of the organization's structure while maintaining leaders' ability to set strategic direction.[2] It is essential, then, to consider its adaptation through a more comprehensive lens. Over the past decade, al-Qaeda's organizational strategy reflects a branching-out model, combining top-down decision-making, decentralized operations, and a strong, clear political direction.

Going beyond the practical interest in al-Qaeda, its actions touch upon two questions of broader theoretical significance. First, why would a transnational terrorist organization seek to expand through the formation of formal branches when alternatives exist? Generally, when terrorist entities try to enhance their power and stature, they focus on expanding their operational reach. Even when they consider expansion through formalizing relationships with other groups, they generally embrace other modes of affiliation, such as integration or the establishment of a looser framework of an umbrella group, rather than a franchising model.

Second, what do a group's structural choices tell us about its leadership's decision-making process? A transnational terrorist organization electing to expand demands numerous strategic decisions, with varying levels of risk—not only the decision of which expansion strategy to follow, but also the particular choice of arenas for expansion (as well as which arenas to avoid), and the specific mode of expansion: starting a new branch or merging with an existing group. Decision-making within clandestine violent groups is notoriously difficult to decipher, primarily due to problems of data availability. The exploration of multiple expansion choices cannot resolve this problem altogether, but it could offer a fresh perspective for thinking about the factors that shape such groups' strategic decisions. And looking at the role of opportunity (in this case, the availability of an arena, as well as potential partners or the group's own forces) and need (a state of pressure on the organization to present success or face decline) could illuminate the extent to which they follow rational decision-making processes.

In this chapter, I begin to address the puzzle of formal organizational expansion—in particular, the reasons that a transnational terrorist group would follow a branching-out strategy. After a brief overview of the literature on cooperation among violent non-state actors, I present a typology of different types of organizational expansion, distinguishing between four types of expansion arrangements—absorption, branching out, unification, and umbrella groups (also known as fronts)—based on the political message that each conveys and the hierarchy and institutionalization manifest in the organizational structure. All four types can also be found when organizational expansion takes place within a national context, although with some modifications. Nevertheless, the transborder dimension affects the message that each arrangement conveys, as well as the operational conditions for its adoption, in distinct ways. This typology will lay the foundation for the following chapter's expanded discussion of a branching-out strategy.

Cooperation among Violent Non-State Actors

The formation of a terrorist group is a complex process, composed of many small steps: individuals band together to form cells, separate cells unite to establish a larger group, and groups join to create a more powerful organization. Therefore, expansion and cooperative measures are both integral to the process of these organizations' formation. As prevalent as expansion and cooperation are in the earliest stages, both become much less common once groups are consolidated and their boundaries become less permeable. Groups may erect walls between them for several reasons, including the hardening of in-group/out-group identities, increased attention to security risks (particularly penetration by enemy agents), and leaders' growing attachment to their positions, which leads them to guard against competition. The result of this process is that among terrorist organizations, organizational expansion through cooperative measures is uncommon.

The terrorism literature notes the difficulty of inter-organizational cooperation. Naturally, formal affiliation, signifying a deeper level of cooperation, is even harder to attain. While raising a few theoretical exceptions, Navin Bapat and Kanisha Bond argue that bargaining theory underscores how the difficulties of demonstrating trustworthiness and the fear of exploitation make collaboration between militant groups difficult to maintain.[3] Tricia Bacon states that terrorist organizations struggle to form enduring relationships due to the structural hurdles of cooperation under anarchy and the absence of mitigating strategies to overcome these obstacles.[4] In addition, the grand sense of purpose and ambition that characterizes many terrorist leaders is hardly conducive to compromise and cooperation.[5] Providing support to these claims, Ely Karmon found little evidence of the existence of coalitions between terrorist groups—let alone official unions—prior to the rise of Islamist networks.[6] If affiliation is rare in national contexts, transnational expansion appears even less likely. Indeed, Kent Layne Oots, writing in 1986, voiced skepticism about the potential for a single transnational terrorist network because it would require an expansive (and unlikely) convergence of interests.[7]

Perhaps the view that strong relationships between terrorist organizations are unlikely explains why they have been so little studied. Only a few scholars have discussed inter-organizational cooperation;[8] interestingly, conflict and competition between terrorist groups has drawn little more attention.[9] Recently, an increasing number of scholars have acknowledged these omissions, leading to studies highlighting questions such as the relationship between terrorist alliances, effectiveness, and longevity.[10] While of considerable value, the present literature has often settled for exploring tactical and operational cooperation between terrorist groups, or the diffusion of strategies and tactics through their interaction. Among scholars of civil wars, discussion of the relationship between violent non-state actors is more common. However, most studies focus on fragmentation within rebel movements,[11] perhaps because shifting alliances between insurgent groups indicate that most relationships are temporary.[12]

Particularly promising is the growing interest in exploring cooperation, coalitions, and alliances among terrorist organizations.[13] Indeed, several recent studies show that many terrorist organizations operating in national contexts have sought to expand their reach and strengthen their position through institutionalizing relationships with other groups. The logic behind efforts to consolidate oppositional forces is straightforward: concentration of power in one group is conducive to the attainment of public goods—specifically, ending occupation and achieving national self-determination.[14] Cooperative arrangements are attractive in a non-hegemonic multi-organizational environment in which eliminating other groups is either impossible or undesirable, and mergers or alternative consolidation strategies appear to be a necessary step in the achievement of political objectives. For this reason, in the late 1960s, Fatah sought to control the Palestinian resistance to Israel by taking over the Palestine Liberation Organization (PLO), which enjoyed wide legitimacy internally and was recognized by Arab states as the representative of the Palestinians.[15] In Algeria, during the 1990s civil war, the GIA (Groupe Islamique Armé, or Armed Islamic Group) attempted to become hegemonic by incorporating some rebel groups and eliminating others.[16] In Iraq, al-Qaeda's local branch prepared for the scramble for power that was expected to follow American forces' withdrawal by attempting to form an umbrella group for the Sunni resistance that would be firmly under its control, thus hoping to overcome competition (but also to appear less foreign and more Iraqi).[17]

Even the prominent Jewish underground movement Hagana—with capabilities far superior to other anti-British terrorist organizations, benefiting from the legitimacy accrued by being the military arm of the Jewish community's central organizations, and supported by the bulk of Jews in Palestine—could not simply ignore its rivals, Irgun and Lehi. It found that the achievement of its political objectives required co-opting them and, at times, taking action against them.[18]

Despite the abundance of examples, the literature on organizational choices of terrorist groups in national settings remains underdeveloped. Naturally, scholars have given even less attention to strategic organizational choices in the much smaller class of transnational terrorist entities. The most detailed discussions of affiliation to date are two studies by Dan Byman on al-Qaeda's franchising.[19] The first of these was written as a policy paper and as such does not aim to construct an analytical framework reaching beyond the al-Qaeda case. The other study theorizes terrorist affiliation but suffers from three shortcomings: it overlooks the availability of alternative strategies as a source for understanding branching out; it overemphasizes organizational theory while underestimating the importance of strategic and ideological factors; and it does not consider cases of arenas to which al-Qaeda opted not to expand its brand name.

Ultimately, there is an obvious need to enhance our understanding of organizational expansion in both national and transnational contexts. On its face, the study of organizational expansion lends itself to two different approaches: we can attempt to create a theoretical framework that brings together shared elements from both national and transnational contexts, or, alternatively, we may study each on its own. The first approach would increase the findings' generalizability; the second offers greater understanding of the particular characteristics of expansion that are unique to each setting.

Acknowledging the trade-off, I see more value in studying organizational choices of transnational terrorist groups separately from those made in a national setting. Despite the similarities between national and international cases, the two settings differ in consequential ways. Indeed, the expansive objectives of transnational terrorist groups, the existence of multiple potential expansion targets, the dissimilar environment that each arena presents (in terms of local culture, state power, and the number, strength, ideology, and cohesion of local opposition groups), and the availability of several strategies for expansion all imply that transnational groups face different considerations when they explore opportunities and means for growth. Thus, focusing on the international dimension, this study seeks to contribute to the theorizing of expansion across borders, while offering specific insights into the key case of al-Qaeda's expansion.

Organizational Expansion

Why do terrorist organizations expand across national borders in the first place? After all, leaders have a wide range of strategies available to maintain or increase power—for example, increasing operational tempo, expanding geographical reach by forming cells, and carrying out attacks beyond the original zone of activity.

Take, for example, the case of the Southeast Asian organization Jema'a Islamiya (JI). The group's origins and the bulk of its membership were Indonesian, but the JI harbored aspirations beyond the archipelago state. Its main political objective was to establish an Islamic emirate in the region, an aspiration that translated into an operational structure in which one governing council exerted control over the heads of four regional divisions, the *mantiki*. These geographical divisions have evolved and expanded over time, adapting to changing circumstances and shifting needs. When the JI was founded, it comprised only two regional divisions: Mantiki I covered Singapore and Malaysia, Mantiki II most of Indonesia.[20] Mantiki III was added in 1997 due to the increase in the significance of the Southern Philippines; the establishment of a military academy in Mindanao produced new logistical needs that in turn required additional administrative support. This *mantiki* covered Mindanao and the two Indonesian provinces of Malukus and Sulawesi. Similarly, Mantiki IV, covering Papua and Australia, was a relatively late creation. While it is unclear when exactly Mantiki IV was formed, it presumably came after the number of JI recruits in Australia had reached a critical mass.[21] Importantly, the JI avoided establishing formal branches despite having the operational infrastructure to support them (at least initially, before counterterrorism measures crippled the organization).

Notably, in this kind of expansion a terrorist organization focuses on internal mobilization, deploying or reorganizing its own resources to expand activities. In looking to grow, it does not partner with other groups (apart from tactical cooperation) or seek to use organizational transformation as a political instrument in and of itself.

As I define it, organizational expansion operates at a higher level than operational adaptation. It concerns the reorganization of a group through publicly announced structural changes that involve relations with other groups and, in the context of transnational groups, that take place across borders.

Although any such strategic reorientation will surely affect the expanding organization's operational and logistical functioning, these are byproducts of the broader shift.

What distinguishes formal organizational expansion, as discussed in this study, is that it involves a transnational dimension: that is, in such an expansion, organization A, operating in country (or countries) X, enters into a relationship with organization B, which operates in country Y. Obviously, these relationships vary, but all represent some level of linking the participating actors' political objectives and building on this linkage to create a new organizational framework. Inherent in such an arrangement: at least one of its participants must compromise its independence, to some extent.

Although organizational expansion generally involves institutionalized relations between previously separate terrorist entities, it may also take the form of one group's strategic expansion to new arenas—for example, al-Qaeda's establishment of a Yemeni branch. Organization A, which operates in country X, announces that it is expanding to country Y. In such an expansion, the geographical dimension—entry into a new arena—remains, but it is not necessarily accompanied by the formation of a formal relationship with other organizations. And in comparison to operational expansion, such enlargement carries distinct political value and emphasizes a certain political message. Consequently, it involves higher political stakes.

There are diverse configurations of expansion and inter-organizational association. Underpinning the distinctions between them are two structural factors: hierarchy and institutionalization. In addition, the adjoining of organizational measures and political motives implies that dissimilar expansion modes also reflect distinct political messages to relevant constituencies such as target states, competing terrorist groups, sympathizers, and uncommitted publics. Hierarchy, institutionalization, and political signaling can each take a range of values along a continuum; together, they form distinctive organizational frameworks. Despite the potential for numerous combinations, for analytical purposes it is useful to emphasize four combinations, which could be viewed as ideal types: absorption, branching out, unification, and umbrella groups (also referred to as fronts). I begin by explaining the three factors that characterize arrangements of organizational expansion, and then discuss how they manifest in each of the four organizational structures. To help clarify the features of these arrangements, I also consider them in comparison to internal restructuring and intergroup cooperation and coordination, two other options that organizations have, even though the first does not involve relationship with other terrorist groups and the latter scores low on institutionalization, hierarchy, and political messaging.

Hierarchy, Institutionalization, and Political Messaging

Hierarchy concerns the authority relations between different groups participating in an organizational arrangement. It is a measure of the equality (or inequality) between the factions participating in the new framework. In order to identify hierarchy, we must examine whether there is one organization to which the others defer as responsible for setting political objectives and designing operational strategy. Likewise, is there one dominant group that issues attack orders on behalf of the new formation, or does each group retain its independence to order attacks, select targets, and choose their timing?[22] The more the collaborating actors accept organizational inequality, the stronger the hierarchy dimension. Similarly, hierarchy characterizes the arrangement when one group assumes general control over strategic orientation, resources, and the planning and execution of operations. Conversely, when actors maintain parity and balk at any one group's leadership aspirations, the arrangement scores low on hierarchy.

The other structural dimension, institutionalization, signifies the permanency of the arrangement between the contracting organizations—that is, whether it could be reversed. Institutionalization also concerns the depth of commitment to a particular arrangement: the more elaborate the cooperative scheme and the greater the interaction among members from the new framework's different components, the more institutionalized it is.[23] Additional indicators: the toppling of walls between the organizations and downplaying of prior organizational affiliations (for example, in shared committees); streamlining that eliminates duplicate pre-unity roles and structures; constraints on members' autonomy and new mechanisms for monitoring and enforcement;[24] and, finally, the substitution of a former organizational affiliation with a new organizational identity by members of the weaker groups, not merely functionally but also at the level of individual emotional identification.

Note that alliances, a central concept in international-relations theory, reflect only low levels of hierarchy and institutionalization. An alliance could exhibit hierarchy when one actor has a more prominent position in the relationship (for example, US dominance in NATO), but usually this primacy is not inked into formal alliance agreements. Similarly, alliances feature some institutionalization, but actors remain independent, even as the relationship restrains allies' behavior and gives them a voice in each other's decision-making.[25] Alliance theory is of only limited use to understanding formal organizational arrangements among terrorist groups because it cannot explain either the presence or absence of affiliation,[26] or the choice between dissimilar organizational arrangements. It also predicts that actors will form relationships in response to threats,[27] whereas the affiliation often *heightens* the threat level.[28]

Distinctions between organizational arrangements may also be viewed through the political messages that they communicate. While acts of terrorism are by definition a form of political statement, formal expansion—especially across national boundaries—carries distinct political messages to foes, competitors, and supporters; the move explicitly communicates (albeit not necessarily accurately) that certain arenas are of greater importance. The value of such a message is less tangible than acts such as forming logistical cells in a new arena. But internal organizational changes, particularly when kept secret, carry no political message in and of themselves. They are instrumental to the strengthening of an organization's fighting abilities and generally reflect no political design for this logistical base; in fact, many times such a base is part of preparations for attacks elsewhere.

By contrast, a strategy of organizational expansion sends a strong, clear, and ambitious political statement. The content of the political message and its strength vary among different types of arrangements. At a minimum, it can express mutual commitment among terrorist groups to fight a shared enemy (for example, left-wing terrorist organizations affiliating against the capitalist West). At the maximum, it is a declaration of focus on a particular arena, a commitment to constituting a new political order there, and a determination to bring all opposition forces to accept the expanding group's ideology, strategy, and full organizational domination. In comparison, a branching-out strategy (this book's central interest) combines a message of commitment to bringing a new order to an arena with one of leadership aspirations, albeit one based on some pragmatism and the acceptance of some divergence between groups and across regions as legitimate.

Types of Inter-Organizational Arrangements
The Absorption Model

The first type of arrangement is the absorption model, in which an organization expands across borders without dividing arenas politically (as would be reflected in separate names to match arenas). To the extent that the expansion involves forming relationships with other organizations, it is lopsided—less a merger than an acquisition. The junior partners relinquish their original identities and organizational roles; they are required to assume the identity of the organization that they joined and to become fully integrated into its structure. Thus, strong inequality and a high level of institutionalization are central characteristics of the absorption model.

The organization's one-size-fits-all approach reveals inflexibility and an uncompromising nature. It allows little room for compromise with other groups. The dominant actor wipes away the smaller groups' original organizational, strategic, and ideological features, along with anything that made them distinctive. The demanding nature of affiliation signals the dominant group's exuberance and self-confidence—as well as hubris. It also broadcasts a message of prowess and momentum—after all, terrorist organizations are unlikely to agree to dissolve, or to be acquired, unless their leaders find the prospect of joining the new framework to be extremely appealing.

Given the obvious obstacles associated with transborder operation, the ability to form such an arrangement while engaged in conflict with more powerful state enemies could also signal that the expanding organization has an overwhelming power advantage, along with, perhaps, both ruthlessness and expansionary ambition. Due to its demanding nature, the absorption model requires the transnational organization to have an exceptional ideological appeal, strong enough to overcome absorbed groups' natural preference for maintaining their independence. Another reason for agreeing to absorption could be a belief that by joining the expanding group, members of the absorbed group would accrue considerable benefits. Absent ideological appeal or the prospects of material gains, absorption necessitates reliance on coercion, which in turn requires the expanding organization to have a strong presence in the arenas it targets for expansion before making the formal announcement, to reduce the danger of resistance by reluctant local groups. This could be the Achilles' heel of the absorption model: overreliance on coercion could undermine the organization's viability in the long run.

Consider the so-called Islamic State (IS), a group that followed the absorption model. Originating in Iraq, where for a decade it was al-Qaeda's designated branch—seven of those years operating as the Islamic State of Iraq—in 2013 it formally expanded into neighboring Syria. In both locations, it compelled other groups to disband and join. IS's expansion into Syria also illustrates how formal expansion has an important political component whose deciphering is necessary to accurately comprehend the events. When Abu Bakr al-Baghdadi announced the organization's new presence in Syria, he called it a new step that reflected progress in the pursuit of the jihadi mission and a message of hope for the umma.[29] He did not have to make any public statement; after all, his group's forces had long operated throughout Syria with great success. But he intended the statement and the renaming of his group—to the Islamic State of Iraq and al-Sham (ISIS)—to signal advancement to his Sunni constituency and prowess to jihadi rivals whose independent existence the IS would not tolerate. Moreover, in proclaiming the birth of ISIS, al-Baghdadi implied that his organization has independent political aspirations, separate from those of al-Qaeda, and that his objectives stretch far beyond Iraq's borders. This was a message of defiance against al-Qaeda and a signal to sympathizers that they now have a viable alternative.

The name change also signaled the level of control the organization's leadership intends to exert over all areas of operation. The declaration, one year later, of the establishment of a caliphate was perhaps the strongest sign that al-Baghdadi expects to maintain tight control over his subordinates. In comparison, al-Qaeda's franchising strategy signals a perspective that combines centralized political and strategic authority with operational freedom for the franchises. Importantly, it also indicates acceptance that the operation of other organizations (particularly those with similar ideological dispositions), however undesirable, is not illegitimate.

The Branching Out Model

Expansion via a branching-out model is based on the creation of an organization with a central managerial level and, below it, branches that are each responsible for a particular geographical area. Byman argues that terrorist affiliates remain organizationally distinct,[30] though this depiction may be a stretch: branches have considerable organizational and operational independence, but, at least in theory, they are subordinated to the central command, which could impose advisors on the affiliate or even supplant members of the franchise's leadership with handpicked representatives. The public nature of branching out makes this strategy fundamentally distinct from an organization's internal restructuring. After all, when an organization grows, delegation of authority to lower levels of management is inevitable—and, sometimes, a necessary evil. What makes franchising exceptional is the public announcement of the expansion, turning an organizational move into a political communication.

By creating formal franchises, a terrorist organization communicates more strongly than with mere attacks that it has decided to focus energies and resources on a certain front. Moreover, it signals greater resolve and confidence that it is about to make significant gains and bring radical change to the area of expansion in the near future; otherwise it would be better off simply expanding operations in the arena. Indeed, it is an explicit pronouncement of forthcoming political change, to be achieved through violent means. This message is directed at the group's foes and is designed to terrorize, demoralize, and, as a result, compel them to change their behavior.

By announcing the formation of branches, terrorist organizations may also seek to create a greater sense of urgency among their enemies either to comply or to escalate their reactions in a way that, the terrorists hope, will generate backlash from the general population. The reliance on public communication is a relatively cheap way to raise the stakes in the conflict. To some extent, such a move can even substitute for attacks. At the least, it can allow the organization to direct resources toward fewer operations. Moreover, the founding of a franchise could produce meaningful political effects while reducing the risk to the group's image from terrorist attacks' brutality and indiscriminate mass killing. The combination of a strong political statement that might lead enemies to overreact, while simultaneously mitigating the risks of losing public support, could be an effective means to promote a terrorist organization's political agenda.

In its essence, branching out sends state enemies a message that differs little from an announcement of expansion through the absorption model. However, the dissimilar organizational structure reinforces a distinct message regarding the group's view of local actors and the broader population. Similar to the absorption model, branching out is a public call to arms, launching a mobilization campaign, though it differs by acknowledging the unique characteristics of the area and its people. Whereas strategic direction remains in the hands of the central leadership, the franchises run daily operations, including the production of propaganda, recruitment procedures, specific target selection, coordination and cooperation with other anti-regime groups, and public relations.

The ability to use different forms of affiliation makes the franchising model's greater flexibility particularly evident. Indeed, branching out may involve the establishment of a franchise by using the organization's own cadre of people, but it may also take the form of a "deep merger" with a group that already is active in the arena. In essence, such a relationship suggests incorporation of the joining group under the authority of the expanding organization. In contrast to the absorption model, branching out could, in this way, feel significantly less threatening to other groups because the expanding actor communicates greater willingness to retain elements of the smaller groups' original structure. When two organizations enter into an institutional relationship, they communicate that they share a similar worldview and pursue same political objectives. Moreover, they demonstrate that their commitment to the cause is much stronger than any particular organizational interests.

Such flexibility may come with a price; although in principle, mergers suggest the establishment of hierarchical and institutionalized relations, command-and-control problems, as well as the stickiness of pre-merger identities, may stand in the way of a full union. These kinds of obstacles can limit a merger's impact. Rather than a complete operational and organizational incorporation, manifested in strategic leadership combined with ground-level flexibility, the outcome could be limited to a shift in the new branch's declared political objectives.

Forming a franchise based on an organization's own cadre, rather than merging with a local group, requires already having an operational infrastructure in place—otherwise many will see the move as empty rhetoric. Concurrently, an organization does not announce a franchise simply because the arm of the group in the designated location reaches a certain operational capacity; after all, organizations continually adjust to changes in their capabilities through internal reorganization, with no press releases involved. Therefore, observers should view the announcement of a branch in political terms; it is best to perceive it as a declaration that matured capabilities and a perceived political value emanating from the prioritization of the target arena, combined, have led the parent organization to establish the franchise.

The Unification Model

Unification (or integration) is a third type of organizational arrangement. Whereas a strategy of expansion through franchising aims to maintain the expanding group's dominance, a unification arrangement grants the transnational terrorist organization considerably less authority. In this type of arrangement, groups merge under a power-sharing agreement and adopt a new name to signal the transformation. As part of the unification, the merging groups form a new leadership structure in which members of both organizations assume leadership positions and meaningful roles in decision-making. Expansion through unification indicates that the contracting groups share political objectives and agree on a confrontation strategy. It also signals that they view each other as ideologically compatible (and thus leave no option to separate once their mutual enemy is defeated). To some extent, a unification arrangement could also signal to both foes and sympathizers that the commitment to the cause surpasses any disparate organizational interests, that the actors see each other as equal and none seeks dominance, and finally, that they share a high level of mutual trust.

One may see al-Qaeda's merger with al-Zawahiri's Egyptian Islamic Jihad (EIJ) as an example of such an integration. Following the agreement, leaders named the emerging organization Qaedat al-Jihad, bringing together elements of each group's name. However, the formal unification did not lead to any noticeable reorganization; indeed, members of the EIJ had begun integrating into al-Qaeda's ranks a few years earlier. Neither did Osama bin Laden's dominance decline. Even the new name failed to catch on; few besides al-Zawahiri used it.[31] In public perception, the post-unification organization remained al-Qaeda.

The Umbrella Group Model

Finally, the fourth type of organizational arrangement is the establishment of a front or umbrella group. In an umbrella group, multiple independent organizations come together, although each retains its identity, internal structure, and a broad set of political objectives, including some goals that other members of the front do not support or perhaps may totally reject. In terms of the characteristics presented in the preceding sections, one may say that in an umbrella group both hierarchy and institutionalization are low. Contrary to formal branching-out strategy, establishing an umbrella group suggests that the groups linking together do not accept one particular organization's seniority as a foundation for the emerging relationship. In reality, unavoidably, some groups exercise a more dominant role in the umbrella group, whether due to their size, financial resources, military equipment, or prestige. One can identify some signs of primacy within a front, as when certain factions get the prestigious and most visible positions on the "board," while other groups settle for fewer positions and low-profile roles. For example, Ahrar al-Sham enjoyed a unique position among the seven founding factions of the Syrian rebel umbrella group the Islamic Front (formed in November 2013), and members of the group headed both the front's Shariah Office and Political Office.[32] Notwithstanding disparities among front members, in principle the formation of such an umbrella group implies power sharing under a decentralized structure. Such an arrangement allows aggregating an opposition's power with relatively little sacrifice by the front's constituent groups. Maintaining their organizational structure and leadership, as well as their distinct ideological orientations and political identity, organizations can ally without paying a high price. However, low costs usually also imply small benefits. The front members fall far short of maximizing the full potential of unity.

In national struggles, an umbrella group's strongest member may join it (and even initiate its formation) with the intention of unifying its members, at a later stage, under its control. A transnational organization may seek to establish such a bloc for a similar reason, although it is likely to find substantially greater operational obstacles that would hinder its path to primacy.

Ultimately, umbrella groups are best seen as a transitional stage. Their utility, particularly in a transnational setting, is short-lived and often is limited to a message of unity, with little tangible impact beyond that. They are oriented toward consensus building instead of hierarchy, characterized by a low level of institutionalization, and are easily reversible. Failing to move to greater hierarchy and institutionalization, their viability is low.

In 1998, al-Qaeda founded the World Islamic Front for Jihad Against Jews and Crusaders as such a front. In practice, that framework meant little beyond a public message of increased unity among jihadis and the declared reorientation of those member groups—previously identified with a nationalist agenda—toward a transnational frame and the fight against the "far enemy."

Alternatives

It is useful to remember that instead of adopting one of these four formal organizational arrangements, actors could settle for inter-organizational coordination. Coordination can be understood as a strategy with an even lower level of commitment, focused on enhancing operational effectiveness. Organizations boost each other's capabilities by transferring resources and knowledge, tapping into each group's particular advantage. Such a strategy seems consistent with new models of networked terrorism and flatter structures, even if it does not take the flat network logic to its extreme: the abolition of organizations altogether. But while it may be an efficient way to utilize resources, it reflects weak foundations for cooperation that are likely to undermine its effectiveness. Organizational interests (or the interests of organizations' leaders), as well as strategic and ideological differences, often hinder groups' ability to adopt such an arrangement, even though it comes with relatively low cost.

Such cooperative arrangements signal mutual interests and perhaps even shared enemies. But they also indicate that the organizations have dissimilar political agendas and ideological visions, as well as only limited levels of trust and an unwillingness (at least at that point) to abandon claims for leadership for the sake of the greater power that comes from a tighter relationship.

Theoretically, a terrorist group can transform into an organization whose role is restricted to advisory missions and propaganda. In reality, groups are likely to retrench only if the move guarantees the group's survival, since it represents a scaling down of the group's profile and acknowledges its vulnerability and declining power. A retreat from active operations reduces the ability to provide economic and reputational goods for the organization's rank and file; any measure that could be interpreted as acknowledging a decline risks accelerating that process.

Conclusions

For terrorist actors, formal organizational expansion is hardly an obvious move. Generally, organizations that are looking to expand will focus on operational expansion by forming cells and carrying out attacks in new locations. Even when they decide to focus their expansion efforts on organizational measures—forming institutional relations with other terrorist outfits and announcing a formal presence in new arenas—they have a menu of options from which they can choose. Absorption, branching out, unification, and umbrella groups or fronts are four distinct configurations that a transnational terrorist organization can pursue. While overlapping in some aspects, the combination of their levels of hierarchy, institutionalization, and political messaging reveals their distinctiveness (see Table 2.1).

Of the four models for formal organizational expansion, this study is mostly interested in branching out. Exploring this model in depth, while keeping in mind the organizational paths not taken, would serve two objectives: the first, theory development; the second, the study of al-Qaeda.

Academic research generally advances through the critical discussion of existing theories. But in the absence of theories to explain patterns of formal expansion among transnational terrorist organizations, and given the complexity of this phenomenon, I have chosen to make the central contribution to the development of a theory by highlighting branching out at the expense of the alternatives. This choice does not reflect only methodological considerations—it is informed by the importance of addressing the empirical

Table 2.1 Characteristics of Expansion Models

	Hierarchy	Institutionalization	Signal
Absorption	Strong	High	Power and public appeal of the expanding organization; ideological uniformity; centralization of power; absolute domination.
Branching out	Strong	Medium	Public appeal of the expanding organization; ideological uniformity; operational flexibility; recognition of different regional characteristics.
Unification	Medium	High	Willingness to share power; ideological compatibility.
Umbrella group (Front)	Weak	Low	Shared enemies; mutual interests.

puzzle of al-Qaeda's organizational expansion, and explaining how creating an image of a very broad organization nevertheless resulted in its weakening. Therefore, the discussion focuses now on the puzzle of branching out and identification of the factors that are likely to drive a transnational terrorist organization to pursue that path.

3

The Puzzle of a
Branching-Out Strategy

IN THEORY, WHEN a transnational terrorist organization is seeking to expand, it can choose from several options. Whichever arrangement the organization selects reflects more than its preferences, of course—it must take into account costs, benefits, and viability. When al-Qaeda decided to expand, it adopted a branching-out strategy, preferring it to absorption, unification, or the broadening of the umbrella group it had established in 1998.

During a decade of organizational expansion, al-Qaeda established and publicly announced new franchises throughout the Muslim world. But while its preferred mode of expansion can be classified as branching out, the manner in which it formed these franchises varied. The branches in Saudi Arabia and Yemen were based on al-Qaeda's own infrastructure in those locations, while its penetration of the "markets" of Iraq, Algeria, and Somalia came through mergers.

Al-Qaeda's behavior is particularly intriguing because the organization has neither formalized links with all jihadi groups nor established an official presence in all potential locations. Moreover, its announcement that it had incorporated the Egypt-based Gama'a Islamiya (GI) and the Libyan Islamic Fighting Group (LIFG) was swiftly denied by the leaders of those groups. And in the highly prized Palestinian arena, al-Qaeda did not even claim to present a franchise, despite repeated invocation of the Palestinian cause, promises of action, and the availability of jihadi outfits in the Gaza Strip expressing identification with al-Qaeda.[1]

The organization's decision to adopt franchising as its expansion mode gives special impetus to studying branching out, and this chapter lays out a theoretical framework for the exploration of a branching-out strategy. In later chapters, I will use this framework to explain al-Qaeda's choices and the dissimilar faces that its expansion has taken in different locations.

Many may question the wisdom of a franchising model, since the strategy can easily backfire; I begin this chapter by discussing the risks of branching out. Afterward, I discuss the factors—strategic, ideological, and organizational—that lead a transnational group to pursue formal organizational expansion in general and the franchising model in particular. While the three dimensions are theoretically distinct, in reality they often overlap in important ways: for example, strategic success also advances organizational interests; ideology shapes which strategies and means are viewed as viable; and the promotion of organizational interests often depends on the group's ideological cohesion. While one might be able to assess the relative importance of each factor in some instances, I suggest that it is more useful to view them in unison as multiple, often interacting, and even overlapping factors whose presence makes a branching-out strategy among transnational terrorist groups more likely.

The Risks of Branching Out

A branching-out strategy offers potential gains, but its notable drawbacks render its adoption, by al-Qaeda and other groups, a puzzle worth examining. Expansion through franchising brings four main risks: higher reputational costs in case of a failure; the strengthening and internationalization of counterterrorism efforts; damage to the transnational parent organization's image and the coherence of its ideology due to preference divergence with the originally more narrowly focused affiliate; and increased threat to the organization's cohesion and its leaders' authority.

Franchising raises the stakes for a terrorist organization, creating audience costs by publicly putting the organization's reputation on the line.[2] Naturally, any investment of resources that results in a visible failure hurts an organization, but when a terrorist group focuses on operational expansion, setbacks are easier to overcome—it can retreat, regroup, and then redeploy its assets. The stakes are higher with franchising: the publicity accompanying formal organizational expansion—with its message of greater interest, commitment, and self-confidence—implies that in the event of failure the organization will incur high reputational costs, on top of the material costs.

Franchising is a force multiplier, albeit a risky one: it can trigger the formation of opposing alliances between states, which might offset the expanding organization's growing power. When a terrorist organization opens a new front, it inevitably increases the number of its enemies. Those enemies may seek to deal with the terrorist threat separately, but they may have strong incentives to collaborate. Moreover, formal affiliation among terrorist organizations reduces a target state's ability to deal with the terrorists through accommodation. The historical record shows some states giving tacit consent to locally based terrorist operations in exchange for a promise that any targets will be outside national borders. For many years, European countries tolerated an array of groups so long as they did not cross implicit red lines, essentially tolerating terrorist activity outside the organizations' host states.

Some Middle Eastern countries have tolerated particular jihadi activity within their borders—the Saleh regime in Yemen, for example, occasionally utilized local jihadis to do its bidding against some of Saleh's local enemies.[3] But when a group announces a formal presence, it takes away the host regime's flexibility in its treatment of the group—the government must explicitly designate the organization as an enemy, leaving it little choice but to confront the terrorists. Even if the state were willing to bargain with the group, declaring a formal presence makes it extremely difficult, since any compromise would damage the regime's image. Domestically, critics would interpret negotiations as an acknowledgment of weakness. Externally, other states would doubtless demand that the government meet its responsibilities as a member of the international society. Reluctance to do so would draw allegations of complicity, particularly if the terrorist organization uses the state's territory to stage attacks on neighboring countries, and may even result in sanctions.

Thus, even if the organization is selective in its targeting strategy, focusing on foreign targets and avoiding attacks on its host regime, a state that falls within the terrorist franchise's "jurisdiction" is unlikely to accept such a challenge to its authority. It will perceive the organization as a threat that must be confronted and, as a result, will be amenable to greater interstate cooperation. The injection of much-needed and specialized resources serves as a force multiplier and strengthens states' ability to counter terrorist threats.

Meanwhile, a terrorist group's expansion via merging with a local group does not always lead to the hoped-for augmentation of power and could even weaken the franchise, reducing its ability to defend itself. Such a scenario is likely when a local organization's members do not overwhelmingly accept a transnational group's tutelage.

When it considered launching a franchise in Syria, al-Qaeda weighed the dangers against its eagerness to join the country's civil war. Ultimately, it chose to keep its involvement in the war a secret. While its branch, Jabhat al-Nusra (JN), proved capable, al-Qaeda's leaders were apprehensive that revealing the relationship would elicit negative attitudes by local Syrians,[4] help the regime to break its isolation by increasing other states' willingness to keep Assad in power as a "lesser evil," and motivate the United States and other actors hostile to al-Qaeda to intervene in Syria directly.[5] Syrian allies of JN shared these worries[6] and reinforced al-Qaeda's commitment to this path.[7] Fear of enhanced international cooperation affected the choices not only of al-Qaeda but of would-be affiliates. Indeed, one factor that reportedly delayed al-Shabab's decision to ask to join al-Qaeda was the fear of attracting US counterterrorism.[8]

Branching out can also generate internal risks: a transnational terrorist organization must contend with branch leaders who are tempted to use the relationship to challenge and even take over command of the broader movement. Because affiliation offers franchise leaders considerable public visibility but gives the parent organization only limited control (or limited ability to remove undisciplined or disloyal leaders), those local leaders are sometimes in a strong position to threaten the central command. A branch can take advantage of the benefits of the affiliation—greater legitimacy, public support, and expanded resources—to nurture independent aspirations; the open challenge of al-Qaeda's Iraqi franchise to the parent organization's authority exemplifies this threat. The transnational organization may be able to mitigate these threats by forming branches based on its own cadre of fighters, or by nominating operatives with proven loyalty to the organization's central command to lead a franchise, but because transnational terrorist groups usually lack a robust infrastructure in all arenas, such restrictions would considerably limit expansion potential. Furthermore, affiliates may reject the imposition of new management at the expense of the groups' original leadership.

Branching-out strategy carries other internal risks because it accentuates conflicts stemming from the contradiction between the imperatives of secrecy, decentralization, and compartmentalization, on the one hand, and discipline, on the other.[9] In a seminal book, Jacob Shapiro elaborates on this "terrorist dilemma": in terrorist organizations, a small number of managers determine goals and policies and then delegate the implementation of the plan to lower-level operatives. When the rank and file do not fully understand how violence is linked to particular political objectives, disagree with the methods and targets dictated by their leaders, or simply act based on their own interests, they may use violence beyond the leadership's given parameters and abuse the organization's scarce resources. Such excesses jeopardize the success of the entire enterprise. Therefore, terrorist organizations need oversight to reduce the risk of undesirable actions by operatives, even though such monitoring increases the risk of state detection and countermeasures. Terrorist leaders must strike a balance between control and security, though achieving their delicate task often requires that they keep a high level of both.[10]

Such principal-agent problems are common among relatively tightly knit organizations that operate in contained geographical areas and, due to members' shared culture, enjoy considerable internal coherence. They are amplified in mergers between terrorist organizations that originate from disparate arenas and exhibit considerable cultural differences and ideological gaps. Because the parent organization's understanding of local conditions is deficient, it must allow the branches considerable freedom of action. Moreover, forming an affiliation with an actor accustomed to operating independently allies the parent organization with local leaders who are likely to be particularly sensitive to oversight and any restrictions of autonomy. These disconnects may increase if the franchising organization's leaders are under siege and are unable to exercise their authority. As a result, the central leadership risks losing control over both operations and the general message. In al-Qaeda's case, all these factors reduced AQC's ability to address problems that stemmed from affiliates' excesses and, ultimately, to utilize its affiliates effectively. The leaders of the group's central command, isolated in the border region between Afghanistan and Pakistan, found it increasingly difficult to communicate quickly with subordinates in the franchises, as security considerations limited communication technology and forced them to rely on safer but much slower means, such as couriers. As a result, the franchises gained a high level of freedom, reducing AQC's ability to control its messaging and target selection.[11]

Gaps between the central command and the organization's franchises both reduce the group's appeal to potential recruits and create opportunities that can be exploited by state rivals to undermine all the groups. Opportunities are particularly significant when a franchise's leader (most likely from a formerly independent group) vies for leadership with the central organization's senior command. Indeed, in Iraq, AQC's eagerness to co-opt al-Zarqawi led the organization to bring into the fold a leader who was generally unwilling to defer to higher authority. When al-Zarqawi's anti-Shia agenda severely damaged the organization's image, Osama bin Laden and his close circle had few tools to constrain him.

Preference divergence may further exacerbate principal-agent problems. Such adverse consequences are particularly likely when a transnational organization brings into its fold groups that do not fully share either its ideology or its strategy to attain its stated political objectives. The parent organization and its franchises may rank their enemies differently, hold dissimilar views regarding who constitutes a legitimate target, and diverge on means of violence. AQC differed from its Iraqi franchise in prioritizing attacks on American targets instead of Iraq's Shia, attacks on military and government personnel over common people in the markets, and bombings and shootings over beheadings.[12] On its face, the parent organization can minimize this danger by closely monitoring its branches; its ability to rein in a wayward franchise increases if the latter depends on the parent organization financially. However, as al-Qaeda learned time and again, the difficulty of monitoring—inherent within clandestine violent organizations—increases dramatically when organizations expand. Ultimately, whether a franchise will follow the parent group's instructions often depends on the affiliate's goodwill. Thus, ironically, while the parent organization is supposed to have authority over the branch, in reality its fate hinges largely on the franchise's commitment to respecting its superiors' wishes.

When a transnational organization begins franchising to nationally based organizations, it also risks undermining its transnational (or anti-national) agenda by legitimating existing borders or localizing transnational ideologies. Franchising may constitute a particular challenge to an organization committed to a transnational religious ideology. Such an ideology rejects the placement of sovereignty in all but God and denies the legitimacy of the state-based international order. By fighting states, the terrorist group is inevitably reifying its role as a cornerstone of world order. Even when the organization rejects the institution of the Westphalian state and seeks to fight a war that ignores national borders, its battle still takes place in a territorial space and, thus, is of this world. By franchising, the organization strengthens the territorial dimension that is so central to the Westphalian system,[13] inadvertently legitimizing the existing international order. This dilemma is less pronounced in organizations that seek to form a regional power by eliminating some state boundaries but are willing, after achieving their territorial goals, to obey the rules guiding all members of the international community.

This ideological challenge has posed a dilemma for al-Qaeda, a revisionist force that rejects the Westphalian order, and has led it to avoid ever naming its branches using state names. In this way, it sought to avoid legitimating the state-based ontology that it vehemently opposes—and even views as an anti-Islamic conspiracy.[14] But by creating local franchises, al-Qaeda has risked diminishing one of its greatest achievements: the creation of a transnational entity based on religious, not national, affiliation. Although its ideology remains transnational and franchising has the potential to spread that ideology, the effort's segmentation risks returning to the decried nationalization of jihad. Indeed, since al-Qaeda's aspirations, at least for the Middle Eastern countries, are transparent, one may wonder why it did not settle for the model that the Southeast Asian Jema'a Islamiya adopted, in which segmentation focuses on operational considerations. The Islamic State's criticism that al-Qaeda is reaffirming illegitimate state borders in the Middle East, discussed in Chapter 9, underscores the risk.

The Logics of Branching Out

Given the substantial risks associated with a branching-out strategy, why would a terrorist organization take this path? As noted earlier, international relations (IR) scholars lack a solid theory to discuss formal organizational expansion, and the literature's underdeveloped state regarding cooperation among violent non-state actors offers a shaky foundation for theoretical work. Given this state, it would be beneficial to apply scholarly insights to the logic directing terrorist operations as a cornerstone upon which to construct an explanation of formal expansion, and articulate the conditions under which a transnational terrorist group would prioritize a certain arena over others.

This direction seems more useful than traditional economics-based frameworks that draw parallels to multinational corporations. The economic comparison is tempting, particularly in light of some works that successfully use the business analogy (though without substantive theory) to shed light on and offer interesting insights into the innovative workings of al-Qaeda.[15] However, this analogy has severe limitations. Indeed, terrorist organizations and business enterprises differ in the most fundamental aspect: businesses focus on increasing their return, whereas terrorist organizations emphasize political and social change through the use, or threat of using, violent means. Corporations may have multiple second-order interests, but ultimately they are all subordinated to one essential purpose: making a profit. Terrorist organizations, on the other hand, pursue a wider range of primary interests: influencing state economic, social, and foreign policies; toppling regimes; repelling invading forces; and even shaping world order. And an illegal and clandestine status constrains an expanding terrorist organization in ways that legal business organizations never have to contemplate.

Business theory also can be difficult to apply because its insights, while thought-provoking and enlightening, tend to be short on specifics. For example, Robert Grant and Charles Baden-Fuller determine that mergers, acquisitions, and business alliances can promote organizational learning through the transmission of ideas and best practices.[16] Obviously, such an insight is valuable, but because dissimilar organizational arrangements among terrorist groups carry different political messages, greater specificity is required.

The economic analogy's limitations are also evident in its use to explain the motives guiding individuals and groups engaged in terrorist activities. Even if one assumes that some individuals join terrorist organizations for material reasons rather than political causes, ideological appeal, or social solidarity, providing economic benefits to its members is extremely low on the list of goods that terrorists claim to seek and openly boast that they provide. Terrorist organizations often resort to criminal activities, instrumentally, as a way to fund their operations. However, by definition, a focus on the economic interests of the group and its members—as opposed to seeking to address the economic grievances of the organization's constituency, a much broader category—would transform an organization from a terrorist to a criminal syndicate.[17] It is no wonder that while some terrorist organizations have taken up criminal activity[18] to the point of practically abandoning their political orientation, none has ever declared its raison d'être as increasing organizational and individual wealth.

Thus, while some insights from economics are useful for understanding the phenomenon of terrorism, we should treat them with caution and accept them for their true value, rather than as a guide for a comprehensive theory. Instead, it would be more useful to use the terrorism literature—which has already incorporated some ideas from economics—as the best starting point.

In what follows, I suggest that a general explanation for organizational expansion through branching out, and the issues that shape whether franchising takes the form of a merger or an "in-house" expansion, link three factors: strategic value, ideology, and organizational interests. On its face, each factor reflects a distinct logic for the behavior of terrorist entities in general and for decisions concerning organizational expansion in particular, and sometimes each clearly plays an independent role in an organization's decision to designate a specific location, or a particular terrorist organization, as a target for expansion. Often, though, the three factors are interrelated. Rather than seeking to judge the importance of each logic separately, it is more useful to transcend the debate about which factor is more important and, instead, to examine them in unison.

Strategic Logic

The foundation for the theory of strategic logic is the traditional economic view of people and groups as rational actors, with action based on calculations of costs and benefits. Adapted to terrorism theory, strategic logic presupposes that terrorists are motivated by relatively stable and consistent political preferences and take action based on a comparison of expected utility and costs, turning to violence when it appears to offer the greatest political returns.[19] Observers would expect terrorist organizations to take measures that increase their power, raise their lethality, enhance their standing among their constituencies, undermine their opponents' ability to confront them, and generally strengthen their bargaining position.

Scholars have invoked the theory to explain a variety of puzzles, including why actors turn to terrorism, why they adopt particular tactics, and what explains the timing of terrorist campaigns. Based on their study of airline hijacking, Michael Horowitz and Phil Potter see terrorist organizations as highly instrumental when it comes to adopting tactics, demonstrating responsiveness to the benefits and risks associated with their tactical choices.[20] Similarly, Ami Pedahzur argues that suicide terrorism is a product of a political strategy and that a terrorist group's decisions stem from rational considerations of its tactics' effectiveness and its constituency's support for these tactics.[21] Robert Pape, too, emphasizes the strategic aspect of suicide bombings: They have a proven record as a successful coercive instrument.[22] In a final example, Navin Bapat employs a game-theoretical model based on strategic logic to explain some terrorist organizations' decision to internationalize their campaigns.[23]

The strategic-logic theory proposes parsimonious and straightforward explanations—indeed, for many critics, *too* straightforward. Some dispute the view of terrorist organizations as truly strategically driven: Max Abrahms, for example, maintains that terrorist behavior is not consistently strategic and that the pursuit of political objectives is not most groups' primary motivation.[24] Moreover, one doubts these organizations' ability to accurately assess whether a certain strategy would promote their interests more effectively than alternative strategies. Even if an organization could make precise assessments, the requirements for short-term success might hinder the attainment of longer-term goals.[25] It is also unclear how such organizations would treat a potential strategy that might promote some interests but jeopardize other equally important objectives.

Strategic logic also poses severe methodological challenges. In theory, it should be assessed against an organization's strategic plan at the outset of its campaign. But such evidence is rarely available, and few terrorists would want to make it available—after all, publicly revealing tactics would generate immediate countermeasures. Flexible strategic planning is warranted even if the group's initial plans are not exposed. Once the conflict breaks out, the terrorist organization must be sensitive to its opponents' actions and must adjust its behavior accordingly. It must also assess the success of its actions and shift strategy if prior assumptions prove flawed, or when opponents' tactics counter particular moves. All this makes it difficult for observers to measure terrorists' success against their strategic plans.

Notwithstanding strategic logic's limitations as a sole explanation of terrorist actions, it can have considerable value when understood more modestly as a lens to highlight certain motivations. Adapting the strategic-logic perspective to the question of organizational expansion suggests that terrorist groups expand in general, and try to expand into a certain arena in particular, when they perceive it, first, as the best course of action toward achieving political objectives, and second, as a strategy superior to all other alternatives. Particular patterns of expansion are expected to follow the organization's strategic plan.

The terrorism literature provides some indirect support to the idea that expansion serves as a force multiplier. For example, Victor Asal and Karl Rethemeyer found that terrorist organizations become more lethal when they cooperate with other groups.[26] As they adopt a broad definition of cooperation, Asal and Rethemeyer do not explicitly suggest that formal expansion leads to greater lethality, but this conclusion appears to be a natural extension of the argument.

Expansion using the branching-out model is designed to tap a reservoir of human resources local to the area of expansion. Not only does it give greater access to new potential recruits—it leads to their training, indoctrination, and acquisition of battle experience without having to travel abroad. Indeed, keeping new recruits at home is more efficient. Localization reduces the security risks involved in crossing borders, as well as lowering the logistical complexity and financial burden. During the 1990s, al-Qaeda opened its training camps to volunteers from all around the world, but in the post-9/11 security environment, it no longer had that privilege. Indeed, the US invasion of Afghanistan and the international crackdown on travel to training camps abroad led jihadi groups to emphasize training in their countries of origin.

When a transnational terrorist organization relies on native operators, its effectiveness in that arena is also likely to increase. In contrast to foreigners, such individuals possess deep knowledge of the new arena and its culture, residents, governing regime, and geographical conditions. Similarly, a relationship with a local terrorist group offers the expanding organization specialization advantages. The affiliate's comparative advantage could be a particular military innovation, whether a weapon system or a tactic. More often, it takes the form of stronger knowledge of an arena.[27]

Importantly, these factors by themselves do not adequately explain the announcement of a formal branch. On its face, merely expanding a group's operational capacity in a certain location could offer similar benefits. Perhaps an official presence attracts a greater number of new recruits. On the other hand, a formal franchise will surely lead local authorities to greater scrutiny of the group's sympathizers and will deter many potential recruits. Although this example illustrates the difficulties of coming up with a clear and compelling determination, it also demonstrates that to account for an organization's decision to take the step of forming a franchise, we must consider the benefits that the group expects to gain from sending such a message versus the benefits from alternative courses of action.

Branching out may promote a transnational organization's strategic interests by putting greater political pressure on enemy regimes. If leaders aim to advance political goals, then organizational expansion signals the terrorist group's increased potency. It suggests that the group has become better organized and more bureaucratized and thus more capable not only of fighting its enemies but of promoting an alternative political order.

Franchising also increases the costs that states must pay to counter the threat. A transnational terrorist organization may seek to stretch the battlefield in order to drain its foes' resources. In increasing their enemies' costs, terrorists expect to persuade targeted states that they cannot win and should concede to demands. However, although terrorist acts are comparatively inexpensive, organizations sometimes lack the resources—financial and human—required to extend the front. Organizational expansion is a viable substitute; franchising in particular is a cheaper and safer way to exhaust enemies while exposing the group's infrastructure and operatives to only moderate risk.

Therefore, branching out can complicate and undermine states' counterterrorism efforts, forcing them to rethink their strategies and resource deployment. Governments may mitigate these advantages through more robust interstate collaboration, though international cooperation is tricky, even when states' interests coalesce. States are just as likely to exhibit increased friction, trading accusations of doing too little to counter the threat and even of outright free riding. Thus, a terrorist group could multiply the benefits of expansion by moving into states that are prone to conflict and unlikely to collaborate effectively.

In an arena where other terrorist groups have already established themselves, the announcement of the transnational group's entry could also shift the dynamics by triggering a unification drive. By creating an organizational platform—in effect also a political platform—rather than merely carrying out a few attacks, the expanding group makes it easier for others to join forces against state authorities. When the arena gets increased attention due to the transnational organization's announcement, these groups may also be encouraged to enhance their anti-regime campaigns. In addition, formal expansion can accrue dividends if the move generates enthusiasm among sympathizers and leads potential supporters to give the transnational group a more serious look. Meanwhile, it might motivate active cells and supporters in other locations to take action and therefore create conditions for the group to upgrade operation or expand further.

As I discuss in Chapter 5, the existence of other terrorist groups in an arena does not always lead a transnational terrorist organization to join the fray. The danger of competition, even outright resistance to its entry, would be central to its calculations regarding which expansion strategy it should adopt, whether the introduction of a branch is advisable, and what form the franchise should take. If expansion would pit the transnational organization against established groups that perceive it as a competitor, simple cost-benefit considerations would militate against assuming the risk. The transnational group, with finite resources, will likely enter the arena where it faces the least resistance.

Note that a terrorist organization would prefer absorbing other groups to franchising—after all, acquiring external groups would augment the organization's power while securing affiliates' loyalty through assimilation, dismantlement of its pre-unification structure, and incorporation of its members as individuals into the larger structure. But this is hard to accomplish in a national setting, let alone in a transnational context. Targets for absorption generally resist such unification, and it is doubtful that the initiator can coerce them into submission because its transnational character implies that its power is also decentralized. Because successfully coercing other groups to join the cause typically requires the expanding organization to concentrate considerable force in one location, it will likely have to rely on persuasion instead. Thus, although the absorption model tends to offer greater benefits, an expanding organization must take into account the low prospects of success and the risk of heavy costs.

Given the obstacles to absorption, a relationship in which a local group becomes a formal branch of the transnational organization could be a satisfying second-best option. The expanding group maintains the benefits of low start-up costs relative to forming a franchise based on the organization's own

operatives,[28] while avoiding a fight with groups who could thwart its encroachment into their turf or make it too costly. From the franchise's perspective,
affiliation, which preserves the original organization, could be appealing. It
may offer a valuable brand name and as a result open doors to new and immediately available audiences; members may attain weapons, learn new fighting
skills, and adopt more effective training programs. Affiliates find particularly
valuable the parent organization's logistical infrastructure, propaganda apparatus, and financial resources (either direct assistance or access to the parent
organization's donor network). At times, when a transnational agenda is more
popular than a local one, affiliation could keep a branch in business until the
opportunity to revive its particular objectives presents itself once again.

According to strategic logic, an expanding transnational terrorist organization should consider arrangements with more limited hierarchical elements and weaker institutionalization only if absorption and branching-out
options are unavailable. Focused as this logic is on strategic benefits rather
than organizational interests, in theory a more decentralized and less hierarchical structure could be more efficient; this would be the case when all
groups participating in the arrangement agree on a common political objective and a unified strategy. However, actors rarely manage to efficiently utilize
flatter and more decentralized structures. The principal-agent problem that
undermines effectiveness among coherent national organizations is particularly acute in arrangements without hierarchy, as well as when state borders
complicate coordination and limit the possibility of control.

Ideology

Ideology, too, can play an important role in an organization's decision to
expand through establishing formal branches. Scholars of terrorism have
debated the importance of ideology, and several discount its significance.
For example, Martha Crenshaw has pointed to terrorist organizations' weak
or inconsistent commitment to their declared ideologies: some organizations shifted their orientations; others lacked theories to guide their strategy,
instead cherry-picking fragments of doctrines from other contexts.[29] Max
Abrahms maintains that organizational interests may lead an organization to
alter its ideology to justify a certain type of attack or its operations' continuation in general.[30] And Jessica Stern suggests that the drive to ensure a group's
survival may lead to ideological flexibility, with the group altering its stated
cause, either because the original cause was achieved or to attract a wider variety of recruits.[31] Elsewhere, Stern, together with Amit Modi, notes that terror

organizations may form alliances with groups they once described as infidels or enemies, pursuing very different objectives.[32] Considering al-Qaeda specifically, Dan Byman notes that ideology is insufficient for explaining the organization's relationships because it does not affiliate with all, or even most, Salafi-jihadi groups.[33]

While these findings demonstrate ideology's limitations as a full and overarching explanation for terrorists' choices, it nevertheless remains a key factor. Indeed, elsewhere I show how al-Qaeda's ideological rigidity constrained its ability to take advantage of the global-governance discourse.[34] Ideology can also account, at least partially, for the rift between al-Qaeda and Hamas.[35] So scholars should seek to identify the various ways in which ideology influences the actions of terrorist groups, as well as the conditions under which it is more, or less, likely to have an impact. For example, overwhelming operational constraints often trump ideology, even in highly committed groups, whereas minor operational constraints may allow even the least ideological terrorist groups enough freedom to act in accordance with their declared ideology.

Ideology does not always remain constant; exposure to different lines of thought and diverging perspectives can lead an organization to modify its ideological stance. During the Afghan war against the Soviets, interaction at the individual level between mujahideen from different countries led to numerous debates and mutual ideological fertilization.[36] Thomas Hegghammer identifies "ideological hybridization" among jihadi groups as a genuine process of ideational change, resulting in ideological convergence.[37] Hybridization points to ideology's malleability and the need to explore factors, especially the level of interaction between terrorist organizations and inter-organizational ideological debates, that may lead actors to shift certain ideological positions.

Ideological shifts can be also affected by the nature of the location and the formal role of a group's ideological (often religious) authority—specifically, whether the individuals who guide its ideological direction are part of the organization or external to it. Many times, the group's leader fulfills the role of ideological authority, but such an authority could also reside outside the group. The leadership of jihadi organizations often serves as the designers and interpreters of Islamist ideology. But jihadi scholars outside the official ranks (for example, the Jordanian Abu Muhammad al-Maqdisi) also hold considerable sway, and group leaders must take their positions into account. Such religious authorities are often less isolated than an organization's ideology-setters and, therefore, less susceptible to adverse small-group dynamics, more sensitive to the way terrorism affects the group's constituency, and more attentive to the way in which ideologically driven actions affect the public interest and the prospects of realizing the ideology. Thus, they may lead to ideological shifts as part of a feedback loop between the organization's activities and its ideological authorities' assessment of the legitimacy and consequences of these activities.

Hence, an organization may alter its ideology, and not necessarily for instrumental reasons. This shift can manifest itself at both the strategic and tactical levels, for example in driving an organization to abandon a certain tactic deemed incompatible with ideological restrictions. For our purposes, these factors suggest that a shift in ideology from local to transnational orientation, and unification with a transnational group, does not a priori refute ideology's role or confirm the primacy of organizational considerations. Empirical work is required to determine whether the ideological shift preceded the group's organizational orientation, rather than the other way around. One must also avoid confounding ideology and strategy and assess whether the observed change was the former or the latter. After all, an organization may change its strategy without transforming its ideological goals.

Although jihadi groups are the most obvious example of ideological terrorist organizations, the importance of ideology to their strategies must still be scrutinized rather than assumed. Financial difficulties and diminished manpower were major reasons why Ayman al-Zawahiri steered the Egyptian Islamic Jihad (EIJ) toward al-Qaeda.[38] In another case, immense pressure from Algerian authorities weakened the Salafi Group for Preaching and Combat (Groupe Salafiste pour la Prédication et le Combat, or GSPC) considerably and contributed to its decision to join al-Qaeda, adopt that organization's rhetoric of global jihad, and expand operations beyond Algeria to the broader Sahel region.

Furthermore, one could argue that adopting a West-centered perspective following a merger with al-Qaeda may not even indicate an ideological change. If a group attributes its orientation shift to US responsibility for the group's failed efforts to topple a local regime, then seeking to drive the United States out of the Middle East could be plausibly viewed as a change of strategy, not of ideology. Additionally, the argument that ideology drives al-Qaeda's actions is weakened if, as a few authors maintain, al-Qaeda has pursued inconsistent political goals.[39]

Even if ideology guides al-Qaeda's actions, observers should not equate its ideology with its religiosity and religious worldview. Religion provides al-Qaeda and analogous organizations an ideological focal point, but it is hardly the only ideological element. In al-Qaeda's case, Nelly Lahoud aptly warns that while religion defines the group's ideological paradigm, it would be a mistake to view its ideology solely through a theological lens and ignore the important ways in which al-Qaeda's militancy also defines its ideology.[40]

How might ideology affect an organization's formal expansion decisions? It could play three roles. First, ideology could delineate the boundaries for a group's efforts to implement its views and, as I discuss later, shape the priorities that certain arenas receive. Most basically, formal expansion across national borders depends on whether the organization envisions the creation of a transnational political community or is focused on change within one country. Ideology determines the scope of the group's potential for expansion. A terrorist organization with a national liberation agenda is unlikely to be interested in expanding organizationally to a foreign country (as opposed to carrying out attacks on foreign targets that belong to the primary enemy, or attacking that country to deter it from providing support for the target state). Such a move would be incompatible with the organization's agenda, would distract from its main objectives, and could generate opposition from within. By contrast, a group with broader aspirations would be naturally inclined to promote its ideology and interests in locations that it views as part of the cause; its ideology would also more easily justify expansion efforts.

Second, ideology may give certain arenas greater significance and push the organization to expand in that direction. Certain locations carry greater historic, symbolic, and religious value, and a terrorist organization will likely identify these spots as its raison d'être. Ideologically driven formal expansion may exist even when purely strategic considerations suggest that an alternative location would offer greater operational payoff. Indeed, to preserve its claims for authenticity among its constituency, an organization may expand reluctantly to an ideologically charged arena with low prospects for operational success. This carries intriguing implications for counterterrorism policy: it may be worthwhile to challenge a terrorist organization that fails to follow its credo, suggesting that its absence from a primary arena is a sign of either weakness or disingenuous rhetoric.

Note that the question of expansion to a particular arena often mixes ideological factors and instrumental ones. Entry into an arena of considerable ideological resonance can be consistent with strategic considerations, and absence from such an arena may be due to lack of capabilities rather than insufficient ideological commitment. Terrorism scholars struggle to disentangle the strategic from the ideological: How does one determine whether an action consistent with an organization's ideology resulted from ideological commitment or instrumental factors? After all, for the group, avoiding ideological imperatives could produce undesirable strategic consequences. Alternatively, if ideology is the primary catalyst for mobilization, then adhering to an ideological logic is a sound move, consistent with strategic logic. Consequently, few groups adhere to ideology so rigidly that they won't bend when operational interests conflict.

A third way in which ideology may impact formal expansion concerns the organization's view of its role in the struggle to attain its political objectives, and its place in the new order that would follow victory. A transnational ideology, on its own, inadequately explains any particular organizational strategy. An ambitious terrorist organization is more likely to establish branches across borders if it believes that the encouragement and support of other groups are insufficient, and that its brand name is necessary for promoting its agenda. A group that sees itself as destined to lead may also go beyond promoting its political agenda and actively seek to expand, placing itself in a leadership position.

Organizational Imperatives

Several scholars have demonstrated that organizational considerations—increasing power, resources, and prestige—are central to terrorist organizations' decision-making, even trumping strategic and ideological objectives.[41] Survival imperatives can, according to this view, lead to diverse strategies, including creating unlikely alliances or even splintering.[42]

The paramount motivation, of course, is organizational survival. Mia Bloom argues that even the most religious group is pragmatic and power-seeking and therefore will prioritize political survival over ideological considerations.[43] Crenshaw asserts that since survival is the fundamental objective of a terrorist organization—or any other political organization—the operational interpretation of ideology will vary according to the requirements of self-preservation.[44] Abrahms, too, highlights the importance of the organization's survival, although he sees it as a necessary means of facilitating delivery of the organization's affective function.[45]

While all of these explanations underscore the importance of survival, they inadvertently stretch the conditions under which it plays a role beyond the extreme situation in which an organization faces imminent elimination. Extreme threat to a group's survival may make the organizational explanation more easily distinguishable from behavioral shifts due to strategic considerations, but organizational factors also operate under less restrictive conditions.

Byman enthusiastically supports using the organizational perspective to explain al-Qaeda's formal relationships; he sees this perspective as offering insights into the causes of cooperation as well as the decision to favor affiliation over lesser forms of cooperation. It explains variation when strategic and ideological variables are stable, and it highlights dangers for the organization in branching out.[46]

An organizational perspective can offer a number of reasons for a terrorist group's drive for formal expansion. On its face, the drive to expand is natural for any organization. However, it is perhaps counterintuitive that not only successful groups but also groups in distress may seek expansion. A terrorist group could envision forming branches as a way out of a crisis, real or perceived. Branching out beyond prior boundaries would be a declaration of prowess that, theoretically, could arrest its decline. If this interpretation is correct, we would expect to see predictable choices in groups' particular targets of expansion: a troubled organization would expand to arenas in which it is most likely to succeed, or to locations that would offer it the greatest prestige, which in turn would assist in its rejuvenation.

Students of terrorism in general, and of al-Qaeda in particular, have noted that for an organization to survive, it must continuously move. In the words of Bruce Hoffman, "al-Qaeda is much like a shark, which must keep moving forward, no matter how slowly or incrementally, or die."[47] Many scholars interpret "moving forward" as groups carrying out terrorist acts, but this logic can be extended: al-Qaeda's ambitious agenda requires it to show not only that it can use violence on an ever-widening geographical scale but also that its ideas have broad appeal that can translate to expanding its ideological and political apparatus. Hoffman argues that since al-Qaeda wants to promote its durability as an ideology and a concept, expansion can serve as a way to remain in the news when the organization's central command fails to carry out regular attacks.[48] Similarly, expansion can temporarily substitute for operations, to meet the constant need to sell the group's mission to donors and patrons.[49]

A branching-out strategy could be particularly beneficial if it allows a besieged group to attack its enemies in new theaters and force them to relieve pressure on the group elsewhere. Expansion is especially attractive against an enemy that is already spread thinly. Thus, similarly to the logic behind operational escalation,[50] organizational expansion may stem from a need to adapt to a changing strategic environment under growing state pressure. Note that such a need can be seen as reflecting strategic, not organizational, needs;

furthermore, it does not require organizational expansion—only operational expansion. Therefore, this factor is more likely to account for the behavior of an organization seeking to enter an arena in which other terrorist groups already operate, rendering operational shift a less viable option.

In competitive conditions, when a terrorist organization fears the loss of members, declining public support, or a competing organization attracting potential recruits, it often seeks to raise its profile and increase its appeal through escalating terrorist activity.[51] When operational constraints limit the group's options, it may adopt a strategy of formal expansion in an effort to distinguish itself from other groups and reduce the threats to its existence.

Another organizationally centered explanation focuses on the interests of the organization's leadership. A terrorist organization's actions may reflect leaders' need to maintain members' approval.[52] The primary objective is to assure members, many of whom joined for reasons other than ideology,[53] that the group continues to offer members individual and social goods. Normally, this would translate into terrorist attacks, but when the ability to carry out operations is limited, formal expansion may signal organizational health.

In the case of al-Qaeda, constraints on its ability to attack the United States and other favorite targets, as well as limited success in recruiting and absorbing new volunteers in the battlefields of Afghanistan and Pakistan, led its leaders to pursue organizational expansion. Such an approach aimed to boost members' morale and maintain leaders' status and reputation.

Seth G. Jones argues that as security concerns overwhelmed al-Qaeda's central leadership and prevented it from playing a major strategic and operational role, franchising was critical to the group's survival. He views this strategy as being fairly successful in expanding al-Qaeda's global presence, although it could eventually create fissures among increasingly autonomous groups.[54]

Financial difficulties may force an organization to seek alliances and even mergers with richer groups. For example, money drove the EIJ into bin Laden's arms. Given al-Qaeda's request for financial assistance from its Iraqi branch,[55] one can speculate that the financial pressure on its leadership, isolated in Pakistan's tribal areas, and the riches of al-Zarqawi's group in Iraq likely had at least some impact on al-Qaeda's attitude toward expansion to Iraq. Once again, we see the difficulty of disentangling the factors behind terrorist operations: searching for financial resources can result from organizational factors but also from strategic considerations, under which funds serve the achievement of the organization's political objectives.

In-House Expansion versus Merger

The three logics presented in the preceding sections also offer important insights about the particular form that franchising should take, but disentangling them is difficult and arguably distracting. As interwoven as strategy, organization, and ideology are in any organization's decision to branch out, they are even harder to separate when considering the two franchising options of mergers and in-house expansion. Such decisions, because they more explicitly involve relationships with other groups, inevitably bring forward issues of ideological compatibility and of each group's particular organizational interests. Thus, I combine elements from all three logics as I discuss considerations for each form of branching out.

Mergers and internal franchising advance an organization's strategic interests in similar ways: both foster an image of increased capabilities and greater commitment, intended to demoralize state enemies and attract potential supporters. However, in-house franchising is, above all else, a political move made by an organization upgrading its operation in a certain arena simply by proclaiming that it now operates a branch. A central attraction of in-house franchising is that it gives the parent organization an affiliate that it knows and generally trusts. An in-house franchise is more likely to understand and follow the strategy its central command has articulated. The ability to understand the wishes of the parent organization is especially important considering that security concerns prevent the latter from exercising robust oversight. Trust built over the years also enables the parent organization's leaders to ask an in-house franchise to undertake more complex missions (or to assume a more central role in the organization) when the leadership is unable to perform them. These advantages suggest that the formation of in-house branches should be the preferable mode for branching out.

In comparison, expanding through a merger can be seen as an off-the-shelf option for increasing the capabilities of the organization, saving start-up costs by providing an already established infrastructure and human resources in locations where the parent organization lacks them. The expanding organization may avoid the usual missteps involved in learning a new arena by gaining a trained force already familiar with the geography, local population, social structure, culture, and enemy. As a result, it can quickly launch a terror campaign, with greater prospects of effectiveness.

When is a merger preferable? When a group lacks the resources to establish a solid base and wishes to avoid competition with other organizations. It provides the group with an already existing infrastructure and local knowledge but, naturally, reduces the organization's ability to exert control. The added symbolic value may offset this downside: a merger signals the appeal of the expanding group and its ideology, particularly if the local organization adopts the name of the transnational one, thereby strengthening the expanding group's reputation.

The principal-agent problem looms large in the case of franchises that existed independently prior to merging with al-Qaeda. At the most basic level, the central leadership faces information problems. Contrary to in-house branches in which communication channels predate their public introduction, merger-based expansion involves their establishment. Both organizations must create such channels while trying to evade detection and overcome distrust. As a result, information from the franchises is often tardy and incomplete, making it more difficult for the leadership to utilize its franchise effectively. Insufficient information exacerbates the center's challenges when problems in a branch demand intervention.[56] Lacking the level of familiarity that exists between a parent organization and an in-house branch, it is particularly hard for the central command to interpret accurately the meaning of the information it receives.

Franchising an organization also puts its brand and reputation at the mercy of groups and leaders over whom it has limited influence and who may end up hurting its cause. Indeed, the pleas by Ayman al-Zawahiri and other leaders to Abu Musab al-Zarqawi, the leader of its Iraqi franchise, underscore al-Qaeda's awareness that the franchise's blunders could undermine public support and thereby risk its enterprise in the country.[57] Franchising means that the central leadership not only gets credit for its agent groups' successes—it also owns their failures.

Moreover, when a merger brings a group that was previously oriented toward toppling a particular regime into the fold of a transnational organization, the central command may find it difficult to assure that the franchise embraces the parent organization's agenda more than rhetorically and half-heartedly. It may be disappointed to find that the franchise enjoys the benefits of the affiliation without meaningfully committing itself to the path charted by the central command. The franchise may choose to follow the central command's instructions only haphazardly. Insufficiently committed to the objectives of the center, the franchise might carry out only attacks that it perceives to be in its own interest.

Organizational expansion through mergers may particularly appeal to declining groups who worry that their weakness may undermine their overall endeavor and thus seek to create symbiotic relationships with local actors that enjoy greater support and legitimacy. According to Jones, this consideration shaped al-Qaeda's policies in Afghanistan in the post–9/11 era.[58] We can also see this explanation as compatible with the ideological logic: if a group's political objectives are in line with its ideology, measures undertaken to enhance the former inherently also promote the latter.

Note that the potential for competition with other terrorist groups may lead an actor to look to expand elsewhere. However, when rival groups constitute a barrier to entry to a strategically valuable location, merger may be an indispensable strategy. Turf wars, particularly against already entrenched contenders, can exhaust organizational resources and hurt the group's reputation in its constituency's eyes. Additionally, by diverting the organization's attention from its primary target, they further endanger the general enterprise. The resilience of local identities and agendas makes the threat of conflict between the transnational organization and local groups, adhering to locally focused objectives, particularly daunting. Mergers, then, can be a way to shift local groups' operational focus toward a transnational agenda. Co-opting, or swallowing, a competitor group is therefore a rational way to pursue the organization's strategic goals while reducing harmful and unsuccessful friction, which could deteriorate into terrorist fratricide.

Ideology could impact an organization's decision to form its own branch or to opt for a merger option. When ideological commitment is strong, an organization will be unable to ally with groups following a conflicting ideology. Thus, ideology could determine which organizations may be seen as potential partners. When a transnational terrorist organization wants to expand into an arena dominated by groups holding radically different ideological orientation, it is likely to build its own branch. Granted, some differences between organizations are inevitable if they have fundamentally different origins (that is, transnational versus national), but sometimes the dissimilarities are not too deep. Differences over strategic outlooks, views regarding the most effective ways to attain political objectives, and the ranking of the organizations' priorities can often be bridged without compromising core beliefs.

Conclusions: Relationship between Logics for Expansion

Despite our best efforts to analytically distinguish among strategic, ideological, and organizational logics, success in separating them is modest. For example, formal expansion that serves a group's organizational interest in bolstering its power and stature may equally work as a force multiplier and enhance its strategic objectives. An organization fighting for its survival may at the same time fight for the survival of its strategic objectives. Consequently, measures designed to save the organization will be compatible with actions dictated by strategic logic.

On its face, it appears easier to identify the independent impact of ideology. When ideological logic directs an organization to an arena with unique ideological appeal despite high strategic obstacles, one may infer ideology's comparative strength as a driving force. There are exceptions to this claim: in extreme cases, one can legitimately portray divergence from a group's ideology in order to guarantee its survival as compatible with ideological commitment. After all, if the organization dies, it can no longer champion its ideology, pure or otherwise.

The confluence of the three logics is notable when an organization branches out to an ideologically valuable arena. Such a move is rarely incompatible with the strategic and organizational logics. As long as ideology is a central mobilization tool, measures in line with it can promote the organization's objectives and enhance its power and stature. True, in some cases, the decision to enter an arena with unique ideological appeal undermines the organization, but such an assessment is often made in hindsight. Since strategic decisions are always shrouded in uncertainty, success and consequences are rarely sufficiently clear to allow a prediction that the planned move will be counterproductive. Finally, even when organizational interests appear to violate ideological commitments, sometimes they may reflect genuine ideological transformation or a shift in strategy, rather than an abandonment of the group's ideology.

One could assess the relative importance of strategy, ideology, and organizational interests in those unique cases where each would point at different expected behavior. Such studies are valuable for explaining these particular incidents but cannot claim generalizability, since these cases are unrepresentative of the full scale of terrorist behaviors. Reading too much into a narrow pool of cases would skew findings and thus be counterproductive. Scholars may be better off accepting the three logics as interacting and even overlapping, and should seek ways to utilize all in unison in order to address particular research questions.

This chapter has followed this holistic approach for the purpose of identifying the conditions that are conducive to the adoption of organizational expansion through a branching-out strategy. Which conditions, or mix of them, are necessary for the adoption of a branching-out strategy is a question that cannot be answered without examining a large set of cases. At this stage it would suffice to suggest that a transnational terrorist organization is likely to pursue this strategy under the following conditions:

1. Branching out is viewed as conducive to the attainment of the group's political objectives and superior to alternative modes of expansion.
2. The organization is committed to an ideology that surpasses states' boundaries. Its expansion will cover territories that its ideology calls for controlling.
3. It perceives itself as a vanguard, superior to other groups and destined to lead the emerging political entity.
4. The organization sees decentralization as a more effective management strategy than centralization, given dissimilar cultural settings and operational constraints.
5. The organization and its leaders are experiencing considerable success and seek to capitalize on it to reorganize and boost their resources. Success will lead the organization to expand to arenas offering the greatest political returns.
6. The organization and its leaders are experiencing great distress. When that happens, branching out could substitute for operational success. The threat of decline will lead a transnational organization to expand to locations simply based on the ability to enter them.

In the following chapter, I propose an explanation for al-Qaeda's general interest in formal expansion. This explanation links strategic, ideological, and organizational logics. I maintain that al-Qaeda has preferred organizational expansion based on its view of itself as the obvious leader of the jihadi movement and its conviction that jihadis would willingly accept its primacy. Moreover, the organization's weakening, the decline in its popularity, and increased competition from other jihadi groups have pushed al-Qaeda to a more gradual approach for mobilizing the umma, based on the force of local identities. In fact, the worse al-Qaeda did, the greater the pressure it felt to formally expand.

Subsequent to that discussion, I will suggest that in order to understand al-Qaeda's specific expansion choices, it would be more fruitful to examine the intrinsic value of potential jihadi arenas alongside considerations of opportunity and need. I will then explore how these potential explanations perform in nine jihadi arenas.

4

Explaining al-Qaeda's Franchising Strategy

IN THE WAKE of 9/11, al-Qaeda inspired both groups and individuals—sometimes with no direct connection with the organization—to commit acts in line with its ideology, leading to what Marc Sageman calls "leaderless jihad."[1,2] It was flattering to the egos of al-Qaeda leaders that observers suggested that the group has transformed itself, turning into a social movement, an ideology, and an idea.[3] But in its essence al-Qaeda remained an organization, directing and carrying out violent operations in pursuit of its strategic goals. It tried to adapt to the expansion of the battlefield and rejuvenate in the face of the aggressive American campaign to hunt down its leadership. As part of this evolution, al-Qaeda's senior leadership delegated authority to increasingly autonomous lower-level commanders, becoming less involved in managing daily business than it had been prior to losing the group's base in Afghanistan in late 2001. Yet there remains a clear hierarchy within the group, supported by clear (although not as effective as AQC hoped) command-and-control processes.[4] Moreover, since the group reconstituted itself in Pakistan's tribal area, it has been consistently trying to expand.

This expansion goes beyond strengthening al-Qaeda's ability to operate on a much broader geographical scale. It involves the establishment of a public and permanent presence, in the form of branches carrying the al-Qaeda name. Whether carried out through the formation of local groups based on al-Qaeda operatives, as in the case of al-Qaeda in the Arabian Peninsula (AQAP), or by mergers with existing jihadi groups such as the Algerian Salafist Group for Preaching and Combat (GSPC), franchising is not merely a bureaucratic organizational act but a political statement. It is usually marked by official announcements through *al-Sahab*, al-Qaeda's media production company, and the naming (or renaming) of the branch.[5]

This development, intriguingly, is neither an obvious course of action for al-Qaeda nor an inevitable outgrowth of its ideology. For many years, leaders declared that they viewed al-Qaeda's main mission as inciting the Muslim public to action; formal organizational expansion was merely one possible way to advance this objective. Moreover, according to Leah Farrall, al-Qaeda's branching-out strategy diverged from previous efforts to enhance the group's standing among jihadis. These efforts focused on a predatory approach, bullying weaker groups or buying their allegiance and attempting to divide and conquer the stronger ones.[6] Therefore, because organizational expansion can—and did—take different shapes, al-Qaeda's choice of the franchising model should be considered not inevitable but, rather, problematized. The branching-out drive is particularly puzzling because of its potential costs. By creating local franchises, al-Qaeda risked diminishing one of its greatest achievements: the creation of a transnational entity based on religious, not national, affiliation. Although its ideology remains transnational and franchising has the potential to spread it, the segmentation of the effort risked reverting jihad back to the era of national-based Islamist resistance, which al-Qaeda has always decried.

One may also wonder about the timing of al-Qaeda's pursuit of this organizational strategy. Although it was established in 1988, al-Qaeda did not start forming franchises until 2003. Foreshadowing the beginning of its violent campaign (the bombing of the American embassies in Nairobi and Dar al-Salam) in 1998, al-Qaeda pursued expansion through an alternative model, forming an umbrella group, the World Islamic Front for Jihad Against Jews and Crusaders. Why would it follow this route for expansion and then shift to the branching-out model? In the same vein, al-Qaeda did not follow the 9/11 attack—the most remarkable demonstration of its aptitude—with a franchising drive. In fact, in its scramble to survive after 9/11, al-Qaeda relied on other jihadi groups, such as the Southeast Asian Jema'a Islamiya, that had benefited from its largesse in the past but were never incorporated into al-Qaeda.[7] Why, then, did al-Qaeda not capitalize on its astounding success to start franchising, choosing this path only after the United States considerably degraded its capabilities?[8]

Consistent with my earlier argument that separating ideological, strategic, and organizational factors would limit, rather than strengthen, our ability to understand formal organizational expansion among transnational terrorist organizations, in this chapter I weave these factors together to explain why al-Qaeda adopted a branching-out strategy. I argue that this move, which some scholars view as a demonstration of al-Qaeda's prowess,[9] was in fact a sign of its weakness. The organization's mounting difficulties did not stem only from the United States' military might—they also reflected shortcomings in its strategic thinking, as well as the hubris of its leaders. In turn, these factors shaped al-Qaeda's response. Unable to sustain a battle with the United States solo, and seeing its claim to leadership of the jihadi movement diminishing, al-Qaeda chose organizational expansion that would not only bolster its image of prowess, but also allow it to claim affiliates' actions as its own (in contrast with its approach during the 1990s, when it was content to offer uncredited aid to other groups). However, the power that came with franchising was an illusion and in fact proved to be a Faustian bargain, as poor affiliation choices undermined al-Qaeda's standing among Muslims worldwide and accelerated the group's decline.

Expansion

Al-Qaeda was established as the Soviet presence in Afghanistan was coming to its end and the war began subsiding. Though its leadership's strategic thinking was still unformed, they knew they wanted to tap the jihadi zeal to accomplish new objectives. The idea was to create a mobile force that would support Islamic and Muslim causes. This orientation, further developed and strengthened throughout the 1990s, distinguished al-Qaeda from most other jihadi groups and was reflected not only in its multinational membership but also in its ability to transcend nationalism and elevate the notion of resistance to the Western international order.

Although al-Qaeda provided support for terrorist activities, throughout most of the 1990s it focused on building an independent infrastructure. Building relationships with many nationally based jihadi groups was essential for this strategy, including forming or strengthening ties between al-Qaeda and other organizations' leaderships while establishing strong interpersonal relations with members of these groups who passed through al-Qaeda's training camps in Sudan and Afghanistan; al-Qaeda recruited the most promising talents for its own ranks.[10] Then, in 1998, when leaders felt ready to advance to the next phase in their agenda, al-Qaeda announced the establishment of the World Islamic Front for Jihad Against Jews and Crusaders. Still leery of provoking resistance from other jihadi groups, the new front was an umbrella group that brought together Egyptian, Pakistani, Bangladeshi, and Afghan groups. Al-Qaeda and its leader Osama bin Laden were the prominent actors in this front, but al-Qaeda did not claim to have merged operationally and structurally with these groups.

A few months after announcing the front, al-Qaeda bombed the American embassies in Nairobi and Dar al-Salam as its coming-out operation, killing more than two hundred people in the process. Retaliatory US strikes on training camps in Afghanistan and a pharmaceutical factory in Sudan were resounding busts, failing to kill large numbers of al-Qaeda members or any of its leaders and proving to be a huge propaganda coup. Al-Qaeda's popularity increased, attracting many new volunteers to its training camps and expanding its donor base. The October 2000 bombing of the USS *Cole* in the port of Aden, Yemen, was the group's second significant attack on an American target. This time the United States elected not to retaliate, avoiding another potential fiasco but further boosting al-Qaeda's self-confidence and its conviction that US power was a myth.

A few months later, al-Qaeda made its first formal "acquisition," merging with Ayman al-Zawahiri's Egyptian Islamic Jihad (EIJ).[11] Whatever the particular reasons for this union, it does not appear to reflect a strategy of expansion. Nevertheless, the move may have planted the seeds for future moves.

Emboldened by its rising stature and popularity, al-Qaeda was ready to launch a cataclysmic event that would expose the "Western war on Islam" and US "occupation" of the Middle East, an attack that the world could not ignore. The 9/11 attacks successfully provoked the United States to heighten its military involvement in the region. But al-Qaeda's plan underestimated American power as well as resolve; its leaders were surprised that the United States did not settle for limited retaliation along the parameters of its response to the embassy bombings, instead aiming to topple the Taliban regime. Al-Qaeda was also surprised and disappointed to reveal that the Taliban and the foreign jihadi contingency in Afghanistan were unable to robustly resist the invading forces.[12] Nearly decimated by the US attack, al-Qaeda encouraged its affiliates and its existing cells outside Afghanistan to carry out attacks against Muslim regimes and Western targets, while al-Qaeda was preoccupied with its survival in Pakistan's tribal areas.

Al-Qaeda's fortunes improved after the United States attacked Iraq in 2003. The invasion redirected important US operational and intelligence assets from Afghanistan to Iraq, providing al-Qaeda and the Taliban breathing space (that would later result in a comeback) and ammunition for its propaganda campaign. While the 9/11 attack was generally unpopular among Muslims, the invasion of Iraq appeared to confirm al-Qaeda's claim that the United States was an expansionist aggressor, waging a war against Islam and seeking to take over the Middle East. Though al-Qaeda was unable to participate in the military resistance to the invading forces and had to watch enviously as Jordanian jihadi Abu Musab al-Zarqawi established an organization of foreign jihadis (later joined by many indigenous Iraqis) to fight the American occupation, it identified this event as an important lifeline.

The success of al-Zarqawi's group, al-Tawhid wal-Jihad (TWJ), in Iraq represented a breakthrough for the global jihadi movement: for the first time, a jihadi organization with a transnational agenda had created a base in the heart of the Middle East, one that could become the nucleus of the caliphate. Al-Qaeda was excited by this accomplishment, even though it was not of its own making.

As resistance to US operations in Iraq grew, al-Qaeda began looking to formally expand into "markets" in the Middle East. The organization still aimed to incite Muslims to action while also planning and executing terrorist attacks, but forming branches carrying its brand name became another central priority. Over the next 11 years, al-Qaeda established branches in Saudi Arabia, Iraq, Algeria, Yemen, Somalia, Syria, and the Indian subcontinent, along with claimed mergers with jihadi groups in Egypt and Libya.

The Tension between al-Qaeda's Strategic Objectives and Branching Out

Expansion appears an obvious strategy for a transnational group with an ambitious agenda spanning a wide geographical space encompassing multiple countries. But al-Qaeda adopted this strategy only gradually and in a manner inconsistent with its declared objectives.

Al-Qaeda's stated objective is to create an Islamic state modeled after the medieval caliphate. The restored caliphate, ruled according to *sharia* law, would include all currently and formerly Muslim countries; it would stretch from Indonesia to Spain and would serve as a launching pad to spread Islam and Islamic rule throughout the rest of the world. Thus, the restoration of a caliphate is part of an even grander plan to bring all human society under the Muslim umbrella.[13]

In the shorter term, al-Qaeda seeks to terminate US influence in Muslim countries, liberate Muslim lands under foreign occupation, topple insufficiently Islamic regimes, and implement *sharia* in Muslim countries—all political objectives that appear compatible with organizational expansion. As I will show in the following, a branching-out model is a less comfortable match with al-Qaeda's strategy to attain these objectives.

Over the years, leaders have clearly laid out the group's strategy.[14] In al-Qaeda's view, the demise of the United States is essential to bring change to Muslim lands. The rulers of Muslim countries serve American interests and in return enjoy American protection. Even in the unlikely case that a corrupt regime collapses, Islamists are unable to take concrete steps because the US military will surely move to thwart it, with the United States seeking to form a new puppet regime if necessary to serve its interests. While the US ability to impose its agenda is limited when facing a resolute army of jihadis, experience has taught that even when the mujahideen emerge victorious from a battle, Washington simply will not allow the establishment of a radical Islamist state and is powerful enough to topple any Islamic emirate.

Therefore, the jihadi movement will be able to achieve its political objectives only if it first severely cripples the United States. Al-Qaeda's strategy is directed against the United States and is focused on attrition; it seeks to bleed its Western adversary by inflicting great human, military, and financial losses. Leaders reason that the United States will loosen its grip on Muslim lands only after its power is diminished. At that point, the jihadis will make decisive moves to topple the hated regimes and establish in their stead enduring Islamic states and, eventually, a caliphate. Not only is a focus on Muslim rulers futile as long as American power remains intact—it will lead to under-utilizing jihadi resources and will exacerbate the tremendous existing power imbalances between the jihadis and their enemies.

In internal correspondence, bin Laden echoes this strategy:

> The plague that exists in the nations of Muslims has two causes: The first is the presence of American hegemony and the second is the presence of rulers that have abandoned Islamic law and who identify with the hegemony, serving its interests in exchange for securing their own interests. The only way for us to establish the religion and alleviate the plague which was befallen Muslims is to remove this hegemony which has beset upon the nations and worshippers and which transforms them, such that no regime that rules on the basis of Islamic law remains. The way to remove this hegemony is to continue our direct attrition against the American enemy until it is broken and is too weak to interfere in the matters of the Islamic world. After this phase comes the phase in which the second cause—rulers who have abandoned Islamic law—are toppled, and this will be followed by the phase in which God's religion is established and Islamic law rules.

The focus must be on actions that contribute to the intent of bleeding the American enemy. As for actions that do not contribute to the
intent of bleeding the great enemy, many of them dilute our efforts and
take from our energy. The effect of this on the greater war in general is
clear, as is the resulting delay in the phases leading to the establishment
of an Islamic caliphate, God willing.[15]

Given this analysis, al-Qaeda and its affiliates must concentrate on attacking the main enemy—the United States—and cannot be distracted by the
local regimes. Fighting individual governments may gain primacy under only
particular conditions, primarily when these regimes facilitate Western occupation of Muslim lands, and when they attack jihadis. In short, al-Qaeda coun-
sels jihadis to avoid directly confronting the regimes unless for self-defense. In
a document titled the "General Guidelines for Jihad," al-Zawahiri also warns
his followers to avoid distractions such as fighting "deviant sects" such as the
Shia unless they attack first. Even then, the response must be measured and
restricted to those directly engaged in the fight. Areas of public gathering
such as markets and houses of worship must be avoided, and the lives of other
members of the community must be spared.[16]

If the focus must remain on the United States, why would al-Qaeda establish franchises in Muslim countries? After all, the existence of local branches,
with operational infrastructures in place, makes attacks on local targets
more likely. By launching an affiliate, al-Qaeda raises expectations among its
constituency—and especially among its operatives—for new terrorist operations. Moreover, since some franchises comprise the remains of local terrorist
groups co-opted by al-Qaeda, affiliation presumably requires the parent organization to persuade the contracted group to forgo violence altogether—a
highly unlikely scenario. Finally, by announcing branches, al-Qaeda puts the
regimes in the affiliates' designated regions under domestic and international
pressure to assert their sovereignty. Consequently, even if al-Qaeda would
prefer to avoid fighting local regimes, by forming branches it often creates the
conditions that make fights of self-preservation, distracting the jihadis from
the main battle, more likely.

One may argue that establishing a branch makes sense in locations in
which Muslims are under foreign occupation. When non-Muslims conquer
a Muslim land, jihad to liberate it becomes an obligation; such a defensive
jihad is an individual duty for all capable Muslims, and in its pursuit, common
restrictions, such as requiring parents' permission to join the fight, are lifted.
The problem with applying this logic to al-Qaeda's branches is that although

one may argue that Iraq and Somalia fit the criterion, other Muslim countries into which the group has introduced franchises do not.

Franchises may serve other purposes. The guidelines document emphasizes the importance of propaganda to realizing al-Qaeda's objectives. The organization seeks to educate and cultivate a jihadi spirit and a vanguard that will shoulder "the responsibility" of confronting "the crusaders and their proxies." And it wants to create awareness among the masses and mobilize them so that they would revolt against their rulers.[17] This *da'wa*, the call to follow Islam and its tenets, is of utmost importance to al-Qaeda; it is not just a means to an end but constitutes an objective of its own. But franchises never exist merely for propaganda reasons. Moreover, in the age of global communication, it is doubtful that a propaganda campaign, even one tailored to suit specific local conditions, cannot be effectively organized from a distance, without a local office.

Because al-Qaeda views jihad as the best way to cultivate jihadi spirit, it is hard to imagine it abandoning the active pursuit of jihad. Education for jihad must, therefore, involve actively supporting jihadi efforts—if not in the country of origins, then in a different jihadi front. Again, the question arises: Does preparation for jihad elsewhere require the announcement of a formal branch?

An alternative theory suggests that the affiliates' main mission has been to attack Western targets in each branch's area of responsibility. In the case of al-Qaeda in the Islamic Maghreb (AQIM), this indeed seemed to be the main difference in the group's operations after the GSPC merged with al-Qaeda. Yet most affiliates' attacks have targeted local regimes and public spaces frequented by simple Muslims.[18]

Interestingly, in a letter bin Laden wrote a month before his death, he objected to attacks on American targets in Islamic countries if the jihadis were not poised to topple the regimes in those locations. He maintained that such attacks would result only in confrontations for which they were unprepared, increased government suppression, and the imprisonment of many devoted Muslims. In addition, violent escalation might cost al-Qaeda public sympathy, especially as it endangered innocent Muslims.[19] Thus, bin Laden's clear preference for attacks in non-Muslim countries appears inconsistent with formal expansion through franchising to Muslim countries.

Granted, one must consider the possibility that, isolated, bin Laden was not in control over the organization, and thus his words should be taken as musing rather than mandate. But the Abbottabad documents depict a leader who is trying to be involved, and while bin Laden could not communicate freely and regularly with the franchises, he retained a considerable level of control over AQC. Moreover, at least from the few documents that have been declassified, the franchising strategy (and in fact, even particular franchising decisions) seems to have been adopted with bin Laden's blessing.

The possibility that bin Laden originally envisioned different roles for al-Qaeda's branches and later changed his mind may discount his letter as indicative of a stable al-Qaeda strategy. In the absence of conclusive evidence from internal correspondence among members of al-Qaeda's central command, it is impossible to determine with certainty whether AQC always held such a restrictive view of its franchises' obligations, or whether notions of affiliates' role evolved after AQC witnessed the damage its agents caused. But it is certainly plausible that AQC's thinking underwent change—after all, on several occasions, al-Qaeda leaders called for attacks on American and Western targets in countries where the group had branches.[20] Such an explanation would also resolve the inconsistency between establishing branches and seeking to concentrate attacks on the "head of the snake." Considering al-Zawahiri's unconvincing explanation for direct confrontations between al-Qaeda branches and local regimes—worked up, ad hoc, to justify the branches' existence[21]—it seems clear that al-Qaeda's post-2010 positions imperfectly reflect its original stance regarding franchises' role.

But even if we assume that AQC changed its position about the franchises' mission, an important question remains: Why did al-Qaeda adopt a strategy with such inherent internal contradictions, one that ended up causing the group's image immense damage?

The Need for Unity and Organizational Expansion

An initial factor in explaining al-Qaeda's branching-out strategy concerns its view of the importance of unifying the jihadi camp and its own (major) role in bringing about that unity. This perspective led al-Qaeda to invest greater efforts in consolidating a broad-based jihadi organization, dedicated to a US-centered strategy, under its leadership. Indications that its efforts were going awry only led the organization to strengthen its commitment to expansion, including through mergers with groups whose battlefield successes were quickly undermined by their uncontrollable nature, ultimately harming the al-Qaeda brand.

Long before it began expanding, al-Qaeda encouraged unity among the various jihadi groups, calling for the umma to come together. It saw power in unity and attributed failures on the battlefield to dissension and rifts among the diverse Muslim groups.[22] Al-Qaeda saw itself as the vanguard exposing the Western campaign against Islam, inspiring oppressed Muslims, and offering resources to those joining the fight. As the front line in the war, al-Qaeda's actions focused on propaganda efforts, religious indoctrination, providing professional information online (on topics such as bomb construction and forming and operating cells), and training youth seeking to join the fight. Even its greatest operational success, the 9/11 attack, was intended to inspire and empower Muslims by destroying the myth of American power and showing what even a small cadre of dedicated Muslims armed with rudimentary weapons can accomplish.[23]

Yet by presenting itself as merely a vanguard, al-Qaeda clarified that it sees significant limits to its role; it cannot achieve its objectives—the objectives of the umma—on its own, and therefore needs the support of its co-religionists.[24] In the December 2002 words of spokesman Suleiman Abu Ghaith, the mujahideen are

> the vanguard that has pledged itself to spark the confrontation between our enemies and us. Thus it is not fighting instead of the umma but it is working as an activator for the umma against its enemies so that it may rise altogether to face the occupying and invading enemy.[25]

The central command of al-Qaeda has never explicitly declared leadership, and on some occasions has even declared that the group does not seek to rule.[26] Its rhetoric has always emphasized the primacy of its political and religious objectives, frowning upon organizational jockeying, at least outwardly (and when it concerned other groups). Al-Qaeda has seen its primary role as articulating an ideology, demonstrating the "correct" methodology, and facilitating jihadi operations. Moreover, it declared jihad an individual duty that can be carried out without organizational affiliation or structure.[27] Nevertheless, calling for individuals to take action was never meant to substitute for organized action in which al-Qaeda would play a critical role.

Al-Qaeda has always believed that any means are justified in promoting its agenda. In his book *The Management of Savagery*, al-Qaeda strategist Abu Bakr Naji states clearly that the struggle demands total mobilization of the Muslim masses and the Islamic groups, and that mobilizing believers on such a scale may require taking extraordinary measures:

> We must drag everyone into the battle in order to give life to those who deserve to live and destroy those who deserve to be destroyed.

We must drag all of the movements, the masses, and the parties to the battle and turn the table over the heads of everyone. We will become a single power by uniting our groups, improving the organization and systematizing the spread of our groups, giving allegiance to each other, assisting each other to the ends of the earth and to its East, and by dividing our enemies and dividing their interests and their goals (by the permission of God). [This single force] will be able to impose the rule of the sharia and preserve its rights and the rights of humanity which the Taghuts of unbelief and apostasy toy with.[28]

Prior to 9/11, al-Qaeda labored to shape the jihadi discourse on the problems of the umma and the way to resolve them, emphasizing the United States as the source of the umma's state and the necessity of confrontation to restore Islamic rule. This discourse gained greater appeal as the two alternative ways to pursue jihad, which dominated the jihadi scene in the early 1990s, failed to live up to their promise. Jihad against the Algerian and Egyptian regimes brought disastrous results and discredited the wisdom and viability of campaigns against rulers of Muslim states, the "near enemy." In Bosnia, the less controversial jihad to save oppressed Muslims under occupation had greater success on the battlefield, but jihadis were booted out of the country following the US-brokered Dayton Accords (1995), and they watched with dismay as Bosnia eschewed Islamic rule and pursued the path of multi-ethnic democracy. Therefore, al-Qaeda had a window of opportunity to persuade jihadis to follow its proposed third way.[29]

Al-Qaeda also sought to shift the operational focus of other jihadi groups to the United States. But the organization did not use its brand name to promote its perspective more widely. Establishing the World Islamic Front was a comparatively tame effort to build a jihadi coalition committed to fighting the "far enemy," representing a step up from the organization's ongoing efforts to build relationships with other jihadi groups through providing training and financial resources to a more formal commitment to al-Qaeda's strategic orientation. However, in such a coalition there is no formal hierarchy, and no single leader holds authority over all groups. Indeed, Michael Scheuer argued that in this coalition bin Laden's role was of the "inciter-in-chief," not the commander-in-chief.[30] This architecture is distinct from the franchising of al-Qaeda that we see today.

Formed prior to the launching of its campaign of violence, the World Islamic Front was based on member equality and minimal institutionalization.

Participation required little commitment from al-Qaeda's partners, with little risk of costly action. In reality, al-Qaeda's main achievement was that it
succeeded, for the first time, in convincing several regional jihadi groups to
declare their commitment to a transnational and anti-American campaign.
This was not an easy task. Shortly after the announcement, the Gama'a
Islamiya denied that it had joined the front and declared that Rifa'i Taha, who
signed the founding document, acted without authorization; senior members
in the EIJ were outraged that al-Zawahiri would make what they viewed as a
reckless decision and commit the group to the new front without consulting
them.[31] It appears that even bin Laden came to see the front as a burden rather
than a benefit; he reportedly admitted that his hope that the front would
push groups and individuals to join al-Qaeda's cause had been frustrated.[32]

Al-Qaeda was in a better position to expand once it started executing
spectacular attacks. The bombings of African embassies and the USS *Cole*
burnished its credentials in the jihadi "market" as an effective group capable of carrying out lethal operations and hitting highly symbolic targets. It
was no longer a group whose role was restricted to facilitating and assisting
others' work but an important power in its own right. Moreover, the mea-
ger American response seemed to validate al-Qaeda's claims that fighting and
even vanquishing the United States was feasible. Importantly, the group's
expansion between 1998 and 2001 focused on the individual level, attracting
young Muslims to join.

Then, a few months before the 9/11 attacks, al-Qaeda merged with
al-Zawahiri's EIJ. Al-Zawahiri had already been managing many aspects
of al-Qaeda's operation, with other EIJ members also holding central roles
in al-Qaeda's bureaucracy. The merger came as the EIJ underwent a period
of turmoil: its terror campaign in Egypt had failed, and a crackdown by
Egyptian authorities and the arrests of many members abroad had decimated
its ranks even as financial mismanagement exacerbated a resource drain.
Infighting even temporarily removed al-Zawahiri from his leadership position. With the group's survival at stake, al-Zawahiri presented the union to
disgruntled members as a way to overcome its financial difficulties and operational setbacks.

It is unclear what prompted bin Laden to formalize the connection with
his lieutenant's organization; there are no indications that the merger was
conceived as part of a broader strategy of systematic expansion. The absence
of a media campaign to accompany the merger indicates that its objective
probably was not to make a direct and immediate impact on al-Qaeda's political enterprise. Al-Zawahiri likely viewed strengthening ties with bin Laden as

the only way to guarantee the EIJ's survival; bin Laden, who was interested in beefing up his organization yet conscious of the failure of expansion through the World Islamic Front, was receptive to the idea of formalizing the relationship.[33] Thus, the new arrangement was a one-time event and a response to a close associate's problems, which had the added value of bolstering al-Qaeda's numbers just before launching the 9/11 attack and escalating the confrontation with the United States. It also reduced the odds that the EIJ would return to its previous focus on fighting the Egyptian regime.

Notably, the merger was based on the principle of equality between the two groups, manifested in renaming the organization Qaedat al-Jihad. Yet this theoretical equality did not translate to significant change in al-Qaeda's organizational structure, except for formalizing al-Zawahiri's role as bin Laden's lieutenant. Even the name change—intended to highlight the Egyptian group's importance within al-Qaeda—failed to stick in the collective memory of both supporters and foes. In following years, al-Qaeda's affiliation agreements focused on explicit hierarchical relations, no longer interested in equality (or even the façade of equality). Interestingly, there are some important similarities between the merger's very limited success and al-Qaeda's later efforts to expand into Egypt and Libya. Al-Zawahiri was unable to deliver the whole EIJ—while many of the members present in Afghanistan followed him, others did not. And given the collapse of the organization's Egyptian infrastructure, the merger did not give al-Qaeda a foothold in that prominent Muslim country. Similarly, al-Qaeda's expansion plans, based on forming relationships with the segments of the Gama'a Islamiya (GI) and the Libyan Islamic Fighting Group (LIFG) that had operated alongside al-Qaeda in the Afghan and Pakistani arenas, did not provide al-Qaeda footholds in their home countries. However, whereas those among the EIJ who opposed the merger promised not to reveal their position in public and to maintain an image of a united organization,[34] the leadership of the GI and the LIFG chose a different path: they immediately acted to suppress al-Qaeda's hostile takeover and made sure that al-Qaeda was unable to "steal" their members or appropriate the groups' operational infrastructure.

The attack on the American homeland further escalated al-Qaeda's campaign to unite (or, for some, to force) the jihadi camp under its leadership and mobilize the Muslim masses. While expecting the umma to respond to US actions with large-scale mobilization was overly optimistic, bringing together diverse jihadi groups seemed realistic. Indeed, the United States' inability to distinguish between the multitude of actors and positions in the jihadi camp led it to put pressure on all jihadi groups. The imperatives of international collaboration strengthened this inclination: states tried to link their domestic opposition groups to al-Qaeda to make them targets in the war on terrorism. Al-Qaeda's strategy had some success, mostly in Afghanistan and Pakistan's tribal areas, where the American assault drove diverse jihadi groups sheltered in Afghanistan to fight together in defense of the Taliban and for their own lives. But outside the warfront, leading figures in the jihadi camp were less forgiving; they were angry that al-Qaeda had forced all jihadi groups into a confrontation with the United States that they did not want and were unprepared for.[35]

Al-Qaeda did not settle for triggering a worldwide clash between the US-led international community and the jihadi movement—it envisioned itself in a leadership role in the next stages of this struggle and in the emerging new world order. Al-Qaeda believed that demonstrating its ability to conduct an operation on such a large scale would lead Islamic groups and Muslims around the world to naturally view it as a potent force worthy of leadership.[36] Its quest for leadership was also fed by its belief that the process launched with the attacks and the subsequent American response was reversible; thus, to sustain it, al-Qaeda must lead.

The organization demonstrated some willingness to lower its public profile when circumstances required; its Iraqi branch gave up the brand name for the name Mujahidun Shura Council and, later, Islamic State of Iraq (ISI). Far from embodying al-Qaeda's readiness to relinquish power, though, these formations were fronts intended to create an image of harmony among the multitude of jihadi groups in the country, while in reality al-Qaeda planned to swallow them. In addition, the leaders' goal was to establish facts on the ground in preparation for the war to control Iraq following the departure of US forces. They included a few other small jihadi outfits but remained dominated by people from al-Qaeda's Iraqi franchise. Moreover, al-Qaeda used intimidation and coercion to encourage jihadi groups to join and continuously tried to force perceived competitors to succumb to its authority.[37]

Al-Qaeda's actions in Syria, a few years later, support the claim that observers should view this apparent flexibility as tactical, rather than as evidence of al-Qaeda abandoning its leadership aspirations. Equipped with lessons from its debacle in Iraq, al-Qaeda entered Syria determined to follow a much more accommodating approach vis-à-vis other groups. Al-Qaeda avoided using the brand name when establishing its branch, Jabhat al-Nusra (JN), and instructed JN's leaders to deny any relationship. Furthermore, it declared a willingness to share power in the governance of liberated areas, publicly emphasized the people's right to choose their leaders, and formed cooperative relationships with a wide array of rebel groups, including some with moderate nationalist agendas.[38] However, al-Qaeda's restrictive view of what constituted legitimate leadership left a shallow pool of potential chiefs and positioned al-Qaeda itself as the de facto leader. The limits of the organization's willingness to deepen cooperation based on equal relationships with other groups was evident in November 2013 when jihadi rebel forces—but not JN—came together to form an umbrella group, the Islamic Front, and when in May 2014 JN refused to sign the "revolutionary covenant" initiative.[39]

Even Naji, while acknowledging that there may be regions liberated from non-Islamic rule that will be governed for a while by tribes or other Islamic groups and suggesting that the local al-Qaeda branch may have to accept other elements' leadership, views such situations as temporary: if the administrator of these "savage" regions is genuinely interested in ruling according to *sharia*, it will form a union with al-Qaeda, and if it participates in what al-Qaeda views as acts of infidelity, it will be challenged and fought.[40] In this way or the other, whether because other groups willingly adopt al-Qaeda's worldview and strategy or because al-Qaeda operates to thwart wrongful direction, the result is al-Qaeda expanding its authority.

The statements of al-Qaeda leaders and former allies suggest that, not unlike other jihadi figures, the leaders, and bin Laden above all, have harbored a sense of moral superiority and infallibility, justifying any action the organization takes and reaffirming the command's vital role in the inevitable Islamic renewal. While al-Qaeda leaders have sometimes admitted mistakes, they have been slow to see them as reflecting more than tactical-level errors. Particularly in the case of the excessive violence emerging from its ranks, al-Qaeda has preferred to dismiss transgressions as the result of insufficient knowledge of individual fighters on the ground and pressing circumstances.[41] Some of al-Qaeda's admitted mistakes have concerned the permissibility of particular operations, but, at least until the ISI imploded, they were not treated as strategic blunders. Ultimately, al-Qaeda's leaders have failed to address these problems in a comprehensive manner. When they have had adverse strategic ramifications (for example, when the death of Muslim civilians hurts the image of the jihadis), al-Qaeda speakers have generally shifted blame to critics who, they charge, bought into a campaign of deceit orchestrated by the umma's enemies and intended to smear the mujahideen, instead of offering advice and trying to improve the jihad from within.

As some of the internal debates among al-Qaeda's leaders reveal, a handful of AQC members have supported a more self-critical approach. Of particular interest is a group, including the Egyptian Saif al-Adl, that opposed 9/11 and in its aftermath was particularly vocal in its criticism, arguing that bin

Laden was leading the organization in the wrong direction.[42] Little came of this group's calls for a reassessment of al-Qaeda's strategy. One of them, Abu Hafs al-Mauritani, who had a reputation as a religious authority,[43] returned to his home country of Mauritania to retire. Others fared no better: They were sidelined, possibly because their criticism centered on the shortcomings of bin Laden himself.

Al-Qaeda's leaders display total confidence in their understanding of the umma's condition and of the strategy required to revive it. Groups following the "right path" understand the correctness of al-Qaeda's interpretation of reality, the effectiveness of its strategic plans, and its solid religious foundations. Such groups will inevitably accept al-Qaeda's emphasis on the need to join forces and unify all righteous jihadi organizations. Jihadi groups failing to accept al-Qaeda's interpretation and leadership become targets of the organization's subversive and predatory efforts to change their orientation.

This worldview led al-Qaeda to damaging public fights with Hamas and other Sunni insurgent groups in Iraq,[44] as well as intense quarrels with the growing crowd of repudiators, including prominent jihadi individuals and leaders of other Islamic groups, especially from Egypt and Libya.[45] Indeed, observers should consider al-Qaeda's declarations of unification with remnants of the LIFG and the GI in the context of its desperate efforts to discredit repudiations from these organizations' traditional leadership. Al-Qaeda's branching-out strategy thus appears to be another step in its escalating efforts to steer the umma and the jihadi movement in the "right" direction. The greater the difficulties in promoting this mission, the more forceful al-Qaeda's moves have become.

AQC appears to have grasped the transgressions' systematic nature and the extent of their harm to al-Qaeda's cause and reputation only after the Sunni Sahwa (Awakening) groups and American forces crippled the Iraqi branch. Although AQC took no responsibility for the perverse actions of franchises and allies such as the Pakistani Taliban, it was forced to take a hard look at its actions and figure out a way to avoid repeating such harmful actions, deal with the wayward branches, and restore al-Qaeda's image. Notably, bin Laden and al-Zawahiri remained reluctant to renounce undisciplined affiliates, even as some members began advocating for al-Qaeda to severe ties with rogue branches.[46] It took al-Zawahiri nearly two years to expel the ISI from al-Qaeda, even though the latter publicly refused to respect his authority and defied his instructions to hand over responsibility for the Syrian arena to JN.

Indeed, once it entered these new arenas, al-Qaeda found retreat hard to swallow. The central command in Pakistan could have sent trusted members to the problematic affiliates to strengthen its control and steer them in the right direction, were leaders not focused on their personal survival and facing a depleted bench of senior leaders. An attempt to send a "fixer" to the ISI proved very costly when AQC's emissary, the very senior Abd al-Hadi al-Iraqi, was caught as he was trying to return to Iraq.[47]

Strategic Miscalculations and Organizational Response

Branching out is the most recent example of al-Qaeda's escalating commitment to actively leading the umma, but observers cannot understand this strategy without considering flaws in the group's original design for the conflict. These defects helped transform the strategic landscape: the organization's weakening and the threat of competition from other jihadi groups pushed al-Qaeda to change its plans. Despite numerous American mistakes (the invasion of Iraq in particular) that created opportunities, the war did not evolve in the way the leadership had expected, and al-Qaeda found itself in a difficult overall position. In a prescient assessment of the group, written before the Arab Awakening, Jason Burke noted al-Qaeda's failure to promote its strategic interests: it failed to rally the Muslim masses or to unseat even one despotic leader (although when al-Qaeda finally recovered from the initial shock that demonstrators had managed to topple Tunisia's Zine El Abidine ben Ali and Egypt's Hosni Mubarak, it gave itself credit for creating the conditions that facilitated the removal of these leaders[48]). Burke noted that al-Qaeda had produced no spectacular attack since the 2005 London bombing and suggested that, in the fragmented world of global jihadi militancy in which groups compete for donations and air time, al-Qaeda risks becoming "the aging rock-star or director who once produced some good work but has done nothing for a long time."[49]

To some extent, al-Qaeda's problems are of its own making. Notwithstanding bin Laden's carefully polished image, some in jihadi circles dismissed him as an inept strategist substituting wishful thinking for planning.[50] Such claims seem to be substantiated by the inherent tension in al-Qaeda's operational plan as well as the contradictions between its strategic objectives and its organizational interests. The tension stems from the gap between a political and ideological focus on the Middle East and a strategy prioritizing the West as a target for attacks. On the face of things, with the United States dragged into greater regional involvement, al-Qaeda should have felt less of a need to operate in non-Muslim regions and should have redirected its resources to the Middle East. Such a shift, however, risked diminishing al-Qaeda's uniqueness and pitting it against local jihadi groups. The conflict's transformation to one focusing on battles between jihadi outfits and regimes, supported by the United States, would have put local opposition groups in a better position than al-Qaeda to take the lead. Thus, in the absence of goodwill from local competitors, even a strategic success could have spelled the organization's demise.

Al-Qaeda lacked a plan for such a transition. As a result, it was left with two ways to achieve both its political objectives and its organizational interests. The best-case scenario involved the United States' rapid decline, equivalent to that of the Soviet Union, which informed bin Laden's strategic thinking (according to Abu Walid al-Misri, bin Laden expected that three blows would suffice[51]). Alternatively, a very receptive Muslim street would rush to join al-Qaeda en masse, convincing other jihadi groups to accept its leadership or, at least, to offer sufficient human and material resources to prevail in any internal competition. Both scenarios depended on unrealistically fast developments and were the product of wishful thinking.

The reality was different. Despite failing to bring down the United States or excite the umma, al-Qaeda did draw America into the region and became a symbol of resistance to Western hegemony. This partial success justified al-Qaeda's continued existence but came at a heavy price, with supporters pressuring the group to further escalate operations and take actions it was unable to sustain. Al-Qaeda miscalculated: the 9/11 attacks expanded the battlefield, but the organization lacked the capabilities to fight on such a broad front. It felt tremendous pressure to follow its success with successive blows in the West while simultaneously promoting the jihadi cause in the Middle East. But it never had the resources to support those plans, and the attacks failed to bring in the expected new resources. Moreover, the punishing American onslaught seriously degraded its existing capabilities, to the extent that when the Iraqi front opened, al-Qaeda was unable to lead the insurgency and saw al-Zarqawi fill the gap.

Thus, while al-Qaeda looked to attack the West and establish Islamic emirates in the Muslim world, it lacked the resources to simultaneously and effectively do both. Yet the organization no longer had the privilege of choice: if it simply retreated to the Middle East and abandoned its Western-oriented strategy, al-Qaeda would have lost credibility and would have found itself competing with established and not necessarily sympathetic local jihadi groups. If it moved out of the Arab arenas, it would have risked losing relevance and the most important mass of potential recruits, on whose mobilization its grand strategy depended.

The reasonable compromise was to seek a way to be present in both the West and the Middle East, and to give its operations in Arab countries an anti-Western flavor, mostly via attacks on Western-identified targets—for example, foreign embassies. In the West, al-Qaeda has focused considerable energy on establishing covert cells and plotting terrorist attacks. These cells usually comprise Western volunteers who have made their way to Pakistan.[52] More recently, the Syrian civil war offered al-Qaeda a new stream of Western recruits that could replenish the diminishing ranks of its European network. Conversely, in Muslim countries the organization seeks to cultivate local branches, either by merging with already active jihadi groups or, where none exists, by establishing its own through local al-Qaeda operatives.

The difference in the way al-Qaeda operates in the Middle East and the West can be attributed to each region's political role in the group's strategy and different organizational environments. Al-Qaeda's ideological innovation—portraying the US-led West as the cause of Muslims' unfortunate political, social, and economic conditions and its fall as the key to Islamic renewal—necessitates continuing terrorist operations in the West, with or without establishing formal branches there. The Middle East, by contrast, is the ultimate focus of the organization's political objectives. It is also an environment where al-Qaeda must compete with other jihadi organizations for market share. Thus, its inherently incoherent plan forced it to focus its operational energy on attacking the West while deepening its role in the Middle East via efforts to co-opt struggles in the Arab world.

Branching out offered some tangible and appealing short-term benefits, especially in light of the demands that al-Qaeda's incoherent strategy imposed on the group. Franchising enabled the group to grow at an unprecedented rate and its central command to portray itself as the headquarters of the global jihadi movement.[53] Mergers with like-minded organizations served as force multipliers and gave al-Qaeda a shortcut to growth by acquiring groups with existing human resources, local knowledge, and organizational infrastructure. According to a team of researchers in the US Military Academy's Combating Terrorism Center, al-Qaeda increased its presence in at least 19 countries through mergers. Mergers also created opportunities for new sanctuaries and effectively lowered the barriers of entry to jihad, creating increased opportunity and access for aspiring jihadis and largely releasing AQC from having to vet volunteers on its own.[54]

In addition, al-Qaeda's branches link the global jihad to particular regional grievances and create focal points throughout the Middle East, freeing the central leadership from the need to deal directly with local insurgent groups.[55] All these advantages loomed larger in light of the mounting pressure on al-Qaeda's senior leaders and the organization's diminishing capabilities. Branching out allowed al-Qaeda to show activity even when its leadership was under pressure. It also increased its redundancy and, by stretching the battlefield, probably lifted some of the external pressure on the leadership. In fact, in 2004 bin Laden linked the dispersal of jihadist activities to al-Qaeda's strategy of economically bleeding the United States.[56] While he spoke in the context of small al-Qaeda cells, the logic is compatible with organizational expansion as a way to raise the costs for the US-led coalition as well. Indeed, AQC became increasingly reliant on its franchises, to the point of directing them to initiate attacks in the West.[57]

Nevertheless, branching out carried risks, and AQC soon found itself managing setbacks. At the most basic level, the leadership in Pakistan's tribal areas felt insufficiently informed: information from the franchises was often slow to arrive and tended be incomplete, putting the senior leadership in a difficult position when problems in a branch required its intervention.[58] And as AQC remained under siege, groups that have joined the organization enjoyed significant freedom of action, with the leadership seeing a corresponding loss of control over its messaging and target selection.[59] In fact, by franchising, al-Qaeda put its brand and reputation in the hands of groups and leaders over whom it has limited control and who may end up hurting its cause. The pleas by al-Zawahiri and other leaders to al-Zarqawi, for example, showed al-Qaeda's awareness that the franchise was making blunders that could undermine public support and thus risk al-Qaeda's enterprise in Iraq and beyond. Franchising means that al-Qaeda not only gets credit for success—it also owns the blunders.

Of course, a branch does not need to bring calamity on the parent organization to make the relationship dubious—it may simply fail to meet the expectations of a meaningful contribution to its success. Al-Qaeda has found more than once in Algeria that the branch tasked to carry out attacks lacks the urgency felt by the central leadership, often following the central command's instructions only when it perceives particular attacks to be in its own interest. The discrepancies between the center and the branch appear to vary depending on the nature of their links, with affiliates that emerged organically from the parent group less likely to exhibit preference divergence and more inclined to follow its instructions than those who joined following a merger agreement. For example, AQAP, established by members of al-Qaeda, appears to be more willing to follow AQC's directives[60] than are jihadi outfits that merged with al-Qaeda but whose leaders skipped the indoctrination process aimed at assuring adherence to its ideology, clear understanding of its strategic objectives, and total deference to the leadership. As noted, al-Qaeda's leaders repeatedly tried to direct al-Zarqawi to follow its directives (for example, to avoid targeting the Shia population). The leadership's isolation and communication problems, with messages normally sent via courier, made exerting such control particularly challenging, demonstrating the risks involved in putting the organization's fate in the hands of uncontrollable affiliated groups.[61]

While franchising could help thwart competition from other jihadi organizations through their co-optation, in al-Qaeda's case it actually made such intra-jihadi competition more likely. As the pressure on al-Qaeda rose and made the organization more dependent on its franchises, its leaders discovered that they had become less relevant. Not surprisingly, then, the Arabian Peninsula branch (an al-Qaeda creation and thus more trusted) has been central to efforts to attack targets outside the Middle East;[62] after the death of bin Laden and other leading members of AQC, al-Zawahiri nominated AQAP's emir, Nasir al-Wuhayshi, as al-Qaeda's general manager.[63] Even with trusted branches, however, AQC faces the risk that elements within them will look to individual political objectives at the expense of the global jihad. Moreover, AQAP's high profile gives its leaders—should they decide to seize control of the parent organization—an operational record, organizational infrastructure, and name recognition valuable in mounting a challenge.

But al-Qaeda's Iraqi affiliate has posed a stronger threat to the senior leadership. Chapter 9 will offer a detailed discussion of the Islamic State's challenge to al-Qaeda, but the case exemplifies the threat from a group that was never properly incorporated into the al-Qaeda network yet was able to benefit from the brand name and build its abilities while under al-Qaeda's wing until it felt prepared to directly challenge an ineffectual AQC.

Finally, in franchising, al-Qaeda recognized the power of local identifications and the greater attractiveness of mobilization based on local grievances. But such an approach has endangered al-Qaeda's ideological appeal. Indeed, al-Qaeda's willingness to allow a much greater role for the fight against the "near enemy" represented a 180-degree shift from its prior position that such a development would distract from the main effort. By blurring the line between its ideology and that of national jihadi groups, al-Qaeda is undermining both its credibility and its argument for ideological supporters to favor it over those competitors.

Al-Qaeda has tried to avoid such pitfalls by reformulating the justifications for its strategy. It has repeated allegations that "apostate" Middle Eastern regimes collaborate with Washington, but while in the past its speakers used this connection to justify shifting the battle to the United States, they have appropriated it to explain attacks against these regimes. Because of America's defeat at the hands of the mujahideen, they argue, it has opted for an indirect strategy of standing behind "agent regimes" who do its bidding. In the words of top al-Qaeda leader Abu Yahya al-Libi, "What pushed the United States to follow this method and to avoid confrontation were the massive losses that it suffered on the fields of jihad that it dared to enter. . . . Thus, it moved to another experiment, which is war by proxy and the exporting of agent forces."[64]

Attacking the regimes and attacking the United States thus serve the same objectives of undermining Western designs for the region. Al-Qaeda declared, "the mujahideen must strive to overcome the protecting barrier [the local forces] in order to strike at what is hiding behind it."[65] Rather than reflecting ideological adjustments, this reversal appears to be self-serving, a natural outcome of internal contradictions in al-Qaeda's strategy, and an excuse for transformation. Unsurprisingly, when the Islamic State denounced al-Qaeda, one of its arguments was that the organization had lost its original ideology under al-Zawahiri and had abandoned its support for an Islamic caliphate for the despised Sykes-Picot borders.[66]

Conclusions

Al-Qaeda's quest for expansion reflected the group's escalating efforts to unite the jihadi camp behind its agenda, with al-Qaeda standing at the front of this greater movement—not simply showing the road forward, but leading there. This chapter has showed how al-Qaeda's choice to expand through a branching-out strategy stemmed from internal tension in the leadership's strategic thinking, conflict between its strategic objectives and organizational interests, leaders' detrimental hubris, and an aggressive American campaign that severely constrained AQC's operations.

But if al-Qaeda was so committed to uniting all jihadi forces, why did it not pursue alternative organizational arrangements? Whereas in its early years al-Qaeda moved cautiously to spread its vision and persuade other jihadi groups that the road to restoring the caliphate passes through direct confrontation with the United States, after 9/11 the organization has found itself unable to sustain that fight in the same manner. Unwilling to accept defeat but unable to unite the jihadi camp under its leadership, al-Qaeda chose to pursue a piecemeal approach in which it sought expansion through franchising. In this way, it was able to forge an image of success in which organizational expansion compensated for its inability to strike the American homeland again. At the same time, it offered groups that wished to benefit from al-Qaeda's reputation, operational and logistical networks, and donor base a way to join the group without losing much of their own autonomy.

Al-Qaeda probably preferred to expand through the absorption model, but while 9/11 increased the urgency of unification, it denied the group the power to pursue it effectively. Important jihadi groups did not rush to join al-Qaeda, and the organization lacked the ability to coerce them into accepting its authority, especially with its leadership blockaded and far from all target arenas. Indeed, consent was the only way to affiliation. Attempts to rely on Middle Eastern allies, present alongside AQC in Pakistan, to push leaders of these regional groups to accede to al-Qaeda have failed.

While affiliation required consent, could not al-Qaeda change the organizational arrangement to one of absorption? As AQC's ability to control its franchises has only weakened over time, there is little reason to believe that absorption would be feasible. In locations where al-Qaeda formed in-house branches, it should have been easier—albeit still far from guaranteed—to change the organizational arrangement. But to fully integrate some branches without doing the same with the others makes little political sense: it creates organizational incoherence, diminishes the importance of the arenas and leaders who appear to have lost autonomy, and may push branches leery of an AQC takeover to break with it altogether. As AQC lacks the power to force this organizational change on unwilling affiliates, it would be a gamble with no realistic chances of success.

5

Explaining Arena Choices

TWO PERSPECTIVES

AL-QAEDA'S FIRST ORGANIZATIONAL expansion took place prior to the 9/11 attacks when, in 2000, it united with the Egyptian Islamic Jihad (EIJ). But it was only in 2003, with the announcement of the organization's Saudi branch, that formal expansion emerged as a central strategy.

The next year, al-Qaeda announced a second branch, following its merger with Abu Musab al-Zarqawi's Iraq-based organization, al-Tawhid wal-Jihad (TWJ), later renamed Al-Qaeda in the Land of the Two Rivers. In 2006, al-Qaeda brought the Algerian GSPC (the French abbreviation for the Salafist Group for Preaching and Combat) into its fold and renamed it Al-Qaeda in the Islamic Maghreb (AQIM), followed shortly by the establishment of a franchise in Yemen. In January 2009, this branch was rebranded and assumed the name of the defunct Saudi branch Al-Qaeda in the Arabian Peninsula. In the following year al-Shabab joined al-Qaeda, but the merger was not announced until two years later. Jabhat al-Nusra (JN) was formed as al-Qaeda's Syrian branch in 2012, although it denied the nature of the relationship for well over a year. Finally, in September 2014, al-Qaeda announced the formation of Al-Qaeda in the Indian Subcontinent (AQIS).

Notwithstanding this impressively broad deployment, al-Qaeda's expansion has fallen short of expectations. The organization has neither formalized links with all major jihadi groups nor established an official presence in every potential high-impact location. Most strikingly, it has failed to launch a franchise in the highly prized Palestinian arena, despite repeated invocations of the Palestinian cause, promises of active support, and the availability of Gaza Strip jihadi outfits that have declared identification with al-Qaeda. Moreover, in two cases, al-Qaeda's efforts to expand suffered setbacks when its declarations of mergers with the Libyan Islamic Fighting Group and the Egyptian Gama'a Islamiya were rebuffed publicly by those groups' leaders.

The previous chapter explained why al-Qaeda chose a strategy of branching out. Spreading the organization's brand name is a logical, albeit counterintuitive, response to the combination of growing expectations and diminishing capabilities. I argued that al-Qaeda preferred organizational expansion, based on its self-image as destined to lead a greater jihadi movement, but the organization's weakening and threat of competition from other groups pushed al-Qaeda toward a branching-out strategy. Having failed to mobilize the Muslim masses through its attacks on the United States, and acknowledging the force of local identifications, al-Qaeda sought to mobilize the umma in a more piecemeal manner. Overall, the worse it was doing, the greater the pressure it felt to formally expand. Branching out was hardly an illogical move: by co-opting other jihadi groups, some of them potential competitors, al-Qaeda could have enhanced its survival prospects and perhaps even continued to move toward its dream of leading the jihadi camp. But as al-Qaeda learned, the hazards of franchising have been no less significant.

While incoherent strategy and impending decline may encourage an organization to expand, they still do not explain the form and direction of al-Qaeda's franchising. After demonstrating how al-Qaeda's blunders and delusions of grandeur prompted its decline and drove its expansion efforts, in this chapter I offer two perspectives on particular expansion choices, applied to the al-Qaeda case. The first focuses on the ways in which a target arena's characteristics explain franchising choices; the second links branching-out choices to modes of decision-making.

An arena-based analysis looks at the value of specific locations. Some are attractive because of their intrinsic importance, particularly their religious significance and historic symbolism. A transnational terrorist organization may also enter arenas for their strategic value—that is, their role in the organization's comprehensive plan. An arena's particular characteristics, such as its terrain, the strength of the state (and its ruling authorities), and the number and identity of opposition groups, present another category of determinants of franchising choices.

The second perspective is actor-oriented. It looks at the way in which situational factors—specifically, the level of pressure-group leaders' experience— inform decision-making regarding expansion choices. When an organization is enjoying a period of success and operating under tolerable levels of pressure— after all, pressure is inevitable in the life of a terrorist organization—affiliation

decisions are shaped by leaders' ability to discriminate between different arenas, to judge costs and benefits of taking action in potential locations, and to
decline those promising insufficient or negative returns. By contrast, an organization under extreme pressure, facing strategic weakness, will naturally make
lower-quality affiliation decisions, seeking to expand to whichever location it
can, even if entering the chosen arena would result in harm.

Applying this framework to al-Qaeda's franchising decisions, I suggest
that when it operates under conditions of "need," we would expect to see it
scrambling to spread the brand name, even at grave costs. When "opportunity" drives its decisions, it should follow a more deliberate and rational
decision-making process, entering an arena only if success is likely. Working
from this actor-based perspective requires a rich store of information that is
often hard to come by. However, the addition of such situational and psychological dimensions to the study of transnational terrorist organizations
strengthens our understanding of these groups in general and of their affiliation choices in particular.

Arena-Based Perspective

The discussion of a transnational terrorist organization's decision to adopt a
branching-out strategy views the entire area that the group seeks to dominate
as one, implicitly seeing all states (or territories) located within it as equally
important. Such an assumption is useful for understanding the broad strategy, but in order to grasp particular affiliation choices, it is imperative to
acknowledge the dissimilar value of different locations and the various conditions that make expansion into some arenas more attractive than others.
Some characteristics—for example, geographical conditions and religious
importance—are stable over time. Others, such as regime capabilities and
competing groups' size, are transient. In this section, I discuss three broad categories of arena-based factors that shape the particular franchising choices of
a transnational terrorist group such as al-Qaeda: a location's symbolic value,
its importance to an overarching strategic plan, and particular characteristics
that affect feasibility calculations.

Ideational Value

Some arenas have great ideational value. Ideational value refers to sticky qualities such as religious meaning and historical importance, but an area can also
assume ideational significance indirectly, usually as actors frame particular

events taking place in certain locations in ideological terms and in this way magnify their significance.

While all territories that Muslims have ever controlled can potentially evoke symbolism, some locations possess particularly strong religious and historical value. These places are inscribed in the minds not only of the jihadis but of all Muslims. Consequently, religious and historical appeal generates incentives for establishing a formal presence. Such lands occupy a central role in the organization's identity: it cannot credibly declare itself a transnational Islamist movement, dedicated to returning Islam to its glory days, without openly working to assume control and, in some cases, to liberate the places at the core of Islamic identity.

The organization's expansion decisions can offer insights into the balance between ideological commitments and practical considerations. Locations central to Islam are obvious expansion targets but can pose serious challenges and can undermine the organization's pursuit of broader strategic objectives. While an organization can demonstrate considerable flexibility in its operational decisions, and even its decisions of where to establish branches, arenas infused with religious importance test a group's ideological essence. Naturally, pursuing those locations should be prioritized, but if conditions for entry are not ideal, following ideological imperatives could undercut an organization's broader agenda by, for example, diverting resources from other fronts. The challenge can be particularly acute if entering a religiously central arena has little chance of outright success. Thus, such a location can present a dilemma: the organization may be unable to promote its objectives there—and yet it needs to maintain a presence or risk losing support, since some would see its absence as indicating a lack of capabilities or insufficient commitment to the group's declared ideology. For a jihadi group such as al-Qaeda, avoiding a religiously prominent arena risks undercutting its ideological legitimacy, undermining its ability to achieve strategic goals, and threatening its organizational interests.

Thus, an arena's symbolic value could make al-Qaeda gravitate in its direction not only due to its centrality to the organization's identity but also because its importance to the umma compels al-Qaeda to continuously demonstrate a commitment to its liberation, regardless of—and even in spite of—operational considerations. On the Palestinian question, the criticism leveled against al-Qaeda for the gap between its rhetoric and its miniscule actual activity shows how the organization's ideological commitment shapes its operational needs and imposes constraints that it ignores at a high price. The group may try to tamp down expectations and explain the practical limitations in the hope of avoiding the need to choose between operational failure and loss of credibility; it may also try to portray its activities elsewhere as serving the interests of the umma in the symbolically laden arena.[1]

Two places hold supreme religious importance for Sunni Muslims: the Arabian Peninsula (particularly the area now known as Saudi Arabia) and Palestine (mostly territory currently controlled by Israel). Saudi Arabia is the cradle of Islam, where the Quran was revealed to the Prophet. It is the location of Islam's two holiest places, Mecca and Medina, and the place in whose direction all Muslims pray. Moreover, it is from the heart of the Arabian Peninsula that the Islamic empire spread at an unprecedented pace throughout the world.

As a *Waqf* land, dedicated to God and required to be under Muslim control, all Palestine is highly important, but Jerusalem (or *al-Quds*) is imbued with a unique religious significance. It is the religion's third most sacred place and the original direction of Muslim prayers. Moreover, according to Islam's teachings, the Prophet made his "night journey" to heaven from the city's al-Aqsa mosque. The contestation with Judaism and Christianity—the monotheistic religions that Islam intended to replace—further enhances Jerusalem's importance. Although Islam allows tolerating the People of the Book (Jews and Christians) as protected minorities under Islamic rule, equality between the religions is impossible. Consequently, particularly for the jihadis, no arrangement can resolve these religions' claims to holy sites in Jerusalem—especially a deal granting them sovereignty. This problem is particularly acute in the case of the Wailing Wall, the last remains of the Jewish Temple that is located on the same spot as the Muslim mosques. Israel's control of Jerusalem further strengthens the importance of the city: not only has a Muslim holy site come under occupation—its physical existence is under severe threat. If the Muslims do not thwart the "evil" designs for al-Aqsa, the Jews will destroy the mosque.

Iraq has symbolic value as well. The nation served as the seat of the Abbasid dynasty, a caliphate that ruled supreme for five hundred years, seeing great successes as well as painful historical memories. The Mongols' 1258 C.E. capture of Baghdad signifies a low point for Islam and carries memories of internal weakness and external hostility.

Although religious and historical value naturally appeals to Muslims, such symbolism in and of itself is unlikely to boost mobilization. After all, their ideational value is constant, and they have failed to move Muslims for many decades. In fact, one may argue that, with the exception of the most radical fringes, Muslims grew accustomed and accepting of the status quo in these locations. Periods of great religious revival among Muslim societies could boost age-old symbolism, but given their rarity, symbolism is more likely to prove potent when combined with salient and recent Muslim grievances, primarily foreign occupation.

Al-Qaeda has used ideological frames to portray American actions as a continuing assault on Islam and part of an ongoing cosmic battle between falsehood and truth. It frames particular events in a religious context, aiming to strengthen its broad narrative as well as encouraging mobilization and justifying jihadi actions in urgent crises. In that way, jihad in Saudi Arabia is important not only because of the country's centrality to Islam but also because it must be liberated from the occupying "Crusaders," a reference to US forces deployed to the kingdom in the early 1990s and still embedded there long after the Gulf War ended. For Osama bin Laden and his followers, repelling this occupation has religious meaning that goes even beyond the imperative to liberate Muslim territories: in the jihadi view, American presence in Saudi Arabia is a greater humiliation to Muslims than in any other location. It also violates a religious decree (understood expansively, in geographic terms, by the jihadis) that prohibits non-Muslims from entering the land and contaminating its holiness.[2]

For jihadis, events in Iraq following the American invasion have been ripe with religious symbolism and historical lessons. The belief, held by many Sunni Muslims, that the Abbasid caliphate fell to the Mongols as a result of Shia betrayal made it easier to propose an ideological frame. Jihadis viewed the US invasion of Iraq, and the Shia's subsequent ascendance to power, as a repetition of this bitter history. The vivid analogy confirmed fundamental Shia antagonism and underscored the importance of confronting the Americans with full force. It served as a rallying cry for Sunnis to join the insurgency in Iraq and led the most radical elements—al-Zarqawi and his followers—to view all Shia as collaborators and enemies who could be legitimately killed.

The above lessons from Iraq's history bring to light how the presence of occupation forces and Muslim repression under non-Muslim rule fit al-Qaeda's ideological narrative and make some places particularly attractive candidates for expansion. Muslims must resist foreign occupation; in al-Qaeda's view, the regimes in all Muslim countries are apostates; thus, essentially, all Muslim states are occupied. However, although Muslims have voiced general dissatisfaction with their rulers (as the Arab Awakening clearly shows), they appear to reject the blanket inference that all Muslim countries are de facto occupied. Furthermore, had this frame gained currency, the urgency of establishing al-Qaeda branches would have been equal throughout the Middle East.

These radical jihadi claims have generated little support among Islamic scholars and Muslim publics; therefore, we should focus on a more widely accepted argument regarding foreign occupation: when non-Muslims invade a state that is populated and ruled by Muslims, Islam comes under attack and, consequently, defensive jihad becomes mandatory. Under the doctrine of defensive jihad, fighting the foreign aggressor is a religious duty, lifting many limitations and conditions on who may join the jihad.[3] Thus, entering an arena that is recognized as being under foreign occupation is not only ideologically justified—it is an imperative.

Indeed, foreign occupation plays a central role in al-Qaeda's narrative that it seeks to protect Muslims, that Islam faces coordinated attack, and that jihad has become an individual rather than a collective duty (one that could be satisfied when a Muslim ruler sends some forces to fight on behalf of the whole umma). It is essential to al-Qaeda's position that it is justified in taking action, particularly in raising arms, regardless of Muslim leaders' stance or preference. When a Muslim land is under occupation but the leaders of Muslim states decline to declare jihad and send their forces to war, al-Qaeda is entitled—in fact, obligated—to appropriate the right to use force. The inclination, expressed in most interpretations of Islam, to grant rulers authority for the sake of the general interest and order, even when they do not exemplify ideal Islamic behavior, is more easily challenged when these rulers fail to assist Muslim brethren under foreign occupation. Moreover, by establishing a franchise in such a location, al-Qaeda could amplify its role as the true carrier of the banner of Islam, taking action where apostate leaders are too timid and/or corrupt to fulfill their obligations.[4]

The 2003 invasion of Iraq made it an obvious location for establishing an al-Qaeda franchise. Palestine is another place that most Muslims view as occupied. The 2006 Ethiopian invasion of Somalia to depose the Islamic Court Union regime also reinvigorated the country's appeal for al-Qaeda. Following this logic, the oppression of Chechnya's Muslim inhabitants would make it a potential target for al-Qaeda expansion as well.

A decision by al-Qaeda to enter an arena under foreign occupation is not merely religiously sanctioned—and thus consistent with the organization's ideological logic—but will also be consistent with its strategic logic. In fact, bin Laden acknowledged in internal communications that American occupation was uniquely instrumental in awakening Muslims to fight.[5] Thus, foreign occupation creates fertile ground for al-Qaeda activity. Moreover, absence from such an arena, especially if the foreign occupation began after the group started operating and propagating, would undermine al-Qaeda's credibility and religious credentials. Foreign occupation may even produce greater salience for the jihadi cause than religiously symbolic locations whose status has not changed in many years, forcing al-Qaeda to respond by deploying to the occupied land or to risk becoming marginalized.

Note that al-Qaeda's conception of what is a Muslim country and, consequently, which countries are under foreign occupation is quite expansive. Moreover, the group's memory is long. Spain was marked, at least rhetorically, as a territory that must be freed, even though Muslim control of Andalusia ended in the fifteenth century. However, leaders understand that the group's prospects for success depend on its claims' appeal to the broad Muslim populace—in this case, the extent to which the arena represents an injury to Islam and the umma. As this "foreign occupation" has little salience, the likelihood that it will become a primary target for formal expansion is relatively low.

Islamic traditions could also guide al-Qaeda's arena selections. One important tradition (or *hadith*) predicts that forces coming from the Hindu-Kush, the mountain range stretching between central Afghanistan and northern Pakistan, will lead the umma in its fight against "falsehood."[6] Another hadith promises that a force will emerge from Aden-Abyan, in Yemen. In addition, there are apocalyptic visions of the battle on the "day of judgment," which, if taken as a guide for al-Qaeda's expansion, should lead the group to establish a formal presence in Syria[7] and Israel, where the final battles are prophesized to take place. But although al-Qaeda has an operational presence in most of these locations, it has branches in only some. Meanwhile, the organization has established franchises elsewhere—for example, merging with the Algerian GSPC—undercutting the explanatory value of religious traditions.

Indeed, reading too much into these traditions underscores the danger of after-the-fact rationalizations. Rather than a guide for expansion, Islamic traditions appear to have served as motivational and mobilization tools, particularly by reinforcing the narrative of inevitable and unstoppable ideological force rising from the periphery, and suggesting that al-Qaeda is that prophesied force. They do not mandate organizational expansion or the creation of a ruling authority.

It bears noting that while symbolic appeal could contribute to expansion decisions, it is unlikely to be the sole reason for arena selection. Indeed, al-Qaeda strategist Abu Bakr Naji notes that the organization marked Saudi Arabia as an arena for change only in response to post–9/11 circumstances, thus indicating that the country's religious value alone was insufficient to make it an expansion priority.[8] Even if religious value increases arenas' importance, the difficulty of ranking territories based on that criterion weakens this explanation's predictive power. As Thomas Hegghammer argues, there are no clear criteria suggesting that Iraq, as the seat of the Abbasid caliphate, should be a more important expansion target than Syria, the first location outside the Arabian Peninsula that Muslims conquered. Trying to identify the ranking of places based on religious symbolism, he warns, may lead us to post-facto rationalizations.[9]

Strategic Value

An arena has strategic value when it is vital to realize the organization's general objectives, and organizations may identify certain fronts whose capture is a prerequisite for mission success. Thus, an arena's strategic value and its place in a group's plans can influence expansion decisions and even determine their sequence.

Following a carefully planned strategy is particularly important for an actor with ambitious territorial aspirations that require navigating an intricate environment encompassing multiple fronts. Obviously, organizations need a measure of flexibility in case initial assumptions prove to be off the mark or circumstances change. But adjustments rarely alter strategic thinking; actors often settle for a shift in tactics or redirecting their focus from one front to another, while retaining the same identified enemies and assumptions about which actions would appeal to constituencies and promote mobilization, how enemies would react to these moves, and what conditions are most conducive to operational progress. Thus, barring radical reshuffling of the strategic conditions (for example, the acquisition of game-changing weapon systems), an organization will likely adhere to its initial designation of essential arenas.

It is possible, even likely, that more than one location will emerge as a viable base for spreading into neighboring areas. When considering which of these locations will become an expansion target, leaders will take into account several factors, including the prospects of success, freedom of operation within the arena, and the potential for controlling territory, all of which I address in the following. Changing circumstances could lead the group to shift its focus between arenas of similar importance, but a shift from core areas to peripheral ones is less probable.

Al-Qaeda's primary region of interest, the Middle East, has experienced radical environmental changes since 2003. First came the US invasion of

Iraq, which created favorable conditions for fighting a guerrilla war against al-Qaeda's central enemy in the heart of the Middle East, rather than in the peripheral state of Afghanistan. Then came the Arab Awakening. Unlike the Iraq war, which made that country a center of attention but ended up causing only small disturbances elsewhere, the Arab Awakening shook the entire region and required revising the group's strategic thinking. It eroded central assumptions undergirding al-Qaeda's strategy, such as the balance between violent and nonviolent means to attain objectives, the extent to which the United States hinders change in the Middle East, and the necessity of targeting that nation to begin mobilizing the umma, toppling the Arab regimes, and re-establishing the caliphate. From a strategic perspective, while we should expect al-Qaeda's postwar franchising logic to change little, the magnitude of recent changes in the region could have led to a more substantial shift in the manner in which al-Qaeda ranks arenas.

A state may become a candidate for the establishment of an al-Qaeda branch when it is strategically located—that is, when it could serve as a launching pad for further expansion. Al-Zawahiri stated as early as 2001 that al-Qaeda needed a base in the heart of the Middle East.[10] Such an arena provides greater visibility and, more important, could serve as a nucleus of the future caliphate. Thus Iraq, bordering the Levant states and the Arabian Peninsula, has unique strategic value, and its long, porous borders make it an even more attractive target. Syria is another central location; its importance increased as its civil war brought it forward as a place where Sunnis, subjected to oppression and death at the hands of the Alawite Assad regime and his Shia backers, needed defense.

Strategic value influences not only where a transnational terrorist group may consider formal expansion but also where it may prefer to maintain a lower profile. Certain places are designated as rear bases, logistical hubs, and important passageways to other, more vital, arenas. Consequently, an organization may prefer not to open a franchise that would lead its state enemies to refocus their efforts and thus endanger these locations. During the 1990s, al-Qaeda considered Kenya to be such a location, important to sustaining its effort in Somalia. As a result, its operatives in the region opposed attacks there until the circumstances in Somalia changed and Kenya's value decreased.[11] Yemen, too, had such a value: its extensive and largely uncontrollable perimeter offers not only a safe haven but also easy access to Saudi Arabia, as well as to the Horn of Africa (particularly to the chaotic Somalia). Note, too, that operational success could allow an arena to become a support base for operations in neighboring countries as well.[12]

One must approach the question of strategic value with caution. When multiple locations fit the description of a "strategically important" arena, biased confirmation of this hypothesis is all too likely. Notwithstanding such danger, franchising decisions that fail to conform to an arena's strategic value could be very revealing. In al-Qaeda's case, its franchises in the less prominent areas of North Africa and Somalia, as well as its absence from Jordan, indicate that strategic importance is only one factor and insufficiently explains specific expansion decisions.

Perhaps a more robust way to assess particular arenas' value is by viewing them through the lens of the organization's strategic plan. Naturally, such an approach would require knowledge of that plan, and in al-Qaeda's case, there is little reliable information. This could be simply a matter of knowledge gaps or, alternatively, because al-Qaeda never formulated an elaborate blueprint. It is likely that al-Qaeda's leaders preferred opportunism to rigid planning and, thus, settled for identifying parameters to guide the group's expansion.

A less generous explanation of the absence of strategic planning might attribute it to schisms in al-Qaeda's thinking. Bin Laden was largely fixated on attacks on the United States and its Western allies. Despite the organization's support for attacks on Western targets wherever they might be, including in the Middle East, he preferred strikes on Western countries in their own territories. Yet al-Qaeda gradually shifted its operational focus to Middle Eastern countries (in large part due to the inability to replicate its 9/11 success). This may have resulted in stagnated strategic thinking, as bin Laden failed to resolve the conflict and his lieutenants were unwilling or unable to release al-Qaeda from its bind.

One may see Naji's *Management of Savagery* as a step toward formulating a strategy for expansion. The book articulates a road map for how al-Qaeda should operate in Muslim countries, from operations designed to bring down a regime, to the subsequent phase of managing liberated areas (while taking into account the interplay with other actors, often local tribes, operating in the same space), to expansion through the borders to locales in their vicinity.[13] However, Naji does not clarify which locations he views as the most prominent destinations. There are several potential explanations for this omission. It may be that al-Qaeda's leaders disagreed on the ranking of important arenas or preferred constructive ambiguity to avoid revealing its plans to foes. It may also be the case that Naji's document was more conceptual than practical.

Jordanian author Fu'ad Husayn comes closer to presenting the group's strategic plan. In a 2005 book about Abu Musab al-Zarqawi, Husayn lays out a 20-year, seven-stage plan that would involve fighting the Arab regimes of the Middle East, confronting the United States and Israel, and expanding the battlefield to involve Turkey and Iran. Husayn envisions al-Qaeda's triumphant establishment of a caliphate in Iraq.[14]

The first of the seven stages is "the awakening stage" that began when al-Qaeda attacked the "head of the snake" (the United States) and, allegedly, led that nation to act chaotically; as a result, the Muslim umma has awakened and finally has realized the true nature of the war. The stage ended with the American occupation of Baghdad. Then, Husayn explains, would follow the three-year "eye-opening" stage, in which the umma wakes up to the reality of "occupation" and builds a jihadi army in Iraq. In the third stage (2007–2010), that jihadi army redeploys to neighboring countries, at first focusing on the Levant. With presence on Israel's borders, al-Qaeda is able to launch attacks against that country, increasing the group's standing and resources.

The fourth stage (2010–2013) focuses on overthrowing the "subservient" regimes, as the expanded battlefield makes it difficult for the United States to defend its allies, exposing the regimes to jihadi attacks. Economic warfare results in the dollar's drop and eventual collapse; the country's economic decline—due in part to the "schemes of the Jewish economists"—results in public pressure on American leaders to abandon Israel. In the fifth stage (2013–2016), the regimes' hold loosens further, and Israel weakens. The US decline is accompanied by China's rise as a superpower less hostile to Islam. The following phase sees the onset of an all-out confrontation between the forces of faith, led by a strong al-Qaeda, and forces of global atheism; the fight starts immediately after the establishment of the caliphate. In the final stage, the war ends, with the Muslims victorious.

Although this is the only known blueprint laying out al-Qaeda's long-term strategic plan, it appears less an AQC battle plan than a reflection of al-Zarqawi's ideas and his independent agenda. Husayn's book is written in a manner suggesting shared strategic understanding between AQC and al-Zarqawi, even though in reality al-Qaeda's leadership rejected many of his actions and even maintained that they reflected an inability to grasp the broader picture.[15] The chapter dealing with this overarching plan reads as if it reflected al-Zarqawi's analysis, with al-Qaeda's name added primarily to add credibility and bolster al-Zarqawi's standing within the organization. The fact that people in his close circle were the main sources for Husayn's book raises additional suspicions about whether this 20-year blueprint represents an authentic al-Qaeda plan.

The plan emphasizes Iraq and the Levant states of Syria, Jordan, and Lebanon, all central to al-Zarqawi's agenda. Bin Laden and al-Zawahiri's vision of success must have included these same countries, but they had an even greater interest in their home countries of Saudi Arabia and Egypt, on which the 20-year blueprint is surprisingly ambiguous.[16] Another reason for doubt stems from the plan's reliance on a confrontation between the United States and Israel and the forces of Iran. Bin Laden himself envisioned a fight that follows a chain of events that al-Qaeda's actions would trigger. Drawing the United States into the Middle East and exposing the true nature of its relations with the Arab regimes were central objectives for the 9/11 attack and necessary for the umma's mobilization against its enemies. But Husayn's plan is even more reliant on developments well out of al-Qaeda's control.

The notion of a war between two powers, both hostile to Islam, that leads to their exhaustion and facilitates the Muslims' success is reminiscent of Islam's early days, when it benefited from the wars between Byzantium and the Sasanian Empire. Al-Qaeda's strategic thinking, as portrayed in Husayn's book, sees as practically inevitable a war between the United States and Iran that weakens both considerably and serves al-Qaeda's objectives. But despite a substantial number of al-Qaeda documents and internal communications coming to light in recent years, there is surprisingly little to confirm that AQC ever shared al-Zarqawi's intense hostility to Iran, or even that it viewed Iran as playing a vital role in the defeat of the United States.

Internal Characteristics

Although symbolic and strategic value could determine a terrorist organization's level of interest in a particular arena, that region's viability depends on additional considerations. The high cost of failure demands that the organization carefully weigh a new franchise's success prospects.

What conditions are likely to shape an organization's assessment of the feasibility of introducing a branch in an arena? First, the existence of operational infrastructure in the target country obviously makes a branch a more attractive proposition. A terrorist infrastructure comprises several factors, including the number of operatives both in fighting and supporting roles, media apparatus, logistical assets such as safe houses, access to weapons and explosives, and a steady flow of financial resources from reliable sources. An existing, ready infrastructure lowers start-up costs and allows immediate operational impact and the quick use of propaganda machinery to maximize

operations' political impact, as well as greater ability to withstand the anticipated government onslaught.

In the absence of strong presence of its own members, a large constituency of sympathizers may encourage an organization to formally expand.
Transplanted fighters depend on local supporters to shelter and guide them
in an unfamiliar cultural, social, and political environment. Such assistance
is particularly important considering that the authorities, with a great power
and knowledge advantage over the foreign fighters, can be expected to hunt
them down. The immigrant fighters (*muhajirun*) require local assistance, at
least until they become strong enough to stand on their own. When promising to join the struggle against Israel, al-Qaeda called its local supporters to
prepare to receive the brethren who would cross the borders into Gaza.[17]

A supportive environment offers not only shelter but new recruits. Local
support is necessary to strengthen the base of the group, particularly since
fighting typically leads to attrition outpacing the arrival of new foreign volunteers that would allow full force substitution (let alone growth). Over the
years, al-Qaeda learned that attracting local support, preferably by recruiting
locals to join (and even lead) the branch, is critical for gaining acceptance and
legitimacy among the indigenous population and, consequently, for success.

Al-Qaeda can look back in time as it tries to gauge the potential for support among local communities. A populace that contributed volunteers for
jihadi causes in the past is likely to continue offering a deep recruitment pool.
Even if only a few individuals joined jihadi causes in the past, countries in
which considerable segments of the population subscribe to radical interpretations of Islam present high recruitment potential. Indeed, the prominence
of Salafism in Saudi Arabia makes its population particularly vulnerable to
radicalization—though, as al-Qaeda found out, despite Saudis' enthusiasm
for jihad, their conservative roots often lead them to prefer jihad against foreign occupiers rather than the Saudi regime.[18] To support its mobilization
efforts, al-Qaeda often sends members back to their original communities.
These members' familiarity with the target arena makes them particularly
effective in speaking to youth of similar background and in attracting new
recruits.

Second, geography is essential to franchising decisions. Difficult terrain
can complicate efforts to build local resistance to a regime, or it can aid a
group's campaign. Mountainous regions may provide hiding places and limit
government access; by contrast, terrorists will likely have trouble defending
safe havens in flat and exposed lands as governments use their technological
advantage to trace and attack them. Indeed, Afghanistan and Yemen provided

al-Qaeda with ample sheltered areas from which it could operate with relative safety, while in Egypt, the desert and flat terrain forced jihadi groups to operate from within cities, making them more vulnerable.[19]

Geography relates to the question of accessibility—that is, how difficult it would be for forces to enter an arena. Accessibility has several elements: geographical conditions that allow undetected movement, the distance between the group's current position and the new arena's location, and the number of borders that terrorists must cross in order to reach an arena. Naturally, establishing a new branch in a neighboring country with porous borders should be easier than crossing multiple well-guarded boundaries where movement is easy to detect. The mountainous terrain straddling the border between Afghanistan and Pakistan allows Taliban fighters familiar with the region to cross it with ease. Smuggling routes across the porous border separating Iraq and Syria facilitated al-Qaeda's expansion into the latter after civil war erupted. Large bodies of water also can make expansion difficult, whereas narrow straits can be conducive to moving undetected. Al-Qaeda operatives have regularly crossed the Bab al-Mandab Strait, the waterway between Yemen and Somalia, and Jema'a Islamiya fighters regularly traveled between the numerous islands of Indonesia and the Philippines. A geographically inaccessible area could still see the establishment of a branch, although such an obstacle would probably require the expanding organization to forge an arrangement with a local group.

Third, state power is central to terrorists' expansion decisions. A strong state can invest considerable resources, providing citizens with services and limiting terrorists' ability to exploit economic and social grievances for support and recruitment. Power is particularly essential for providing security to the population: as the examples of Afghanistan, Iraq, and Somalia demonstrate, terrorism flourishes when the state cannot provide security. The local population often resignedly accepts the authority of radical, violent non-state actors when that authority is accompanied by a greater sense of personal security. Strong states are also better able to confront terrorist groups by thwarting their plots, identifying and arresting their members, and denying them funding sources, weapons, and the ability to enter the country undetected. A strong state can also deny terrorists safe haven and can launch effective counterterrorism operations.

In contrast, a weak state is less able to prevent an organization from entering and establishing its presence; it is less likely to be able to guard its borders and to prevent terrorists from carving out a safe haven for training and operations.[20] Because state weakness often manifests in an inability to provide citizens basic services, a deep-pocketed terrorist organization can offer an attractive alternative, increasing the territory under its effective control and recruiting locals to its ranks. Even when terrorists are unable to provide many services, the ability to provide personal security and to stop predation from corrupt state authorities can be a tangible advantage. A safe haven may also allow the organization to expand its operations into neighboring states.

Weak states may be conducive to jihadi penetration, but weakness by itself cannot explain why an organization would choose to establish a new branch rather than simply expand its operations. It appears that a group prefers formal expansion when seeking to send a political message of vitality to its enemy states and to constituencies and donors outside the region. While falling short of an emirate—a political and administrative unit with official responsibility for delivering goods, justice, and law and order to the people living under its authority—a branch suggests movement toward assuming such a role. Importantly, announcing a franchise can be as much about creating an image of success as about realizing the organization's governance aspiration. After all, a group can control a territory using a considerable governance apparatus without declaring either a formal branch or an emirate.

Fourth, whether a transnational terrorist group enters an arena often depends on its competitors there. Any organization would prefer an arena with no other organizations operating to engaging in a struggle for dominance. A competitive environment carries greater start-up costs: the group must overcome considerable barriers to entry, since both the regime and local terrorist competitors will view it as a threat. For the expanding actor, the greater the number of organizations operating in the arena, the more complex and uncertain its calculations become. Even if the group can establish a presence, it will have to fight over market share. That inevitable competition would lower the probability that the organization can beat the regime and achieve its political objectives and, thus, might serve as an argument against expansion.

When only one other anti-regime force operates in the target state, the transnational terrorist organization might be inclined to join the arena via merger. Whether it pursues this path depends, obviously, on the local group's identity—for instance, whether the organizations share an ideology. Groups across an ideological divide might still cooperate, but since a branching-out strategy involves relationships between a core leadership and affiliates and is characterized by relatively high levels of hierarchy and institutionalization, it would require basic ideological compatibility.

Over the years, al-Qaeda sought to establish an image of itself as a unifying force for jihadi organizations. By hosting other group's members in its training camps in Afghanistan and Sudan during the 1990s, al-Qaeda sought to strengthen the capabilities of the broad jihadi movement, to identify individuals with unique qualities—who it then tried to recruit—and to cultivate links with jihadi groups worldwide. By waiving the requirement to join al-Qaeda or allowing for conditional membership, the organization has been able to forge ties to diverse jihadi groups through loose, overlapping memberships. Indeed, Jema'a Islamiya military leader Hambali was a high-ranking al-Qaeda operative while serving with JI.

When al-Qaeda began its expansion drive, these relationships facilitated affiliation arrangements that might have been impossible otherwise. Averse to splitting the jihadi camp in arenas housing other groups, al-Qaeda has proved amenable to merging with local organizations rather than establishing its own branches. In cases of highly fragmented jihadi scenes, al-Qaeda weighs the benefits of entering each arenas against its reluctance to increase division. It prefers to use its willingness to enter an arena as an incentive for the other groups to bridge their differences and unite. In Syria, al-Qaeda found a highly important cause but a fragmented jihadi scene. In some respects, the existence of several groups forced al-Qaeda's hand by preventing it from preferring one over the others. Al-Qaeda could have settled for sending fighters to augment the anti-Assad forces without forming a formal organization, but with rebels divided into several groups, formal presence seemed required for involvement in the civil war, thus pushing al-Qaeda to form its own organization and to make its existence public faster than it would have without such clear organizational boundaries between the many rebel factions. As I show in Chapter 9, al-Qaeda made substantial efforts to ensure that its Syrian branch would not undermine the country's broader jihadi movement—that it would build bridges rather than divide further.

Notwithstanding al-Qaeda's affinity with other jihadi groups, there are many theological differences that could separate them—for example, their attitudes toward the state-based order and nationalism: Al-Qaeda's rejection of the Westphalian system and of nationalism as heretic approaches puts it in opposition to organizations that restrict their fight to certain governments and national boundaries. Some jihadi groups may accept al-Qaeda's anti-Westphalian vision but, as they prioritize bringing about change in a localized struggle, pay only lip service to the broader agenda. Mergers would require al-Qaeda to turn away from a central tenet of its ideology or the local group to shift its orientation outward, toward al-Qaeda's global agenda. Jihadi groups might reject al-Qaeda's overtures due to other theological differences, including divergent views regarding the permissibility of attacks likely to result in the death of Muslim innocents (as in the case of the Gama'a Islamiya in Egypt), al-Qaeda's efforts to force an Islamic state on other groups and the public (a central source of resistance to al-Qaeda's Iraqi branch after 2006), and the imposition of harsh Islamic laws on the population (Iraq again).

Differences of this kind also have a practical dimension. Some jihadi groups with strong roots in local communities may fear—not without foundation—that uniting with al-Qaeda and adopting its tactics would cost them public support. Lingering grudges about al-Qaeda's past behavior could be another obstacle to unity. Some jihadi leaders found it particularly irksome that al-Qaeda carried out the 9/11 attacks without consulting them first, practically dragging even disapproving jihadi groups into the war on terrorism and making them targets of the ferocious US-led counterterrorism campaign. Reluctance to join can also be very personal: local leaders may not want to become subordinate to AQC's leadership and see their own authority weakened. Interestingly, opposition from leadership elements of a group with which al-Qaeda would like to merge does not necessarily mean that al-Qaeda will halt its overtures. As the Egyptian and Libyan cases, discussed in Chapter 8, demonstrate, al-Qaeda could try to overcome the opposition by allying with the local organization's more supportive factions and through appeals to its rank and file.

Of course, notwithstanding local groups' resistance, al-Qaeda could introduce branches based on its own cadre of fighters, perhaps believing that ideological affinity would constrain competitors' ability and willingness to stop al-Qaeda. Alternatively, it could open a branch and then try to co-opt other jihadi groups to join it. However, expanding into an inhospitable environment is risky. Ideological affinity hardly guarantees that local groups will not try to sabotage its efforts; entrenched in the area, they are in a strong position to thwart al-Qaeda's efforts, particularly while it is still in a start-up phase. A less risky option that al-Qaeda could pursue is to create an operational infrastructure but stop short of announcing formal presence. Peer groups might see such a move as less threatening and thus may avoid undermining it.

Introducing a franchise over local objections is even harder in arenas dominated by non-jihadi groups, because they are likely to view al-Qaeda as an existential threat, feel greater urgency to thwart its entry into their theater, and accept fewer constraints in their dealing with al-Qaeda. Organizations that do not identify themselves as Islamists or jihadis could go beyond expression of objection to al-Qaeda to outright opposition. As established forces, and free from ideological constraints on handling rival forces, they are in a strong position to inflict high costs on al-Qaeda and thwart its entry attempt, particularly if they take action early enough.

Establishing a branch in an arena dominated by Islamist forces that are not jihadi or Salafi groups carries its own distinct challenges, putting al-Qaeda in a tense ideological competition with groups that are defined by their religious ideology but have significantly different views on central issues, including governance, piety, attitudes toward minorities, and international relations. The competition with organizations associated with the Muslim Brotherhood is particularly fierce, as each Islamist strand sees itself as the authentic conveyer of the correct understanding of Islam and seeks the support of pious Muslims.[21] Moreover, in contrast to intra-jihadi competition, non-Salafi Islamists tend to view al-Qaeda's presence as a threat rather than a potential opportunity. The threat goes beyond the prospect of losing resources: al-Qaeda's radical ideology and stern rejection of the Muslim Brotherhood guarantee that if capable, it would seek to suppress its ideological opponents.

More moderate organizations have acted accordingly: following rhetorical skirmishes, Hamas vowed to deny al-Qaeda entry into the Gaza Strip, effectively quashing the group's aspirations for an effective jihadi presence in that key arena.[22] (In addition, Hamas is taking measures to assure that none of the local Salafi groups becomes too prominent and threatens its dominance there.) Thus, whether or not al-Qaeda attempts to branch out into an arena dominated by non-Salafi groups will depend on their level of effective control, their willingness to accept al-Qaeda (or commitment and capability to resist it, including through collaboration with state authorities), and the organization's appeal to the local audience.

Actor-Oriented Perspective

For scholars, an actor-oriented approach offers an alternative to the arena-based perspective. It highlights how the interaction between organization-specific factors and environmental conditions shapes franchising choices. This approach does not imply that an arena's particular value is unimportant, but it considers the factors associated with arenas as input factors that by themselves cannot fully explain the output—that is, franchising decisions. Instead, it attributes affiliation choices to the psychological pressures affecting the leaders' decision-making processes. This approach goes beyond the core questions regarding branching-out strategy by demonstrating that exploring formal organizational expansion can provide insights into the type and quality of decision-making among transnational terrorist groups. However, due to space constraints, I do not develop this approach fully, settling for a cursory discussion.

An actor-oriented perspective is situational in nature, distinguishing between affiliation decisions and examining each on its own. It does not reject the possibility that some overarching guidelines may inform franchising decisions but, rather, assumes that actors have the flexibility to evaluate each potential arena in light of situational conditions and to compare options. An important advantage of this approach is that it allows for a learning process in which actors' actions are informed by lessons from their earlier moves; it also incorporates psychological factors, such as the level of pressure that terrorist leaders feel, and how these pressures shape cost-benefit analyses.

Studies in political psychology underscore the role of psychological factors in shaping decision-making. Leaders are not machines capable of calculating exact utilities—they are humans exposed to motivated and unmotivated biases,[23] experiencing emotions that inevitably influence their decisions.[24] When operating in a group, they are affected by social pressures.[25] Although individuals have personal dispositions, most psychological approaches to decision-making highlight the power of the situation. Situational factors and the way they manifest in the decision-maker's psychology determine the choices she makes.[26]

What constitutes a situation is open to debate. It can refer to a stimulant that operates for only a brief period and elicits a nearly instinctive response, but it can also refer to a significantly longer period of time. Given that terrorist organizations decide to enter an arena after internal discussions and, in the case of mergers, negotiations with the other groups, the latter understanding of what a situation means is more appropriate.

Before elaborating on the psychological roots of franchising decisions, it is imperative to clarify that, despite the use of vocabulary suggesting that organizations act like human beings, they are not. Thus, organizations, as this work refers to them, are the leaders that lead them. This view is particularly appropriate for affiliation decisions, which reflect strategic policymaking that only top leaders can make.

Prospect theory offers a way to link situational psychological factors to actors' decision-making, and could be applied to franchising decisions. It links risk-taking with the decision-makers' psychological state. Individuals' risk propensity hinges on their domain—that is, whether they face prospects of gains or losses. The theory asserts that when people are in a domain of gains, they tend to be risk-averse; a person is risk-averse if he prefers a sure outcome to a risky prospect with an equal or greater expected value.[27] On the other hand, when people are in a domain of losses, they tend to be risk-acceptant, more willing to adopt risky behavior intended to recoup losses. In a seminal application of prospect theory to international relations, Rose McDermott shows how leaders (in her study, US presidents) who experience loss exhibited a greater tendency to take risks. Rather than following the prescriptions of rational decision-making, they were more likely to "double down" and, in the process, further endanger the achievement of their desired objectives.[28] Note that prospect theory does not treat risk as inherently negative—after all, if the gamble succeeds, the decision-maker reaps greater rewards than when following a less risky behavior.

Applied to franchising decisions, prospect theory would predict that a transnational terrorist organization (or, more precisely, its leaders) in a domain of gains will likely move to enter an arena if it assesses the likelihood of success as high and potential costs in case of failure as low. It is also likely to prefer in-house franchising that not only allows for closer oversight but increases the likelihood that the leadership's preferences align with those of the franchise. However, when in a domain of loss, an organization may be expected to take greater risks, entering into arenas where the odds it would succeed are lower and the potential costs higher. Importantly, it might forge a relationship with unruly organizations whose preferences differ on important dimensions, threatening the brand name.

In an alternative approach, psychological factors are manifested in the quality of the decision-making process. Quality could refer either to the decision's outcome or to the manner by which an actor adopts a decision, and the distinction is important: An actor can follow a methodical decision-making process and yet see her policy fail, while a poor process does not preclude the possibility that the chosen policy brings positive returns. While tempting, we must be careful not to infer decisions' quality from their outcomes; instead, we should assess the process's quality by its thoroughness, considering both the full range of relevant policy options and the seriousness in which leaders analyze each. A choice made after a consideration of all available options and a thorough comparison of their utilities and costs represents better decision-making than a choice made after examining a few or no alternatives at all and making only a shallow survey of their expected consequences. Leaders may fail to engage in a vigorous decision-making process because of psychological pressures.

Arjen Boin and his colleagues note that while moderate levels of stress often improve decision-making, excessive stress is associated with declining performance. Among the negative effects of stress on decision-making, they note an inclination to emphasize short-term interests at the expense of long-term strategic considerations.[29] Margaret Hermann contends that stress leads decision-makers to consider only one policy option, consequently undermining their performance during foreign-policy crises.[30]

Similarly, Richard Ned Lebow shows how pressure can affect the number of alternatives that decision-makers consider and can distort their assessment of the chosen policy's feasibility. He proposes that when leaders feel a need to attain irreconcilable objectives, psychological pressures often produce suboptimal decision-making and lead them to adopt risky policies. Wishful thinking distorts these leaders' calculations; they undervalue the extent to which the objectives they are pursuing conflict and overestimate the probability that their policies will achieve their desired goals. Importantly, Lebow determines that such deficient decision-making is not limited to any specific type of decision. Leaders have exhibited it both in cases of crisis brinkmanship and when they have pursued accommodations with rival states.[31] For Lebow the main issue is not risk but, rather, how a leader's delusion that an inherently unworkable policy might succeed leads her to try to square a circle.

Extrapolating from Lebow's work, I suggest that policy-makers experience varying levels of pressure, affecting the quality of their decision-making. The proposed approach can enhance our understanding of an actor's particular franchising decisions. As these decisions, in turn, affect an actor's state, they allow a more comprehensive analysis of the organization and even shed light on its life cycle. I differentiate between decisions reflecting "opportunity" and those reflecting "need." Opportunity decisions are associated with a proactive approach that refers to an organization that is making strides (or believing it is doing so) and seeks to further improve its position. For that reason, leaders attempt to shape the organization's fate by exploring a variety of options and adopting those that offer the greatest positive returns. In contrast, need-based action is a reactive mode of decision-making, referring to choices made under considerable pressure. Often, these decisions manifest greater risk propensity than opportunity-based decisions. Instead of seeking the optimal choice, an actor takes action that may satisfy short-term needs but is likely to inflict, as a result, significant long-term damage.

Opportunity and need offer distinct approaches to terrorists' franchising decisions. "Need" explains the general policy preference for spreading the brand name, suggesting that an organization in distress feels pressure to display its vitality. Whereas in theory it could fight an image of decline in various ways, if its distress reflects a declining ability to carry out terrorist attacks, spreading the brand name could be seen as a preferable alternative.

Need may also account for more specific choices: when need arises, the organization will seek to enter the first available arena, paying less attention to the long-term prospects of success there, opportunity costs, or fit with the organization's grand strategy. Need might also lead a terrorist organization to seek expansion into a certain location because it identifies developments in that arena, or groups within it, as primary threats to its existence. In this case, formal expansion could be seen as a preemptive measure intended to thwart such dangerous developments, to reduce competition, or to discredit critics. With al-Qaeda representatives exposed to repeated attacks by Gama'a Islamiya leaders in Egyptian prisons, announcing a merger with those GI elements favorable to al-Qaeda potentially served three objectives: discrediting the critics, undermining the perception that the authors of the GI's recantation books (in which they revisited and rejected the jihad against the Egyptian regime) reflect the views of the group's broad membership, and dissuading GI members and sympathizers from turning their back on the jihad.

Such a specific need-driven action tends to be risky. It is often rushed, premature, and counterproductive, and even if potentially useful, taking the action under suboptimal conditions will likely squander the opportunity. When a group declares affiliation with another but lacks a sound plan or ability to translate rhetoric into reality, it can undermine the organization's credibility, antagonize members of the group in whose affairs it intervened, and threaten its ability to penetrate the arena at a later stage. Need-based affiliation could generate even greater costs when a premature attempt to enter an arena results in the branch's defeat. Similarly, when an organization, pressured by the threat of decline, enters into a relationship with a group that is a poor fit, the relationship could harm the brand name, distance potential supporters, and undermine the organization's ideological coherence. The expanding organization may also reveal that its partner not only refuses to accept its authority but is taking advantage of the relationship to supplant the organization's leadership.

Of course, not all decisions guided by need are a priori doomed to failure. Theoretically, a flexible organization following rational decision-making procedures may reverse its misfortune by "broadening the tent" and bringing new elements into the movement. However, for such measures to succeed, the expanding actor must remain selective: it should integrate only with actors likely to contribute to promoting its goals, rather than settling for the first candidate available, a choice that could undermine the organization from within or tarnish its image externally. Successfully responding to need may also require some ideological flexibility and willingness by the expanding group's leadership to share power with the newcomers. In reality, it appears that need produces psychological biases that amplify the already harsh psychological pressures stemming from life underground, thus reducing the quality of the decision-making process.

Expansion stemming from "opportunity," on the other hand, manifests less urgency, and is characterized by a more robust decision-making process. When it comes to a general interest in expansion, opportunity-informed action could, similarly to need-based decisions, reflect a response to external pressures. The difference is that leaders choose the direction of expansion after a more measured and selective decision-making process. They examine all options for expansion and potential candidates for mergers. They then select the location that offers the greatest prospects of success and the partners that offer the greatest resources, match best with the organization's ideology, and are most likely to follow its instructions. Inhospitable arenas and poor partners are avoided. Thus, opportunity as a cause for expansion suggests less urgency and greater ability to be selective in one's choices. When opportunity is the primary causal factor behind expansion decisions, we can anticipate that, all else equal, strategic logic will be more salient than the organizational.

Conclusions

This chapter presents two approaches to understanding franchising decisions, enhancing our understanding of al-Qaeda's expansion choices. In the first, an expanding actor's actions derive from the value of particular arenas, manifested in their symbolic value, their importance to the organization's strategic plan, and a host of internal characteristics. In the second, psychological pressures shape the way an organization contemplates its branching-out choices. Under intense psychological pressure, leaders are less diligent about decision-making and take highly risky expansion decisions. On the other hand, a transnational terrorist organization operating under favorable psychological conditions would follow more rigorous decision-making and expand to arenas only after carefully evaluating costs and benefits.

Viewing al-Qaeda's decisions from these perspectives can be revealing for students of terrorism as well as those leading counterterrorist efforts. Scholars can move beyond the debate regarding whether strategy, ideological commitment, or organizational interests shape such choices. At the very least, it will allow them to consider additional variables that would lead to a more nuanced understanding of how these three logics interact, and under what conditions a particular logic may be the primary cause for the organization's decisions.

For practitioners of counterterrorism, these perspectives offer another way to assess al-Qaeda's strength. The organization's expansion suggests a stronger and more capable organization, but a nuanced, comprehensive study of the motivations behind its branching-out strategy—and of its specific expansion decisions—offers a more reliable and, in fact, counter-intuitive explanation. It also offers insights into the quality of al-Qaeda's decision-making, particularly whether leaders manage to adhere to ratio-nal procedures and assess costs and benefits before branching out, or whether "need" undermines rationality and is leading the organization to rushed and self-destructive behavior. Practitioners will also benefit from understanding al-Qaeda's commitment to particular locations and under what conditions it may be expected to compromise areas with symbolic value. Designers of counterterrorism policies can also identify and take advantage of contradictions between particular ideological commitments, organizational need, and practical considerations, utilizing them to erode the group's reputation and credibility.

In the following chapters, I will examine the role that this broad set of factors played in al-Qaeda's franchising choices. In Chapter 6, I exam-ine al-Qaeda's first franchising moves: the founding of its Saudi branch and its merger with al-Zarqawi's TWJ group, in Iraq. In Chapter 7, I ana-lyze the processes that led al-Qaeda to bring North Africa's largest jihadi group, the GSPC, under its wing, to introduce al-Qaeda's Yemeni branch, and to merge with the Somali group al-Shabab. In Chapter 8, I look at cases of failed affiliation and absence from a theater, beginning with the intriguing cases in which al-Qaeda's claims to have merged with the LIFG and the Egyptian GI were rejected by those groups' leaders. I then discuss the negative case of al-Qaeda's avoidance of producing a franchise in the Palestinian arena. Finally, in Chapter 9, I explore al-Qaeda's entry into the Syrian theater, where its Iraqi franchise's rebellion undercut the organiza-tion's efforts to learn from past mistakes.

6

Stepping into Uncharted Territory

AL-QAEDA'S FIRST EXPANSIONS

THIS CHAPTER AND the following three explore al-Qaeda's formal expansion into particular arenas. Concretely, I seek to identify what prompts the organization to pursue involvement in any particular state, and under what conditions it is likely to successfully establish a franchise. I also explore why al-Qaeda seeks in some places to merge with existing jihadi groups and, in others, to establish a group on its own. Additionally, I cautiously assess the ramifications of al-Qaeda's branching-out decisions.

It is hardly surprising that actors sometimes miscalculate and pursue policies that in hindsight prove harmful. For al-Qaeda, branching out has often failed to generate the desired outcome due to unforeseen factors—changing strategic environment, effective counterterrorism, or an affiliate's lack of capabilities—rather than ideological incompatibility between core and franchise, affiliates' excesses, or local leaders' personal aspirations. Nevertheless, on some occasions the potential for adverse consequences was obvious in an early stage. I show how the elevated level of pressure since 9/11 led al-Qaeda to take highly risky steps that not only reflected its weakness but exacerbated its decline.

This chapter tells the story of al-Qaeda's first wave of expansion, the launching of branches in Saudi Arabia (2003) and Iraq (2004). These cases present an interesting contrast: al-Qaeda's Saudi branch took the form of in-house expansion; in Iraq, al-Qaeda merged with the foreign-led al-Tawhid wal-Jihad.

Saudi Arabia

Saudi Arabia was the first location where al-Qaeda established a formal branch. The branch, named al-Qaeda in the Arabian Peninsula (AQAP) was an in-house creation, based on al-Qaeda's own forces and led by al-Qaeda operatives. Osama bin Laden, Saudi himself, had many Saudi followers, including highly skilled mid-level operatives whom he could deploy in forming the branch. A couple of years before launching AQAP, he assigned Abd al-Rahim al-Nashiri and Yusuf al-Uyayri, separately, to establish infrastructure for operations in the country. Al-Nashiri was captured in November 2002, but the second effort, led by al-Uyayri, progressed steadily. As clouds of war gathered above Iraq, bin Laden instructed al-Uyayri to prepare the organization's Saudi cells to launch a terror campaign. Feeling that the branch needed more time, al-Uyayri pleaded with al-Qaeda's central command for more time, but bin Laden insisted.[1] Al-Uyayri accepted the verdict and on May 12, 2003, shortly after American forces invaded Iraq, sent operatives to attack three residential compounds in Riyadh that were populated largely by Westerners.

Observers later dubbed this operation AQAP's debut, but in fact al-Qaeda's Saudi enterprise—the group's first official franchise—did not begin using the name AQAP until a few months later, and by that time the Saudi network was already fighting to survive. Al-Uyayri's assessment that AQAP was unprepared proved prescient. The Saudi regime responded to the attack in Riyadh with a brutal crackdown; al-Uyayri himself became one of its first victims, perishing less than three weeks after the Riyadh attack. The branch's efforts to recover and demonstrate its prowess produced some high-profile attacks, but instead of reviving the group, these operations further weakened it. Bombings that killed Muslim civilians and Saudi security forces, along with regime propaganda, proved disastrous to AQAP's nascent image and turned Saudi public opinion against the militants. Hunted down by the regime and rejected and informed on by the public, AQAP suffered attrition and struggled to recruit new members. Although the group's original size was large enough to allow some of its cells to escape the dragnet and carry out operations,[2] by 2006 it became clear that al-Qaeda's campaign in the kingdom was a failure.[3]

Four factors explain al-Qaeda's decision to expand to Saudi Arabia, as well as its timing: Saudi Arabia's ideological appeal, bin Laden's particular connection to his homeland, the availability of a sizable group of al-Qaeda operatives there, and the changes in al-Qaeda's strategic environment—its eviction from its bases in Afghanistan and then the American invasion of Iraq.

Saudi Arabia was always prominent in bin Laden's decision to orient jihad against the "far enemy." In his declaration of war, he listed US "occupation" of Saudi Arabia as the greatest "injustice" that the "Zionist-Crusader alliance" had imposed on the umma: "The latest and the greatest of these aggressions incurred by the Muslims since the death of the Prophet (God's prayers and peace be upon him) is the occupation of the land of the two Holy Places—the foundation of the house of Islam, the place of the revelation, the source of the message and the place of the noble Ka'ba, the Qiblah of all Muslims—by the armies of the American Crusaders and their allies."[4] Indeed, Saudi Arabia is imbued with symbolism for Muslims: it is the birthplace of the Prophet Muhammad, the host of Islam's two holiest sites (the cities of Mecca and Medina), the direction to which Muslims turn when they pray, and the land from which the Muslim armies spread the Prophet's message throughout the Middle East and beyond. The combination of the country's value as the most important place in Islam and the jihadis' resentment of US forces who arrived to protect the kingdom from Saddam Hussein in 1990 and then stayed made the country an obvious arena for al-Qaeda's first branching-out decision.

While al-Qaeda rejected an American presence in any Muslim country, leaders found US forces' deployment in Saudi Arabia particularly outrageous. The sense of humiliation and anger in the face of a foreign "occupation" of the country with the greatest religious value is magnified by the Islamic prohibition of non-Muslims in that land.[5] According to an Islamic tradition, on his deathbed Muhammad ordered, "Let there be no two religions in Arabia." Al-Qaeda interprets this hadith broadly; whereas the Saudi state, guided by the Hanbali school of Islamic jurisprudence, understands it to bar non-Muslims only from the sacred soil of Hijaz but accepts non-permanent residency in the rest of the country, al-Qaeda views non-Muslims' presence anywhere in Arabia as a grievous offense.[6] In a treatise on the Riyadh bombing, al-Qaeda stated, "If we could remove the Americans from the Muslim countries in accordance with the correct and explicit texts that enjoin us to fight the aggressor infidels, we should remove them from the Arabian Peninsula in particular, because this is what our Prophet—God's prayers and peace be upon him—commanded us to do after his death."[7]

Bin Laden's personal connections also played an important role in the decision to start an al-Qaeda branch in Saudi Arabia. From a privileged family, bin Laden grew up in close proximity to the Saudi royal family.[8] After the Soviets invaded Afghanistan in 1979, he traveled to Pakistan to support the Afghan resistance forces. Due to his family connections, he began serving as a liaison and a central node in an apparatus dedicated to channeling Saudi donations and volunteers to the Afghan jihad.[9] Over the years, bin Laden's ties to the Saudi regime frayed, and he became a vocal critic of the royal family—both its morals and its stewardship of the country. The relationship deteriorated to the point that in 1989, after bin Laden returned to Saudi Arabia, officials confiscated his passport, denying him the ability to travel back to Afghanistan.

After Iraq invaded Kuwait in the summer of 1990, bin Laden proposed assembling an army of Afghanistan war veterans to defend Saudi borders from a possible Iraqi attack. The regime rejected his idea offhand and, to worsen the injury, invited US forces instead. Outraged, bin Laden decided to circumvent his travel restrictions and in 1991 escaped the country, returning to the Pakistani city of Peshawar before relocating to Sudan the following year; from the capital of Khartoum, he continued to challenge the authority of the house of Saud. Through family members and friends, the Saudi authorities made several overtures to bin Laden, offering him safe passage home if he renounced his opposition and ended his public criticism. When bin Laden rejected these proposals, Saudi Arabia revoked his citizenship, and his determination only grew. In fact, after Saudi authorities arrested the leaders of the *Sahwa* reform movement, which opposed the regime's policies and demanded reform in line with their view of Islamic law, bin Laden felt compelled to assume an even higher profile.[10]

Bin Laden's Afghan experience and the influence of fellow Arab jihadis he met during the Soviet war made him more amenable to the use of violent means as a legitimate tool of resistance. The failure of the scholars' nonviolent campaign, which included petitions by the movement's scholars as well as public sermons (many circulated as audiotapes), and their subsequent arrest further convinced him that violence might be the only way to bring change. This view led him to designate the kingdom as a target for attacks, although he later reversed his position, deciding that due to its logistical and fund-raising importance, Saudi Arabia should remain off limits.[11] But the decision to spare Saudi Arabia was tactical rather than a rejection of violence as a means to reform the country; as circumstances changed, the option of violence could be revisited.

His deep ties to the kingdom implied more than a unique personal commitment to reforming it—they translated to connections that al-Qaeda used to build an operational infrastructure. Although young Saudis admired bin Laden for his role in the Afghan jihad, at first he was unable to attract a significant number of volunteers. This changed after al-Qaeda started attacking the United States: Thomas Hegghammer notes that after 1999, many Saudis traveled to Afghanistan's jihadi training camps and joined al-Qaeda's ranks, though some of them, he argues, were interested in classical jihad—defending Muslims who are oppressed by non-Muslims—and were manipulated by al-Qaeda to join its ranks.[12]

Bin Laden, and even more so his man in Saudi Arabia, al-Uyayri, also had a vast network of contacts with religious opposition figures that allowed al-Qaeda to tap (or at least believe that it could tap) into their pool of followers. The US invasion of Afghanistan increased both bin Laden's popularity and anti-Americanism in Saudi Arabia.[13] In addition, although bin Laden lost his personal fortune during his years in Sudan, he maintained a vast donor base. Thus, when al-Qaeda considered launching a Saudi branch, his expectations that the organization could build a robust infrastructure that could, with Saudi donations, withstand a regime crackdown and replenish lost human and financial resources were not unreasonable. Recruitment proved more difficult than al-Qaeda's chiefs anticipated, prompting the Saudi network's leaders to plead with their superiors to delay action.[14]

Finally, the changing strategic environment increased Saudi Arabia's appeal as an arena. The US invasion of Afghanistan demolished al-Qaeda's infrastructure there, and the loss of its safe haven forced leaders to rethink their strategy and structure. Unable to operate in the open as it had in 1996–2001, al-Qaeda could no longer accommodate the flood of Saudi volunteers. The international counterterrorism campaign that led states to tighten their borders and crack down on terrorists using the global financial system to transfer money[15] made it difficult to use Saudi volunteers and funds outside the country. At the same time, the Taliban's collapse made investment of resources in Afghanistan pointless. In this way, the new strategic environment led bin Laden to reconsider his views regarding Saudi Arabia's viability as a theater of operations.

Additionally, al-Qaeda fighters, disillusioned by the lost war in Afghanistan, asked bin Laden for permission to return home to Saudi Arabia and launch operations there. As it became clear that al-Qaeda could have little meaningful impact in the Afghan theater, bin Laden instructed many of his followers to head back to their home countries.[16] Thus, the diminishing importance of Afghanistan, the availability of a large cadre of operatives in the Peninsula,[17] and the change in the considerations that had led al-Qaeda to avoid targeting Saudi Arabia before all pointed toward a change in the group's Saudi policies.

In the summer of 2002, it became apparent that the Bush administration had shifted its attention from Afghanistan to Iraq. The change in focus greatly impacted al-Qaeda's strategic environment by giving the organization more breathing space in Pakistan; it also required al-Qaeda to reconsider its next moves if it wanted to stay relevant. With Iraq turning into the next battleground for American forces, al-Qaeda was handed a fresh cause—one that,

unlike Afghanistan, was at the heart of the Middle East and thus could better promote al-Qaeda's agenda, so long as the group could mount a credible
challenge.

Although bin Laden made the strategic decision to attack in the kingdom
and began preparations in early 2002,[18] long before the Iraq war, top al-Qaeda
leadership likely determined the campaign's specific timing in March or April
2003,[19] influenced by events across the border. No doubt al-Qaeda would
have preferred to fight the invading American forces, but its negative opinion
of Saddam Hussein and lack of readily available assets in Iraq meant that the
organization would have to settle for an indirect approach. In the lead-up to
the war, al-Qaeda leaders and strategists used the Internet to offer advice to
the defending forces. Unable to operate in Iraq but feeling pressure to demonstrate its relevance, al-Qaeda had Saudi Arabia—a high-profile arena in which
it could activate its existing assets in a relatively short time—as a second-best
option. Moreover, the close US-Saudi alliance allowed al-Qaeda to construe
a narrative with fighting in Iraq and Saudi Arabia as parallel fronts of the
same war against the United States. Al-Qaeda may have also been driven by
a desire to capitalize on the rise of anti-American Saudi sentiment due to the
war in Iraq.

All of these factors created permissive conditions for the emergence
of AQAP and for turning Saudi Arabia into the first Mideast arena that
al-Qaeda designated as a theater of a concentrated terrorist campaign. But by
themselves, they do not explain why al-Qaeda's Saudi enterprise went beyond
terrorist operations to the announcement of a formal branch. Available information leads to no definitive reason—particularly unfortunate given how
consequential this decision has been for al-Qaeda's organizational moves
since. It charted the way for the group's adoption of branching out as its preferred mode of expansion, shaping its interaction with other jihadi groups
and its subsequent deliberations of possible entry to other locations.

As an organization, AQAP was the result of al-Uyayri's efforts to link
a number of relatively autonomous cells around the country, many established independently by returnees from Afghanistan. Al-Uyayri wanted to
bring those cells together under one command-and-control structure in
order to improve the effectiveness of al-Qaeda's Saudi infrastructure and
to guarantee that none of its components would take action prematurely
and prompt regime countermeasures against the entire network.[20] Thus,
it is possible that al-Qaeda built its Saudi branch not necessarily with a
clear vision for formal organizational expansion but, rather, as preferable to maintaining a loose structure of disconnected cells. In fact, in the

formation of AQAP one may see a chain of events in which operational considerations—primarily the need for coordinated strategic action and a clear command-and-control system—led to consolidating al-Qaeda's Saudi assets into one entity, with the political implications of branch creation following only after violence broke out.

Supporting this explanation is the fact that al-Uyayri attempted to dissuade bin Laden from activating the network because he believed that it was unready—for instance, the militants went on a violent rampage before establishing their media arm. Given the great importance al-Uyayri attributed to propaganda's role in promoting the jihadi cause, the delayed release of the magazines *Sawt al-Jihad* ("the Voice of Jihad") and *Mu'askar al-Battar* ("Military Camp of the Saber"), which did not appear until months after AQAP's first attack, indicates the rushed nature of the branch's inception. The members of al-Qaeda's network in Saudi Arabia referred to themselves as the "mujahideen in the Arabian Peninsula"; they first used the name AQAP about six months later.

Thus, evidence indicates that AQAP evolved into an al-Qaeda franchise only gradually. The group was first understood as an operational structure and, at the time it became public, an incomplete one. The political considerations affecting franchising appear to have come only later. Most likely, they reflected hope that by making such a strong political statement, the branch would be able to attract volunteers and financial resources to offset the enormous losses it incurred due to its premature birth. It is even possible that the decision to give the Saudi network its name—formally linking it to AQC and at the same time giving it organizational distinctiveness—was made by the leaders of the branch rather than the besieged bin Laden. Whether by design or inadvertently, the result of a decision by the core al-Qaeda leaders or the operatives in the kingdom, by presenting its Saudi network as a franchise, branching out became al-Qaeda's most promising arrangement for future organizational expansion.

The decision to introduce a Saudi branch proved disastrous for al-Qaeda. Despite relatively large membership and considerable resources, the AQAP collapsed under the weight of the Saudi regime's counteroffensive. Not only did al-Qaeda fail in a highly symbolic theater, it also lost tremendous public support as well as many irreplaceable seasoned operatives. Moreover, the campaign did what American post–9/11 pressure could not, forcing the regime to take robust and comprehensive action to curb al-Qaeda's financing.

Even more significant, by shifting its attention to the "near enemy," al-Qaeda weakened its ideological and strategic coherence while exposing the limits of its appeal even among bin Laden's compatriots. His conviction that foreign occupation mobilizes Muslims more effectively than wayward local regimes proved accurate, which makes it all the more puzzling that he failed to follow his own advice. Saudis rejected the revolutionary fight against the near enemy and did not accept al-Qaeda's attempts to frame its fight in the kingdom as a battle against a foreign occupation (especially when the United States had already announced plans to withdraw its remaining forces). Young Saudis were much more interested in traveling to Iraq to fight a real occupation—a cause that, unlike the fight against the Saudi royal family, was supported by important Saudi clerics.[21]

Iraq

In October 2004, about a year after al-Qaeda's Saudi branch adopted the name AQAP, Iraq became the second arena for al-Qaeda's formal expansion and the first one to feature a franchise that was based on a merger. The expansion was announced in a message from Abu Musab al-Zarqawi and his group al-Tawhid wal-Jihad (TWJ), which was based in Iraq prior to the American invasion and launched an effective terror campaign in its aftermath; the group pledged allegiance to bin Laden and announced that it had become al-Qaeda's affiliate in Iraq.[22] After this announcement, TWJ began using its new name, Al-Qaeda in the Land of the Two Rivers (commonly referred to as al-Qaeda in Iraq, or AQI). In corresponding messages, including a rare statement from bin Laden himself and an editorial in AQAP's *Mu'askar al-Battar* magazine (which also reprinted TWJ's allegiance message),[23] al-Qaeda publicly acknowledged its new Iraqi branch.

Although the merger expanded al-Qaeda's reach into the most prominent jihad arena, where Sunnis were fighting occupying forces, forming an Iraqi branch proved to be one of the organization's most self-destructive acts. It undermined al-Qaeda's ideological coherence and caused a public-relations disaster that permanently stained its reputation. Nearly a decade later, that branch's leaders would openly rebel against al-Qaeda and upstage it.

Why did al-Qaeda expand to Iraq? The country had great symbolic value. A combination of its history as the seat of the Abbasid caliphate and, in contrast to Saudi Arabia, indisputable foreign occupation made it a highly desirable arena for al-Qaeda penetration. In addition, Iraq appeared to have validated al-Qaeda's narrative that Islam is under attack, primarily from the United States. Even as interest drove al-Qaeda to seek expansion into Iraq, lack of capabilities slowed its entry and forced it to rely on a merger, as opposed to the in-house expansion in Saudi Arabia.

As noted in Chapter 4, al-Qaeda failed to anticipate the events that followed the 9/11 attack: the Taliban's collapse, losing its safe haven, and seeing its operational ability crippled. The organization achieved one of its main objectives as it drew the United States into a greater and much more transparent presence in the Middle East, but al-Qaeda was poorly positioned to confront its named archenemy. Despite ample warning that the United States intended to invade Iraq, al-Qaeda had few assets in place and no plan for facing Western forces there.[24] Even had leaders truly understood the necessity of a plan for Iraq, there was little al-Qaeda could do with its leaders besieged in Pakistan's tribal areas. The best it could do was to direct some operatives to join al-Zarqawi's emerging network in Iraq and to release statements offering tactical advice—highlighting, for example, the usefulness of digging trenches.[25]

Bin Laden's overconfidence, his weakness as a strategist, and his delusions that the 9/11 attacks would galvanize the umma left him on the sidelines, watching the conflict with the United States expand into a global confrontation—one that al-Qaeda had insufficient resources to enter. The organization was unable to deploy to major conflict hotspots; in Iraq it left the niche of a transnational jihadi outfit open for the more farsighted al-Zarqawi and his TWJ. In a combination of luck and shrewd analysis, al-Zarqawi established a presence in Iraq prior to the war. After the jihadis were driven out of Afghanistan, he found refuge in Iran, but when Iranian authorities tightened supervision of jihadi refugees, he moved with his supporters to neighboring Iraq, where he found shelter among Kurdish jihadi groups in the autonomous Kurdistan region in the country's north, far from Saddam Hussein's reach. For al-Zarqawi, Iraq was not just an available safe haven—he anticipated that the country would become the next target in President Bush's war on terrorism, and as war loomed, he traveled to Baghdad and Iraq's Sunni heartland to recruit volunteers and establish an infrastructure for the post-invasion resistance.[26]

Once US forces occupied Iraq, getting involved in the resistance was no longer merely a way to promote al-Qaeda's interests but an imperative; absence from the arena would be damaging to its reputation. Moreover, the insurgency's popularity and its success in inflicting considerable costs on the US-led international coalition forces threatened al-Qaeda's aspirations for leading the jihadi movement and ultimately the Muslim umma. But the organization lacked the necessary resources and was at a disadvantage, since other groups had already established themselves in Iraq and would be able to thwart al-Qaeda's expansion if they so wished. Given these constraints, al-Qaeda had to engineer a peaceful and unthreatening entry through co-optation. By merging with TWJ, al-Qaeda managed to enter a central jihadi arena while avoiding conflict with the most threatening established group. Moreover, by turning a potential competitor into a subordinate, al-Qaeda strengthened its leadership claims. Finally, the merger allowed al-Qaeda to assert that, notwithstanding the American onslaught, the group was flourishing. Indeed, the *Mu'askar al-Battar* editorial boasted that the merger indicated the failure of the American strategy: the United States had launched the war on terrorism to destroy al-Qaeda in Afghanistan only to see the organization actually expand throughout the world. The author also suggested that the unification indicated imminent victory.[27]

Why did al-Zarqawi agree to join al-Qaeda? There are two main explanations. The first emphasizes the connection between strategy and the requirements for its implementation. Al-Zarqawi's ambitious confrontation strategy was based on igniting a sectarian war and necessitated significant boosting of his resources, whether as a bridging measure until he had recruited enough Iraqi Sunnis or to enable the preparation and absorption of new recruits. By joining al-Qaeda, al-Zarqawi would gain an attractive brand name that would strengthen TWJ's legitimacy and give it access to al-Qaeda's logistical and propaganda capabilities, as well as its network of donors from Gulf countries, promising more resources and foreign recruits. The importance of these foreign fighters cannot be overestimated, as the vast majority of AQI's suicide bombers—central to its offensive capability—came from their ranks.[28]

The second explanation highlights how little al-Zarqawi needed to sacrifice by joining al-Qaeda. He avoided giving bin Laden the *bay'a*, pledge of allegiance, before 9/11 in order to preserve his autonomy. But the conditions under which he chose to join al-Qaeda in 2004 were radically different: TWJ joined under the condition that it would be able to pursue a sectarian strategy, which went against bin Laden's less hostile approach toward the Shia and his preference for focusing on the United States. Given that when TWJ announced it had joined al-Qaeda, it claimed that the latter accepted its perspective, and given that al-Zarqawi's subsequent actions clearly show that he pursued sectarian violence, there is little reason to think that TWJ made any significant compromises in merger negotiations. Moreover, with al-Qaeda's leadership in hiding, unable to respond quickly to events or to exercise strong planning or oversight, al-Zarqawi's formal submission to al-Qaeda hardly undermined his actual autonomy.

Although many observers at first saw the merger as a huge coup for al-Qaeda, in reality it was far from that. Its new terrorist partner turned out to be a Trojan horse that further undermined al-Qaeda's strategy, theological coherence, and reputation, while mounting a strong leadership challenge.

There were early signs that the relationship between al-Qaeda and TWJ would be fraught with problems. Although the merger announcement communicated unity, TWJ signaled that the agreement was achieved only after eight months of rocky negotiations, including at least one suspension. Moreover, TWJ's claim that its pledge of allegiance to bin Laden occurred after al-Qaeda came to understand al-Zarqawi's strategy and "its heart warmed" to his group's methods[29] indicated that the Iraqi branch was determined to assert its ways and importance, undermining its own claim that it would follow bin Laden in whatever commands he gave.

The relationship between al-Qaeda and al-Zarqawi was contentious even before the affiliation negotiations and TWJ's tepid declaration of fealty. Al-Zarqawi was familiar to al-Qaeda leaders since arriving in Afghanistan in December 1999, after his release from Jordanian prison.[30] He met with bin Laden shortly after his arrival. According to Mary Anne Weaver, bin Laden immediately disliked the young Jordanian, finding him overly ambitious, arrogant, and abrasive. In a harbinger of future divisions, bin Laden did not share al-Zarqawi's passionate hatred of the Shia. Al-Zarqawi, on the other hand, disagreed with bin Laden urging Taliban volunteers to fight fellow Muslims in the Northern Alliance. Despite the acrimony, following the advice of bin Laden's lieutenant, Saif al-Adl, al-Qaeda's leader gave al-Zarqawi seed money to open a training camp for Jordanian and Syrian radicals near the remote city of Herat. Although al-Adl argued that al-Qaeda clarified in that meeting that it asked al-Zarqawi only for coordination and cooperation—not a full pledge of allegiance—in the next two years, bin Laden, notwithstanding the hostility, reportedly called al-Zarqawi at least five times to come to Kandahar and give him a *bay'a*. Each time, al-Zarqawi refused.[31]

Notably, Abu Muhammad al-Maqdisi, al-Zarqawi's mentor turned critic, suggests that it was al-Zarqawi's lack of flexibility that prevented his incorporation into al-Qaeda,[32] whereas al-Adl ignores al-Zarqawi's refusal to pledge fealty while self-servingly offering a much more positive portrayal of the relationship. In al-Adl's testimony in a book about al-Zarqawi, he proposes that the latter's move to Iraq after the Taliban's fall was taken in consultation with al-Qaeda,[33] insinuating that al-Qaeda shared al-Zarqawi's foresight to see Iraq as the next battlefront, while avoiding the inconvenient discussion of the circumstances that led to the change in the relationship.

There are scant details about the dialogue that led to the merger. The reconstruction of the two organizations' positions relies to a large extent on three letter exchanges captured by US forces: one, intercepted in January 2004, was written by al-Zarqawi months before the merger announcement, and two came from al-Qaeda leaders Ayman al-Zawahiri and Atiyatallah al-Libi, dated 2005, after TWJ had become al-Qaeda's Iraqi branch.

Al-Zarqawi's letter was likely his gambit in the merger negotiations; it lays out his understanding of the conflict in Iraq and TWJ's strategy, identifying the Shia as the main obstacle. His extreme hostility toward the Shia is evident: he describes them as "the lurking snake, the crafty and malicious scorpion, the spying enemy, and the penetrating venom." Fighting the Americans is simple, he maintains, because they are easy to identify, unfamiliar with the land, and short of operational intelligence; they will "disappear tomorrow or the day after."[34] Not so the Shia, who al-Zarqawi saw as the real enemy, composed of fellow countrymen and highly knowledgeable about the jihadis. They had been working to establish control, taking the reins over the military, the security apparatus, and the state's economy. According to al-Zarqawi, Shia leaders had been careful to avoid a sectarian war with the Sunnis, knowing that it would lead Sunnis everywhere to join their brothers in Iraq, resulting in ultimate defeat.

Al-Zarqawi complains that even in the face of this Shia conspiracy, the Sunni masses sat idle; despite the Sunnis' hatred of the United States, they failed to mobilize and fight against it. Their *ulama'* (religious scholars) were composed mostly of despised Sufis who avoid jihad no matter how bad the circumstances. His view of the Muslim Brotherhood in Iraq is hardly more positive: according to al-Zarqawi, they lack a backbone and firm principles, caring only about publicly representing the Sunni population and thus shifting their positions based on political calculations. While holding the Iraqi jihadis in higher esteem, al-Zarqawi criticizes them for lacking jihadi spirit—they are risk-averse, seeking to return home safely even short of victory. Failing to appreciate the importance of martyrdom, they pursue ineffective fighting methods. Additionally, only slowly are they starting to see the need of uniting the efforts of all jihadi forces. The foreign jihadis, in comparison, do not suffer from these malaises, but their numbers are too small and they do not receive enough support from the local Sunni population.

Given this analysis, TWJ's strategy is to target the Shia everywhere and provoke them to retaliate in a manner that would expose their true nature to the slumbering Sunnis. The group believes that by dragging the Shia into a sectarian war it will be able to mobilize the Sunnis, a precondition for success in Iraq. Al-Zarqawi concludes his letter with a direct appeal to bin Laden, telling him that if he accepts the analysis and the proposed strategy for a sectarian war, then TWJ will gladly operate under the al-Qaeda banner and publicly give bin Laden an oath of allegiance. But he also makes clear his intention to proceed with his strategy with or without al-Qaeda.[35]

Although TWJ maintained that it joined al-Qaeda only after the latter came to accept its strategy, evidence indicates that al-Qaeda was not entirely sold on al-Zarqawi's plan. This is not surprising given bin Laden's US-focused strategy and his significantly weaker hostility toward the Shia.[36] The letters from al-Zawahiri and Atyiahallah reveal great dissatisfaction with the Iraqi branch's harmful actions and show how al-Qaeda's leadership sought to reign in al-Zarqawi, including on those aspects of his strategy that al-Qaeda supposedly adopted with the merger.

Al-Zawahiri's letter, dated July 2005, criticizes al-Zarqawi for focusing on fighting the Shia instead of the more urgent priority of attacking and expelling the American forces. The al-Qaeda lieutenant does not engage directly with al-Zarqawi's view that triggering a sectarian war would awaken the Sunnis to action, but he argues that the Sunni masses "do not rally except against an outside occupying enemy." To the extent that Iraq's Sunnis have mobilized against the Shia, it has not been a robust movement, and whatever strength it did have should be attributed to the Shia's cooperation with the Americans, not to fundamental sectarian hostility. Al-Zawahiri is also critical of the affiliate's expansion of its Shia targets beyond leaders to include ordinary people. He objects to targeting the Shia masses on both strategic and doctrinal grounds. From a strategic perspective, he suggests that opening a front against the Shia population diverts resources from the anti-American campaign and undermines the primary objective of expelling the US forces.[37] The theological differences with al-Zarqawi are at least as important and reveal the extent to which bringing TWJ under al-Qaeda's wing undermined the organization's ideological coherence.[38] In al-Zawahiri's opinion, the Shia should be viewed as Muslims and deserve the protections awarded to Muslim sinners. They cannot be deemed heretics if their sinful behavior is the result of ignorance; instead of being condemned to death, they should be educated and guided to the truth.

In Zawahiri's words:

Indeed, questions will circulate among mujahedeen circles and their opinion makers about the correctness of this conflict with the

Shia at this time. Is it something that is unavoidable? Or is it something that can be put off until the force of the mujahed movement
in Iraq gets stronger? And if some of the operations were necessary
for self-defense, were all of the operations necessary? Or were there
some operations that weren't called for? And is the opening of another
front now in addition to the front against the Americans and the government a wise decision? Or does this conflict with the Shia lift the
burden from the Americans by diverting the mujahedeen to the Shia,
while the Americans continue to control matters from afar? And if the
attacks on Shia leaders were necessary to put a stop to their plans, then
why were there attacks on ordinary Shia? Won't this lead to reinforcing false ideas in their minds, even as it is incumbent on us to preach
the call of Islam to them and explain and communicate to guide them
to the truth? And can the mujahedeen kill all of the Shia in Iraq? Has
any Islamic state in history ever tried that? And why kill ordinary Shia
considering that they are forgiven because of their ignorance? And
what loss will befall us if we did not attack the Shia?[39]

Al-Zawahiri's letter, albeit critical, is couched in positive references, in a
clear effort to avoid offending al-Zarqawi. Al-Zawahiri repeatedly praises the
work of AQI, allowing that because of his distance from the front, he is less
familiar than al-Zarqawi with conditions on the ground. He thus cautiously
frames his letter as a request for additional information and as advice that is
based on general principles but incomplete knowledge of the specific facts.[40]
    Atiyatallah's letter, written in late 2005, is much more explicit in its criti-
cism of al-Zarqawi and in demanding that he change his ways and follow
AQC's orders. In contrast to AQI's attempts to secure the leadership of the
Sunnis in Iraq by exacerbating sectarian fears, Atiyatallah emphasizes the
importance of soft power. He urges AQI to attract Iraq's Sunnis by exhibiting
goodness, mercy, and justice; instead of forcing its leadership, AQI should
capture Sunni hearts. It must therefore avoid intra-Sunni conflict, show
respect for all Sunni leaders (even those with whom it disagrees), and consult
them, especially in major decisions such as declaring war on Iraq's Shia. AQI
must be especially careful not to kill any religious scholar or tribal leader with
a good reputation and followers. Atiyatallah also rebukes al-Zarqawi for overreaching in authorizing an attack in Jordan's capital, Amman, which led to
the death of scores of common Muslims and turned public opinion in Jordan
strongly against al-Qaeda. According to Atiyatallah, the decision to expand
operations into a new arena is strategic and therefore AQC's responsibility.

A branch leader must not take such an initiative without consulting his better-informed superiors, who have greater understanding of the way military action serves the organization's political objectives.[41]

The letters make clear that the merger did not resolve fundamental differences between al-Qaeda and al-Zarqawi. The merger agreement was largely on the latter's terms, with al-Qaeda reluctantly consenting to his Shia-focused strategy, probably believing—or at least hoping—that after TWJ's incorporation into al-Qaeda, the parent organization's leadership would be able to assert its authority and advance its own strategy.

Once the disastrous costs of al-Zarqawi's insistence on targeting the Shia became clear, al-Qaeda tried to persuade him to moderate his ways and stop the indiscriminate killing. The February 2006 bombing of the Shia's al-Askari mosque in the city of Samarra, which led to an unprecedented escalation of the sectarian violence in Iraq, demonstrates how patently AQC's efforts to rein in al-Zarqawi failed. And gaps between AQC and the Iraqi franchise continued to widen. In October 2006, a few months after al-Zarqawi's death, AQI announced the establishment of an Islamic state, which it named the Islamic State of Iraq (ISI).[42] This announcement, understood at the time as in line with al-Qaeda's ideas concerning the future of Iraq, can in retrospect be seen as another AQI challenge to the authority of al-Qaeda's senior leadership.[43]

In his 2005 letter, al-Zawahiri asks al-Zarqawi to prepare for the United States' imminent departure, lest a vacuum be created into which rivals would enter, stealing the fruits of the jihadis' victory; he also suggests establishing an emirate after the Americans' expulsion.[44] Later, in his eulogy to al-Zarqawi, al-Zawahiri urged his "mujahid brothers in Iraq" to "establish an Islamic state in Iraq, then make your way towards captive Jerusalem and restore the Caliphate."[45] But AQC did not favor its branch's confrontational approach in its dealings with fellow Sunni groups and would have probably preferred to postpone the establishment of an Islamic state until dominant groups among the Sunni insurgency were persuaded to join it. Moreover, al-Qaeda was surprised when al-Zarqawi's successors actually moved ahead and announced the establishment of a state without receiving the explicit approval of al-Qaeda's senior leadership—in fact, without even consulting it.[46] Astonishingly, communications between AQC and the branch suggest that the former was unfamiliar with Abu Umar al-Baghdadi, the individual nominated to head the ISI, and that for a long time it lacked any way to directly communicate with him.[47]

AQC's displeasure with its rogue branch grew after prominent jihadi actors inside Iraq and beyond voiced disapproval of its moves.[48] In response to the criticism, ISI leaders insisted that they were justified in announcing the state because during wartime, a Muslim who overpowers enemies is allowed to establish an Islamic state through imposition, alluding to (and embellishing) the group's military success. Moreover, the ISI argued that during war the fighters who are leading the jihad—rather than scholars and other Muslim leaders—become the "influential leaders" who are authorized to pledge allegiance to a person they choose who meets the desired qualities of an imam.[49]

Al-Qaeda's Iraqi franchise distorted its superiors' instructions in additional ways. Al-Zawahiri proposed that the branch might benefit from an Iraqi leader, to fend off accusations of being a foreign organization. The January 2006 establishment of the Mujahideen Shura Council (MSC) could be viewed as al-Zarqawi's response.[50] The MSC was billed as a union between AQI and six other jihadi groups, but al-Zarqawi's MSC associates represented tiny organizations and had practically no operational significance. Their only value was in legitimating AQI and its Islamic-state project, as well as shielding it from accusations of a unilateral power grab. By joining AQI, these groups' leaders facilitated the larger organization's independent aspirations. Thus, in a book prepared by the ISI to justify its founding, it deceptively argued that the MSC displayed great strength and control over a large territory and that, as the product of groups joining to work as a single army, it was worthy of setting up an Islamic state. At the same time, AQI used the MSC to challenge the legitimacy of other groups' resistance to the ISI, based on the argument that these groups—many of whom were much bigger and more powerful than any of AQI's allies—had failed to unify.[51]

In establishing the ISI, the Iraqi franchise put AQC in an uncomfortable position: bin Laden could not restore the original balance of power without exposing schisms within al-Qaeda, as well as his own inability to control his franchises. He also risked being openly rebuffed and disobeyed had he rejected the ISI after its public launch. So al-Qaeda reluctantly offered approval of the ISI, only to see the ISI cynically use this support to further proclaim its state's legitimacy. Strong public endorsement from some of al-Qaeda's leaders suggests that they might have even come to see value in the Islamic state, once established, though it is also noteworthy that bin Laden himself continued to emphasize unity within the jihadi camp without demanding that Iraq's Sunni groups submit to the ISI's authority.[52]

The cost of siding with the ISI mounted over time, including straining AQC's relationships with other Sunni insurgent groups in Iraq. A few years later, the ISI (by then renamed ISIS, the Islamic State of Iraq and al-Sham) argued that, with the establishment of the state, it was no longer subordinated to bin Laden and therefore could not be seen as violating its oath to al-Qaeda (more on this in Chapter 9).[53] The excesses of al-Qaeda's Iraqi franchise and its failed strategy incurred additional costs on the parent organization, primarily by harming its image among Sunni Muslims worldwide.

Atiyatallah was prescient in his 2005 warning to al-Zarqawi that the Iraq affiliate's actions would project on the whole organization: "Your success in your field projects success onto our plan, and to us as the faction waging jihadi in general. If you suffer defeat, and if mistakes occur, then we all bear its consequences as well."[54] Thus, although al-Qaeda did not support AQI's focus on instigating a sectarian war, its supposed authority over the Iraqi franchise meant that it could not dissociate itself from this effort. Moreover, it could not wash its hands of responsibility for the outcome. Al-Zarqawi gambled that Iraq's Sunnis would accept AQI's leadership in the face of a salient Shia threat and, importantly, that it would be able to deliver victory to its followers. But he was overly optimistic about AQI's power: it was unable to radicalize the Sunni population and ultimately win the civil war it had started, and its failure to protect the Sunnis whom it dragged into the war led them to blame AQI for Shia groups' retaliatory violence.[55] Although this was primarily AQI's failure, there was no way it would not stick to the parent organization as well.

The franchise's brutality against fellow insurgent groups further hurt the al-Qaeda brand name, especially when directed against likely allies subscribing to Salafi-jihadi ideology. The hostility between AQI and most other groups, including Ansar al-Sunna (later renamed Ansar al-Islam), which had close relations with AQC leaders, increased following the ISI's introduction. The ISI declared itself the sole legitimate ruling authority and called all other Sunni groups to join it,[56] but those groups did not view its establishment as benign—rather, it was seen, accurately, as an attempt to bully them into submission. Because the quarrel played out in public (often through statements released online) and was closely followed by Muslims worldwide, al-Qaeda was unable to control the fallout and contain the damage to the Iraqi arena. Its branch's misdeeds undermined al-Qaeda's image far beyond Iraq's borders.

The Iraqi case supports the arena's intrinsic role in al-Qaeda's expansion decisions. Iraq's importance, particularly given the American occupation, rendered the country not merely an attractive target for formal expansion but an arena al-Qaeda had to join or face reputational costs. Eager to enter Iraq but lacking sufficient operational capabilities to establish itself, especially in an already saturated market, al-Qaeda was pushed into a merger. Therefore, need forced al-Qaeda into an alliance with a brutal and unruly leader about whom it had long harbored reservations. Not only did the merger drive al-Qaeda into strategic compromises, saddling it with doctrinal positions to which it did not subscribe—it resulted in a public relations disaster from which the group has not recovered.

Conclusions

In 2003 and 2004, al-Qaeda formed its first franchises. Although its branching-out strategy created the impression of strength, over time it became evident that not only did this expansion not significantly bolster al-Qaeda's power—it also inflicted devastating costs. Al-Qaeda's formal expansion to Saudi Arabia and Iraq took place under the condition of "need," leading the group to take risky and, as it turned out, self-defeating choices. The US-led "war on terrorism" in general, and the American invasion of Afghanistan in particular, caused al-Qaeda severe losses. It was desperate to prove its relevance but lacked the ability to pull off another spectacular terrorist attack against the United States. The Iraq war presented al-Qaeda with a cause and an opportunity to recover but simultaneously increased the pressure to prove its viability.

As a result, al-Qaeda launched a campaign in Saudi Arabia that backfired resoundingly, leading to its infrastructure's destruction in a prized arena. Need then pushed al-Qaeda into a merger with TWJ, with even more devastating consequences. Al-Qaeda's expansion into Iraq—a response to both general pressure to act and the specific pressure to show up in the central front against the United States—undermined its already shaky strategy because its agent in Iraq, al-Zarqawi, prioritized a counterproductive sectarian approach that undermined al-Qaeda's US-first strategy. The TWJ affiliation would end up haunting al-Qaeda for years to come, as the rogue franchise first tarnished al-Qaeda's reputation among Sunni Muslims and later took advantage of the conditions in Iraq and Syria to challenge AQC and upstage it.

7

Spreading

AL-QAEDA'S BRANCHES IN ALGERIA,
YEMEN, AND SOMALIA

PRESSURE TO RESPOND to the international dragnet and the Iraq war led al-Qaeda to introduce its first franchises, in the center of the Middle East. In subsequent years, the group expanded into several new arenas: it reached the Horn of Africa, the Maghreb, and the Indian subcontinent, and, despite its failures in Saudi Arabia and Iraq, did not abandon its efforts to establish itself in the Levant and the Arabian Peninsula. This chapter examines al-Qaeda's branching out to Algeria (2006), Yemen (2007), and Somalia (2010) and how, following the two cases discussed earlier, al-Qaeda franchised in diverse ways—introducing an in-house branch in Yemen and using mergers to branch out elsewhere.

Algeria

The Algeria-based Salafist Group for Preaching and Combat (GSPC) joined al-Qaeda at the end of 2006, becoming its third franchise. This was the second branch to result from a merger agreement but the first to rely on local leaders, in contrast to TWJ's mostly non-Iraqi leadership.

The GSPC's origins can be traced to the Armed Islamic Group (GIA), an Algerian jihadi outfit composed of returnees from the war against the Soviets in Afghanistan, bolstered by a large contingent of local radicals. The GIA emerged as the dominant opposition force during the Algerian civil war of the 1990s. But its radicalism—manifested primarily in declaring the entire Algerian population apostates for not actively supporting the GIA's agenda and, as a result, the indiscriminate killing of ordinary Algerians—was extreme even by jihadi standards. By the decade's end, GIA's excesses led most of the global jihadi community—including the Libyan Islamic Fighting Group, the Egyptian Islamic Jihad, Osama bin Laden, and the former GIA enthusiasts Abu Qatada and Abu Musab al-Suri—to renounce it. Inside Algeria, numerous GIA members who disapproved of the group's massacres of common Algerians and feared that they themselves would become victims of the purges abandoned it.[1] Some of these jihadis banded together in 1998 under Hassan Hattab's leadership to form the GSPC, which would focus attacks on government and military targets rather than ordinary Muslims.

Ayman al-Zawahiri announced the merger between al-Qaeda and the GSPC in an interview with al-Qaeda's al-Sahab media-production wing on the fifth anniversary of the 9/11 attack.[2] The affiliation process was completed four months later when the GSPC announced, in January 2007, that it had changed its name to al-Qaeda in the Islamic Maghreb (AQIM).[3] The merger's operational implications were first revealed when, three months after al-Zawahiri's announcement, the GSPC carried out an attack on a bus shuttling employees of a Halliburton subsidiary.[4] The attack was the first in a few years to aim at Westerners rather than regime targets and reflected al-Qaeda's focus on Western targets (albeit locally located); additional such operations followed in subsequent years. The group's internationalization was also manifest in the spread of its attacks beyond Algeria's borders to neighboring countries, primarily Mauritania, Mali, and Niger.[5] The merger influenced GSPC tactics, as the group carried out more frequent and more sophisticated attacks; importantly, it introduced suicide bombings—al-Qaeda's hallmark—to the arena.

Following al-Qaeda's Saudi and Iraqi ventures, its expansion into the Algerian theater was less rushed and the result of a longer and likely more deliberative process. Although the organization was under persistent pressure to continue expanding, no location presented the urgency to intervene in the way Iraq did. Furthermore, there was no particular pressure on al-Qaeda to choose Algeria as an expansion target. So why did leaders decide to enter the Algerian arena?

By adopting a branching-out strategy, al-Qaeda made expansion into new arenas a public indicator of its success. Al-Qaeda's implied inability to carry out further spectacular attacks in the West gave formal expansion oversized significance; entering a new arena signaled power. Taking the form of a merger, it could also bolster the impression that al-Qaeda's appeal to Islamist groups was increasing and that more people viewed the group as a natural leader. This, in turn, would signal al-Qaeda's success in "awakening" the umma to the fight against the United States and, like a self-fulfilling prophecy, would encourage more Muslim youth to join it. Finally, the perception of success, al-Qaeda hoped, would increase its Western enemies' anxiety and deter countries from cooperating with the United States in fighting the group.

Despite the perceived value of formal expansion, al-Qaeda was constrained: it lacked sufficient capabilities to establish in-house branches in new Middle Eastern arenas and had to partner with other groups to realize its branching-out strategy. In theory, al-Qaeda could have targeted Syria and Jordan, where its Iraqi branch had spread its tentacles; however, given AQC's distrust of that branch and reports about its excesses, relying on al-Qaeda in Iraq seemed too risky. Al-Qaeda preferred to look for partners elsewhere. It claimed to have merged with the Libyan Islamic Fighting Group and the Gama'a Islamiya, but only marginal factions from these groups—located alongside al-Qaeda far from the Middle East, not in their home countries—welcomed joining it. That left Algeria and the GSPC as the best available alternatives.

Al-Qaeda and the GSPC have always had some ideological affinity, a prerequisite for going beyond cooperation to affiliation. Both organizations espouse a Salafist worldview, aspire to establish an Islamic state modeled after the one founded by the Prophet and his immediate successors, and emphasize jihad not only as a political strategy but as a religious imperative. At the same time, while sympathetic to the objective of Islamic rule in Muslim countries, in practice the GSPC pursued a less ambitious and more narrowly focused nationalist agenda. It sought to topple the Algerian regime and replace it with a government that would rule according to Islamic law.

Over time, this original divergence blurred. Observers saw signs of the GSPC's reorientation toward al-Qaeda as early as 2003, when senior members of the group who supported a more internationalist outlook compelled Hattab to step down.[6] His successor, Nabil Sahraoui, openly declared support for al-Qaeda.[7] The group also shifted its rhetoric toward internationalist and anti-American discourse.[8] In parallel, the GSPC made overtures to al-Qaeda: through diverse communication channels—directly through al-Qaeda leader Younis al-Mauritani and indirectly through al-Zarqawi and the Iraqi branch—al-Qaeda and the GSPC discussed cooperation and the possibility of deepening the relationship further through a merger.[9]

Although Algeria was a low US priority, the country still fit into al-Qaeda's narrative of a fight against the "far enemy"—after all, France still plays a weighty role in its affairs, decades after its independence. The GIA proffered the connections between France and the Algerian regime a decade earlier to justify carrying out terrorist attacks on French territory, in an attempt to compel Paris to stop its support for the regime. From al-Qaeda's perspective, focusing on France would be beneficial because of its "meddling" in Muslim affairs (primarily in Africa) and its role as a junior partner in the American-led "crusade." But teaming up with the GSPC was also compatible with al-Qaeda's efforts to present itself as the protector of oppressed Muslims and its expressed interest in relieving the plight of France's Muslims. Al-Qaeda sought to exploit tensions surrounding the French headscarf ban by spearheading action in support of Muslims in France, using the ban to unite Muslims against this alleged conspiracy to hinder their worship of God. Given that many of France's Muslims are of Algerian origin, and that the GSPC had an active infrastructure in the country, al-Qaeda could find the GSPC a valuable asset.[10]

Al-Qaeda envisioned additional operational benefits from bringing the GSPC under its wing, such as access to that group's European pool of jihadis and criminal contacts.[11] Branching out to Algeria was also in line with al-Qaeda's interest in spreading its influence throughout North Africa and the important Sahel region. Smuggling routes through the Sahel became important sources of income for al-Qaeda as AQIM became involved in trafficking and providing security for smugglers in the area.[12] The desolate area proved particularly conducive to the group's hostage-taking business. Ransom paid, primarily by European states, to release kidnapped citizens became a central source of revenue for al-Qaeda.[13] Finally, al-Qaeda expected that its expansion into North Africa would lead the United States to divert resources from the Afghan arena and, consequently, would relieve pressure on the organization's senior leadership.

In explaining its reasons for joining al-Qaeda, the GSPC maintained that the merger was based on ideology. In a *New York Times* interview, emir Abdelmalek Droukdal (also known as Abu Musab Abdel Wadud) denied that material interests were a factor for the GSPC. Islamic imperatives, he argued, require Muslims to unite, particularly when their enemies have banded together to wage a war against the umma. The main objective of unifying jihadi forces is to please Allah.[14]

Ultimately, neither an ideological shift, nor a strategic calculation concerning the requirements for achieving its political objectives, determined the GSPC's direction. Rather, its jump on the al-Qaeda bandwagon appears to have been motivated primarily by organizational interest—above all, fear for the group's survival.[15] Numbering 4,000 fighters in 2002,[16] membership declined rapidly. The regime's amnesty offers caused the GSPC considerable attrition as many fighters, tired of the struggle, choose to defect.[17] Regime crackdown augmented the pressure on the group: in 2005 and 2006 the Algerian government captured or killed some 500 jihadis, practically halving the organization's available members.[18] Unsurprisingly, these developments also impacted the remaining fighters' morale. With public support for the anti-regime insurgency slipping ever further, the battle appeared lost. A former leader of the GSPC's media wing admitted that the group needed the merger to justify continuing its activity. Algeria's national-reconciliation process and public rejection of the jihadis put tremendous pressure on what was left of the group. By joining al-Qaeda, the GSPC believed that it could reinvent itself and gain authority and new legitimacy.[19]

The GSPC also had good reason to believe that adopting a more international approach would increase its appeal among Algerian youth. While its anti-regime struggle was faltering, the group learned that young Algerians found the fight against the United States in Iraq a much more appealing cause.[20] To some extent, the GSPC's embrace of the Iraqi jihad gave the organization a new lease on life: it opened training camps for volunteers and used its logistical networks to send them to fight under al-Zarqawi's leadership. The relationship with al-Zarqawi improved the GSPC's reputation within the global jihadi community and brought the group closer to al-Qaeda. GSPC stature was also elevated by activating Saharan smuggling routes for militants from Morocco, Tunisia, Mauritania, and Libya and opening camps for them to train before they headed to Iraq.[21] And by adopting the Iraqi cause, the GSPC was able to sustain the fight within Algeria, since, in order to gain military experience, some volunteers were deployed in the Algerian arena before being deemed ready to head to Iraq.[22] Other volunteers, who could not leave Algeria due to government crackdowns, ended up adopting it as their theater of operations.[23] Clearly, then, the GSPC acknowledged and embraced the lore of global jihad in the hope that an affiliation with al-Qaeda would enable it to revitalize.

Christopher Chivvis and Andrew Liepman suggest that joining al-Qaeda also served the interests of GSPC leader Droukdal, who likely hoped that this step would strengthen his own position with the group's rank and file.[24] That al-Qaeda gave its branches' leaders great freedom to run their organizations magnified the merger's appeal for Droukdal. Indeed, although al-Qaeda determined the group's strategic direction, leading to an operational shift toward the "far enemy," it neither tried to assume control over the group's management nor sent its own representatives to oversee the GSPC's leadership (although it did send a senior trainer to assist in the Sahel region).[25]

Despite a perception that a merger would be mutually beneficial, it could not proceed before the GSPC persuaded al-Qaeda that it would be a dependable partner, not another iteration of the notorious GIA. Lingering hostility toward Algeria's jihadi community—stemming from the killing of foreign jihadi volunteers who had gone to Algerian during the civil war, only to end up targets for the GIA's madness—made building such trust essential. Formal affiliation also required that the GSPC prove that it could contribute to al-Qaeda in a meaningful way, a task complicated by the group's declining power and its original focus on the "near enemy." A 2005 attack on a Mauritanian military base, far from Algeria's borders, and a shipment of fighters to join the insurgency in Iraq helped convince al-Qaeda senior leadership that the GSPC was indeed committed to the cause of global jihad.[26]

Less than a month before Droukdal announced his group's name change and completed the affiliation process's public stage, he released a statement directed at bin Laden. Although the message's purpose is somewhat unclear, it appears designed to assuage possible doubts regarding the franchise. Its public nature may have been prompted by communication problems, particularly with the al-Qaeda leader isolated in Abbottabad. In the message, Droukdal assures bin Laden that the GSPC is in a good state, recovering from earlier setbacks and seeing growing membership. According to the statement, the group was regularly carrying out attacks following a well-studied plan and inflicting heavy losses.[27]

Droukdal also had to overcome some internal resistance to the merger. The main points of contention among members were the required shift from focusing on the overthrow of Algeria's secular regime to global jihad, and the permissibility of targeting civilians rather than restricting operations to regime targets. Some GSPC members left over its decision to ally with al-Qaeda.[28]

A Rand Corporation study portrayed the merger as a "marriage of convenience" between organizations that shared some fundamental views but did not fully align their objectives.[29] The unification was a definite win for the GSPC, which gained renewed relevance, rejuvenating—at least in the short term—its image and enhancing leaders' self-confidence.[30] In public statements, AQIM officials also declared that the group became stronger as a result of the merger, with an influx of recruits from neighboring Maghreb states.[31]

From al-Qaeda's perspective, the relationship failed to live up to its operational promise. In contrast to its negotiations with the TWJ, al-Qaeda had greater leverage in its dealings with the GSPC because the latter was more eager to reach an agreement; this allowed AQC to test its new partner and set the terms of the affiliation. But AQIM's contribution to al-Qaeda has been more limited than expected. AQIM's media intensified the focus on international themes,[32] but apart from a few high-profile attacks on Western targets, the shift from the "near" to the "far" enemy has been largely rhetorical. While AQIM's kidnap-for-ransom enterprise contributed to the parent organization's finances, the branch's war chest has translated to very few spectacular terrorist attacks. The increase in attacks on Western targets was relatively short-lived, and by 2013 close to 90% of AQIM's violent activity was concentrated in Algeria, with about 80% of attacks directed at state security forces.[33] The efforts to mobilize the GSPC's European networks essentially failed,[34] and while it was conceived as a vanguard to push north to Europe, AQIM has proved incapable or unwilling to attack France or Spain.[35] The goal of integrating the various North African jihadi groups into one structure also has remained unmet; contact with the Tunisian Combatant Group, for example, has remained limited.

AQIM's disappointing performance reflects, in part, organizational dysfunction[36] and the resilience of its original anti-regime proclivities, but a capabilities deficit has probably played a more central role. The Abbottabad documents reveal certain disapproval among AQC toward some of the franchises but not much with regard to AQIM. Documents found in 2013 after French forces pushed AQIM and its Islamist allies out of the main cities of northern Mali show that while AQIM members were responsible for some excesses, Droukdal rebuked them and directed his representatives to act with moderation and not offend local sensibilities.[37] Notably, his guidelines are compatible with bin Laden's instructions[38] and are similar to those followed by al-Qaeda's branches in Yemen and Syria.[39] Looking ahead, AQIM may still prove invaluable, especially in light of the new opportunities to increase its penetration throughout North Africa, created in the aftermath of the Arab Awakening.[40] Indeed, confirmed AQIM attacks in Tunisia and its use of Libya as a training, logistical, and transit hub are ominous signs.[41]

Yemen

Yemen was the fourth country to have the dubious honor of hosting an official al-Qaeda franchise. The branch was an in-house expansion, based on Yemeni al-Qaeda members and reinforced by Saudis who had escaped government crackdowns; it operated as a branch since mid-2007, using the names "The al-Qaeda Organization of Jihad in the South of the Arabian Peninsula" and "The al-Qaeda Organization in the Land of Yemen."[42] Demonstrating operational maturity, the group carried out daring operations—including attacks targeting oil facilities and Western tourists and even two failed attacks on the American embassy—as well as publishing a magazine titled *Sada al-Malahim* ("Echo of Battles").[43] And yet al-Qaeda saw it as peripheral until January 2009, when the Yemeni leaders, joined by two former Guantanamo Bay Saudi detainees, announced in a video message the unification in Yemen of al-Qaeda's Saudi and Yemeni networks under the name al-Qaeda in the Arabian Peninsula (AQAP).[44] This rebranding signaled a new phase and the assumption of a much higher profile.

Over time, AQAP became al-Qaeda's most important branch as well as its most dependable affiliate, owing to its origins, coming from al-Qaeda's own ranks. Not only was it more in tune with the parent organization's strategy—it also was highly capable. When AQC could not successfully execute foreign operations in the West, AQAP assumed this role: its plan to down a Northwest flight over Detroit (on Christmas Day 2009) failed only because the bomber failed to ignite the bomb properly, and a plan to explode two cargo planes 10 months later was thwarted at the last moment. Both operations came closer to success than any planned by al-Qaeda's senior leadership lately, and their high profile allowed al-Qaeda to claim them as victories, particularly in circumventing Western security measures and drying up Western resources. As a sign of AQAP's importance, in 2013 al-Zawahiri nominated its leader Nasir al-Wuhayshi to the post of al-Qaeda's general manager. It was the first time this position was filled by a branch leader and not an AQC figure.[45]

Why did al-Qaeda form a formal branch in Yemen? The country was important to al-Qaeda long before the branch was introduced; in fact, Yemen—the homeland of bin Laden's father—was on al-Qaeda's radar soon after the organization came into being and before bin Laden even formulated al-Qaeda's strategy. At first, he planned to use al-Qaeda to counter the socialists in the country's south. By December 1992, his interest in Yemen converged with his anti-Americanism upon learning that US soldiers intended to use Yemen as a transit state on the way to the UN humanitarian mission Restore Hope in Somalia. Determined to prevent the United States from using Somalia as an excuse for keeping forces in Yemen—bin Laden still smarted over US forces, two years earlier, using the Iraqi threat as a rationale for deploying forces in Saudi Arabia—he ordered an attack on the Marines. The December 29 attack was al-Qaeda's first act of terrorism, and although it missed its target, killing instead a local hotel employee and an Austrian tourist, bin Laden credited it for the US decision against using Yemen as a support base.[46]

Seven years later, Yemen was the site of a spectacular al-Qaeda terrorist attack, the bombing of the destroyer USS *Cole* off the shores of Aden, followed two years later by an attack on the French tanker *Limburg*. But al-Qaeda's infrastructure in Yemen was fragile and did not survive the drone-strike death of its commander, Abu Ali al-Harith. Al-Qaeda's Yemeni operation was revived after 23 members, including al-Wuhayshi and other prominent operatives, broke out of prison in February 2006.

In an interview on the occasion of AQAP's introduction, al-Wuhayshi offered justifications for waging armed conflict in Yemen. He argued that the West's "Crusader campaign" against Islam relied on bases in the Arabian Peninsula for logistical support, pre-deployment of forces, and staging ground for strikes. In the interview—conducted in the midst of another round of violence between Israel and Hamas—al-Wuhayshi also maintained that fighting in Yemen and other Middle Eastern fronts was necessary to break the siege that prevents jihadis from coming to the aid of their Palestinian brothers.[47] He clearly tailored these justifications to align with al-Qaeda's emphasis on the "far enemy," but the rationale seems forced and its validity dubious. In particular, arguing for a hybrid approach, in which the Palestinian cause requires dealing with the "near enemy" as well, demands rhetorical gymnastics. Moreover, there had been no meaningful change in the deployment of US forces in Yemen and, as al-Wuhayshi admitted, Hamas did not want AQAP's help, sending away jihadi volunteers.[48]

Regardless of the veracity of these claims, they can at best explain al-Qaeda's interest in operating in Yemen and only insufficiently explain the organization's decision to present its network in the country as a branch, and why it elevated its status with the 2009 rebranding. A more compelling explanation would link the expansion to al-Qaeda's efforts to project success and to demonstrate increased appeal in convergence with an opportunity for a public-relations coup following the arrival of prominent Saudi operatives in Yemen.

Originally, al-Qaeda perceived Yemen as a refuge and a support base for jihad in Saudi Arabia and the Horn of Africa, not as an intrinsically valuable jihad arena.[49] Therefore, initiating a terrorist campaign in the country and elevating the Yemeni network to the status of a formal franchise, in a direct challenge to the Ali Abdullah Saleh regime, was a non-trivial change. In the 2009 interview, al-Wuhayshi was compelled to address this strategic shift and justify its pursuit despite its conflict with Islamic traditions that the Prophet himself viewed Yemen as the land of "support." Al-Wuhayshi claimed that turning Yemen into a jihad arena was a defensive move that was forced

on the group because foreign interests sought to prevent it from continuing
its supportive role.[50] The actual reasons for the transformation were different. It was not pressure on al-Qaeda's activity in Yemen that led it to alter
its plans there and expand its forces' responsibilities—it was the existence
of new capabilities in the country and al-Qaeda's weakness elsewhere. The
injection of new blood following the 2006 prison break provided conditions
conducive for establishing a Yemeni branch. The escapees included capable
and highly committed operatives who, in contrast to their predecessors, were
uninterested in cutting deals with the regime. Al-Wuhayshi himself proved to
be a charismatic and effective leader; his association with bin Laden, whom
he had served as a personal secretary, gave him clout and likely assisted him in
both recruitment and eliciting loyalty. Al-Wuhayshi painstakingly established
a decentralized infrastructure, and, despite some lapses, his subordinates were
disciplined, making the group not only robust but resilient.[51]

One cannot separate the group's rebuilding and public rise from the collapse of al-Qaeda's franchise across the border in Saudi Arabia. The failure in
the prized Saudi arena was a devastating blow for the group. Downplaying
national borders as a matter of principle and eager to demonstrate its prowess in the cradle of Islam, al-Qaeda set its sights on the kingdom's backyard.
Yemen was a cherished second-best choice not only because of its symbolically significant Arabian Peninsula location. The country also offered tangible operational benefits, as an arena with a mountainous terrain, weak state
structure, an abundance of available armaments, and a substantial number of
al-Qaeda sympathizers but no strong or already entrenched jihadi group.[52]
Additionally, due to the government's inability to extend its power over considerable parts of its territory, its authority often depends on agreements with
tribes that enjoy broad autonomy. As a result, the lawless areas where the population is unsympathetic to the government represent spaces in which actors
such as al-Qaeda can establish strongholds.[53]

The Yemen refuge facilitated the Saudi jihad's continuation even as
al-Qaeda increasingly turned its weapons against the Yemeni regime. The
porous border between the two countries allowed operatives under pressure
in the kingdom easy access to a safe haven from which they could plot against
that regime (as the daring 2009 attempt to assassinate the Saudi counterterrorism chief, Prince Muhammad bin Nayyif, demonstrates).

The inextricable connection between the two arenas, bin Laden's homeland Saudi Arabia and his ancestral country Yemen, is evident in the new
branch's adopted name. Although none of the leaders of the defunct Saudi
branch survived, and the Saudi operatives who joined the new AQAP's

leadership were imprisoned at Guantanamo Bay during AQAP's failed campaign in the kingdom, al-Qaeda sought to create an image of continuity while glossing over its earlier defeat and its rejection by Saudi society.[54]

And yet the considerable time that passed between the Saudi AQAP's failure and the Yemeni chapter's rise indicates the importance of al-Qaeda's general well-being to its reasons for introducing the new AQAP. The group's supporters were becoming impatient, and this pressure built with every manifestation of al-Qaeda's weakness. When the group established AQAP, al-Qaeda in Iraq had been defeated, the Algerian affiliate had failed to deliver on its promise, and al-Qaeda's core could do little more than release tedious and uninspiring statements. The Somali al-Shabab could have been an alternative, but despite that organization's considerable success, bin Laden's envoys to the country deemed al-Shabab unreliable and advised against such a merger. Under these conditions, refocusing al-Qaeda's expansion on the already proven Yemeni branch, rebranding it along the way, appeared a promising and prudent way to convey vitality.

In contrast to merger-based expansion, in-house branches require no complicated lengthy negotiations or compromises regarding strategy and degree of affiliate autonomy. They can be announced as soon as the parent organization believes it has sufficient assets in the target arena; under severe distress, the parent can proclaim a new franchise even prematurely. Hence, the Yemeni branch's steady and slow evolution indicates that its formation and rebranding were calculated rather than panicky responses to external pressures.

The Abbottabad documents raise interesting questions about AQAP. The picture emerging from the few released documents suggests that bin Laden was preoccupied with AQAP's affairs. This is unsurprising, given his personal ties to the country and the greater authority he had over the group because it was born out of al-Qaeda. Nevertheless, it is intriguing to see the concern and dissatisfaction reflected in the documents, as well as the divergence between bin Laden's expectations of the Yemeni branch and its actions. Even after announcing the unification of al-Qaeda's Yemeni and Saudi elements, bin Laden adhered to his view that Yemen's primary role should be support to other fronts. Specifically, he maintained that the country was the launching point toward all other oil nations, whose control he viewed as the key to dominating the world. Consequently, he warned that escalation in Yemen would disrupt al-Qaeda's plans and thus would be counterproductive. From his hiding place, bin Laden viewed developments in Yemen and, particularly, AQAP's response to them with alarm and displeasure. He perceived as mistakes the branch's apparent focus on Yemen and Saudi Arabia, the targeting of Yemeni armed forces and police, operatives' risky entanglement in Yemen's bitter inter-clan conflicts and cycles of revenge, and the branch's ill-timed and misdirected media efforts.[55]

To the greatest dilemma facing AQAP—whether to aim to topple the regime and take control of territory in the country's southern provinces—bin Laden had a clear negative answer. He sent instructions to al-Wuhayshi, lecturing him that it was not enough to bring regimes down—one must also maintain control and provide services to the public under its authority. Haunted by the decade-long war with the United States and the Taliban's post–9/11 collapse, bin Laden noted that the United States had managed to topple every state that jihadis had established. He also warned that the Saudi interest in preventing the emergence of a *sharia* state in Yemen would lead it to invest considerable resources in undermining the jihadi project.[56]

Despite al-Wuhayshi's belief that the establishment of an Islamic emirate in Yemen was at hand, bin Laden thought that the project was doomed and should therefore be postponed. Where al-Wuhayshi saw opportunity, bin Laden envisioned overreach that would lead to chaos and pain, pushing the Yemeni public to compromise on its desire for (or tolerance of) an Islamic state in return for stability, security, and the provision of other basic goods. The al-Qaeda chief warned that establishing a state and then losing it, particularly while it was still in its infancy, would have devastating effects.[57] His aversion to bolder action in Yemen was reinforced by a belief that citizens there would not grant al-Qaeda a second chance.[58]

Bin Laden's stated positions do not seem to correspond to AQAP's actual actions. While the branch did not abandon its efforts to target the United States, it moved forward to occupy territory. Through alliances with local tribes and secessionist forces in south Yemen, in 2011 AQAP managed, under the name Ansar al-Sharia, to assume control over large swaths of land in the southern provinces. It is unclear, therefore, how much authority bin Laden had at the time; there is little doubt that his ability to control his organization had been greatly diminished.[59]

His position against attacking the regime was incompatible with the preferences of many rank-and-file operatives, who were much more interested in bringing about immediate change in their home countries. Moreover, some of al-Qaeda's senior leaders—most importantly, al-Zawahiri—were less willing to abandon domestic agendas in favor of attacks on American targets.

Granted, it is possible that communication problems prevented al-Wuhayshi from receiving bin Laden's instructions in the first place.[60] But the most likely explanation for AQAP's actions is that changing conditions on the ground, due to the Arab uprisings, presented new opportunities that AQAP leaders were irresistibly tempted to exploit and unable to forfeit. With government forces in Yemen severely weakened, large areas were ripe for the picking. In the absence of sufficient and credible information, we cannot yet determine whether AQAP's leadership acted independently or followed new instructions from AQC. Regardless, AQAP's experimentation with controlling territory justified bin Laden's pessimism regarding the ability to establish and preserve an Islamic emirate. Military pressure by the Yemeni regime and local militias, backed by US power, forced AQAP to retreat after only one year.[61]

This episode offers important insights regarding the viability of al-Qaeda's program. AQAP's governing style reflected efforts to maintain good relations with local tribes and a relatively cautious approach to the imposition of harsh social controls and the implementation of Islamic law. Later, after AQAP was driven out of the cities it briefly controlled, al-Wuhayshi imparted to Droukdal, his Algerian colleague, the lessons he had learned from this experience. He warned Droukdal that governing and defending a territory is expensive. And while underscoring the importance of developing close relations with the local population, he also noted that when it became evident that standing ground, in the face of intense military pressure, would cause intolerable pain to the civil population, AQAP felt compelled to melt away.[62]

It also sheds light on the inherent weakness of al-Qaeda's branching-out strategy. As Bryce Loidolt eloquently notes, al-Qaeda's franchises "must remain true to the contours of their immediate surroundings, deriving legitimacy and credibility by articulating a local cause."[63] A cell may be able to focus its attention on striking "Crusader" targets, but a franchise cannot altogether avoid localizing the fight. And when the environment in which an affiliate operates becomes chaotic, as happened in 2011 in Yemen, it is virtually impossible to preserve the local restraint that bin Laden's global jihad seems to require.

Notwithstanding the questions surrounding its "occupy and hold" attempt, there is little doubt that AQAP remains al-Qaeda's most important affiliate. It is the only franchise to vigorously pursue the parent organization's commitment to target the United States. In a demonstration of its resilience and dedication, it continued these efforts even after its external-operations unit suffered a blow with the US assassination of the American-Yemeni preacher Anwar al-Awlaki and his fellow American Samir Khan, editor of AQAP's English-language journal *Inspire*.[64] Less than a year after their deaths, a plot to bomb another American airliner was foiled at an advanced stage,[65] and new editions of *Inspire* appeared.[66]

Importantly, AQAP did not taint the al-Qaeda brand name. In fact, it even helped rehabilitate al-Qaeda's image, rewriting the narrative regarding the group's ability to maintain positive relations with the Sunni community it claims to defend. It assumed a particularly important role in the post–bin Laden era, playing a central role in coordinating between al-Qaeda's franchises (particularly al-Shabab, AQIM, and Jabhat al-Nusra) and helping the organization navigate its way through the Middle East turmoil.

Somalia

In February 2012, al-Qaeda's media arm, al-Sahab, released a video publicly celebrating the introduction of a Somali branch. The video featured al-Shabab leader Ahmed Abdi Godane (also known as Abu Zubeyr) pledging allegiance to al-Qaeda, and the acceptance of that oath by al-Zawahiri, who only eight months earlier had succeeded bin Laden as al-Qaeda's chief.[67] In reality, al-Shabab joined al-Qaeda two years earlier, but the affiliation was kept under wraps.[68] This appears to be the first time that al-Qaeda decided to postpone the formal introduction of a branch. It would later repeat this approach when it expanded to Syria.

The merger followed the consolidation of al-Shabab's rule over vast territory, but its announcement took place under a very different atmosphere; in 2012 both al-Qaeda and al-Shabab were under severe pressure and, to their disappointment, the announcement did little to arrest the decline of either. Although al-Zawahiri was able to show that al-Qaeda could not only survive bin Laden's demise but even grow, al-Shabab contributed little to al-Qaeda's war against the "far enemy." Internal purges and the assassination of foreign fighters who disapproved of Godane left al-Qaeda with a formal affiliate in Somalia but only a few reliable allies. On the other hand, the legitimacy that al-Shabab drew from al-Qaeda failed to offset the loss of standing incurred by Godane's purges, and it certainly did not reverse al-Shabab's territorial losses and the resulting shrinking of its revenues.

Al-Shabab originated as a prominent military force within the Islamic Court Union (ICU), a loosely structured organization that united separate *sharia* courts around the country and ruled from June 2006 until early 2007. In its rise to power, the ICU wrestled control from abusive warlords who had dominated the Somali scene since the country's civil war began in 1991. Generally, the local population welcomed the ICU: where Islamic courts were established, they stopped warlord predation and brought Somalis some order, a modicum of justice, and personal security. But the ICU regime's decentralized nature and somewhat heterogeneous composition, advantageous at times, also proved to be its undoing when radical elements within the movement challenged neighboring Ethiopia, leading it to invade Somalia and quickly topple the ICU regime.[69]

While the ICU's political leadership disintegrated in the face of the assault, al-Shabab continued to function. Despite considerable fatalities, damaged morale, and the departure of fighters who elected to return to their homes, al-Shabab soon regrouped. It began a highly effective insurgency and gradually gained new power, taking control of large territories and attracting new recruits. By framing the struggle against the Ethiopians as a defensive jihad to rid Somalia from a foreign occupier, al-Shabab increased its appeal. At its peak, following Ethiopia's 2009 departure, al-Shabab ruled most of central and south Somalia, including Mogadishu.[70] But by 2011, its fortunes had reversed: it lost territory and in August of that year was even forced into a humiliating retreat from the capital.[71]

Why did al-Qaeda merge with al-Shabab, and why did it announce the merger two years later, at a time when both groups faced declining effectiveness, not to mention attractiveness as partners? Ideology does not seem to be the reason for the merger, since al-Shabab's objectives matched al-Qaeda's only imperfectly. Al-Shabab shared al-Qaeda's commitment to Salafi precepts and had clear sympathies with the broader jihadi movement and jihadi fights outside the Horn of Africa. Many of its leaders trained and even fought in Afghanistan.[72] And yet, even while paying tribute to the dream of a pan-Islamic caliphate, al-Shabab's actual objectives were essentially local, diverging from al-Qaeda's global agenda. Publicly, al-Shabab sometimes tried to position its struggle within the context of the broader jihadi fight, but its actions were aimed at defeating the UN-mandated Transnational Federal Government (TFG) and its African Union backers and, then, establishing an Islamic state in Somalia. Even the occasional US drone strike targeting al-Shabab and al-Qaeda commanders did not lead al-Shabab to go beyond threats and aim at Western targets.[73] Al-Shabab's claims that it was fighting a foreign occupation—the African Union Mission in Somalia—and the countries comprising and supporting it aligned more closely with al-Qaeda's commitment to remove foreign occupiers, but it must be noted that those claims did not lead to a merger when al-Shabab faced a full-scale Ethiopian invasion in 2006, and they were less convincing after the Ethiopian retreat.

Alternatively, one might assume that al-Shabab's success would lead al-Qaeda to co-opt the group, to benefit from its success and preempt its emergence as a threat to al-Qaeda's image as the jihadi movement's indispensable leader. The empirical record provides only limited support to this interpretation. In fact, not only was it al-Shabab that sought to entice al-Qaeda, its efforts were not received enthusiastically.[74] Al-Shabab had appealed for a merger a couple of years prior to the actual announcement; in September 2009, it even released a video titled "At Your Service O Osama," in which its chief, Godane, proclaimed that the group awaited bin Laden's guidance.[75] Bin Laden welcomed the message of unity and acknowledged a "brotherly Islamic connection" between members of al-Qaeda and al-Shabab, but through private channels he suggested to Godane that a public merger would be counterproductive for two reasons: a formal merger would lead al-Shabab's enemies to escalate their assault on the movement, and the suffering and immense poverty of the people of Somalia requires aid programs. Bin Laden informed Godane that he was encouraging wealthy merchants from the Arabian Peninsula to launch development projects in Somalia, but he maintained that these people would be unable to offer support unless they could deny an official connection between al-Shabab and al-Qaeda.[76]

It is hard to determine with certainty whether bin Laden's reluctance to formalize and openly admit al-Qaeda's relationship with al-Shabab was strategic, reflecting the benefits of maintaining secrecy given Somalia's enormous challenges, or the result of doubts that it would benefit al-Qaeda. In its statements, al-Qaeda frequently celebrated al-Shabab's success and called on Muslims to come to its aid.[77] One of its chief operatives, Saleh Ali Saleh al-Nabhani, even appeared in one of al-Shabab's video messages in August 2008 (a year before a US strike killed him).[78] Other senior al-Qaeda operatives were also stationed in Somalia and kept regular contact with al-Shabab's leadership; they assisted al-Shabab in training but maintained organizational and operational independence. However, according to Nelly Lahoud, these operatives, who had bin Laden's ear, generally did not favor a merger.[79] Bin Laden's confidant and formal liaison to al-Shabab, Fazul Mohammad, was critical of al-Shabab's break from the ICU in 2006 and regularly warned of the danger of infighting among the various Islamist groups.[80] When al-Shabab's violence became increasingly disturbing, bin Laden himself urged Godane to moderate the group's harsh methods.[81]

And yet, forging a formal relationship with al-Shabab had its upside. Al-Shabab had some assets that al-Qaeda may have found attractive: Christopher Anzalone suggests that al-Qaeda's main motivation was likely al-Shabab's real estate; he maintains that "the control and governance of territory has long been a transnational jihadi dream." Even in al-Shabab's weakening position at the time of the announcement, it controlled large swaths of land.[82] Thus, al-Qaeda may have believed that the affiliation would allow it to project an image of success, realize its goals of performing Islamic governance, and, *inter alia*, demonstrate what an Islamic state can do.

Bin Laden could hardly pass on an opportunity to bring a group that had established an emirate and ruled over millions of Muslims into al-Qaeda. Moreover, he believed that given the gravity of the task facing al-Shabab, it must be guided to assure it would not fail. Tellingly, al-Shabab's need of Islamic guidance contributed to bin Laden's decision not to nominate Abu Yahya al-Libi to a position with greater managerial responsibilities to free him to focus on religious research.[83]

Striking a balancing act, al-Qaeda's ambivalence toward al-Shabab led it to seek strong links with the organization while avoiding publicly admitting the unification. Since franchising became the yardstick to measure the closeness between al-Qaeda and fellow jihadi groups, rejecting al-Shabab could alienate it, causing a rift within the jihadi movement and endangering al-Qaeda's influence over Godane's actions. It is possible that by bringing al-Shabab under al-Qaeda's fold and then dangling the public announcement, bin Laden hoped to make them more receptive to his counsel.

Bin Laden's death improved al-Shabab's chances of making its entry into al-Qaeda formal, since his successor, al-Zawahiri, set a lower bar for mergers with other jihadi groups and was more receptive to branches' pursuit of local agendas. Lahoud suggests that Godane removed Fazul Mohammad from the scene to increase the chance of strengthening the relationship between the groups. Mohammad died under suspicious circumstances a month after bin Laden—instead of reaching an al-Shabab checkpoint for a meeting with fellow jihadis, he happened upon a checkpoint manned by the TFG. Whether or not Godane was responsible, Mohammad's departure—followed by the death of his successor, Bilal al-Berjawi, in January 2012[84]—removed local al-Qaeda operatives' last known significant opposition to the merger. With al-Zawahiri at the helm and most al-Qaeda leaders in Somalia dead, opposition within the organization to the merger considerably weakened.[85]

Abdi Aynte raises the possibility that al-Qaeda considered Somalia a potential safe haven, particularly needed at a time when the group was being squeezed out of its strongholds in Pakistan's tribal areas.[86] This explanation is unpersuasive. Al-Qaeda did not send its leaders to Somalia after the merger, even before the country's value as a safe haven declined when the veil on the relationship was lifted in 2012. Moreover, even as the pressure to leave Pakistan increased after bin Laden's death, Somalia was hardly an ideal alternative. Indeed, al-Qaeda had considered moving to Somalia during the 1990s but found the terrain unsuitable and the local environment dominated by complex tribal relations and hostility toward foreigners.[87] Additionally, relocation to Somalia would hardly lessen the danger from American drone strikes, particularly with Djibouti offering the United States a base for operations in the Horn of Africa. And it is doubtful that al-Qaeda leaders would leave the security of its reliable allies in Pakistan in the hands of power-hungry Godane.

Clint Watts speculates that al-Zawahiri might have been interested in access to Western foreign fighters;[88] there is no information to confirm or refute this explanation. However, if al-Qaeda indeed hoped to tap al-Shabab's reservoir of Western recruits, it would soon find this ambition overly optimistic. Reports regarding foreign fighters' problems in Somalia surfaced prior to the merger announcement but became widespread when the saga of Omar Hammami—the American volunteer who emerged as the face of al-Shabab's Western contingency—played out in the public sphere.[89] Hammami's strained relationship with Godane, his accusations of mistreatment of foreign fighters (confirmed publicly by prominent al-Shabab officials),[90] and eventually his killing at the hands of Godane's assassins effectively warned foreign volunteers to stay away from Somalia. Moreover, by the time al-Zawahiri accepted al-Shabab's *bay'a*, Western governments were fully aware of the foreign fighters' danger and acted to stem it.

One could find elements of both "opportunity" and "need" in al-Qaeda's expansion to Somalia. As an arena, Somalia held no special importance, only difficult conditions: underdevelopment, tribalism, and harsh weather. However, Somalia became more attractive when it underwent clear occupation by a non-Muslim country and, later, when al-Shabab was at the zenith of its power and public support, ruling over most of Somalia, including the capital and revenue-rich coastal cities. In the absence of credible information we must settle for speculations. It appears likely that al-Qaeda did not expand to Somalia during the Ethiopian occupation because it was preoccupied with launching branches in more prominent arenas, and that al-Shabab did not show serious interest in a merger. In contrast, by the time the Ethiopian forces retreated, al-Shabab's value increased, but bin Laden was cautious, accepting tutelage over it but reducing the potential costs by not owning the volatile group publicly.

To some extent, the weakened state of both al-Qaeda and al-Shabab made the announcement more likely by minimizing the risk of losses.[91] At the time when al-Qaeda publicly accepted al-Shabab into its ranks, both groups had much less to offer. Al-Qaeda was still reeling from the loss of bin Laden and was pressured by the events of the Arab Awakening. It was desperate to prove that it remained relevant and to reassert its role as the umma's vanguard. In the merger announcement, al-Zawahiri linked the alleged defeat of the "Crusader enemy" in Iraq and Afghanistan to the revolutions in the Middle East, maintaining that the United States was losing its grip on the Arab region while the jihadi movement "is increased in its solidity by the events, and ferocity by the tribulations, and strength by the incidents." He presented the merger with al-Shabab as the latest evidence of the jihadi movement's continuing ascendance.[92] The Arab revolutions' impact on al-Qaeda's actions can also be seen in the group's efforts to put forward a softer side, manifested in a videotaped ceremony in which an al-Qaeda representative handed al-Shabab humanitarian aid for victims of the Somali drought.[93]

Bin Laden's death exacerbated the pressure on al-Qaeda and on its new leader in particular. Pressed to show that under his reign al-Qaeda remained the leading jihadi organization despite its inability to launch attacks, al-Zawahiri turned to expansion to show al-Qaeda's continued growth. And by upgrading and exposing al-Qaeda's involvement in a country that was arguably under foreign occupation, its propaganda would gain additional impetus.

The Somali side of the story is also ambiguous. There is no consensus among al-Shabab watchers as to what led the movement to join al-Qaeda. Some speculate that the step was driven by prospects of financial support and recruits, possibly from al-Qaeda itself but, given that organization's own needs, more likely from its sympathizers. This explanation attributes al-Shabab's interest in the merger to the crisis it underwent due to a severe famine, declining financial and manpower support from the diaspora, and growing military pressure from the African Union forces, Ethiopia, and Kenya.[94] Al-Shabab may also have hoped that the merger would help it to compensate for declining local support.[95]

These explanations presuppose that the merger took place in early 2012. Recent information regarding the timing of affiliation indicates that al-Shabab asked for a merger even before it fell into a downturn spiral, though it is possible that its leaders knew that unless they took preemptive measures the group would face a decline. Indeed, according to Christopher Harnish, Godane understood—even before al-Shabab's precipitous decline—that the group's own resources would not suffice to achieve and sustain its goals. It required external resources—funding as well as specialized knowledge and personnel. To appeal for assistance beyond al-Shabab's original circle of supporters, al-Shabab added global themes to its propaganda and recruitment efforts.[96] The formation of a formal relationship with al-Qaeda had the potential to bolster these efforts. A merger would raise the profile of the Somali arena and change its image from a marginal backwater to an essential front in a broader conflict against infidelity. Godane hoped that with al-Qaeda's support, his group could enhance its legitimacy and strengthen its credentials on the jihadi scene, which in turn would give it steady access to the jihad movement's resources.

Whether or not those were indeed al-Shabab's considerations, they failed to materialize. Although the group's status received a short-term boost, there is no evidence that its finances improved. Furthermore, the bin Laden documents include hints that instead of being the beneficiary of al-Qaeda's largess, it was al-Shabab that provided AQC some financial support.[97] Perhaps both groups believed they would gain similar types of resources from each other; in that case, at least one of them was bound to end up disappointed.

Expectations of additional resources constitute only part of the story. Al-Shabab's decision was also influenced by internal dynamics, against the background of growing divide among its leaders and fears of splintering. Mounting disagreements between Godane's "globalist" section and rival leaders Mukhtar Robow Abu Mansour and Sheikh Hassan Dahir Aweys, who were promoting a more Somalia-focused agenda, threatened the organization's effectiveness. Abdi Aynte speculates that by merging with al-Qaeda, Godane sought to neutralize his rivals, who had signaled support for beginning a dialogue with the TFG. In linking al-Shabab to al-Qaeda, Godane may have believed he could block any channels for talks, since the United States would object to negotiations with al-Qaeda.[98]

One must be careful, though, not to exaggerate the role of ideology and strategic differences at the expense of clan politics and leaders' power considerations. The merger was central to Godane's efforts to establish absolute control over al-Shabab. A few months after the merger announcement, Godane issued a decree that for the sake of unity, establishing new groups in Somalia would be forbidden.[99] The main targets of this decree were Godane's rivals within al-Shabab, whom he feared might break with al-Shabab and undermine his power. Those rivals, unsurprisingly, did not respond well to Godane's attempt to monopolize power and, in fact, his demand for submission. One of al-Shabab's prominent officials, the elder jihadi Aweys, even condemned it publicly, declaring,

> Jihad is mandatory and it is an Islamic duty; therefore no one should
> have the right to take over or lead the movement. It should not be

modified after one's thoughts and opinions. You cannot deny one his jihad. The jihad can be done in any way, whether it is done individually, in groups of two, three, five, or even amongst clan lines. Only after we expel our enemies is when we should unite. But even after that, no one should be allowed to say they are leading the only legitimate supreme authority over Muslims.[100]

Ultimately, the merger with al-Shabab has done al-Qaeda more harm than good. Al-Shabab is focused on change in Somalia and contributes little to the fight against the West. Its defeats pushed al-Shabab to expand its attacks to neighboring Kenya and even to Uganda, two countries with forces fighting al-Shabab inside Somalia, but this is a shift in targeting, not in objectives. Even its usefulness for al-Qaeda as a symbol for success—and as a model for Islamic governance—is in decline, due to al-Shabab's territorial losses.

At the same time, the costs of affiliation have risen. Godane's authoritarian tendencies led him to consolidate his power through brutal repression of internal dissent, liquidating prominent rivals such as Ibrahim al-Afghani, and chasing away Mukhtar Robow and others. They damaged the al-Qaeda brand name. Illustrating how bleak the situation became, Aweys chose to surrender to the government rather than die at the hands of Godane's assassins.[101] The purges led former al-Shabab members to compare Godane's actions to those of the Algerian GIA, an analogy that expressed jihadis' strong disapproval of his methods and that reflected poorly on al-Qaeda. Jihadis did not blame al-Zawahiri for Godane's actions, but they expected him to intervene and rein in his new partner. Al-Zawahiri's silence, thus, brought disappointment and exposed his weakness. To make matters worse, the inability to reach out to AQC through secret channels—a result of both security considerations on al-Zawahiri's side and Godane's absolutism, denying his lieutenants access to AQC—forced al-Shabab leaders to make public their appeals to al-Zawahiri.[102] Consequently, al-Shabab's internal fissures, Godane's excesses, and AQC's impotence were on display for jihadi sympathizers and enemies alike.

Nevertheless, it is too early to write off al-Shabab—it still controls territory and has both access to funds and a proven record of resilience. In light of the grave challenges al-Qaeda faces, even a declining al-Shabab allows al-Qaeda to argue that it remains a vital force. Additionally, the organization contributed to al-Qaeda's effort to stem ISIS's momentum among jihadis when, after Godane was killed in September 2014, his successor Ahmad Umar (also known as Abu Ubayda) resisted the temptation to jump on the ISIS bandwagon and renewed al-Shabab's oath of allegiance to al-Zawahiri.[103] And if al-Shabab's fortunes reverse once again—not an unlikely development in dysfunctional Somalia—it could offer al-Qaeda even greater benefits.

Conclusions

The three cases discussed in this chapter illuminate the considerations shaping al-Qaeda's franchising decisions and their consequences. Notwithstanding the inherent problems associated with al-Qaeda's branching-out strategy, in-house expansion brings meaningful benefits, lowering the threat of preference divergence at the same time that it reduces oversight requirements. Al-Qaeda's Yemeni affiliate was fundamentally supportive of al-Qaeda's global jihad. Originating from within al-Qaeda and led by members who had accompanied bin Laden in Afghanistan, AQAP was al-Qaeda's most trusted franchise. Even while directly engaging the regime, AQAP did not neglect the larger struggle against the United States. It got closer to successfully carrying out spectacular terrorist attacks than had any branch, or even AQC's foreign-operations wing. Moreover, through al-Awlaki and its English-language magazine, it encouraged lone-wolf operations in the West. These efforts led Nidal Hassan, an American follower of al-Awlaki, to kill 13 American soldiers and civilians on a US Army base in Fort Hood, Texas, in 2009.

But al-Qaeda's weakness severely limited its ability to establish in-house branches throughout the Middle East and drove it to seek partners. The cases of the GSPC and al-Shabab prove that long after 9/11, some prominent jihadi groups—though not all, as Chapter 8 shows—still found the al-Qaeda brand name attractive and were eager to pledge allegiance to bin Laden. By taking in these two groups, al-Qaeda tried to form an image of success and prowess. But the mergers had little value beyond the symbolic, and the purges within al-Shabab have even harmed al-Qaeda's reputation.

Al-Qaeda did learn some lessons from the Iraqi quagmire and in general was more cautious in its expansion decisions. Contrary to the negotiations with TWJ, in the Algerian case al-Qaeda had leverage that permitted it to set the terms of engagement. Although ultimately its expansion into North Africa failed to yield the anticipated benefits, this decision was less damaging. And with the change in the strategic circumstances in the region, AQIM may yet prove to have greater value.

Al-Qaeda initially resisted al-Shabab's appeals for a merger, and when the latter was at the peak of its power, al-Qaeda accepted its allegiance without giving the relationship publicity. But bin Laden's death changed the equation; under pressure to demonstrate the organization's relevance as revolutions challenged governments throughout the Middle East, al-Zawahiri gambled, publicly bringing into al-Qaeda a group now in decline, one whose leader handled internal dissent via purges. Under new leadership, al-Shabab may one day contribute meaningfully to al-Qaeda, but as of yet it has only tarnished al-Qaeda's image and exposed al-Zawahiri's inability to exert control.

Even when it has bargained from a position of strength and has been able to dictate the terms of affiliation, al-Qaeda has soon found that it has limited ability to guarantee that its branches adhere to its charted strategy and comply with its instructions. The isolation of al-Qaeda's senior leadership and communication problems have further compounded its difficulties when dealing with AQIM and al-Shabab. Messages were normally sent by couriers and took time to reach their destination, making it particularly challenging to exert control and putting al-Qaeda's reputation at its affiliates' mercies. The comparison to al-Qaeda's franchise in Yemen is instructive: when merging with a jihadi group originally focused on the "near enemy," al-Qaeda found that the newcomers tended to fall back on their old habits, and there was very little AQC could do to redirect them to fight the "far enemy."

8

Absent

AL-QAEDA AND THE EGYPTIAN, LIBYAN, AND PALESTINIAN ARENAS

OVER THE LAST dozen years, observers have paid considerable attention to al-Qaeda's franchises. The reason for the interest is obvious: they constitute new facets of the al-Qaeda threat, with repercussions for the countries in which they operate and to the security of the United States and its Western allies. Looking at the organization's formal expansion into Saudi Arabia, Iraq, Algeria, Yemen, and Somalia identifies important clues regarding the conditions under which al-Qaeda decides to enter an arena, and the form it chooses for its expansion. Valuable as such insights are, looking at "positive" cases in which al-Qaeda branched out explains only part of the story.

A lot can also be learned from "negative" cases—that is, arenas that the group avoided and relationships that it did not form. Indeed, as Sherlock Holmes showed, taking note of "the dog that did not bark" is often critical in solving a mystery. This chapter explores three cases in which al-Qaeda failed to establish a formal branch. To begin with, there are no al-Qaeda franchises in Egypt and Libya. This is not for lack of trying, considering that AQC announced mergers with groups from the Egyptian Gama'a Islamiya and the Libyan Islamic Fighting Group. But those organizations' leaders rebuffed al-Qaeda's claims, and the expansion efforts quickly dissolved, casting doubts on their seriousness. In the Palestinian arena, on the other hand, al-Qaeda did not even make a pretense of expansion, forfeiting the opportunity to enter a highly prized arena.

Egypt

In August 2006, two years after al-Qaeda's last formal expansion (the merger with Abu Musab al-Zarqawi's TWJ), its media arm al-Sahab released a message announcing an al-Qaeda merger with a faction from the Gama'a Islamiya (GI). The message included three parts: a formal communiqué from "those adhering to the covenant" in the GI, declaring that they had merged with al-Qaeda; an Ayman al-Zawahiri statement welcoming the group; and an interview with a GI member, Muhammad Khalil al-Hakaymah, the initiative's public face.[1] With its entry into al-Qaeda, al-Hakaymah's contingent adopted a new name: the al-Qaeda Organization in Egypt.

It's hardly surprising that al-Qaeda sought to establish a franchise in Egypt. The country has been political Islam's most important center for at least a century; it produced the strongest Islamist movement, the Muslim Brotherhood, as well as prominent jihadi thinkers—above all, the late Sayyid Qutb—and jihadi groups that left their mark in Egypt and beyond. During the 1980s and 1990s, the Egyptian Islamic Jihad (EIJ) and the GI carried out high-profile attacks, most notably the 1981 assassination of President Anwar al-Sadat. For a period of time, Egypt's jihadis even created Islamic zones off-limits to Egyptian authorities.[2] The arrival of many Egyptian jihadis at Peshawar during the Afghan jihad against the Soviets invigorated the Arab mujahideen and was instrumental to the evolution of a global jihadi community. The Egyptians' predominance was observed once again when they swelled the high echelons of the ascendant al-Qaeda organization.

Why, then, did al-Qaeda pursue such a limited extension drive into Egypt? Given that al-Zawahiri's EIJ had united with al-Qaeda in 2001, it would have been the obvious choice to lead the organization's branch. Such an arrangement—an in-house expansion—would have given al-Qaeda a more dependable affiliate than it could get through a merger. Perhaps even more puzzling is that the merger and the formation of al-Qaeda in Egypt turned out to be bogus. Not only did al-Hakaymah represent only a small fraction of the GI, but al-Qaeda's new acquisition was based on operatives located far from Egypt, cohabitating with al-Qaeda in Pakistan's tribal area and with its contingency in Iran.

The merger is better understood as another round in a long and bitter conflict between al-Zawahiri and GI leaders. Notwithstanding the EIJ and GI's shared desire to topple the Egyptian regime, epitomized in their cooperation in the assassination of Sadat, negotiations discussing unification faltered several times.[3] The divide between the two organizations deepened following the jihad's failure in Egypt. In the face of an aggressive and highly effective regime crackdown and the loss of public support due to the targeting of civilians and tourists, both groups had to rethink their strategies. As it happened, they came up with two radically different reactions: al-Zawahiri (who had assumed the leadership of the EIJ in the early 1990s) oriented his considerably shrunk and devastatingly poor group toward bin Laden and global jihad and, as discussed in Chapter 4, formalized the relationship with al-Qaeda; in contrast, the GI decided in 1997 to unilaterally halt all armed operations.

The GI's ceasefire initiative enraged al-Zawahiri, even though the EIJ had ceased its attacks in Egypt two years earlier. Viewing the move as detrimental to the jihad in Egypt, he violated the informal agreement against intervening in other groups' internal affairs and personally tried—and failed—to persuade GI leaders, especially those located outside Egypt, to continue planning violent operations.[4] Al-Zawahiri then used his close relationship with one of the GI's senior officials, Rifa'i Taha, to claim that the GI had joined the World Islamic Front for Jihad Against Jews and Crusaders. The GI quickly denied the claim, and its Shura Council forced Taha to clarify that when he signed the declaration on the establishment of the front he had not been representing the GI.[5]

The acrimony continued. Over the next decade, GI leaders in Egyptian prisons did not settle for a ceasefire between the groups, also producing more than 20 studies revisiting the organization's ideology and presenting a "corrected" Islamic view on the conditions for jihad.[6] In the studies and in newspaper interviews, GI leaders criticized al-Qaeda in strong terms. They declared that the GI, unlike al-Qaeda, sees jihad as a means, not an objective, and only one way to achieve the central goal of bringing Islam to the lives of Muslims. The GI leaders maintained that Islamist groups must consider whether in their particular circumstances jihad is likely to have a harmful impact on the umma. Even when organizations decide to launch a jihad, its execution must correspond to restrictions imposed by *sharia*. The GI accused al-Qaeda of violating Islamic law—for example, by relying on an excessively broad interpretation of the conditions under which killing is permissible. Furthermore, the leaders argued, al-Qaeda was mistaken when it expanded the categories of people who may be legitimately killed to include Western Muslims, infidel tourists, and noncombatant women and children.[7]

Additionally, the GI faulted al-Qaeda for building a strategy around its view of the United States as inherently anti-Islamic. According to the GI, America is motivated by self-interest, not religious fervor. In fact, on some important occasions, its interests have aligned with those of the umma, leading it to policies benefiting Muslims; American opposition to communism, for example, led the government to support the Afghan jihad against the Soviets. In a sense, by targeting the United States, al-Qaeda created a self-fulfilling prophecy, pushing Washington to adopt a strategy aligned against Muslim interests. In the Egyptian leaders' view, by failing to comprehend the nature of

US behavior, al-Qaeda entered into a fight with a power much stronger than it could handle, exacerbating its situation by turning nearly every country in the world into a foe. According to the GI, al-Qaeda found itself pitted against the whole world as the result of an inadequate strategy and an inability to set priorities, and, inevitably, it resulted in defeat. Al-Qaeda's fatal mistakes are even more deserving of condemnation because the group did not bear the costs alone: it dragged the entire umma into an unwinnable and damaging war. Among the negative repercussions of al-Qaeda's blunders, the GI listed the toppling of the Taliban regime, a global dragnet for jihadis, the widely seen characterization of Muslim minorities resisting occupation as terrorists, and the promotion of Israel's interests.[8]

Facing this stinging critique, al-Zawahiri, known for his vindictiveness, had an open account to settle with the GI. Given that one of the main objectives of al-Qaeda's branching out was to create an image of success, the organization could pursue an expansion even if it would not necessarily translate to operational effects. Therefore, claiming a merger could serve al-Qaeda's interests while giving al-Zawahiri an opportunity to strike back at his former brothers-in-arms for their criticism of his character and actions,[9] as well as for what he saw as their responsibility for abandoning jihad in Egypt. By announcing a merger, he would exploit differences within the group to undermine his antagonists. Moreover, if all went well, he might even gain a foothold for al-Qaeda in the place for which he still cared deeply, as evidenced by the disproportionate number of statements he dedicated to Egypt.[10]

The hostility between al-Qaeda and the GI was evident in the merger announcement, in which al-Hakaymah accused the recanting senior officials of changing the group's methodology. The statement presented joining al-Qaeda—"the symbol of the umma's jihad"—as the reaffirmation of the GI's original ideology and as fulfilling the "obligation" of all jihadi groups to join forces. Al-Hakaymah took pains to justify his move against the traditional leadership; he rebuffed them for allegedly acting without authority by neglecting to consult many of the group's leaders and ignoring vast opposition to the ideological reversal. In an effort to establish his legitimacy, al-Hakaymah, a mid-level operative at best, claimed that he was speaking on behalf of the majority of the group's membership and reflecting the stance of household GI names such as Muhammad al-Islambouli, the brother of al-Sadat's killer. Al-Zawahiri's portion of the statement echoed al-Hakaymah's words, focusing on the divisions within the GI, the betrayals of the authors of the ideological revisions, and the steadfastness of those remaining committed to the "correct" path.[11]

Al-Qaeda's gambit collapsed quickly. The leadership of the GI in Egypt quickly began a public-relations blitz denying the merger; it posted a statement on the group's official website and gave interviews to Arab media outlets. The message was one of unequivocal rejection of the claimed merger, and of distance from al-Qaeda. The GI argued that most of the names al-Hakaymah offered as supporting an affiliation with al-Qaeda were, in fact, strongly behind the GI leadership. It also dismissed al-Hakaymah's importance, denying that he had ever occupied a leadership position in the organization and clarifying that his association with al-Qaeda represented only his own personal stand. The GI reaffirmed its commitment to reconciliation while characterizing al-Qaeda as seeking to sabotage the process. It also reiterated the organization's position that—in contrast to al-Qaeda's thinking—jihad should be reserved for fighting foreign occupation, not attacking Muslim-ruled countries.[12]

In the following months, al-Hakaymah tried to raise his profile by releasing statements on a range of political and religious subjects, including the need to unify the jihadi camp, support for the establishment of the Islamic State of Iraq, and a rebuttal of a revisionist book written by the former EIJ leader Sayyid Imam. Al-Hakaymah also penned two books on tactical and operational aspects of intelligence and warfare.[13] But these efforts gained little traction.

Rhetoric notwithstanding, al-Qaeda itself did not appear particularly invested in the Egyptian project. There is little evidence to suggest that, ahead of the attempted merger, the organization attempted to enlist GI members, though many were released from Egyptian prisons following the revisions process and were, therefore, potentially available for mobilization. Moreover, al-Hakaymah generally published his statements on his personal website, with no connection to al-Qaeda's media wing, another indication that the alleged merger was little more than a phishing attempt by al-Qaeda. Al-Hakyamah himself held an important position within al-Qaeda, serving for a while as its spy chief, but his incorporation was personal rather than part of a more ambitious move to integrate the GI into the organization. When he died in a drone strike in November 2008,[14] al-Qaeda did not bother naming another former GI operative to replace him; instead, it quietly dropped the charade.

Ultimately, although Egypt remained dear to al-Zawahiri, its native, operational considerations militated against the prospects of an Egyptian branch. Al-Zawahiri's conclusion, following the Egyptian jihad's failure, that the country's terrain makes it inhospitable to jihadi groups appears to have counterbalanced his urge to bring al-Qaeda to his homeland. After all, the desert and flat terrain that had forced jihadi groups to operate from within the cities, making activists more vulnerable,[15] is a constant feature. Absent a breakthrough that would help overcome this fundamental weakness, al-Qaeda could not establish a successful formal branch in Egypt. With the EIJ's Egyptian infrastructure largely decimated and the GI senior leadership holding together in their resistance to the resumption of violence, al-Qaeda lacked the capability to operate in so central a location. Even though there were jihadi cells in Sinai that carried out some vehicle-borne suicide bombings on tourist attractions frequented by, among others, Israelis, al-Qaeda did not move beyond the gimmicky merger with al-Hakaymah's faction.

Libya

It was only a year before al-Qaeda tried another dubious expansion, this time announcing a merger with the Libyan Islamic Fighting Group (LIFG). Although it chose a considerably more senior partner within that organization than the GI's al-Hakaymah to be the merger's face, the move was similarly audacious. Al-Qaeda promoted an agreement reached with a faction of the organization that had been fighting alongside it in Afghanistan and Pakistan's tribal area; these fighters did not receive the blessing of LIFG leaders in Libyan prisons and Europe before proclaiming their allegiance to al-Qaeda, and their move conflicted with LIFG's new initiative for ideological revisions. Ultimately, the results of the Libyan expansion resembled the Egyptian: the group's established leaders publicly rejected the claims of a merger as bogus, and al-Qaeda was denied a formal affiliate in the Libyan arena and suffered another embarrassing blow to its image.

Libya has had a long tradition of jihadism. The LIFG was an important actor within the jihadi scene during the 1990s: it led a bloody though ultimately unsuccessful rebellion against the Qadhafi regime in the mid-1990s and had an influential and enduring presence among the jihadi diaspora in their refuge countries in Sudan and Afghanistan, where it established training camps and guest houses and participated in debates on the condition of the jihadi movement and its future. LIFG members also aided jihadi fights in other countries—most notably, they sent fighters to support the GIA in Algeria, only to learn later that their paranoid and ultra-radical jihadi hosts had murdered them soon upon their arrival.[16] Outside the LIFG, Libyan jihadis held high-ranking positions within al-Qaeda since that organization's early days.

The LIFG's centrality within the jihadi scene made the group and the arena from which it emerged an attractive expansion target for al-Qaeda. And yet it was not inevitable that al-Qaeda would try to form a formal branch in Libya, or that it would rely on the merger pathway to expansion. Libya has no unique religious importance, and even though its past includes a revolt against a colonial power (Italy), this episode resonates with Muslims no more than similar rebellions elsewhere in the Arab world and left no significant mark on the collective memory of Muslims outside Libya.

Additionally, because Libya is sparsely populated and its desert terrain is not conducive to asymmetric warfare, the value of channeling scarce resources to open a Libyan front is low. To compensate for these shortcomings, the jihadis would need a large force and broad popular support. As the LIFG's failed uprising proved, short of that, the regime would use its greatly superior power to isolate and then decimate the rebel forces.

The wisdom of establishing a Libyan al-Qaeda franchise was also questionable due to the complicated relationship between al-Qaeda and the LIFG. Despite friendly, even close, personal connections between both organizations' senior leaders and a fundamental ideological affinity, the groups held conflicting positions on important subjects. A major source of disagreement concerned the attitude toward the Taliban regime: after the LIFG's struggle against the Qadhafi regime collapsed, many of its members fled the country and resettled in Afghanistan, where they developed close relationships with the Taliban and felt great appreciation for its support. The LIFG's loyalty to the Taliban put it in opposition to al-Qaeda; leaders objected to al-Qaeda's US-focused agenda, in part because they feared it would hurt the Taliban.[17] But the differences were about more than respect to their hosts' wishes—the LIFG opposed the 9/11 attacks on principle.[18] Moreover, it found bin Laden's ultimate goals of a pan-Islamic state unrealistic and in conflict with its own nationalistic desires. Notably, when al-Qaeda formed the World Islamic Front in 1998, the LIFG declined to join.[19] The gap between the groups became even more difficult to bridge when in 2007 the LIFG began a dialogue with the Qadhafi regime, revisiting its ideological position.

It, therefore, was not trivial that, in November 2007, al-Zawahiri and the LIFG's Abu Layth al-Libi released an audio message in which they declared that the LIFG had joined al-Qaeda. In the message, al-Zawahiri pompously portrayed the jihadis as leading a supportive Islamic nation to victories as they confronted numerous enemies. After constructing a narrative of "the pioneering mujahideen" who are gaining in strength and are drawn ever closer together, he announced that a group from the "elite" of the LIFG had joined al-Qaeda. Speaking directly to the imprisoned LIFG leadership, al-Zawahiri declared that the merger was good news because it showed how their brothers were marching in the leaders' footsteps. But whereas the LIFG traditionally had focused on fighting the Libyan regime, al-Zawahiri sneaked the United States into the message. By alleging that the American government controls Qadhafi, he deceptively implied continuity between the LIFG's past struggles and its post-merger orientation.[20]

In his part of the statement, Abu Layth echoed al-Zawahiri by suggesting that he and his colleagues were continuing on the path the LIFG's leaders had initiated and were adhering to the group's methodology. He maintained—without explicitly admitting that the merger could be viewed as a shift from the organization's Libyan focus—that the rapprochement between Qadhafi and the international community had turned Libya into a base for the "Crusaders" war on Islam. Consequently, jihad must be not limited to the regime but, rather, waged against the United States and other "infidels of the West."[21]

What explains the merger announcement? Al-Qaeda's move was not a serious effort to enter the Libyan arena—more likely, it was driven by fear that LIFG leaders were about to follow the Egyptian GI's example and publicly renounce violent jihad and al-Qaeda. Presence in Libya could have had some operational value for al-Qaeda; had the merger been received well by the LIFG, al-Qaeda would have gained access to its operatives not only in Libya but in other Middle Eastern countries and, most important, in Europe. According to former LIFG leader Noman Benotman, al-Qaeda had eyed the LIFG's extensive infrastructure and over the years had requested to utilize it, and was denied, multiple times.[22] Given the announcement two months earlier that the Algerian GSPC had joined al-Qaeda, one could even imagine that bringing the LIFG under al-Qaeda's fold was part of a concentrated organizational push to destabilize North African countries. Al-Zawahiri and Abu Layth both put the merger within the context of a regional confrontation.[23]

In reality, al-Qaeda made few preparations for a meaningful penetration into Libya, indicating that the explanation lies elsewhere. Al-Qaeda feared that the reconciliation initiative might lead another veteran group to abandon the battlefield, sapping the morale of jihadis elsewhere and reinforcing a narrative of the movements' decline and defeat. Therefore, al-Qaeda felt pressure to thwart the LIFG's dialogue with the regime or at least to mitigate its adverse impact. Al-Zawahiri knew about the dialogue after LIFG leaders sent an emissary to consult their contingency in Iran and Pakistan's tribal area.[24] Nevertheless, al-Qaeda did not criticize the outreach to the

Libyan government, instead trying a different approach. In the announcement, al-Zawahiri encouraged LIFG leaders to remain steadfast in the face
of conspiracies to make them recant, suggesting that the merger would allow
the prisoners to stab "Qadhafi's dogs, agents of the world Crusade" in the
chest. Abu Layth al-Libi praised the group's leaders for "rejecting deals and
concessions."[25]

It is important to note that the LIFG's post–9/11 organizational fragmentation created the conditions for al-Qaeda's effort to halt the reconciliation
initiative. Despite the LIFG's opposition to the attack, it found itself, like
many other jihadi groups, a target of the US-led "war on terror." Many of
its members fled Afghanistan, only to be arrested in hiding places throughout the world. Meanwhile, a few field commanders, most prominently Abu
Layth al-Libi, decided to stay behind and organize remnants of the Arab
fighters to support the embattled Taliban.[26] As the fighting wound down,
they relocated to Pakistan's tribal areas alongside fighters from other groups,
including al-Qaeda. This close proximity and the experience of direct cooperation in battle brought the remaining members from both groups closer
together. Gradually, those relationships led many of the Libyan fighters to
join al-Qaeda, although when they did, it was on an individual basis.

Thus, when al-Qaeda sought to halt the LIFG's drift from the jihadi cause,
it turned to the faction that shared its experience in Afghanistan and Pakistan
and that was genuinely outraged by the prospects of reconciliation with
Qadhafi.[27] Al-Qaeda hoped that by presenting this splinter group as representative of the whole organization, it would be able to persuade the LIFG rank
and file that the merger was uncontroversial and to pressure its senior leadership to withdraw from its dialogue with the Libyan regime. Moreover, if this
maneuver succeeded, al-Qaeda would have another base in North Africa, one
created with little to no investment of the organization's own resources. In a
testimony to al-Qaeda's eagerness to bring in Abu Layth's group—or perhaps
evidence of bin Laden's flexibility in setting unification terms—the Libyans
were allowed to retain financial independence.[28]

Despite the star power of Abu Layth and his fellow Libyan Abu Yahya
al-Libi, al-Qaeda's scheme faltered. Perhaps the steady stream of volunteers
from the eastern Libyan cities of Benghazi and Darnah, jihadis who heeded
Abu Yahya's call to head to Iraq while relying on LIFG recruiting and logis-
tics networks, led to a false sense of confidence.[29] But LIFG leaders swiftly
quashed the plan by denying the merger, and the group's followers in Libya
did not challenge that denial. The group's leaders asserted that Abu Layth had
not consulted them and that, regardless, he lacked authority to speak for the

group. If he had indeed joined al-Qaeda, it was as an individual.[30] The rejection was not merely procedural: The LIFG, its leaders explained, opposed bin Laden's extremist beliefs and the use of violence. Later, in the group's own repudiation manual—released in 2009 and presented as aiming to deter Libyan youth from extremism in general and al-Qaeda in particular—leaders argued that sharia prohibits fighting Muslim regimes. The manual also denounced jihadi groups' use of excommunication outside of a restrictive set of conditions.[31]

The denial and strong rebuke from LIFG leaders, both from those incarcerated in Libya prisons and those living in Europe, exposed the announcement as a ploy. Abu Layth al-Libi's death, in a January 2008 drone strike, emptied the merger of the little tangible meaning it may have had. Although al-Qaeda invested no significant resources in expanding into Libya, the botched effort proved costly: The group's leaders, appearing desperate and deceptive, failed to create the impression that al-Qaeda was doing well and expanding, and instead of preempting the LIFG's repudiations, they probably forced the Libyan group to take an even clearer stance in rejecting violence.

Nevertheless, al-Qaeda's cause—if not necessarily the group itself—still enjoys considerable support in Libya. The recent establishment of an ISIS Libyan extension demonstrates that there is a considerable contingency eager for jihad at home. Libyans have also maintained enthusiasm for jihad abroad, whether in Iraq or in Syria.[32] Al-Qaeda took advantage of the nation's chaos after Qadhafi's October 2011 death to expand its presence and to form links with various groups, especially Ansar al-Sharia. Notably, this is an operational expansion. By the time this book went to press, al-Qaeda had yet to establish a formal Libyan branch, even as the threat that such a move would lead to a direct US intervention practically vanished. Instead, the group included Libya under AQIM's areas of responsibility.[33]

Palestine

In contrast to al-Qaeda's attempts to form the impression that it is expanding into Egypt and Libya, conditions in the Palestinian arena denied the group even that façade. Al-Qaeda's absence from this highly prized arena shows how practical constraints can hinder the realization of ideological commitments. The group was able neither to reach the Palestinian-controlled territories nor to use a local jihadi force as a proxy. And unlike the previous two cases, there was no Palestinian faction present in Central Asia to bring into the group's fold. Al-Qaeda's involvement in the Palestinian arena was essentially limited to rhetoric.

On its face, establishing a Palestinian branch should have been a priority for al-Qaeda. From a religious perspective, Palestine is second in importance only to Saudi Arabia: al-Quds (Jerusalem) was the direction Muslims faced in their prayers before the Prophet instructed them to turn to Mecca; it was also the site of Muhammad's "night journey," in which he ascended to heaven from the al-Aqsa mosque. Palestine's symbolic value does not end there—many Muslims view it as occupied land whose inhabitants are oppressed by non-Muslims. While that alone could have led al-Qaeda to focus on the Palestinian cause, surely an even more important incentive is the fact that, more than any other issue, the Palestinian people's plight resonates among Muslims worldwide.[34]

The Palestinian arena indeed took a prominent place among the grievances bin Laden and al-Zawahiri listed. Bin Laden invoked Palestine's occupation and its Muslims' plight in his Declaration of War and in the World Islamic Front's fatwa, though for him those outrages took a back seat to American forces' presence on Saudi soil.[35] The collapse of the Israeli-Palestinian peace process and the second intifada's beginning in the fall of 2000 led al-Qaeda to invoke Palestine much more prominently. Palestine appeared in more than 200 statements by al-Qaeda leaders; more than 80 statements noted Muslims' obligation to liberate it, while about 60 referred to Palestine in the context of the oppression of Muslims.[36] Famously, bin Laden repeatedly stated that Americans would not be safe until the United States guaranteed the Palestinian people's security.

Fu'ad Husayn's book on al-Zarqawi clearly indicates that al-Qaeda's leaders saw Palestine as part of a larger goal—the real target was the removal of Israel. In addition to this objective's intrinsic appeal, attacking Israel would weaken the Western-friendly Arab regimes, win al-Qaeda credibility among Muslims and prove its eligibility to lead the umma, and attract recruits as well as financial and moral support. To some extent, beating Israel—the spearhead of the West planted in the heart of the Middle East—would be key to the entire jihadi project. Indeed, a confrontation with Israel features in some of the seven stages of al-Qaeda's strategic plan, as presented by Husayn. In the second, "eye-opening" stage (2003–2006), al-Qaeda was supposed to engage in direct confrontation with Israel in Palestine. The goal of a comprehensive direct confrontation with Israel would be further advanced in the third stage (2007–2010), when "eyes are opened and the movement's power is multiplied." And in 2016—when, following the establishment of an Islamic state, the all-out confrontation between the "forces of faith and the forces of global atheism" would begin—the assault on Israel will intensify considerably, with the country buckling under Islamic power.[37]

An al-Qaeda ideologue, using the pseudonym Asad al-Jihad2, is another source indicating that the group anticipated a war with Israel. In a 2008 essay posted to a jihadi website, he predicted that by the end of the following year, al-Qaeda would complete the long preparations for jihad in Palestine and launch several years of fierce battle, beginning in 2010. The author advised Palestinians on preparations for the arrival of foreign fighters, including practicing martial arts, building bombs and rockets, acquiring weapons, storing food, and learning ways to accommodate and protect the fighters streaming in from abroad.[38]

And yet the primacy of the Palestinian issue did not translate to prioritizing direct action in that arena. Although al-Qaeda carried out several attacks against Jewish and Israeli targets, including in Tunisia, Kenya, and Turkey, it launched no attacks within Israel's borders and was able to manage only a few unimpressive attempts to strike the country from Egyptian and Lebanese territories with rudimentary rockets. Its few attempts to form cells were amateurish and were thwarted in their early stages. Furthermore, at a time when al-Qaeda introduced branches across the Middle East, it made no serious effort to form one for the Palestinian front.

Al-Qaeda's absence from the Palestinian arena demonstrates how practical considerations mitigate ideological commitments. The West Bank is not conducive to establishing a meaningful al-Qaeda presence: it borders no Arab state and therefore cannot be accessed without going through Israeli-controlled territory and evading the eyes of its robust security services, which also have denied local jihadi sympathizers space to organize. The Gaza Strip, bordering Egypt and since 2005 free from Israeli military presence, seems far more hospitable, but a different problem—the dominance of Hamas—halted any plans there.

Although both Hamas and al-Qaeda identify as Islamist, important questions of doctrine and strategy separate the groups. Their differences were not salient in the early 2000s, when the Palestinian intifada was at its peak and Hamas assumed a leading role in attacking Israel. But as Hamas gradually moved away from its uncompromising and narrow focus on violence and showed interest in assuming a formal role in the Palestinian polity, the divide between the groups increasingly came to light, leading al-Zawahiri to disappointedly conclude that Hamas had transformed from "a mujahid movement to part of the Arab consensus which surrenders to America, the Arab consensus which sells the lands of the Muslims."[39]

The scope of Hamas's agenda, the means for Islamist groups to achieve their objectives, and the permissibility of politics and compromise emerged as highly contested subjects between al-Qaeda and Hamas. In light of casual observers' tendency to equate all Islamist groups, it is worth further explaining al-Qaeda's critique of Hamas.

Whereas Hamas is focused on the Palestinian cause, al-Qaeda sees a broad conflict between Islam and the West that transcends state boundaries: since all Muslims are part of one borderless umma, nationalist agendas must be rejected. Consequently, al-Qaeda called upon Hamas to broaden its restrictive focus. Hamas, al-Zawahiri declared, has a stark choice: it can be a local, nationalist movement presiding over a small piece of land, separated from the goals of the umma and engaged in a quest for the international community's acceptance, or a leader in an Islamic jihadist movement that "seeks to establish God's way on earth, to fight so that God's religion becomes supreme, and to represent the central cause of the jihadist Muslim Nation."[40]

Al-Qaeda and Hamas also differ on the question of the role of violent jihad. Hamas views violent resistance as a primary tool for advancing the liberation of Palestine, but it is receptive to nonviolent measures as well. Such an approach conflicts with al-Qaeda's worldview, which elevates jihad to a pillar of faith and rejects any solution falling short of the group's maximalist goals. Consequently, al-Qaeda demanded that Hamas adhere to jihad and the goal of Israel's destruction, declaring the unacceptability of negotiating with the Jewish state, much less conceding any territory.[41]

Al-Qaeda found Hamas's decision to participate in the Palestinian political system especially reprehensible. Two major Hamas decisions, in particular, drew al-Qaeda's ire: its participation in January 2006 elections for the Palestinian legislative council and its February 2007 power-sharing agreement with Fatah. Al-Qaeda rejected Hamas's participation in the political process because it was conceived under a secular constitution (rather than an Islamic one) and entailed sharing a legislative council with secular and nationalist Palestinian forces that supported a compromise with Israel. Such a decision, al-Qaeda argued, implied acceptance of the council's authority and the legitimacy of the agreements that the authority had signed. Furthermore, it amounted to "slaughtering the sharia by agreeing to follow the infidel religion of democracy."[42]

Democracy, al-Qaeda representatives argued, represents the rule of the people and as such is incompatible with *sharia*. The right to legislate is God's alone, not a parliament's. By elevating human judgment, democracy puts men's rule above God's: a believer can under no circumstances choose to follow human decisions, particularly when they clash with God's decrees. In al-Qaeda's perspective, the danger of such conflict is especially alarming because the majority of Palestinians might vote to reach a settlement with Israel, including territorial concessions that jihadis see as violating Islamic imperatives.[43]

When Hamas agreed to form a national unity government with Fatah, al-Zawahiri accused Hamas of selling out Palestine "for a third of the cabinet with a fourth of sovereignty and a tenth of a homeland." He lamented that for a minority of positions in a government that does not control Palestine's borders and whose members cannot even move between the West Bank and Gaza without Israel's permission, Hamas had abandoned *sharia*, ceded most of historical Palestine, and ceased its military resistance.[44] Hamas further enraged al-Qaeda when in June 2007, the former, after ousting Fatah loyalists and gaining full control over the Gaza Strip, refused to impose *sharia* rule.[45]

Al-Qaeda could harshly criticize Hamas or try to enter the Palestinian arena, but it could not do both. Turning Gaza into an al-Qaeda base hinged on how Hamas rulers might view this enterprise. The louder al-Qaeda's criticism of Hamas, the more openly hostile Hamas leaders were to the idea of an al-Qaeda presence in their territory. This became evident when in February 2008 a statement by Islamic State of Iraq's leader Abu Umar al-Baghdadi hit an exposed Hamas nerve. Al-Baghdadi accused Hamas's leaders of betraying their religion and the umma. What made his statement more provocative than previous al-Qaeda declarations was not only its harsher claims but the call to action that accompanied them: al-Baghdadi called on members of Hamas's military wing, the al-Qassam brigades, to split from the organization and isolate its leadership.[46]

Hamas's leaders were enraged and responded with a statement attributed to a commander in the al-Qassam brigades declaring that al-Baghdadi was trying to undermine Hamas's jihad, split the ranks of its mujahideen, and permit the spilling of their blood. Moreover, using derogatory language, the speaker labeled al-Baghdadi and the ISI as "fascist *takfiri*" and for the first time denounced al-Qaeda as responsible for crimes against fellow jihadis in Iraq. Adding further insults, the message stated that "your intelligence betrayed you, and your sense of honor and your manliness betrayed you. We found out that you have a soul that commands you to do evil." Importantly, the statement maintained that Hamas remained united, declaring al-Baghdadi persona non grata and making clear that neither he nor his followers would ever be allowed to enter Palestine.[47] Al-Qaeda backed down: in future references to Palestine, leaders were careful to maintain a more moderate tone.

Of course, Hamas's determination to prevent al-Qaeda from establishing a foothold in Gaza cannot be attributed solely to its leaders' anger at al-Qaeda's criticism—it is based on a broader cost-benefit calculation. Cautiously, Hamas tried to turn to its advantage the threat of al-Qaeda gaining traction within the Gaza Strip. For example, spokesman Samy Abu Zehry warned Israel and its supporters that attempts to economically suffocate Hamas's government only played into extremists' hands and increased the appeal of bin Laden's ideas about religious war.[48] Hamas also characterized itself as a moderate force—indeed, the last bastion against jihadi infiltration into the Palestinian territories. One of its officials declared, "It is time for the West to decide whether it wants to deal with Hamas which believes in reform and wants to have good relations with the whole international community or with the people of this kind [al Qaeda] who don't believe in those kind of relations and believe in burning the whole system."[49] Hamas's efforts had some success: the fear of more radical elements controlling Gaza appears to have convinced Israel, the United States, and Egypt that it was not in their best interest to forcibly topple Hamas.

Overall, Hamas leaders saw little gain from a relationship with al-Qaeda and repeatedly tried to distance the groups;[50] they viewed identification with al-Qaeda as a threat to Hamas's interests as well as to the Palestinian struggle. Hamas has a significantly larger fighting force and greater financial resources and military expertise, and the cost of an alliance with al-Qaeda would be high, deepening Hamas's isolation and increasing the number of actors actively confronting the group. Under these circumstances, Hamas would find it more difficult to deliver on its promises to the Palestinian people, undermining its hold on power.

Another factor deterring al-Qaeda from establishing a Palestinian branch was the lack of unity among jihadi groups in the arena, apart from Hamas. Al-Qaeda is generally reluctant to enter fragmented jihadi scenes—self-styled as a force for unity, it prefers to join arenas after its jihadi groups have come together and requested its leadership as a stamp of approval. Al-Qaeda's approach is all the more reasonable when power disparities put the jihadis in a particularly inferior position vis-à-vis their opponents; they cannot afford to be sidetracked by intra-jihadi rivalry.

Introducing a franchise in the Gaza Strip was unlikely to put al-Qaeda in direct conflict with other jihadi groups—in fact, some of these groups had explicitly declared identification with al-Qaeda.[51] However, being the home to multiple groups—all small in size and none with a real potential for unifying al-Qaeda supporters—made Gaza an unappealingly complex and therefore unattractive expansion target.

Hamas's superior power and its determination to suppress any challenges to its authority made unity of all jihadi forces pertinent. If there were any doubt that Hamas would not tolerate subversion, it was put to rest when, in August 2009, the group quelled a challenge by Jund Ansar Allah (JAA). Hamas had tolerated that group's presence for a while, but JAA leader Abdel Latif Moussa's proclamation of an Islamic emirate in Gaza crossed Hamas's red line. When the JAA refused to submit to Hamas, the latter went on the offensive and killed Moussa and more than 20 JAA members.[52] Interestingly, an ISIS supporter in Gaza noted in 2014 that the self-styled caliph Abu Bakr al-Baghdadi had declined pledges of allegiance from jihadi groups because they failed to unite first.[53]

Considering the very real constraints al-Qaeda faced in the Palestinian arena and the high likelihood of failure, its decision not to introduce a Palestinian branch appears calculated and rational. But the decision—and, more broadly, al-Qaeda's failure to show up to the fight against Israel—came with a price and over time became a major source of criticism of al-Qaeda. When as part of a charm offensive in which al-Qaeda tried to explain its positions and actions, al-Zawahiri held an online town-hall session, he faced tough questions on the subject. A number of questioners challenged him over al-Qaeda's record in Muslim countries, pointedly noting the group's absence from the Palestinian arena:

> Who is it who is killing with Your Excellency's blessing the innocents in Baghdad, Morocco, and Algeria? Do you consider the killing of women and children to be jihad? I challenge you and your organization to do that in Tel Aviv. Why have you—to this day—not carried out any strike in Israel? Or is it easier to kill Muslims in the markets? Maybe it is necessary (for you) to take some geography lessons, because your maps only show the Muslims' states.[54]

Al-Qaeda responded by explaining that operational difficulties prevented it from joining the Palestinian resistance. It maintained that a protective wall surrounds Israel—its Arab neighbors prevent jihadis from coming to the Palestinians' aid—but argued that despite these obstacles, al-Qaeda was still laboring to assist the oppressed Palestinians. In an attempt to de-territorialize the struggle for Palestine, al-Qaeda linked its efforts elsewhere to the advancement of the Palestinian cause. It maintained that weakening the United States is key to bringing down apostate regimes and with them an end to the protection Israel enjoys; by extension, then, al-Qaeda's fight against America serves the Palestinian cause. The group even used this rationale to encourage Muslims, particularly Palestinian refugees in Arab countries, to join al-Qaeda in Iraq.[55] Ultimately, bin Laden promised, once the fighters emerged victorious in Iraq, "legions" would march to liberate Palestine from Israeli hands.[56] Ironically, then, al-Qaeda's failed anti-American strategy provided it with a coherent—albeit unpersuasive—excuse for its practical decision to stay out of the Palestinian front.

Conclusions

This chapter discussed al-Qaeda's absence from three high-profile arenas and its puzzling claims of affiliation with jihadi groups from Egypt and Libya. Such "negative" cases offer some insights into the considerations behind al-Qaeda's branching-out decisions and allow for a more complete understanding of the strategy. In the Palestinian arena, al-Qaeda avoided organizational expansion because it could not compete with the Muslim Brotherhood–affiliated Hamas, particularly with the local jihadi scene so fragmented and weak. Notwithstanding Palestine's symbolic value, al-Qaeda understood that an attempt to establish a franchise there offered exceptionally low prospects of success. Thus, the group preferred to face criticism and questions regarding its commitment to the Palestinian cause over an inevitable failure that was likely to be even more damaging to the al-Qaeda brand.

In comparison, the cases of al-Qaeda's announced mergers with factions from the Egyptian Gama'a Islamiya and the Libyan Islamic Fighting Group show that lack of capabilities does not preclude al-Qaeda's intervention. Feeling compelled to fend off growing attacks on its religious interpretations, methodology, and actions, particularly through refutation documents produced by former allies, leaders attempted to use mergers as a tool to stop jihadi groups from abandoning jihad or, at least, to limit the damage from their ideological reversals. To do so, al-Qaeda relied on factions from these organizations that operated alongside the group since they were driven out of Afghanistan in 2001. Rather than make serious attempts to enter Libya and Egypt, al-Qaeda was focused on producing political effects; leaders hoped that with the assistance of these allies—which they presented as the genuine representatives of the jihadi spirit of the LIFG and the GI—al-Qaeda would be able to isolate the two groups' traditional leadership and discredit their criticism of the organization. In both cases, al-Qaeda discovered that, located far from their homelands, the group's allies were unable to advance its interests in Egypt and Libya. The GI and LIFG factions were detached from the reality of their peers back home—the same reality that led to those reconciliation initiatives in the first place. Ultimately, instead of serving al-Qaeda, the merger claims increased expressions of animosity toward the organization from former friends and exposed the depth of its isolation.

9

Upstaged

AL-QAEDA AND THE SYRIAN CIVIL WAR

THE EVENTS OF the Arab Awakening unexpectedly turned Syria into a viable jihad arena. Beginning as a series of peaceful demonstrations in March 2011, in the southern city of Dar'aa, resistance to Bashar al-Assad's regime was met with government brutality. As violence rapidly spiraled into civil war, al-Qaeda saw an opportunity to enter a new arena and began transferring operatives from Iraq to Syria; they built a branch there and in January 2012 felt ready to make their existence public. Named Jabhat al-Nusra (JN, the Support Front), the group was led by a Syrian national, Abu Muhammad al-Joulani, who had fought for al-Qaeda's Iraqi branch.

Al-Qaeda's entry into the Syrian arena does not fit neatly into any of the categories discussed earlier; JN emerged from the ranks of al-Qaeda's Iraqi branch. Although AQC authorized the expansion into Syria,[1] it played a much less significant role in JN's establishment than did the ISI. The decision to keep secret the relationship between the branch and AQC was also unique—and especially intriguing, given that around the same time al-Qaeda publicly welcomed al-Shabab as its Somali branch. Despite the discrepancies between the announcement of al-Qaeda's Syrian branch and the experience of its organizational expansion elsewhere, the case of Syria is illuminating. As with the decision to merge with al-Shabab, the Syrian expansion took place against the background of the Arab Awakening's turbulent events and the dawn of the al-Zawahiri era. But Syria's centrality gives this theater an importance surpassing that of Somalia.

Syria presented al-Qaeda with a chance for a comeback, after seeing its Iraqi branch collapse, its leader killed, and the peaceful removal of the leaders of Tunisia and Egypt seriously challenge its prescription for Mideast change.

But while involvement in Syria was necessary to prove the organization's relevance and Ayman al-Zawahiri's leadership, the nature of that involvement was open for discussion. Al-Qaeda could have sent forces to either augment the opposition to al-Assad or operate its own Syrian franchise, whether through merger with existing jihadi networks or by forming an independent branch. Al-Zawahiri also had to decide how much publicity al-Qaeda's involvement in Syria should seek. The size of the prize—the civil war was on front pages worldwide—offered a major opportunity for attention, but that same publicity could risk external support for the uprising and even generate a backlash from certain Syrian actors. Although al-Qaeda could not afford to be seen as irrelevant when an enemy regime was toppled by force, it also could ill afford the perception of responsibility for a failure to liberate the Syrian people.

Al-Qaeda chose to form an independent franchise but sought to learn from past mistakes by avoiding short-term political scores that would accompany an early announcement of the relationship between the new group and AQC. Leaders gave the franchise sufficient deniability to enable it to form cooperative relationships with the other jihadi groups that mushroomed throughout Syria. By avoiding the brand name, it hoped to escape anti-al-Qaeda sentiment and, through its actions, to garner positive public opinion that would allow al-Qaeda to assert its role more publicly at a later stage.[2] This refined strategy proved quite successful: when the United States designated JN an al-Qaeda affiliate, most rebel formations in Syria—including some identified as secular—criticized the American move and expressed solidarity with the group.

To al-Qaeda's chagrin, the lessons it learned did not save it from the lingering consequences of its past mistakes. Although the bulk of JN's leadership was loyal to al-Zawahiri, the group was vulnerable to the power hunger of the Iraqi branch from which it originated. Thus, when the ISI decided to strengthen its position in Syria and within the jihadi camp, it declared, in April 2013, that JN had been a subsidiary of the ISI but from that point on would cease to exist as the ISI stepped in to assume full responsibility for the Syrian arena. In this way, the Iraqi franchise exposed al-Qaeda's role in Syria while challenging al-Zawahiri's authority and revealing the weakness of his position. The move by the ISI—which, following its expansion, renamed itself the Islamic State of Iraq and al-Sham (ISIS)—opened a rift that could not be contained. Abu Muhammad al-Joulani rejected this announcement and openly declared his allegiance to al-Zawahiri, but ISIS did not relent and brazenly denounced al-Zawahiri's edict that JN would retain its autonomy as a separate al-Qaeda branch.

For a few months, then, al-Qaeda recognized two separate franchises in Syria. But when Syria's other Islamist groups finally decided to confront ISIS to stem its predatory encroachment into Syria, JN found itself largely on the side of the forces fighting its al-Qaeda brethren. The rift within al-Qaeda could no longer be stopped, and in February 2014, al-Zawahiri finally renounced ISIS, making it the first al-Qaeda franchise to be dropped. But ISIS's meteoric rise continued: its stunning advances in Iraq (including the capture of its second-largest city, Mosul) were followed by additional gains in Syria. Most audaciously, ISIS proclaimed itself a caliphate, using the name the Islamic State (IS), and dubbed its leader, Abu Bakr al-Baghdadi, Caliph Ibrahim.

Given the importance and complexity of the Syrian case, I diverge from the structure of earlier chapters to discuss it elaborately. I begin with the reasons for al-Qaeda's entrance into Syria and for the particular form it took. But the bulk of the chapter discusses the internal fissures within al-Qaeda, which culminated in its splintering and extensive fighting between JN and ISIS.

Al-Qaeda Coming to Syria

Syria has always been a highly desirable area of expansion for al-Qaeda; it has great symbolic value as the seat of the Umayyad caliphate (661–750) and the primary stage for the eventual Day of Judgment battles.[3] The country's modern strategic value is no less significant: not only does it match al-Zawahiri's general quest for a base at the heart of the Middle East, it also borders Iraq, Lebanon, Jordan, and Turkey and thus presents multiple avenues for further expansion. And perhaps the icing on the cake: Syria's border with Israel could offer access to a high-priority target and, potentially, the key to gaining the support of Muslims worldwide. Al-Qaeda's leaders have long been frustrated and censured for the organization's inability to match virulent anti-Israel rhetoric with deeds. Syria could remedy this disconnect.

Among the first generation of Arab-Afghans were a number of important jihadis from Syria. In the early 1980s, the Syrian Ba'ath regime crashed an Islamist uprising; a small group of survivors fled abroad, and some reached Afghanistan. Over time, some of these individuals, such as Abu Musab al-Suri and Abu Khalid al-Suri, became household names in jihadi circles, even as for the next three decades the Assad dynasty's firm hold on power rendered the resurgence of jihad in Syria no more than a remote dream. The events of early 2011 suddenly changed the situation, dangling an enchanting opportunity before al-Qaeda.

The beginning of the uprising coincided with a dramatic leadership change: on the night of May 2, 2011, an American team killed Osama bin Laden in the Pakistani garrison city of Abbottabad. His lieutenant, al-Zawahiri, immediately faced the challenge of tailoring the organization's response to the Arab revolutions, somehow reconciling al-Qaeda's past endorsement of violence as the only viable path to change with mass demonstrations' success in bringing down entrenched rulers. And he had to do so while establishing his authority over an organization that was reeling from the loss of its iconic leader and whose members faced the temptation to abandon violent transnational jihad in favor of newly vital national movements. The new al-Qaeda chief had to identify opportunities arising from the region's new strategic environment. And indeed, after demonstrators managed to topple the Tunisian and Egyptian regimes, anxious dictators began reverting to brutal oppression in an effort to cling to power, thus creating opportunities for al-Qaeda to reassert itself.

JN was established in mid-2011, only a few months after the militarization of the Syrian revolt, by a group of operatives who had fought in Iraq under the ISI's command. According to JN leader al-Joulani, expanding to Syria was an idea of a small group of primarily Syrian ISI operatives; they presented a plan to the Iraqi branch's leadership and gained its approval,[4] and for a few months, the group focused on building its organizational infrastructure and operational capabilities. Given Syria's geographical location and the readily available logistical network the ISI had established in the country years earlier, JN had to rely at first on the Iraqi franchise's logistical services and financial resources. Then, on December 27, it launched an attack on the State Security branch in Damascus. A month later, it finally made its presence public in a video message featuring al-Joulani that was released to the jihadi online forum Shumukh al-Islam.[5]

The branch differed from most al-Qaeda affiliates in two meaningful ways. First, under strict order from al-Zawahiri, JN concealed the true nature of its relationship with al-Qaeda.[6] There is little doubt that other jihadi groups knew of the relationship between al-Qaeda and JN, and those who needed further confirmation could have gotten it from declarations to that effect made by the United States and the UN Security Council. Yet JN continued to deny a formal relationship with al-Qaeda, admitting only a shared worldview and objectives.[7]

A second difference was JN's positive relations with other opposition groups. JN not only tried to avoid conflict with other anti-regime forces, including the secular Free Syrian Army, but in many locations throughout the country actively pursued coordination and cooperation with them. Although it was committed to the idea of re-establishing the caliphate (as one would expect from an al-Qaeda franchise), JN was clear that in the short term it was fully focused on the Syrian arena, toppling the Assad regime and establishing a state governed by *sharia*. It also gained other groups' trust by focusing on battlefield success rather than trying to consolidate independent control over swaths of territory.[8] Even after acknowledging its relationship with al-Qaeda, JN tried to assuage other opposition groups' fears regarding its agenda by clarifying that it did not see itself as the exclusive ruler of a post-Assad Syria.[9] JN's approach was quite successful: when the United States designated JN as a terrorist organization, in December 2012, many members of the Syrian opposition denounced the United States, and many people across Syria protested in support of JN.[10]

In many ways, JN's policy reflected a new al-Qaeda approach: the bitter experience of past failures and the sense of unprecedented opportunity created with the Arab Awakening translated into a greater level of pragmatism. JN tried—as had al-Qaeda's Yemeni branch—to establish a softer image; it labored, with relative success, to attract public support and avoid alienating the people on whose behalf it claimed to fight. And while the organization was dedicated to fighting the Assad forces, it shied away from open interest in creating fiefdoms under its control and augmented its military efforts with the provision of social services. In cooperation with other rebel groups, it established "Sharia Committees," responsible for meeting the basic needs of the population in locations under its primary rule. Among their roles were the distribution of food and clothing and maintaining local civilian infrastructure such as water and electricity; JN also operated health and education services.[11] Moreover, contrary to jihadis in Iraq, Mali, and elsewhere—who, once in control of a territory, focused on regulating all behavior according to a radical interpretation of Islam—JN was careful not to overreach. It sought popular legitimacy before exercising social control. Thus, the organization took responsibility for policing and legal institutions and emphasized the provision of security, but it largely avoided imposing harsh punishments traditionally accompanying its beliefs about appropriate Islamic personal behavior and dress.[12]

Splitting al-Qaeda in Syria

AQC intended its Iraqi branch to shepherd and support JN—a reasonable expectation, considering that, among al-Qaeda's franchises, the ISI had the easiest access to the Syrian arena. Iraq borders Syria, and the ISI had strong-holds in the Sunni border regions. Moreover, the ISI already had in place supply routes established years earlier to support its fight against the United States and Iraq's Shia-dominated government. Neither the Iraqi and Syrian regimes had much ability to police the shared border; what little capabilities they had diminished as the Syrian civil war escalated.

No strong evidence had yet come to light to suggest that al-Zawahiri feared giving the ISI a central role in Syria—though, given the branch's his-tory, it is hard to believe that such a suspicious individual, still laboring to establish his authority as al-Qaeda's leader, was not apprehensive. On the other hand, at the time al-Qaeda operatives moved from Iraq into Syria to organize JN, al-Zawahiri (and, importantly, the leaders of the new Syrian branch) believed that the Iraqi branch's leaders intended to honor their pledge of allegiance to him.[13] Even if he distrusted the ISI, al-Zawahiri had few alternatives: he was headquartered far from Syria, with no oppor-tunity to supervise the buildup of the new franchise. He may have felt more comfortable knowing that loyal operatives—some of whom he knew personally—were spearheading the Syrian venture. But just in case, he kept open communication channels with other Syrian jihadi veterans, such as Abu Khalid al-Suri, whom he had known for decades and who could keep a watchful eye for him.

Over time, JN became increasingly self-sufficient. According to Rand Corporation's Seth Jones, the branch secured its own funding sources from donors in the Persian Gulf and the Levant, independent of the ISI, developed sophisticated bomb-making capabilities, and attracted a growing number of fighters.[14] Threatened by JN's increased independence, ISI leader al-Baghdadi tried to stem its break from Iraqi tutelage by proclaiming, in April 2013, that JN would heretofore be subordinate to the ISI.[15] The announcement, deliv-ered in an audio message titled "And Give Glad Tidings to the Believers," represented a serious setback for al-Qaeda. Long-standing efforts to pres-ent JN as an independent entity focused on a Syrian agenda were sabotaged as al-Baghdadi revealed details about the group's founding. According to al-Baghdadi, the war in Syria led the ISI to deputize al-Joulani and send him with other ISI operatives across the border; the ISI then drew out strategic plans for JN and provided it with funding, fighters, and operational knowl-edge.[16] AQC, al-Baghdadi implied, was not involved. But the challenge to al-Zawahiri and al-Qaeda went much further than blowing JN's cover and dismissing AQC's role. The statement's real purpose was to declare the merger of the Iraqi and Syrian franchises, which would be renamed the Islamic State of Iraq and the Levant. This move was al-Baghdadi's gambit in establishing the ISI's aspirations as a competitor to al-Qaeda.

The way in which al-Baghdadi structured his argument—paying homage to the first leader of al-Qaeda's branch in Iraq, Abu Musab al-Zarqawi, while ignoring al-Zawahiri and AQC—revealed his aspirations. While declaring himself a follower of al-Zarqawi, al-Baghdadi implied that the ISI was now an independent organization rather than a component of al-Qaeda. Consequently, al-Baghdadi justified his move based on the same logic that had dictated al-Zarqawi's actions. According to this logic, the name of the organization, which Abu Bakr inherited from al-Zarqawi's successors Abu Umar al-Baghdadi and Abu Hamza al-Muhajir, is not merely a way to identify the organization; a name change reflects shifts in the organization's status and advancements in the pursuit of jihad. Al-Baghdadi presented the shift to ISIS as the latest link in a chain that started with al-Zarqawi's al-Tawhid wal-Jihad—renamed al-Qaeda in the Land of the Two Rivers after al-Zarqawi's pledge of allegiance to bin Laden, then altered to the Mujahidin's Shura Council and later to the Islamic State of Iraq. Al-Baghdadi did not state explicitly that his group was not part of al-Qaeda, but his argument came as close to that as possible.[17] He did not explain what happened to al-Zarqawi's allegiance to al-Qaeda once al-Qaeda in the Land of the Two Rivers united with other groups in Iraq; he also did not declare that the unification had annulled the *bay'a*. But the formulation of his argument insinuated that the Iraqi branch's success had transformed the relationship with al-Qaeda.

To the surprise of many, JN leader al-Joulani hurried to reject al-Baghdadi's statement.[18] Al-Joulani opened his statement by challenging the authenticity of the message attributed to the ISI leader, before arguing that if it was indeed authentic, JN was not consulted about the claimed merger and did not accept it. Al-Joulani confirmed important parts of al-Baghdadi's narrative regarding JN's establishment, including being deputized by the ISI leader and receiving support for the Iraqi jihad, but he broke with al-Baghdadi in important ways. Al-Joulani argued that JN could not be the embodiment of an Islamic state in Syria, as the name ISIS would suggest, because JN views the building of such a state as a project shared with all anti-regime factions who seek the implementation of *sharia* law in Syria. This claim echoes criticism that some Salafi and jihadi scholars had directed against the ISI when it was established in 2006. In all likelihood, by using this line of argumentation al-Joulani sought not only to calm the worries of jihadi allies in Syria but to sting al-Baghdadi.

But al-Joulani went further by acknowledging JN's relationship with al-Qaeda and reiterating the group's allegiance to its emir, al-Zawahiri.

The public pledge was probably meant as a first response to a crisis that quickly threatened to overwhelm JN. Given the besieged al-Qaeda leadership's command-and-control problems and the risk that al-Baghdadi's message would be accepted by JN's rank and file as well as by the global jihadi community, al-Joulani needed a stopgap measure to defend his group from the Iraqi assault. That numerous JN members pledged allegiance to al-Baghdadi immediately after his merger announcement added urgency to the situation,[19] pushing al-Joulani to take such a measure without instructions from AQC. At the same time, he sought to mitigate the risk that acknowledging JN's allegiance to al-Qaeda would estrange supporters in Syria by declaring that the group's policies would not change, meaning that its objective would remain the defense of Syria's Sunnis and that it would continue to cooperate with Syria's other jihadi groups. In reaffirming his loyalty to al-Zawahiri, al-Joulani also hinted that al-Baghdadi had failed to honor his obligation to the al-Qaeda leader. After all, the promise of obedience remains as long as there are no signs of clear disbelief.[20]

Central actors in the Syrian arena openly criticized al-Baghdadi's announcement as well as, to a lesser extent, al-Joulani's admission of JN's links to al-Qaeda.[21] The criticism focused on al-Qaeda's controversial ideology and foreign, rather than indigenous, agenda, as well as the danger that by exposing al-Qaeda's direct role in the Syrian civil war, al-Baghdadi might end up drawing into the arena new actors, primarily the United States, hostile to the jihadis.[22] The important Ahrar al-Sham rejected the establishment of a state, or an emirate in Syria, arguing that an emirate must have power and dominion on the ground with which it advances the people's interest—a condition that, it argued, was not met in Syria. In addition, Ahrar al-Sham declared that establishing an emirate is not an end in and of itself; its purpose would be to unify the ranks. But according to Ahrar al-Sham, this was not al-Baghdadi's intention and clearly was not the outcome of his announcement. The group also criticized al-Baghdadi for launching such a fateful project unilaterally, without consulting scholars and factions on the ground. Finally, the group lambasted both the announcement of the new state and al-Joulani's response as disadvantageous, since they would expand the battlefield and bring in new enemies, distracting from the fight against the regime.[23] It is noteworthy that, in contrast to the hostility toward the ISI, criticism of al-Joulani's response was relatively moderate. While largely critical of JN's public *bay'a* to al-Zawahiri, many expressed appreciation for JN's work in Syria. In some cases, rival factions voiced willingness to continue to coordinate with the group.[24]

With conflict aired so publicly, al-Qaeda's leader was forced to intervene. Al-Baghdadi's challenge put al-Zawahiri in a bind. He had to respond, and given the public nature of the challenge, the reaction also needed to have a public dimension. The more significant problem was that al-Zawahiri, still in hiding, could not control the al-Qaeda affiliates. His precarious security forced him into a reactive posture and made orchestrating a solution difficult, even had ISIS been more amenable to resolving the conflict. Al-Zawahiri also lacked the clout bin Laden had enjoyed; what his predecessor may have been able to achieve with words, he could not. And while his ability to effectively respond to the crisis was low, the stakes were sky-high—al-Qaeda's enterprise in Syria needed to be salvaged without inadvertently losing Iraq. In light of these constraints, al-Zawahiri chose an accommodation strategy that he hoped would solve the conflict between the two branches while keeping both under al-Qaeda's fold.

In a letter addressed to al-Baghdadi, al-Joulani, and each group's Shura Council, al-Zawahiri sought to arbitrate the conflict.[25] He begins the letter by rebuking the two for airing their conflict in the media. Ironically, al-Zawahiri's letter first appeared on the al-Jazeera network, probably the result of a leak intended to show jihadi sympathizers that he was still in charge and actively engaged. The letter notes a series of steps that al-Zawahiri took as early as three days after al-Baghdadi released his message, indicating his ability to quickly respond to crises. Then, after praising the ISI for contributing to the jihad in both Iraq and Syria, al-Zawahiri declares that al-Baghdadi was wrong to declare ISIS without consulting AQC—and that al-Joulani was wrong to reject his peer's announcement and expose JN's relationship with al-Qaeda without consulting or even informing AQC. He then proclaims that the ISI should retain its name and its responsibility for the Iraqi arena, with the JN remaining al-Qaeda's designated branch for Syria. In a further effort to assert his authority, al-Zawahiri also affirms that al-Baghdadi and al-Joulani would remain in their current positions for a year from the time of the edict, after which each group's Shura Council would send a report regarding the leaders' work. At that point, the general leadership of al-Qaeda would decide whether to retain or replace al-Baghdadi and al-Joulani. Al-Zawahiri's letter also nominates the Ahrar al-Sham veteran Abu Khalid al-Suri as his personal emissary, with various responsibilities. Should conflicts erupt again between the ISI and JN, he tasks al-Suri with establishing a *sharia* court to judge transgressions. Al-Zawahiri probably hoped that al-Suri's stature and his Syrian origins would make it easier to stop the ISI's overreach and stabilize the relationship between the two franchises.

But al-Zawahiri's hope of ending the conflict was dashed. ISIS did not retreat; in fact, it raised the stakes with another direct challenge to al-Zawahiri's authority. In an audio message released through social-media websites, al-Baghdadi rejected al-Zawahiri's edict.[26] Declaring that he would neither change his decision to rename the ISI nor restrict its involvement in Syria to a supportive role, al-Baghdadi explained that al-Zawahiri's decree suffered from several religious deficiencies that led him, after consulting ISIS's Sharia Committee, to reject it. Al-Baghdadi's statement was stunning—after all, the conditions under which one may lawfully ignore his Islamically grounded pledge of obedience are reserved for severe sins, not any religious shortcomings. Al-Baghdadi's message conveyed disrespect, if not outright denial, of al-Zawahiri's authority.

Further details about the concrete reasons for rejecting al-Zawahiri's arbitration came a few days later—this time in a statement from ISIS's official spokesman, Abu Muhammad al-Adnani.[27] The organization based its defense on five fundamental reasons.

First, compliance with al-Zawahiri's ruling would divide the mujahideen and undermine the fight against Assad's regime. Al-Adnani claimed that acquiescence would lead to sin because it required dividing a jihadi group into two—one Iraqi and the other Syrian. Division would, he argued, grow even further because bands of fighters who had refused to join JN due to what they saw as religious failures by some of its commanders—and who had changed their positions once ISIS was announced and the deviant JN commanders removed—would choose to split from the group. Other battalions that intended to join ISIS but had not yet done so would also be lost; some fighters would return with ISIS to Iraq, while others might abandon jihad altogether. Thus, by construing the existence of the Iraqi-Syrian organization as the natural frame of reference, ISIS presented al-Zawahiri's ruling not as a return to the normal state of affairs but, rather, as a harmful and in fact impossible change that would damage the fight against the Assad regime.

Second, JN was never independent, and its leaders should be denounced as rebelling against legitimate authority. According to al-Adnani, by addressing JN and ISIS as separate entities, al-Zawahiri misrepresented the reality that the first had always been a subset of the second. The name JN, the spokesman insisted, had been used only for security and media purposes. JN never had an independent existence separate from that of ISIS. Consequently, al-Adnani accused al-Zawahiri of committing an even graver offense because he had described "rebellious defectors" as noble and honorable and had rewarded their bad behavior by awarding them governance that was never theirs. Alleging that he was seeking to set the record straight, the spokes-man also claimed that JN's defection from ISIS did not follow al-Baghdadi's announcement—rather, al-Joulani and his followers had merely used the announcement as a pretext. In fact, al-Adnani claimed, al-Baghdadi made his announcement in such haste primarily to deter the expected defection of al-Joulani's people.[28]

Third, al-Zawahiri's judgment reflected an illegitimate process. Al-Adnani questioned the decree's legitimacy because the sides to the conflict were not presented with the evidence that informed it; moreover, a trial in which the two sides are not present and cannot respond to each other's claims does not meet the standards for justice.[29] Once again, in their effort to characterize the al-Qaeda chief's role as a judge, ISIS's leaders sought to diminish the scope of his authority. For al-Zawahiri, his edict reflected an emir's expansive rights to command subordinate soldiers, not the actions of an external and neutral judge.[30]

Fourth, withdrawing ISIS's fighters from Syria is morally inappropriate and thus not feasible. Al-Adnani suggested that the move would be funda-mentally unjust. He distorted al-Zawahiri's message—which focused on creating an organizational division of labor—and instead construed it as requiring all ISIS-affiliated jihadis to retreat from Syria. Based on this con-struction, al-Adnani stated that at a time when Shia are slaughtering and oppressing Muslims in Syria, and while Sunnis all over the world seek to assist their suffering brethren and call for unifying the ranks, al-Zawahiri's verdict was unforgivably unjust. ISIS simply could not comply: "No one will pre-vent us from helping our people in the Levant! No one will prevent us from fighting the Nusayris [Alawites] and doing jihad in the Levant! No one will prevent us from staying in the Levant."[31]

Finally, al-Zawahiri's decision must be disregarded because it imposes a division based on the post-World War I–era Sykes-Picot borders—an argu-ment that is particularly interesting and deserves a lengthier explication. The question of borders became a central tool in ISIS's efforts to distinguish itself from al-Qaeda and justify its reach into Syria, arguing that al-Qaeda, not ISIS, had turned away from the "correct" path. How did national borders become, among jihadis, a point of contention and a potent argument? The borders of the Middle East were drawn by Western colonial powers; the Sykes-Picot agreement—in which Britain and France divided the Levant among them-selves and imposed borders in the process—is the strongest and most vilified symbol of a foreign order. Both al-Qaeda and ISIS reject the current division of the Muslim world into separate territorial units; they decry it as the result of a conspiracy by the Christian West to divide the Muslim umma. Jihadis seek to abolish this "unnatural" division and to reconstitute a caliphate that would encompass all Muslim states under one rule; al-Qaeda articulated a denunciation of the Westphalian order in numerous statements, which I have documented elsewhere.[32] When it formed affiliations, al-Qaeda was careful to name its branches in a way that would not legitimize Westphalian borders: the organization chose to name its franchises Al-Qaeda in the Arabian Peninsula and Al-Qaeda in the Islamic Maghreb, rather than Al-Qaeda in Saudi Arabia, or Algeria. Its choice of names also reinforced the message that al-Qaeda's ambitions surpass current state boundaries.

And yet, in denying ISIS's claim of responsibility for both the Iraqi and Syrian arenas, al-Qaeda offered its rival an effective rhetorical weapon. ISIS unhesitatingly presented its expansion effort as reflecting an ideological commitment to bring together all Muslim states, suggesting that al-Qaeda's call to separate the Iraqi and Syrian branches proves that al-Qaeda is not genuinely committed to destroying the Sykes-Picot borders. In ISIS's narrative, al-Qaeda's position is even more deplorable because the fight in the Levant pits Syria's Sunnis against Shia from Iran, Iraq, and Lebanon, while the Shia are presenting a united front, not dividing themselves based on nationality. Therefore, ISIS's insistence on staying in Syria is a principled one. "Iraq and the Levant will remain one arena, one front, one command, and no borders will separate between them! We swear that we will destroy the barrier, we will fill in the ditch, and we will remove the wires and erase the borders from the map and remove them from the hearts! The booby traps will hit the *rafidahs* [Shia] from Diyala [in Iraq] to Beirut."[33]

ISIS's accusations were not without merit. AQC's statements have made clear distinctions between the nation-state and the Islamic state, but its commentary on political developments in Arab Awakening countries focused on criticizing what it views as those nation-states' neglect of the Islamic dimension of governance.[34] Leaders' statements frequently note the Muslim world's illegitimate division and the objective of unifying all Muslim lands,[35] but they do not emphasize the issue. Thus, one could see AQC's statements as attempting to speak to a broad audience whose frame of reference is the current map of Muslim states. AQC's bet that discussing the Islamic nature of existing states would be better received than would statements denouncing the current order is not unreasonable. Its revolutionary vision notwithstanding, al-Qaeda has learned over the years to be more strategic in its actions. And its post–bin Laden approach has sought to take advantage of the changes in the region by aiming to mobilize the masses. In contrast to ISIS's narrow focus, AQC directs its messages toward an audience far beyond the jihadi community. In fact, whereas ISIS sees moderate Islamists such as the Muslim Brotherhood, who participate in the political process, as apostates, al-Qaeda appeals to their supporters as potential converts to its jihadi worldview. It may criticize Islamist parties' decisions, but it sees them as misguided brethren. The price for this approach is that ISIS was more easily able to portray al-Qaeda as straying from its original course.

Al-Qaeda's leaders could have replied to these allegations by pointing to its record—for example, AQAP's responsibility for both Yemen and Saudi Arabia. But since franchise announcements carry an important political element, once ISIS exposed its connection to JN and JN declared its relation to al-Qaeda, arguing that franchise designation is based on operational or organizational logics would have been unconvincing. The strongest reason to reject ISIS's expansion would have been the group's disloyalty to al-Qaeda, but making this argument explicit would have exposed al-Qaeda's disunity and al-Zawahiri's inability to control the organization he inherited from bin Laden. Moreover, al-Qaeda had to consider the repercussions if it pushed too far—its rift with the volatile branch might become irreversible and cause it to leave al-Qaeda, at the time ISIS utilized the sectarian policies of Iraq's government to make considerable strides among Iraq's Sunnis. But concealing the truth actually strengthened ISIS's narrative that it backs its ideology with action, while al-Qaeda settles for rhetorical denunciations. Thus, facing only negative prospects, al-Qaeda chose to pursue a difficult balancing act—one that ultimately failed.

After the de facto split of al-Qaeda's Syrian franchise, many JN members defected to ISIS—even after al-Zawahiri called on the group to return to Iraq. Whether fearing the costs of escalation or unable to take any decisive measure that would get al-Qaeda out of its bind, for several months AQC seemed weak and ineffectual in the face of ISIS's transgression. Meanwhile, the newly declared organization saw a meteoric rise in its public profile and impact. Despite ISIS's relatively small size compared to other central opposition formations (particularly the groups comprising the Islamic Front), its forces were highly effective. By year's end, fighters had captured vast territory in the north and northwest of Syria, including the vital supply lines connecting Aleppo with Turkey, often wrested from the control of fellow rebel groups.[36] At least 35 municipalities came under its total or partial control in 10 of Syria's 14 governorates.[37] Confrontations between ISIS and other rebel groups continued to escalate and over time became increasingly violent. Meanwhile, JN seemed reluctant to openly criticize the new group, instead calling on the embattled factions to stop the infighting and to direct weapons against their shared enemy. It advocated a *sharia* court as the best way to resolve disputes and even proposed its own services as a mediator.[38] But as the infighting continued, JN found its ability to stay on the sidelines greatly diminished.

Full of confidence, ISIS imposed its own style of Islamic rule, brutalizing its rivals and intimidating aid workers and journalists. In contrast to its previous attempts at ruling in Iraq a few years earlier, in Syria ISIS did not focus only on imposing strict rules for "Islamic" personal behavior but also tried to provide some public services.[39] However, as the group continued to expand, its rule became more oppressive, and the "hearts and minds" element—already a lower priority for ISIS's leaders than for JN's—declined. Despite its battlefield success, ISIS seemed more interested in carving out an Islamic state in already liberated areas than in fighting the Syrian army.[40] While the group's fighters went on a rampage, AQC appeared virtually irrelevant; it was unable to affect events on the ground in Syria, even as it continued to claim authority over ISIS. Given al-Qaeda's passivity, it was no surprise that ISIS's setbacks in Syria first came from the actions of other players.

Disavowal and Its Aftermath

On January 3, 2014, ISIS's overreach finally generated the long-expected backlash. A coalition of three rebel fronts—the largely nationalist Syrian Revolutionary Front, the moderately Islamist Jaish al-Mujahideen, and the Salafist Islamic Front—launched a massive military campaign against ISIS and quickly routed it from many of its strongholds in northern Syria. JN elected to not get too involved in the fighting, although in several locations its forces joined the anti-ISIS coalition, allegedly in self-defense when they came under attack.[41]

A January 7 statement by al-Joulani was critical of ISIS and signaled JN's future direction: it called on ISIS to accept the establishment of a *sharia* court composed of all central jihadi groups, which would arbitrate conflicts before they escalated to violence.[42] JN implicitly admonished ISIS that by refusing to accept its place as one force in a broader camp of equally legitimate members, rather than a superior power with authority over all others, it became the obstacle for reconciliation. Al-Zawahiri confidant Abu Khalid al-Suri echoed al-Joulani's critique, as did leaders of the Islamic Front.[43] Soon JN committed itself fully to the fight against ISIS.

The escalation of the crisis put additional pressure on al-Zawahiri to demonstrate his authority; in jihadi circles, there was great anticipation that he would intervene, rein in ISIS, and put a stop to the embarrassing fratricidal violence. But even as anxiety among jihadis worldwide mounted, al-Zawahiri was slow to publicly address the conflict. When he finally did, in a statement released January 23—three weeks after the infighting began—his message was weak. Al-Zawahiri repeated the futile call for unity among all jihadi groups, reminding them of their shared objective: establishing an Islamic state.[44] But the statement avoided any direct reference to ISIS—or even JN. Overall, al-Zawahiri appeared timid. His endorsement of the call for a *sharia* commit-tee to arbitrate conflicts could be construed as an implicit rebuke to ISIS, and his condemnation of apostasy charges among the mujahideen appear directed at ISIS's extremism. But he stopped well short of explicitly accusing ISIS of misdeeds.[45]

Because the intra-jihadi conflict was no longer restricted to al-Qaeda's competing branches, prominent figures among Syria's jihadis became heav-ily involved in the effort to tame ISIS and stop the infighting. Hours after al-Zawahiri's message was posted, Abdallah Muhammad al-Muhaysini, a popular Saudi cleric who had relocated to Syria to support the jihad, pre-sented a reconciliation plan. In essence, the plan—named the "initiative of the umma"—called for the establishment of a *sharia* court composed of inde-pendent judges agreed upon by all parties. The Islamic Front and JN quickly endorsed the initiative, but ISIS rejected it,[46] leading to al-Muhaysini's call, a few days later, for ISIS's members to defect to other jihadi groups.[47]

After the failure of the reconciliation initiative, on February 2 al-Qaeda issued a statement announcing that it had severed its ties with ISIS and no longer saw the group as one of its branches.[48] Al-Qaeda's central command renounced responsibility for the group's actions and, in a strong rebuke to the disobedient branch, affirmed its commitment to refrain from imposing its leadership on the umma. Unlike ISIS, al-Qaeda would not usurp the umma's right to choose its rulers.[49] In the statement, AQC referred to ISIS as merely a group, implying that the word "State" indicated hubris rather than the authority of an Islamic emirate, with the associated privileges accompanying such a designation.[50]

The decision to disavow the group could not have been easy for AQC. ISIS was its most successful franchisee, controlling large swaths of terri-tory in both Iraq and Syria. By breaking with ISIS, al-Qaeda was not simply making a choice to stand behind its other franchise in Syria—it would be left without an affiliate in Iraq. All that, as Sunni resistance to Maliki's Iraqi government was at an all-time high and territories in the country's Sunni regions—including the prized city of Fallujah—were falling under ISIS control. Al-Zawahiri's choice to forgo the benefits of ISIS's operational success signaled that the damage ISIS had caused to his organization, and to his own personal authority, were so great that al-Qaeda would be better off abandoning the former branch.

It is likely that another reason that it took al-Qaeda so long to distance itself from ISIS is AQC's great reluctance to be associated with internal fighting within the jihadi movement. After years of emphasizing the importance of unity and issuing repeated warnings against sedition and strife—backed by strong references in the Quran and the Sunna—disavowing allies who seek to establish an Islamic caliphate is not a step that can be taken lightly. As the crisis among the Islamist insurgent groups in Syria escalated, many in the jihadi community only strengthened their call for unity and warned against publicly discussing the differences among the groups. To appear responsible for weakening the bond among jihadis could be costly, and al-Zawahiri needed to demonstrate that he had taken all possible measures to avoid fragmentation and gain support from luminary jihadi scholars—the shapers of opinion among jihadis worldwide. In the months preceding al-Qaeda's move, some of the most important jihadi scholars (primarily Abu Muhammad al-Maqdisi and Abu Qatada al-Filistini) harshly criticized al-Baghdadi for assuming a title reserved for a caliph and for calling his group a state, thus refusing to accept other jihadi groups as equals.[51] Moreover, al-Zawahiri refrained from announcing his break with ISIS until after al-Muhaysini had acknowledged the failure of his reconciliation efforts. While some leading scholars maintained their support of ISIS, others' growing criticism probably made it easier for al-Zawahiri to disown the group and put him in a better position to deflect accusations of causing disunity. In fact, given the agreement among the other Islamist groups operating in Syria, al-Zawahiri's disavowal could be construed as compatible with the quest for unity—one between JN and Syria's less extreme Sunni rebel, that is, not the renegade ISIS.

The formal split between al-Qaeda and JN, on the one hand, and ISIS, on the other, did not end their conflict. In fact, the battle only escalated. On the ground in Syria, JN took a much more active role in the coalition fighting ISIS, while the latter proved resilient and vigorously pushed to recover lost territories. The online rhetorical war also continued to heat up, with a back-and-forth argument that ranged beyond determining whose actions were proper and justifiable. Struggling to achieve dominance, each side demanded that the other reverse its actions: ISIS pressed to subordinate JN; AQC called on ISIS to return to Iraq. This battle of statements is fascinating and deserves to be treated at length, as it sheds light not only on the heart of the conflict but on the discourse deemed legitimate in an intra-jihadi rivalry.

AQC explained the decision to distance itself from ISIS as the result of a difference in approaches: it maintained that its focus on fighting against the United States did not allow it to engage in "side skirmishes"; al-Qaeda seeks to unite the umma and establish the caliphate, and these objectives require care to avoid shedding innocents' blood and to maintain a positive image—they cannot be accomplished if the group is viewed as seeking domination and usurping others' rights.[52] The organization's implication: ISIS wastes energy on secondary priorities, failing to identify accurately the central threat to the umma; consequently, its strategy is bound to fail. ISIS's aggressiveness, AQC argued, represents a serious error, damaging its reputation and thus alienating the public whose support it requires.

According to al-Qaeda, al-Zawahiri was forced to renounce ISIS because the group refused to respect its authority, announcing the establishment of an Islamic state without permission and without even informing the parent organization. In going public, ISIS violated the decision to keep secret the relationship between JN, al-Qaeda, and its Iraqi franchise. The decision to maintain secrecy reflected a balance between the need to participate in the Syrian war and help the oppressed, and the assessment that openly admitting al-Qaeda's role in the fighting would be counterproductive. But ISIS ignored this rationale and, in exposing al-Qaeda's work in Syria, played into the hands of the Assad regime and the United States. Moreover, the revelation caused anxiety among Syrians who feared that it would lead to an American military intervention that would, purportedly, bring additional pain to Syria's Sunnis.

Al-Qaeda disputed ISIS's claims that, despite the group's wishes to avoid division, it simply could not comply with al-Zawahiri's edict to designate geographical responsibility for jihad by keeping the Iraqi group in charge of the Iraqi arena and JN as responsible for Syria. Al-Qaeda maintained that had ISIS accepted al-Zawahiri's edict, the lives of thousands who died in jihadi infighting would have been spared. Moreover, forces that ended up fighting each other would have been able to dedicate their energies to fighting the Syrian regime instead.[53]

Clearly, al-Qaeda was adjusting its arguments to fit the new realities in the region. Moreover, its arguments suggest that while the conflict with ISIS was damaging al-Qaeda's brand name, the organization also found it an opportunity to cultivate a new image, one of flexibility and attentiveness to the people. One of the lessons al-Qaeda took from the upheaval in the Middle East is that the region's people had abandoned their passivity and wanted to assume a greater role in determining their own fate. Thus, al-Qaeda criticized ISIS: by unilaterally announcing itself as an Islamic state rather than simply an organization, it appropriated the umma's right to be consulted and participate in its own governance. Rejecting the claim that such a role should be reserved for "specialists among the mujahideen," al-Qaeda declared that only the Muslim community is qualified to decide who will lead it.[54]

AQC also sought to refute ISIS's claims that it had ceased being subordinate to al-Qaeda years prior to the conflict. AQC presented evidence proving that the group, as the ISI, had not been independent; therefore, its current behavior constituted insubordination. The evidence included correspondence showing ISI leaders responding to AQC queries; in one example, the affiliate explains to AQC its reasons for nominating Abu Bakr al-Baghdadi to lead the franchise after the 2010 death of Abu Hamza al-Muhajir and Abu Umar al-Baghdadi without first consulting AQC, and agrees that after a one-year period, AQC would decide whether Abu Bakr was to remain in his post. Among the other examples showing hierarchical relations: an ISI request for instructions concerning the way in which it should respond to al-Zawahiri's nomination as bin Laden's successor, as well as the words of reverence Abu Bakr al-Baghdadi used in his communications with al-Zawahiri. Al-Qaeda noted that even in the correspondence following al-Baghdadi's announcement that his franchise had expanded into Syria, he refers to al-Zawahiri as his commander.[55]

Notably, al-Qaeda's defense also confirms that its central leadership's relationship with the Iraqi group was highly contentious years before the split. Al-Qaeda leaders wrote letters to Abu Hamza al-Muhajir and Abu Umar al-Baghdadi, expressing their displeasure with the franchise's policies, which AQC deemed to be political mistakes. Later, after those two leaders' deaths, the ISI failed to consult and seek approval from AQC for its selection of a successor. Al-Qaeda's leadership did not even know the individuals who would lead the ISI; it had to ask for information about them because it could not gauge their reliability based on personal experience.[56] And as the ISI admitted, it had repeatedly ignored al-Zawahiri's requests to stop targeting Shia masses in Iraq.[57]

In its statements, AQC also struggled to explain the discrepancy between its 2006 consent to the ISI's establishment and its 2013 rejection of ISIS. After all, if, as al-Qaeda declared, it did not support the formation of Islamic emirates, then why had it accepted the establishment of such an entity previously? Al-Zawahiri tried to address this inconsistency by noting that al-Qaeda's senior leadership had not been consulted prior to the foundation

of the ISI either. However, distorting those events and ignoring the contention surrounding the ISI's formation, al-Zawahiri argued that the Iraqi group
had received al-Qaeda's blessing because there was no threat that its founding would cause a rift among jihadis and lead to bloodshed among brethren. While admitting that not all actors in the Iraqi arena were consulted
and asked to join the ISI ahead of its announcement, al-Zawahiri claimed
that such omissions were technicalities, the result of communication problems that are natural in wartime and did not constitute a threat of sedition.
Moreover, in a snipe directed at Abu Bakr, al-Zawahiri noted that AQC had
accepted the ISI's explanations for the steps it took because they were deliv-
ered by the trusted Abu Hamza al-Muhajir, implying that al-Baghdadi was
not similarly trusted.[58]

Despite its ample criticism, AQC left the door open for ISIS to return
to al-Qaeda; in early May 2014, it called on al-Baghdadi and ISIS to "return
to hearing and obeying their emir."[59] Emphasizing the needs of Sunnis in
Iraq, al-Zawahiri urged ISIS to shift its focus back there. Urging a rebellious
franchise to repent and come back to the fold of the parent organization is
not a costly measure, and it is consistent with al-Qaeda's efforts to project a
conciliatory image. At the very least, al-Qaeda may have hoped to mitigate
criticism that it was responsible for strife within the jihadi camp. The appeal
to al-Baghdadi must also be seen in light of al-Qaeda's difficulties in finding
an effective way to deal with the ISIS threat. Given ISIS's rising appeal, both
inside the Syrian arena and—more worryingly to al-Qaeda—outside it, there
was an even greater urgency to halt the group's ascent before it reached a tip-
ping point and consumed al-Qaeda.

Unsurprisingly, ISIS vehemently rejected AQC's claims, laying out a different narrative regarding its relationship with al-Qaeda, aimed at legitimizing
its actions and deflecting criticism. At the core of ISIS's story is the refutation
of al-Qaeda's claim that the two organizations had a hierarchical relationship,
with the Iraqi branch's actions therefore constituting rebellion. Highlighting
elements that had appeared in earlier messages, the group proclaimed that it
had ceased to be an organization back in 2006, once its leaders founded the
ISI. According to ISIS, al-Zarqawi pledged allegiance to bin Laden in order
to enhance Muslim unity and raise the morale of the mujahideen. But when
conditions were ripe, the group—together with others—rose to the next level
by founding an Islamic state, and for all intents and purposes, that shift signaled the end of al-Qaeda in Iraq.[60] Despite disbanding the organization, the
ISI continued to view al-Qaeda as a symbol of the umma—thus, Abu Hamza
al-Muhajir's expression of loyalty was a symbolic measure taken to indicate

respect and acknowledgment of al-Qaeda's role in leading global jihad. It was intended to show the ISI's commitment to the unity of the umma but did not reflect continued organizational subordination. From ISIS's perspective, once it was established, it assumed authority over the arena in which it operated. Moreover, the status of an emirate supersedes that of any organization. Consequently, it would be inappropriate for an Islamic state to pledge allegiance to an organization. ISIS even reminded al-Qaeda that this principle is reflected in its own pledge to Mullah Omar in his role as the leader of the Islamic Emirate of Afghanistan.[61]

In ISIS's view, apart from memories of mutual respect, there was little else in its relationship with al-Qaeda. Spokesman al-Adnani derided al-Qaeda as practically irrelevant to ISIS's operation; he asked al-Zawahiri, "What did you give to the State if you were its emir? With what did you supply it? For what did you hold it accountable? What did you order it to do? What did you forbid it to do? Who did you isolate or put in charge of?"[62] According to al-Adnani, while ISIS did not benefit from al-Qaeda, it acted with some deference as long as it could, albeit without allowing al-Qaeda to encroach on the new emirate's legitimate rights. According to ISIS, its sensitivity to al-Qaeda's interests even led it to avoid carrying out operations outside the area over which it had established direct authority. As an example of respectful deference, al-Adnani noted, the ISI had avoided targeting Iran even though, he claimed, the group had the capabilities and saw strong demand for such action among its ranks. Similarly, it avoided operating in Saudi Arabia or intervening in Egypt, Libya, and Tunisia, where, as the holder of the banner of global jihad, al-Qaeda took it upon itself to operate. Nevertheless, such sacrifices reflected no formal obligation to obey al-Qaeda because, from ISIS's point of view, al-Zawahiri's words were no more than recommendations and guidelines.[63]

ISIS's version of its evolving relationship with al-Qaeda also embellished important parts of its history. Skirting the great controversy over the ISI's establishment as an emirate that all jihadis in Iraq must follow,[64] ISIS declared that all jihadi leaders had praised and supported the new Islamic state and that, with their assistance, its legitimacy grew year by year. Distorting the historical record is important for ISIS because it relies on its alleged legitimacy as an emirate, not simply a jihadi organization, to justify its claims for superior status in Syria. Its actions in Syria are therefore appropriate, embodying the fulfillment of natural rights and the progression of the caliphate project. At the same time, such a frame lends greater authority to ISIS's demands for compliance and the condemnation of rivals' actions as seditious.[65]

Given the power of claims of unity—both with regard to the Muslim umma and more specifically within the ranks of those fighting jihad—ISIS tried to portray itself as the epitome of unity. In fact, the group suggested that for the sake of maintaining unity, it had been patient and endured considerable costs as rival Islamist groups tried to draw it into conflict. Ignoring its own role in generating the backlash, ISIS alleged that it had long tolerated attacks out of concern for the unity of the ranks. But it was unable to maintain this position because of the magnitude of al-Qaeda's ideological transgressions.[66] Thus, ISIS's respect for al-Qaeda evaporated at the point at which AQC's policies radically deviated from the correct Islamic method. Such deviation required those who have always remained loyal to the right path—that is, ISIS—to respond. Framing al-Qaeda as the transgressing party is central to ISIS's rhetorical strategy. The group alleged that it has always adhered to the path sanctioned by the Quran and the Sunna, whereas al-Qaeda overreached; therefore, the responsibility for the infighting should be laid at the doorsteps of ISIS's rivals. Based on this logic, there is essentially only one legitimate solution to the rift with al-Qaeda: since al-Zawahiri is responsible for the bloodshed, it is in his power to stop it by changing his ways. Specifically, ISIS demanded, he must annul the acceptance of JN's pledge of allegiance and renounce al-Qaeda's authority within the Syrian arena.[67]

ISIS was careful to associate the detrimental shift in al-Qaeda's ideology with al-Zawahiri rather than bin Laden. Al-Qaeda's founder remains still a mythical and revered figure; condemning him, especially after his martyrdom, could backfire. Al-Zawahiri is an easier target. ISIS has not shied from using statements made by al-Qaeda leaders bin Laden, Abu Yahya al-Libi, and Suleiman Abu Ghaith to discredit al-Zawahiri; the group presents their words about the dangers of disbelief as evidence that ISIS remained loyal to the ideas of al-Qaeda, which its current leadership betrayed. It called on al-Zawahiri to return to his predecessor's path and to the methodology of the true al-Qaeda, the one that won the jihadi movement's admiration and support.[68]

Along similar lines, ISIS's spokesman noted that the group did not want to openly reveal the deviation of al-Qaeda in the post–bin Laden era but was "forced" to do so by the magnitude of al-Qaeda's sins. Among ISIS's long list of severe accusations were charges that the group had abandoned true jihad, flirted with tyrants, and cooperated with secularists and the "traitorous" Awakening groups—the same groups it had previously fought. Moreover, ISIS accused al-Qaeda of splitting the ranks of the mujahideen when it accepted the "defectors" of JN and "started a war against the Islamic State."[69] It identified al-Zawahiri as the cause for sedition because he chose to accept the *bay'a* of the "traitorous" al-Joulani: "You [al-Zawahiri] made yourself and your al-Qaeda a joke and a toy in the hands of an arrogant traitor-boy who broke the pledge of allegiance that you did not see. You left him to play with you like a child plays with a ball, thus ruining your reputation and losing your history and glory."[70] Stopping short of calling for excommunication, ISIS even contended that al-Qaeda's ideological shift had led it to abandon monotheism. Al-Qaeda "leaving the faith of Abraham" is linked to the act of disowning Abraham's followers—ISIS—and their jihad.[71]

The charges go on: by causing a split in the movement, al-Qaeda weakened the mujahideen while emboldening and strengthening disbelievers; it labeled ISIS members as extremists, the *khawarij*, and thus supposedly made shedding their blood permissible. As a result, ISIS representatives complained, the group cannot leave alone its attackers for fear of losing its own fighters, but when ISIS acts in self-defense, al-Qaeda distorts the story to present the group's actions as evidence that ISIS represents the modern *khawarij*.[72]

The gap in perceptions of al-Qaeda's actions is striking. Decisions that al-Qaeda supporters may view as evidence of greater tactical flexibility and acceptance of varied strategies to bring about change are condemned by ISIS as defeatism, abandonment of the doctrine of *tawhid* (unity of God) by catering to the majority in Muslim states (even though it requires alliances with actors al-Qaeda previously rejected), and even willingness to accept peaceful relations, as equals, with non-Muslims.[73] From ISIS's perspective, al-Qaeda must reverse its new approach of accommodation. Al-Qaeda must also change the new vocabulary it adopted: ISIS demanded that al-Qaeda abandon the use of terms such as "popular resistance" and "mass uprising," which are designed to cater to a broader audience but are not derived from the *sharia* and come at the expense of (non-negotiable) ideological purity. Al-Zawahiri should instead return to the language of jihad and explicitly call true Muslims to bear arms and to shun all peaceful means. In the same spirit, ISIS also demanded that al-Zawahiri stop calling the armies of Egypt, Pakistan, Afghanistan, Libya, Tunisia, and Yemen "Americanized" forces, since such a depiction distorts their true nature. Al-Qaeda must instead use the appropriate terms, which reflect the true Islamic view of such entities: they are "tyrants," "disbelievers," and "apostates."[74] The clear message is that the shift in al-Qaeda's position, as reflected in its discourse and in the changes in its behavior, amounts to compromising core elements of the true understanding of the Islamic faith.

Taken together, ISIS built its case on presenting its actions as a truthful and consistent Islamic stance, portraying conflict as the result of al-Qaeda's deviation from the correct path. ISIS alleges that it adheres to its principles and continues to do so no matter the costs it may incur, because these principles represent the right and only way. In contrast, the group argues, al-Qaeda compromised its beliefs and its methods. Instead of being dedicated to the establishment of the caliphate, al-Qaeda became a tool in "demolishing the project of the Islamic State and the coming caliphate."[75]

The Arrival of the Caliphate

The competition between al-Qaeda and its former franchise reached a new peak when a stunning advance by ISIS forces across north and central Iraq was followed, on June 29, by its announcement of the re-establishment of the Islamic caliphate and declaration of al-Baghdadi as the new caliph.[76] The declaration was part of an elaborate rollout, reminiscent of the way a business launches a new product. As part of this rollout, ISIS—now calling itself the Islamic State—also released a Ramadan message from al-Baghdadi directed at "the mujahideen" and the umma,[77] a reissued short biography of the new "caliph,"[78] and a video statement abolishing the Sykes-Picot borders.[79] The Islamic State has also, through Twitter, released ongoing announcements about jihadis who allegedly pledged allegiance, either as groups or as individuals, to al-Baghdadi (or to his new identity, "Caliph Ibrahim"). This is a new stage in the rivalry that heightens the debate over questions of authority and legitimacy. If the Islamic State's claim for supremacy based on an emirate's authority over an organization was controversial, the claims that it constitutes a caliphate are considerably more audacious.

In announcing the caliphate, ISIS pursued a number of objectives. First, the proclamation elevated the status of ISIS and al-Baghdadi. It was likely an effort to strengthen the group's image as actually delivering on Islamists' aspirations, even as other jihadi groups are mired in discussions of future action.

Second, with the declaration, ISIS attempted to stifle debate among jihadis about the religious legitimacy of its actions. In its prior incarnations, ISIS had already maintained that it was a state and, as such, superior to other jihadi organizations and scholars, imbued with authority that their rivals lacked. ISIS relied on such authority to justify its rejection of arbitration with other jihadi groups in Syria. Thus, the announcement of a caliphate—an even higher level of authority—grants ISIS, in its own view, unchallenged authority and serves as a tool to cast off criticism and allegations that its actions are inconsistent with *sharia* law.

Third, other jihadi groups (for example, the Taliban in Afghanistan and al-Shabab in Somalia) managed to gain control over large swaths of territory yet failed to progress toward the objective of a truly Islamic state unfettered by the rules of the Westphalian state system (primarily international law). Failing to mobilize the Muslim umma, their gains proved reversible. It is doubtful that ISIS fears the same fate; its leaders are too confident to worry it will similarly fail, though their steps reflect an attempt to learn from those experiences.

Fourth, and most important, the announcement is part of a plan to mobilize Muslims at large. Al-Qaeda was disappointed that the masses did not enlist after 9/11. For the Islamic State, mass mobilization is even more urgent: it is imperative for expansion through military means and for effective governance in the territories the group controls. Therefore, by announcing a caliphate, ISIS intensified its efforts to attract volunteers, both foot soldiers and professionals. Indeed, al-Baghdadi's Ramadan message called on Muslims around the world to join the Islamic State.[80] This was not a request: using his title as the "Emir of the Believers," al-Baghdadi declared immigration to the caliphate an individual duty, one that all able Muslims must obey. He utilized the caliph's claimed authority[81] to summon—rather than merely encourage—Muslims to join. The rollout of the caliphate was probably timed to take advantage of the holy month of Ramadan, infusing ISIS's measures with additional religious symbolism and enhancing its appeal to jihadis and the broader Muslim community, and thus strengthening the mobilization drive.

By boldly claiming to have re-established the caliphate, the Islamic State affirmed once more its general approach, according to which military success can precede and, in fact, leads to religious legitimacy and the expansion of religious authority. For ISIS, its advances on the ground put it in a position of power that strengthened its arguments' validity regarding religious legitimacy and justified moving to the next phase of its Islamic project. Naturally, for rivals, the caliphate gambit confirmed claims that al-Baghdadi was in well over his head, driven by self-aggrandizement and short-term military gains. Moreover, while a caliphate and a caliph may excite the imagination of some enthusiastic youth, it could give others cause to consider whether the group is overreaching or, worse, going so far that its actions constitute religious innovations strictly prohibited in their own austere interpretation of Islam.

Testament to the new caliphate's success would be its acceptance among Muslims worldwide, not only among jihadis. In the weeks following the announcement, the Islamic State tried to form the impression that its declared caliphate had been well received; it released numerous tweets showing groups and fighters around the world pledging allegiance to the "Caliph Ibrahim." Despite the group's best efforts, these pledges constituted a stream rather than a torrent. Moreover, prominent jihadi scholars who had previously rejected the group's authority claims refused to reconsider their position.[82]

Conclusions

In Syria, the adverse consequences of al-Qaeda's expansion strategy reached a new level, worse than an affiliate tarnishing the organization's brand name. In the ISI, al-Qaeda faced a franchise that turned fully against it. The group became the most serious organized challenger to al-Qaeda's authority within the jihadi camp, with territorial gains that eclipsed anything its former partner had ever achieved.

Although al-Qaeda did not create this monster, the ramifications of merging with al-Zarqawi's group in Iraq nearly a decade earlier—and helping to nurture it, by virtue of their formal association—came full circle. The ISI's challenge was a power play by a power-hungry competitor seeking to replace the parent organization as the leading group in the global jihadi movement. But the group represents an even deeper threat: under al-Qaeda's tutelage, an even more radical version of jihadism emerged, one so violent that al-Qaeda judged it to be too toxic. Ironically, at the exact same time that AQC concluded that it must exhibit greater pragmatism to remain relevant and take advantage of the opportunities created by regional turmoil, it discovered its own breakaway reactionary forces forging a different, more extreme path.

Importantly, these forces did not become reactionary in response to al-Qaeda's relative flexibility. Their radicalism festered in Iraq for a long time before the Syrian civil war (and the weakening Iraqi regime) offered them, like AQC, new opportunities. ISI used these opportunities to break out of al-Qaeda's shadow and claim its place in the sun.

But looking ahead, the jihadi civil war also offers some hope for al-Qaeda. JN exhibited remarkable resilience under difficult conditions. Despite ISI's success and the defection of many foreign fighters to join it, JN did not disintegrate. Remarkably, it regrouped and, by focusing its efforts on regions not under ISI control and taking advantage of more moderate groups' growing weakness, JN even expanded its territory. It achieved all that without reverting to ISI's brutal methods and, consequently, without losing much public support. By continuing to man the frontlines against the Syrian regime, JN further distinguished itself from ISI—renamed ISIS, the Islamic State—and maintained its image as part of the anti-regime revolution. Moreover, its professionalism made its help irreplaceable for any meaningful rebel offensive.[83]

Meanwhile, al-Qaeda did not lose sight of its fight against the West. AQC sent fighters, known as the Khorasan Group, to Syria, where they seek to take advantage of the flow of foreign volunteers from Western countries and the permeable Turkish border to prepare new attacks against the "far enemy."[84] Although by the time this book went to press, the Khorasan Group has yet to execute any spectacular attack in the West, al-Qaeda appears better positioned to carry out such an attack than it has been in years.

10

Conclusions

Introducing AQIS

"[G]lad tidings to the Muslims in the world in general and the Indian subcontinent in particular. . . . [A] new branch of al-Qaeda was established, and this Qaedat al-Jihad in the Indian subcontinent is seeking to raise the flag of jihad, return the Islamic rule, and empower the sharia of Allah across the Indian subcontinent, which was once part of the lands of the Muslims, until the infidel enemy occupied it and fragmented and split it."[1] With these words, Ayman al-Zawahiri opened a September 2014 video message proclaiming the establishment of al-Qaeda in the Indian Subcontinent, al-Qaeda's seventh openly announced franchise, responsible for a vast territory: India, Pakistan, Bangladesh, and Myanmar.

The founding of AQIS was essentially a political move, since its operational focus (at least at the time this book went to press) is American naval forces in the Indian Ocean, and small terror cells are capable of carrying out such attacks without massive organizational support. In contrast to attacks on soft targets—less prestigious but usually more lethal and attention-grabbing—dispersed over large geographical space, or to attempts to capture and hold ground, AQIS operations to date have required neither amassing large forces (as indicated from AQIS claims to unite several jihadi groups) nor the announcement of a formal affiliate.

The reason that al-Qaeda announced the establishment of AQIS is therefore less about newly acquired operational capability than about the pressure leaders feel to respond to a strategic environment that in 2014 turned decisively against al-Qaeda. Whereas in the past the organization's difficulties came predominantly from the actions of the United States and its Arab allies, this time the main threat came from within the jihadi movement and, to some extent, from al-Qaeda's own ranks. In February, al-Zawahiri was forced to publicly disavow the insurgent Islamic State and drop the façade of al-Qaeda having an Iraqi branch (not that ISIS had ever heeded his commands anyway). Then, in June, he watched as the former al-Qaeda affiliate stunned the world by conquering vast territory in Iraq and Syria—including Mosul, Iraq's second-largest city—establishing control over more than 10 million people, and announcing the re-establishment of the caliphate, headed by ISIS's leader, whom al-Zawahiri had until recently regarded as his subordinate. Al-Qaeda had spent the previous dozen years promising action; ISIS actually delivered.

Making things worse, while ISIS became a magnet for enthusiastic young Muslims from all over the world, captivated by the notion of building a utopian caliphate, al-Zawahiri struggled to keep his organization from collapsing and to prove its ongoing relevance. He was forced to conduct this rearguard battle to the sound of murmurs from al-Qaeda's ranks about his irresponsiveness and impotence, and while hiding from American drones. Unable to seize new territory (not even in less prestigious locations than Iraq and Syria) or carry out spectacular attacks inside the United States or Europe, al-Qaeda turned to expansion (followed by a high-profile, but failed, operation by the new branch) as its third-best option.

The announcement did not mention ISIS by name. Implicitly, al-Zawahiri indicated that the establishment of AQIS had nothing to do with ISIS's swift rise by noting that al-Qaeda had begun working to unite the area's disparate jihadi groups two years earlier. And yet the shadow of ISIS hung over al-Qaeda's message, announced via video: the speakers—al-Zawahiri, appointed AQIS leader Asim Umar, and branch spokesman Osama Mahmoud—all emphasized elements distinguishing al-Qaeda from ISIS. Al-Qaeda explained that the new branch's formation reflected a gradual consensus-building process, meaning that AQIS represents true unity and brotherhood. Contrary to ISIS's practice of imposing itself on others, al-Qaeda coerced no group into joining or accepting its authority; group leaders were allowed to choose their actions independently based on *sharia* considerations and their assessment of what the good of the umma requires.

The statements also challenged ISIS by reiterating that al-Qaeda and its branches operate under the command of the Islamic Emirate of Afghanistan and its leader, Mullah Omar. The obvious implications: Al-Qaeda rejects as a charade Abu Bakr al-Baghdadi's purported caliphate and stands by its oaths of allegiance, in contrast to its wayward Iraq branch. Finally, by noting that jihadis must not transgress against the umma and their jihadi brothers, cannot refuse arbitration in *sharia* court, and must labor to please Allah, rather than seeking power and hastening to claim governance and authority, al-Zawahiri criticized ISIS as oppressors who are unwilling to follow God's rule for fear that a *sharia* court would expose their sins and impede their lust for power.[2]

The debut of AQIS exemplifies this book's central assertion that a terrorist organization's decision to create a franchise is often less operational than political. Although al-Qaeda no doubt eyes its new junior partners' capabilities, operational considerations have played a secondary role in its expansion drive. Indeed, introducing branches has become a central tool by which leaders can respond to pressure to show the organization's continued relevance. Ill-prepared for the international onslaught that followed 9/11, failing to mobilize the Muslim masses to join the fight against the "far enemy," and unable to carry out spectacular attacks, al-Qaeda adopted a branching-out strategy in an effort to create an image of success and to manage its transition into the Middle East.

In theory, al-Qaeda had other organizational arrangements available. It would have preferred to absorb the rest of the jihadi camp, but jihadi groups did not respond to 9/11 in the way Osama bin Laden had expected. To their dismay, the groups not only didn't rush to join al-Qaeda—they actually resented bin Laden for bringing about the collapse of the Taliban regime and pinning American targets on their backs. The only way, then, for al-Qaeda to pursue the absorption model was through coercive means, which the organization lacked. Alternatively, it could have entered into relationships that would integrate it with peer organizations on the basis of equality, or open the World Islamic Front umbrella group to new members. But al-Qaeda fundamentally believed—as it still believes—that it is worthy of leadership, especially after the successful demonstration of its prowess on 9/11. Moreover, leaders were reluctant to share power, convinced that their reading of the strategic problems facing the umma and the derivative focus on fighting the "far enemy" was ultimately correct. Al-Qaeda was determined to lead the umma in the "right" direction.

Thus, in a sense, the branching-out model was the only way al-Qaeda could formally expand while maintaining central aspects of its ideology, strategic view, and self-perception. This model's relative flexibility allowed the organizations that joined al-Qaeda to retain real autonomy. And while no significant terrorist organization hoped to be swallowed whole by al-Qaeda, once it became evident that the group had survived—even if in rudimentary form—the American onslaught in Afghanistan, several organizations were attracted enough to al-Qaeda, and to the resources they believed it has, to contemplate joining it.

Al-Qaeda's Branching-Out Decisions

We cannot determine with confidence whether leaders decided to pursue branching-out as a comprehensive strategy before they moved to establish a Saudi franchise. Bin Laden accelerated the timeline for attacks within the kingdom, overruling local commanders' warnings that they were unprepared. The rush to go on the offensive may explain why, unlike with most subsequent franchises, leaders planned no ceremonial rollout of AQAP; it suggests that al-Qaeda did not consider at that point all elements relating to the franchising model of expansion. Nevertheless, the Saudi experience became a blueprint for al-Qaeda's subsequent growth.

Whether accidentally or by design, after Saudi Arabia, al-Qaeda—which had experimented with alternative modes of organizational expansion—settled on the branching-out model and gradually honed the process of introducing branches to produce the greatest propaganda value. Its expansion into Iraq was marked by separate announcements, first from Abu Musab al-Zarqawi and then bin Laden. The merger with the Algerian GSPC was announced in an al-Zawahiri interview marking the fifth anniversary of 9/11 and was confirmed in separate messages. The introduction of subsequent branches followed a more unified formula, including an announcement by al-Zawahiri on behalf of al-Qaeda's Central Command and a statement from prospective branch leaders, presented together in one slickly produced video message intended to rally supporters.

More important, a learning curve is evident in the way the organization has handled mergers. Al-Qaeda negotiated with al-Zarqawi's al-Tawhid wal-Jihad from a position of weakness, leading it to compromise on core subjects such as involving the Shia community in the fight, which ended up hurting al-Qaeda's cause. But when approaching subsequent mergers, bin Laden was more careful not to rush into dangerous relationships. Pressure may have undermined the quality of al-Qaeda's decision-making when it launched its Saudi and Iraqi branches, but as leaders became more acclimated to operating under an American dragnet, expansion decisions no longer reflected panic. Naturally, some expansions proved to be mixed successes or worse. The merger with al-Shabab was particularly damaging. But overall, al-Qaeda, especially when bin Laden was still alive, was cautious, ready to forgo relationships that it believed could cause more harm than good.

The nine cases the book discusses aim to shed light on the considerations shaping al-Qaeda's affiliation decisions. Al-Qaeda is most likely to enter an arena where it already has a sizable group of its own operatives and when it expects little competition from other organizations. Both Saudi Arabia and Yemen offered al-Qaeda reliable leaders, plenty of fighters who had already proven their loyalty, and no established groups that might try to prevent al-Qaeda's entry. Al-Qaeda's problem was that these were the only locations meeting these conditions. The weakness of its forces elsewhere required the less appealing alternative of branching out through mergers.

The most obvious pattern the merger cases show is that al-Qaeda has looked to bring into its fold only other jihadi groups, meaning that a merger with an organization such as the Palestinian Hamas is vanishingly improbable. But not all jihadi groups are likely partners either, considering the ideological and strategic differences within the jihadi camp. Prior to the war against the Soviets in Afghanistan and the establishment of al-Qaeda, jihadi groups' target was always the ruling government in their home countries. Although all paid lip service to the grand idea of forming a caliphate and uniting the umma, and some were willing to assist their Muslim brethren under occupation, they focused primarily on regime change and implementing *sharia* at home. Moreover, before al-Qaeda, no jihadi group made attacking the "far enemy" a central goal, even though they all harbored hostility toward the United States. Thus, adopting al-Qaeda's explicitly anti-American agenda is a prerequisite for joining al-Qaeda.

Over the years, this requirement became less strict for groups seeking al-Qaeda's patronage. To some extent, the American reaction to 9/11—particularly its increased footprint throughout the Muslim world and difficulty differentiating between the many groups populating the jihadi camp—made it easier for largely nationalistic jihadi groups to reorient their ideology. For many, the United States genuinely became an enemy. That al-Qaeda gave its franchises considerable autonomy to mix fighting the "far enemy" with attacks on the "near enemy" made it easier for jihadi groups to qualify for affiliation.

The softening of al-Qaeda's demands from potential franchisees is linked to its increased interest in attacking Western targets within Muslim countries. But al-Qaeda's flexibility was also due to its need to expand in Muslim lands at a time when it was unable to carry out attacks in the West. Moreover, the 9/11 attack changed the nature of the battle to a broad and incessant confrontation for which al-Qaeda was unprepared. Under attack by a diverse lineup of US allies, the group drifted away from its anti-American focus; leaders began characterizing governments collaborating with the United States as legitimate targets and permitting attacks on local regimes under the guise of self-defense. Getting sidetracked created common ground with nationalistic jihadi organizations, but it weakened one of al-Qaeda's defining features.

Being a jihadi group, willing to at least outwardly adopt the language of fighting the "far enemy" and to carry out some operations on Western targets within the group's area of jurisprudence, is insufficient to warrant a merger. Candidates for joining al-Qaeda also must be the dominant groups in their respective theaters with, preferably, a proven ability to unite a fractured jihadi scene. Thus the odds that al-Qaeda would stand behind a particular jihadi group in Gaza are low because the area is home to too many small jihadi groups. The Syrian case is perhaps unusual given that al-Qaeda entered a fractured scene, but the arena's importance and the cost of failing to show up for such a defining fight were more significant. Notably, al-Qaeda went to great pains to depict itself as a multiplying force rather than a competitor to the other rebel groups; the strategy paid off, raising Jabhat al-Nusra's popularity within the anti-Assad camp.

Religious value may have made some arenas more desirable than others but has thus far not been a determining factor in al-Qaeda's expansion decisions. Although we do not know how important a role Saudi Arabia's religious symbolism played compared with other considerations, it was clearly insufficient to get the group to enter the Palestinian arena. It is also possible that after its bitter experience in Saudi Arabia, al-Qaeda reduced the importance of ideological value. Perhaps leaders revised their calculations of utility and calibrated the assessment of how much public support and recruitment the group would likely gain from pursuing expansion into a religiously symbolic arena.

But symbolism was never far from al-Qaeda's leaders' minds, especially when invoking grievances such as foreign occupation and wide oppression of Sunni Muslims. In Iraq, framing the American occupation in religious terms increased the arena's appeal: it played into al-Qaeda's narrative of Crusaders scheming against the umma and presented a cause that Muslims would be comfortable supporting. Iraq's present-day condition was imbued with historical symbolism because it was easy to draw parallels to the country's past. For this reason, al-Qaeda was strongly attracted—or, more accurately, pressured—to introduce a branch in Iraq, even though entering this arena required bringing a rogue actor, al-Zarqawi, into its fold.

Foreign occupation by non-Muslims has had less symbolic value when the occupier was a nation other than the United States. The Ethiopian invasion did not lead al-Qaeda to present a franchise in Somalia; Russian oppression in Chechnya did not bring a merger with jihadis there. These examples indicate that when the United States is not the occupier, al-Qaeda feels less pressure to intervene and sees fewer potential rewards for intervening, particularly when the arenas at stake receive little media attention. It may suggest that leaders believe that al-Qaeda's anti-hegemonic fight against the United States resonates among Muslims, but also that few accept the group's wider claim that the United States is leading a broader anti-Muslim conspiracy that therefore requires viewing each attack on a Muslim country as directed from the White House. Therefore, where al-Qaeda cannot make a compelling argument that the United States is invading or directly oppressing Muslims, characteristics particular to the arena may play an important role in shaping al-Qaeda's decisions: Chechnya is difficult to access, and in Somalia negative impressions from the 1990s—supplemented by recommendations from al-Qaeda commanders on the ground against joining with al-Shabab—translated to reluctance to admitting the group.

Finally, al-Qaeda views low-cost mergers as a tool to confront rivals. Al-Qaeda was concerned that reconciliation between the Gama'a Islamiya and the Egyptian regime and between the Libyan Islamic Fighting Group and the Libyan state might further weaken the jihadi movement and thus undermine confidence in al-Qaeda's ideology. Consequently, it sought to use assets it had pocketed earlier—its close relationship with factions of these groups who had been operating alongside it—in a strategic way. The marginal resources that al-Qaeda invested in announced mergers with these factions indicates that leaders deemed them low-risk moves with only middling odds of success. Al-Qaeda would see clear gains if its gambit succeeded: it would discredit the traditional leadership of the GI and the LIFG, keep important jihadi actors in the struggle, and perhaps even give al-Qaeda footholds in desired arenas it could not enter otherwise. But when the gambit failed, al-Qaeda simply moved on.

The Consequences of al-Qaeda's Franchising

Although franchising hardly deserves all the blame for al-Qaeda's post–9/11 downward trajectory, the strategy proved dangerous and, ultimately, detrimental. By branching out, al-Qaeda put its fate in the hands of its affiliates. Some served al-Qaeda well. The Yemen branch proved reliable and capable. When attrition in the AQC ranks nearly emptied its bench of the experienced old guard, AQAP stepped in and gradually assumed responsibilities previously reserved to al-Qaeda's core. And in Syria, JN showed impressive resilience: not only did it survive the rise of ISIS, assaults by the Assad regime and its allies, and an American bombing campaign—the branch managed to assume control over territory without alienating other rebel groups or the local Syrian population.

Elsewhere, al-Qaeda's affiliates ended up doing little more than allow leaders to boast that the group had put down roots in new arenas. On balance, for example, its expansion to North Africa has probably proved a net positive: the group lost some members to ISIS, but AQIM has served as a bulwark against that group's expansion in Algeria, and it may prove even more valuable if instability in the theater opens up new opportunities to lead an insurgency.

If some al-Qaeda affiliates have contributed little to the group's operational strength and reputation, others have inflicted real damage. Bin Laden made Saudi Arabia the most important cause in al-Qaeda's struggle and no doubt expected his personal connections to have the greatest impact in his home country. Instead, he saw his branch collapse, exposing the limited appeal of the group's ideology and methods in the country with the greatest religious significance—one in which he expected Islamic piety to attract large popular support.

But whereas the failure in Saudi Arabia was of the organization's own doing, it was the branches in Iraq and Somalia, the product of mergers, that caused the gravest damage to the al-Qaeda brand name. In Somalia, al-Qaeda partnered with a group whose authoritarian leader purged its ranks, killed foreign volunteers in a drama that played out on social media for the whole jihadi movement to witness, and likely contributed to clearing Somalia of AQC's representatives. The repression was so brutal that some of al-Shabab's leaders preferred governmental captivity to death at the hands of Ahmed Abdi Godane's thugs.

In Iraq, ISI brutality led other Sunni groups, including some former allies, to take arms and even cooperate with the United States—their original target!—to fight it. Many observers blamed al-Qaeda for the fratricidal violence in Iraq, shrinking support for the group to new lows throughout the Muslim world. Ironically, although it was ISI's actions that damaged the parent organization's reputation, in its second iteration the branch was able to rebrand itself after battlefield success brought enormous power. Meanwhile, al-Qaeda, rejecting ISI's methods, was unable to show similar fighting prowess and, therefore, to use the Iraq conflict to revitalize. And even when leaders tried to learn from their mistakes by forming closer relations with locals, showing greater sensitivity to their needs and traditions, and soft-pedaling their ideology, al-Qaeda could never completely repair its damaged reputation. The perils of franchising became most evident when the Iraqi branch expanded to the Syrian arena and directly challenged the parent organization; having long benefited from al-Qaeda's brand name in jihadi circles, ISI leaders turned a problematic, unruly franchise into a powerhouse that eclipsed al-Qaeda.

It is no surprise that at one time, and as part of the public war of words between al-Qaeda and (the renamed) ISIS, the latter called on al-Qaeda's branches elsewhere to weigh in and clearly state their position on ISIS's methodology and whether they stood behind accusations that it had become a *takfiri* group.[3] This appeal reflected the extent to which the affiliates accrued status and power independent of al-Qaeda's Central Command, and in fact had separate set of interests that only partially overlapped with that of AQC. At the same time, it demonstrated leaders' difficulty in eliciting obedience from their branches and commanding their respect.

Al-Qaeda's inability to settle the rift between its Iraqi and Syrian branches was also damaging by exposing al-Zawahiri's inability to control the group's affiliates. Control had been a problem since al-Qaeda took in al-Zarqawi's group, but as long as bin Laden was alive, disgruntled affiliates were careful to show—at least outwardly—deference and respect to the icon. Inhibitions were lifted after al-Zawahiri succeeded bin Laden, evidenced by not only ISIS's rebellion but the social-media criticism by members of affiliates who called on al-Zawahiri to exert control over the organization, suppress challengers, and check authoritarian branch leaders' excesses.[4] These public appeals—highlighting the fact that aggrieved members had no direct channels to AQC—exposed fissures within the al-Qaeda empire as well as the leadership's helplessness. Al-Zawahiri responded, hoping to correct the impression that he was not in control, but the crisis continued, and his message proved unpersuasive.

Despite the mixed success of al-Qaeda's branching-out plans, it is hardly clear that expansion by different means would have improved the organization's fortunes. After all, the source of al-Qaeda's problems was its unrealistic strategy and its inability to bridge the gap between its "far enemy" focus and its aspirations for change in the Middle East. Once it became clear that the Muslim masses and the jihadi camp at large were unresponsive to al-Qaeda's message, leaders needed to fundamentally rethink their program. But that would have implied admitting how greatly bin Laden had miscalculated, and he was either too blind to see the problems or, more likely, lacked the courage and humility to engage in such soul-searching. Pursuing a branching-out strategy was therefore an attractive alternative that allowed al-Qaeda to move forward and even claim progress without challenging its core assumptions, but it was an alternative that offered limited benefits and considerable costs.

Regardless of its organizational choices, al-Qaeda's failure to help jihadis overcome regimes' overwhelming counterterrorism efforts—a fight made even more asymmetrical by involving the United States—inevitably endangered the group's ability to remain cohesive. However, in going the franchising route, giving affiliates the benefits of a brand name while preserving their organizational structure, al-Qaeda hastened its own hollowing-out. The group expanded geographically, but its resources did not increase correspondingly to give it sufficient leverage over its affiliates. Moreover, from their hiding places, al-Qaeda leaders could not exert control and assure that the branches were complying with al-Zawahiri's directives.

Threats to al-Qaeda's cohesion have come not only from affiliates through merger, as evidenced in the appeal—and, more important, success—of ISIS's radicalism. Even operatives belonging to AQAP, al-Qaeda's most trusted franchise and an in-house creation, have grown restless; with al-Qaeda stagnating and ISIS delivering, rank-and-file jihadis less immersed in theological debates and more easily impressed by prestige and resources have considered switching sides. AQAP's leadership has not always seemed to fully back al-Zawahiri, sometimes sounding as if the branch sees itself as a neutral third side, not directly involved in the conflict between al-Qaeda and ISIS.[5] In fact, it was not until ISIS announced a Yemen *wilaya* (province) that AQAP came out strongly against the insurgent group.[6]

Between Jihadist Organizations and Islamic Emirates

As problematic as al-Qaeda's branching-out strategy was, its weaknesses loomed even larger when ISIS declared itself a caliphate and its leader a caliph to whom all Muslims must submit. In general, al-Qaeda and ISIS share similar strategic goals—most important, the reintroduction of the caliphate and establishing *sharia* rule over a unified umma. Notwithstanding these elements of convergence, there is a wide ideological gap between al-Qaeda and its former franchise on how to achieve these goals. Al-Qaeda emphasizes fighting the "far enemy" and postponing governance, while ISIS has been all too willing to fight the "near enemy" while simultaneously introducing an Islamic state.

For over a decade, al-Qaeda leaders were confident that the *bay'a* its franchises pledged guaranteed their obedience. Al-Qaeda did not seem to fear that Islamic emirates—localized Islamic states, hierarchically higher than organizations—would release subordinates from their promises of allegiance. The group continued to view its Iraqi branch as a subordinate, even after it announced the establishment of a state and changed its name to the Islamic State of Iraq.[7] When bin Laden rejected Nasir al-Wuhayshi's request to establish an emirate in Yemen, it was due to concerns that by announcing emirates, the group would be raising the stakes too high in the confrontation with the United States, not because emirates might pose a challenge to al-Qaeda's authority.[8] Moreover, the story of al-Qaeda's *bay'a* to Mullah Omar, particularly al-Qaeda's flexible use of its pledge to suit its changing needs, attests to the minor religious importance it attributed to emirates. Notably, the Taliban's authority did not prevent al-Qaeda from attacking the United States against Mullah Omar's express wishes.[9]

A caliphate would pose a greater challenge than an emirate, but al-Qaeda did not believe that the United States would let an Islamic emirate survive, making a caliphate, with its even greater authority and symbolism, a highly unlikely threat. In addition, al-Qaeda's leaders probably did not believe that any actor would be so audacious as to make a claim to the caliphate; no contender would be able to present sufficient capabilities and territorial control and, consequently, convince the umma that conditions are ripe to re-establish the caliphate and that it has legitimate authority to make this move.

ISIS's challenge proved al-Qaeda wrong and put it on the defensive. Despite bin Laden's repeated warnings that the war against the "Zionist-Crusader alliance" has been ongoing for centuries and would not likely end in the lifetime of today's mujahideen, many jihadis lacked infinite patience and approved of interim steps short of re-establishing the caliphate and the victory of "truth" over "falsehood." But while other jihadi leaders settled for forming emirates—using them to encourage donors, followers, and potential recruits in need of tangible evidence of progress,[10] and in the service of the leaders' self-aggrandizing ambition—ISIS aimed at the highest prize, the caliphate. It followed its grand announcement with a demand that other jihadi organizations and, essentially, all Muslims pledge allegiance to the self-styled caliph. In introducing a caliph, ISIS was to become the sole authority, thus voiding the legitimacy of all other jihadi groups. Al-Qaeda—long hopeful that the jihadi camp would accept its leadership en masse and willing to reach merger agreements giving jihadi groups considerable autonomy—ended up facing a powerful foe that refused to share power and did not hesitate to use extreme violence to impose its authority on fellow jihadis.

Jihadi scholars had heatedly debated the legal prerequisites for establishing an Islamic state when the Taliban declared itself the rulers of the Islamic

Emirate of Afghanistan; discussions surged when the Islamic State of Iraq was announced in 2006 and, once again, when the ISI expanded into Syria and proclaimed the caliphate. Scholars who opposed the establishment of the ISI and later ISIS viewed these steps as posturing and self-serving acts by leaders seeking to manipulate a divided jihadi field to put them on top. Critics argued that an Islamic state must have substance by providing security and governance to the populace residing in the territory it controls.

Al-Qaeda's Iraqi branch did not inform AQC before establishing the ISI, essentially forcing bin Laden to go along and give his blessing to the move post facto. But overall, in the post–9/11 era al-Qaeda was inclined to see the establishment of emirates, let alone the caliphate, as premature. The organization's rejection of ambitious governance projects may have been influenced by theological considerations, but strategic and organizational interests were paramount. Al-Qaeda's organizational interest dictated rejecting the establishment of entities that would chip away at its authority (and at what limited power al-Qaeda had over affiliates). Its US-first strategy required sacrificing governance for a focus on fighting, particularly given the lessons it learned from its Iraqi experience. Establishing an Islamic state would put tremendous strain on scarce resources, force fighters to defend assets that could not be protected, and cause division when unity was the ultimate goal.

Expressing its opposition to ISIS's methods and proclamations, al-Qaeda maintained that an Islamic state should be a force for unity, not division,[11] and accused ISIS of imposing itself on people and other jihadi groups. No one can establish an Islamic emirate, al-Qaeda declared, without consulting all mujahideen, their commanders, and their scholars. Moreover, an Islamic state, let alone a caliphate, requires the consent of the broader umma.[12] The group reiterated its commitment to the caliphate project but argued that forming one would be premature before, at least, enemies were driven out of Muslim lands.

Al-Qaeda was hardly alone in this position. The influential Jordanian jihadi scholar Abu Muhammad al-Maqdisi declared that al-Baghdadi's caliphate was a conspiracy to fragment and weaken the ranks of the mujahideen; he strongly criticized ISIS for corrupting the jihadi movement, distorting the project of the caliphate, acting without religious support, and leading jihadis to fight each other instead of focusing on the tyrant enemies.[13]

In another example, the then-leader of the Abdullah Azzam Brigades in Lebanon, Majid bin Muhammad al Majid, wrote an open letter to al-Zawahiri expressing reservations about prematurely establishing Islamic

states. He argued that the jihadi movement must create much greater awareness of its project and attract large numbers of supporters before moving
to establish an Islamic state. What is the point, he wondered, of founding
an emirate before it is able to defend itself from Western assault? In addition, al-Majid worried that in an arena where a number of jihadi groups are
fighting a mutual non-Muslim enemy, the costs of founding an emirate far
outweigh any possible benefits. He maintained that the announcement of
a unified Islamic state for Iraq and Syria had split the mujhaideen, leading
to infighting instead of unity, while strengthening the Assad regime and
its allies. Moreover, al-Majid stated, establishing a state implies assuming a
greater governance role. But taking on more responsibilities requires diverting resources from the fight against the Syrian regime and, thus, endangering
the whole project.[14]

ISIS's 2014 territorial gains gave that organization considerable leverage in
this debate, weakening the argument that ISIS's move was invalid because it
must first exercise control over territory and engage in governance. Moreover,
with the announcement of the caliphate, al-Baghdadi was in a stronger position to dismiss critics' authority and, consequently, their ability to challenge
ISIS's actions. Even as most scholars denounced ISIS, the group's victories
persuaded enthusiastic young jihadis that they no longer needed to patiently
wait, as other leaders insisted, but could realize their dream and actively participate in the historical event of building the caliphate. As ISIS created the
impression that the prize of an Islamic state was within reach, al-Qaeda's focus
on organizational expansion, however prudent, appeared out of touch with
the wishes of a restless generation of radicals.

The Future of al-Qaeda

While al-Qaeda's expansion strategy did little to promote the group's political objectives, it did help al-Qaeda retain its unique status within the jihadi
movement years after the group's last successful mass-casualties attack in the
West. But as the memory of 9/11 faded, al-Qaeda had little to show its constituency and financial supporters. Leaders tried, unpersuasively, to take credit
for the global economic crisis of 2008, which they portrayed as a delayed
consequence of the 2001 attack on the American homeland,[15] and later for
the Arab Awakening, but attracted few new supporters. Franchises kept the
brand name alive, but the costs of relying on branches kept mounting, and a
few uncoordinated campaigns of jihadi violence—indicating a lack of central
strategy—did not reverse the organization's rot.

And then bin Laden was killed and was succeeded by al-Zawahiri. The organization survived its first leadership transition, but its new head was a poor replacement for the iconic founder. It is impossible to know whether bin Laden could have prevented the challenge that ISIS mounted against al-Qaeda; he may have been the dam that stanched a flooding river, but the organization was fracturing even while he was nominally in charge. Bin Laden's stature and authority probably postponed the challenge, but he had an expiration date, not just in death.

Al-Zawahiri, unsurprisingly, has been an easier target for dissent within the jihadi movement. As al-Qaeda's relationship with ISIS collapsed and members of JN and ISIS began fighting and killing each other, misgivings regarding al-Zawahiri's leadership grew louder. Online jihadi forums saw increasingly harsh denunciations; some users went so far as to call al-Zawahiri a "disbeliever"—unthinkable prior to the rift with ISIS.[16]

The open conflict with ISIS exposed al-Qaeda's challenge in maintaining its image as the leader of the global jihadi movement; the organization had lost its edge while savvier actors, standing for even more extreme positions, had risen. This is not simply a matter of an aging organization reaching the boundaries of its power and losing appeal to younger and more agile competitors. Al-Qaeda was unable to pull off another attack on the scale of 9/11, and its leaders' need to stay in hiding no doubt contributed to the group's weakening. But al-Qaeda faces a greater problem: where it once was an ideological innovator, the tip of the jihadi spear, for some al-Qaeda now appears too staid and moderate. In the past it could rely on a supportive cadre of jihadi fighters and scholars, but at present al-Qaeda finds these pillars less certain and their impact greatly diminished.

True, in the struggle with ISIS, al-Zawahiri gained the support of some jihadi heavyweights. The Jordanian al-Maqdisi even issued a strongly worded fatwa against al-Baghdadi and ISIS; his words are remarkably harsh:

> I announce, here, that Tandheem al-Dawla fil-Iraq wal-Shaam [the organization the State in Iraq and the Levant] is a deviant organization from the path of truth; they are aggressors against the mujahideen. They lean toward *ghuluw* [extremism]. They have become embroiled in the spilling of unlawful blood, the sequestration of their wealth, war booty, and [the] regions which they have liberated from the regime. [This group] has besmirched the name of jihad and the elite mujahideen. [They have] turned their rifles from the chests of the apostates and those at war [with the Muslims] to the chests of the mujahideen

and the Muslims, as well as other documented deviances. . . . This statement is the same as retracting the Islamic pretext from this rebellious organization.[17]

But the fragmentation of religious authority that characterized the jihadi movement even prior to 9/11 has worsened in recent years. A decade and a half of fighting raised the stature of jihadi "warriors"—some of whom used their claim to authenticity to assume authority—at the expense of religious scholars. The expansion of social media also contributed to the weakening of the class of jihadi scholars by offering platforms and a vast audience for virulent voices, some with less religious training but greater skill than old-guard scholars for capturing sympathizers' imagination. As a result, it has become even more difficult for al-Qaeda to fend off challenges from ultra-radical competitors.

And so al-Qaeda has found itself in a dogfight over the support of jihadis, forced to depend on scholars outside the organization in a way it did not when bin Laden was alive and al-Qaeda had among its leadership echelon figures with considerable religious clout, such as Abu Hafs al-Mauritani and Abu Yahya al-Libi. Its efforts to solicit statements of support from fighters and scholars who command admiration and followers have been relatively successful, exemplified by al-Maqdisi's messages and letters of support from the likes of Abu Qatada al-Filistini.[18] But the appeal of the extremism of al-Zarqawi and his successors has grown, while fewer jihadis look to veteran scholars for guidance.

One complicating factor is that many experienced jihadi scholars are forced to communicate from prison cells, leaving room for critics to challenge their messages' authenticity and credibility, arguing that the authors lack a complete picture of the situation and that interested regimes may have forged, compelled, or edited the statements. Some imprisoned jihadi scholars have fought back against these accusations. For example, Abu Qatada maintained that prison did not prevent him from gaining all the information he needs but only limited his ability to state it frequently enough; he lamented that these constraints leave the field exposed to "the minors and the fanatics clinging to the Dawla [ISIS] like the ignorant clings to his tribe without understanding or awareness."[19]

When, during the Algerian civil war of the 1990s, the Armed Islamic Group overreached, it suffered tremendous backlash—not least from scholars—and saw all external support dissipate. It is possible that extreme violence and the excommunication of whole communities could again lead to the implosion of the group responsible, but the withdrawal of scholars' support for such groups would likely have less impact than in the past. The radicalization of the jihadi scene suggests that, at present, there is a greater space for "legitimate" violence: a significant segment of the jihadi community accepts and even celebrates higher levels of violence, a broader set of targets, and fratricidal violence.

This is the reason that Abu Qatada lamented the negative consequences of the proliferation of online fatwas that are written, he argued, by people who lack sufficient knowledge and encourage extreme positions instead of fostering unity. In his words:

> I warn my mujahideen brothers, including commanders and soldiers, against listening to fatwas issued by some from afar. They are written by starters among the students of knowledge, or claiming to be students of knowledge, who obligate one group to submit to another.... Disagreement can only be resolved with conciliation.... Those who write these fatwas on websites and elsewhere are completely insignificant. They tempt those who support them to take extreme positions without achieving the purpose, which is to respond to the disagreement and to accomplish reconciliation and unity. It will lead to more division and renewed provocation of hearts. These ignorant fatwas may even rush the brothers to fight one another, as the people of experience before know. You will not fail to find an ignorant who completely invalidates the other with these strange fatwas.[20]

Indeed, while squeezed by condemnations left and right, ISIS still enjoys considerable support among jihadis worldwide, and the stream of foreign volunteers heading to its territory suggests it is even increasing. Its caliphate-building project has captured the imagination of many young Muslims (though one must be careful not to overstate this attraction—tens of thousands of immigrants to ISIS's country represent only a tiny fraction of the 1.6 billion Muslims worldwide). The group is also supported by some popular religious figures such as the Bahraini Turki al-Bin'ali, and the management of several leading jihadi forums,[21] though its controversial caliphate move cost it prominent supporters such as the Mauritanian scholar Abu al-Mundhir al-Shinqiti.[22]

Al-Qaeda's weakness is also evident in the fact that AQC needs its affiliates more than ever, to serve as a bulwark against ISIS's expansion, but can hardly take their loyalty for granted. Thus far, none has defected: in response to ISIS's caliphate bid, al-Qaeda's franchises reconfirmed their support of al-Zawahiri;[23] even Ahmad Umar, who succeeded Godane as al-Shabab's leader, skipped the opportunity to reorient his group and renewed his pledge to al-Qaeda.[24] Retaining the branches' allegiance represents a success for the embattled al-Zawahiri, though it is hard to believe that this loyalty is based only on ideological convictions, adherence to the branch leaders' oaths of allegiance, and rejection of ISIS's extreme brutality. No doubt the leaders weighed their own interests in retaining their positions and autonomy; the branches' loyalty may well be conditional—and temporary.

Moreover, the statements of support for al-Zawahiri hardly quieted al-Qaeda's internal threat. Branches' leaders face pressure from rank-and-file members, and even some in leadership positions, who would like to get on the ISIS bandwagon and enjoy the group's glory and resources.[25] Leaders of AQIM's Central Region, for example, issued a message supporting al-Baghdadi and calling to those fighting ISIS to repent and accept its authority;[26] a few months later, they formally pledged loyalty to al-Baghdadi.[27] Essentially, the future cohesiveness of al-Qaeda has become intricately linked to the fortune of ISIS. The more established the "caliphate" becomes and the more territories and people it brings under its control, the greater the internal pressure al-Qaeda's branches experience.

The rise of ISIS plays into the continuous power shift within al-Qaeda, from its base in Pakistan to the Middle East and to its franchises. Due to the deaths of most of al-Qaeda's first generation of leaders, the limitations on the operational ability of what is left of AQC, the new opportunities for success in the Middle East following the Arab Awakening, and the need to confront the ISIS threat, AQC is now heavily dependent on its branches. The nomination of al-Wuhayshi as al-Qaeda's general manager shows that AQAP has been assuming greater responsibilities, gradually replacing AQC in Pakistan. In transitioning to the Middle East (reflected also in the establishment in Syria of Khorasan cells planning attacks in the West), al-Zawahiri is attempting to take advantage of operational opportunities to revitalize al-Qaeda, but the increasing decentralization makes AQC, and him specifically, more vulnerable to challenges from the branches. Calls in online forums for al-Wuhayshi to replace al-Zawahiri may not have been orchestrated by AQAP,[28] but they reflected a sentiment that the star of al-Wuhayshi (who was killed in a drone strike in June 2015) was rising while trust in al-Zawahiri's leadership was in decline.

Given the high attrition among al-Qaeda's leaders, it is hard to tell how long al-Zawahiri will lead the group, or who will be around to take over if and when al-Zawahiri dies or steps down. A leadership change at a time of crisis, particularly in an organization with autonomous franchises spread over two continents, can easily lead to its disintegration. But if succession progresses smoothly and brings forward a charismatic and savvy leader more capable of reforming al-Qaeda to meet new challenges and to harness new technologies, it may prove to be instrumental to the organization's revitalization.

* * *

Al-Qaeda's position is weaker than anytime since it became a household name worldwide, synonymous with non-state terrorism. It is headed by an uninspiring leader, its strategy is in shambles, the United States routinely targets its commanders from the air, and ISIS—its main competitor—is much more exciting and successful. Yet it is too early to write al-Qaeda's obituary. It remains a dangerous actor. The group's anti-American strategy is bound to fail, but it may still score tactical successes by carrying out attacks on targets in the West. Moreover, the Arab Awakening gave al-Qaeda a second lease on life: although ISIS's meteoric rise represents an existential threat, the disintegration of states in the Middle East (primarily Yemen, Libya, and Syria) offers al-Qaeda an unprecedented opportunity for a second start.

The organization has not revised its fundamental assumptions about the conflict, but it has shown in recent years an ability to learn. In a process that preceded the Arab revolutions but accelerated considerably once they began, al-Qaeda has been making a serious effort to expand its appeal beyond the community of jihadi sympathizers to a wider constituency of Sunni Muslims. As part of an effort to improve the group's image, al-Zawahiri instructed branches to refrain from carrying out attacks that might lead to the death of innocent Muslims. By making these instructions public, al-Qaeda also reminded ordinary Muslims of its code of conduct.[29] Additionally, al-Qaeda quickly apologized for incidents of excesses from within its ranks[30] and denounced operations that resulted in mass civilian casualties, even when carried out by its allies.[31]

Learning is also notable in al-Qaeda's attitude toward the role of violence. While exaggerating its own role in bringing about the revolutions, al-Qaeda took note of the masses' willingness to take to the streets and their ability to effect change peacefully. Consequently, in its statements since 2011, al-Qaeda has emphasized the importance of its jihad as complementary to the work of nonviolent protest movements. In some places, where regimes suppress protesters, violence becomes essential; elsewhere, it supports the masses' interests and helps preserve their political gains.[32] Al-Qaeda has also changed the way it interacts with civilian populations: in Yemen, Syria, and Mali, the group has labored to garner public support by providing services and avoiding the imposition of harsh Islamic punishments. Unlike ISIS's brutal imposition of its version of *sharia*, al-Qaeda has taken a softer approach—though still fundamentally extreme—that emphasizes *da'wa* and education.

Al-Qaeda has a distinct transnational ideology that could appeal to many Muslims seeking common identity beyond their own states' borders. Its assertions that it aspires to establish the coveted caliphate but prioritizes fighting the umma's enemies first and believes that a caliphate cannot be introduced without extensive and broad consultation and the people's support resonate better with ordinary Muslims than does ISIS's worldview. Moreover, al-Qaeda could position itself as a bridge between an umma-oriented perspective and nationally focused groups. It has also benefited from ISIS's extremism, which has made al-Qaeda appear moderate and almost reasonable in comparison.

Under these conditions, one cannot rule out the possibility that al-Qaeda may be able to persuade more people to give it a second look, especially if it revises its unrealistic anti-American platform and focuses instead on the Middle East and North Africa. The Arab Awakening created opportunities for al-Qaeda to get closer to Muslim communities, defend them, and provide services while cooperating with other actors. These experiences are essential—in order to rejuvenate, al-Qaeda must show that it can do more than kill. Governance is particularly important because ISIS has created new standards for success, while regional instability has created ungoverned spaces where jihadi groups could demonstrate their ability to rule.

Ironically, the Obama administration's policies could also contribute to an al-Qaeda recovery. ISIS's overreach has brought the American military back to the region, bolstering al-Qaeda's narrative that it was correct all along when it argued that the United States would never allow the umma to determine its own fate.[33] The American-led intervention in Iraq and Syria could also help al-Qaeda by arresting ISIS's expansion. Were President Obama's declaration that the United States will "degrade and ultimately destroy" the Islamic State to come true, al-Qaeda is bound to gain the allegiance of many ISIS supporters.[34] American bombing of JN positions in Syria strengthened the branch's reputation and facilitated its offensive against US-supported rebel groups in Northern Syria, leading in effect to their eradication and to the expansion of JN's dominance in the area. The administration's reluctance to send ground troops to the Middle East could also aid al-Qaeda's recovery. The parameters of US intervention imply that in locations where al-Qaeda shifted its focus from terrorism to building insurgent forces, the risk to these forces' survival is limited. But al-Qaeda does not rely solely on President Obama's aversion for military interventions: by embedding its branches, primarily in Syria and Yemen, within broad-based Sunni popular movements and forging strong ties with local actors, al-Qaeda makes an American intervention—which would alienate the Sunni population—a more complicated enterprise.

Notwithstanding this silver lining for al-Qaeda, to successfully pursue all the measures that could enhance its position, it must revisit core assumptions, admit its mistakes, and ultimately become a different kind of organization. As long as al-Zawahiri is at the helm, the odds that al-Qaeda would undergo such a radical change are low. Notwithstanding its continuing expansion, al-Qaeda's decline is unlikely to be arrested. It is doubtful that the fearsome organization that Osama bin Laden built will survive to unite the umma and proclaim the caliphate to which it has always aspired.

Notes

CHAPTER I

1. Eli Lake and Josh Rogin, "Al Qaeda Conference Call Intercepted by U.S. Officials Sparks Alerts," *The Daily Beast*, August 7, 2013.

2. "Al-Qaeda Releases Video for 13th Anniversary of 9/11, Denies Reports of Waning Influence," Site Intelligence Group, September 14, 2014.

3. Ahmed Rashid, *Pakistan on the Brink: The Future of America, Pakistan, and Afghanistan* (New York: Viking, 2012), 197.

4. Stephen Tankel, *Storming the World Stage: The Story of Lashkar-e-Taiba* (Oxford: Oxford University Press, 2011).

5. International Crisis Group, *Indonesia Backgrounder: How the Jemaah Islamiyah Terrorist Network Operates*, Asia Report No. 43, December 2002; International Crisis Group, *Jemaah Islamiyah in South East Asia: Damaged But Still Dangerous*, Asia Report No. 63, August 2003.

6. For example, Peter Krause, "The Structure of Success: How the Internal Distribution of Power Drives Armed Group Behavior and National Movement Effectiveness," *International Security* 38:3 (Winter 2013–2014), 72–116; Barak Mendelsohn, "Dominant Violent Non-State Groups in a Competitive Environment: Insights from Israeli and Palestinian experience," Paper presented at the annual meeting of the American Political Science Association, Chicago, August 29–September 1, 2013.

7. Barak Mendelsohn, *Combating Jihadism: American Hegemony and Interstate Cooperation in the War on Terrorism* (Chicago: University of Chicago Press, 2009).

8. David Cook, *Understanding Jihad* (Berkeley: University of California Press, 2005).

9. Quintan Wiktorowicz, "Anatomy of the Salafi Movement," *Studies in Conflict and Terrorism* 29 (2006), 207–239. Note that the division is imperfect; as Joas Wagemakers masterfully demonstrates, even among senior figures within the jihadi movement there are important tendencies associated with the other Salafi strands. See Joas Wagemakers, *A Quietist Jihadi: The Ideology and Influence of Abu Muhammad al-Maqdisi* (Cambridge, UK: Cambridge University Press, 2012).

10. John Mueller, *Overblown: How Politicians and Terrorism Industry Inflate National Security Threats, and Why We Believe Them* (New York: Free Press, 2006).

11. Audrey Kurth Cronin, *Ending Terrorism: Lessons for Defeating al-Qaeda* (London: Routledge, 2008), 59–60.

12. For example, in 2007 Michael Scheuer, the former CIA analyst who created the agency's bin Laden unit during the 1990s, counted 29 al-Qaeda franchises. See Michael Scheuer, "Al-Qaeda's Waiting Game," *The American Conservative*, May 21, 2007. In comparison, a team of researchers in the Combating Terrorism Center (CTC) determined that through mergers al-Qaeda increased its presence in at least 19 countries. "Al Qa'ida's Five Aspects of Power," *CTC Sentinel* 2:1 (January 2009), 4.

13. Hoffman claimed that the category of "affiliates and associates ... embraces formally established insurgent or terrorist groups who over the years have benefited from bin Laden's largesse and/or spiritual guidance and/or have received training, arms, money and other assistance from al-Qaeda." See Bruce Hoffman, "Combating Al Qaeda and the Militant Islamic Threat," Testimony presented to the House Armed Services Committee, Subcommittee on Terrorism, Unconventional Threats and Capabilities (February 16, 2006).

14. For example, see The Abbottabad Documents, Combating Terrorism Center, SOCOM-2012-0000004, and SOCOM-2012-0000007, May 3, 2012. See also Nelly Lahoud, *Beware of Imitators: Al-Qa'ida Through the Lens of Its Confidential Secretary* (West Point, NY: Combating Terrorism Center, June 2012).

CHAPTER 2

1. Marc Sageman, *Leaderless Jihad: Terror Networks in the Twenty-First Century* (Philadelphia: University of Pennsylvania Press, 2008).

2. John Arquilla and David Ronfeldt (Eds.), *Networks and Netwars: The Future of Terror, Crime, and Militancy* (Santa Monica, CA: RAND, 2001).

3. Navin Bapat and Kanisha Bond, "Alliances between Militant Groups," *British Journal of Political Science* 42:4 (2012), 793–824.

4. Tricia Bacon, *Strange Bedfellows or Brothers-In-Arms: Why Terrorist Groups Ally*, Ph.D. dissertation, Georgetown University (2013), 2.

5. Ibid., 9.

6. Ely Karmon, *Coalitions between Terrorist Organizations: Revolutionaries, Nationalists, and Islamists* (Leiden: Martinus Nijhoff Publishers, 2005).

7. Kent Layne Oots, *A Political Organization Approach to Transnational Terrorism* (New York: Greenwood Press, 1986), 118.

8. Karmon, *Coalitions between Terrorist Organizations*; Bacon, *Strange Bedfellows*. On tactical cooperation between terrorist organizations, see Oots, *A Political Organization Approach to Transnational Terrorism*.

9. Mia Bloom, *Dying to Kill: The Allure of Suicide Terror* (New York: Columbia University Press, 2005); Andrew Kydd and Barbara Walter, "The Strategies of Terrorism," *International Security* 31 (2006), 49–80.

10. Michael Horowitz and Phillip Potter, "Allying to Kill: Terrorist Intergroup Cooperation and the Consequences for Lethality," *Journal of Conflict Resolution* 58:2 (2014), 199–225; Brian Phillips, "Terrorist Group Cooperation and Longevity," *International Studies Quarterly* 58:2 (2013), 336–447.

11. For example, Wendy Pearlman and Kathleen Gallagher Cunningham, "Nonstate Actors Fragmentation, and Conflict Processes," *Journal of Conflict Resolution* 56:1 (2012), 3–15; Kristin Bakke, Kathleen Gallagher Cunningham, and Lee Seymour, "A Plague of Initials: Fragmentation, Cohesion, and Infighting in Civil Wars," *Perspectives on Politics* 10:2 (2012), 265–283; Cunningham Kathleen Gallagher, Kristin Bakke, and Lee Seymour, "Shirts Today, Skins Tomorrow: Dual Contests and the Effects of Fragmentation in Self-Determinations Disputes," *Journal of Conflict Resolution* 56:1 (2012), 67–93. For a notable exception, see Paul Staniland, *Networks of Rebellion: Explaining Insurgent Cohesion and Collapse* (Ithaca, NY: Cornell University Press, 2014).

12. For example, see Fotinii Christia, *Alliance Formation in Civil Wars* (Cambridge, UK: Cambridge University Press, 2012); Abdulkader H. Sinno, *Organizations at War in Afghanistan and Beyond* (Ithaca, NY: Cornell University Press, 2009).

13. Assaf Moghadam, "Cooperation between Terrorist Organizations," paper presented at the annual convention of the International Studies Association. San Diego, April 1–4, 2012.

14. Krause, "The Structure of Success."

15. Mendelsohn, "Dominant Violent Non-State Groups in a Competitive Environment."

16. Bárak Mendelsohn, "The Battle for Algeria: Explaining Fratricidal Violence Among Violent Non-State Actors," paper presented at the annual meeting of the American Political Science Association, San Francisco, September 3–6, 2015.

17. Ayman al-Zawahiri, "Letter from al-Zawahiri to al-Zarqawi, 9 July 2005," DNI.gov, October 11, 2005.

18. Mendelsohn, "Dominant Violent Non-State Groups in a Competitive Environment."

19. Daniel Byman, "Buddies or Burdens? Understanding the Al Qaeda Relationship with Its Affiliate Organizations," *Security Studies* 23 (2014), 431–470; Daniel Byman, *Breaking the Bonds between Al-Qa'ida and Its Affiliate Organizations*, Analysis Paper Number 27 (Washington, DC: The Brookings Institution, August 2012).

20. Previously it was responsible for all of Indonesia.

21. Sidney Jones, "The Changing Nature of Jemaah Islamiyah," *Australian Journal of International Affairs* 59:2 (2005), 170.

22. Jacob Shapiro, "Organizing Terror: Hierarchy and Networks in Covert Organizations," Manuscript, Department of Political Science, Stanford University, August 2005.

23. Ibid.

24. Bakke, Cunningham, and Seymour, "A Plague of Initials," 269.

25. G. John Ikenberry, *After Victory: Institutions, Strategic Restraint, and the Rebuilding of Public Order after Major Wars* (Princeton, NJ: Princeton University Press, 2001); Robert Keohane, *After Hegemony: Cooperation and Discord in the World Political Economy* (Princeton, NJ: Princeton University Press, 1984).

26. Byman, "Buddies or Burdens?," 438.

27. Stephen Walt, *Origins of Alliances* (Ithaca, NY: Cornell University Press, 1987).

28. Byman, "Buddies or Burdens?," 438.

29. Abu Bakr al-Baghdadi, "ISI Leader Rebrands ISI and al-Nusra Front as 'Islamic State in Iraq and the Levant,'" Site Intelligence Group, April 8, 2013.

30. Byman, "Buddies or Burdens?," 434.

31. The Abbottabad Documents, SOCOM-2012-0000009.

32. Aron Lund, "The Politics of the Islamic Front, Part 2: An Umbrella Organization," Carnegie Endowment for International Peace, January 15, 2014.

CHAPTER 3

1. Barak Mendelsohn, "Al Qaeda's Palestinian Problem," *Survival* 51:4 (August–September 2009), 71–86.

2. On audience costs, see James D. Fearon, "Domestic Political Audiences and the Escalation of International Disputes," *American Political Science Review* 88: 3 (1994), 577–592.

3. For example, see Gregory Johnsen, *The Last Refuge: Yemen, Al-Qaeda, and America's War in Arabia* (New York: W.W. Norton, 2013), 38–47.

4. Rania Abouzeid, "The Jihad Next Door: The Syrian Roots of Iraq's Newest Civil War," *Politico*, June 23, 2014, http://www.politico.com/magazine/story/2014/06/al-qaeda-iraq-syria-108214.html#.VZ66cvlViko.

5. Ayman al-Zawahiri, "Zawahiri Reportedly Settles Dispute between ISI, al-Nusra Front," Site Intelligence Group, June 9, 2013.

6. For example, see Ahrar al-Sham, "Ahrar al-Sham Criticizes ISI Leader's Declared Islamic State in Iraq and Syria," Site Intelligence Group, May 6, 2013.

7. Until, to the chagrin of al-Qaeda's leadership, its agents in Syria exposed the relationship.

8. Brian Bennett, "Al Qaeda's Yemen Branch Has Aided Somalia's Militants," *Los Angeles Times*, July 18, 2011, http://articles.latimes.com/2011/jul/18/world/la-fg-bin-laden-somalia-20110718.

9. Martha Crenshaw, "An Organizational Approach to the Analysis of Political Terrorism," *Orbis* 29:3 (Fall 1985), 467.

10. Jacob N. Shapiro, *The Terrorist's Dilemma: Managing Violent Covert Organizations* (Princeton, NJ: Princeton University Press, 2013).

11. "Al Qa'ida's Five Aspects of Power."

12. Al-Zawahiri, "Letter from al-Zawahiri to al-Zarqawi."

13. John G. Ruggie, "Territoriality and Beyond: Problematizing Modernity in International Relations," *International Organization* 47:1 (1993), 139–174.

14. Barak Mendelsohn, "God vs. Westphalia: Radical Islamist Movements and the Battle for Organizing the World," *Review of International Studies* 38 (2012), 589–613.

15. For example, see Peter Bergen, *Holy War, Inc.: Inside the Secret World of Osama bin Laden* (St. Ives: Clays, 2001); Brad McAllister, "Al Qaeda and the Innovative Firm: Demythologizing the Network," *Studies in Conflict & Terrorism* 27 (2004), 297–319.

16. Robert Grant and Charles Baden-Fuller, "A Knowledge Accessing Theory of Strategic Alliances," *Journal of Management Studies* 41:1 (January 2004), 61–84.

17. Bruce Hofmann, *Inside Terrorism* (New York: Columbia University Press, 2006), chapter 1.

18. ETA is a prominent example of such a slide to criminalism. See Fernando Reinares, "Who Are the Terrorists? Analyzing Changes in Sociological Profile among Members of ETA" *Studies in Conflict & Terrorism* 27:6 (November 2004), 465–488.

19. Max Abrahms, "What Terrorists Really Want: Terrorist Motives and Counterterrorism Strategies," *International Security* 32:4 (Spring 2008), 79; Martha Crenshaw, "Theories of Terrorism: Instrumental and Organizational Approaches," in David C. Rapoport (Ed.), *Inside Terrorist Organizations* (London: Frank Cass, 2001), 14 and 27.

20. Michael Horowitz and Phillip Potter, "The Life-Cycle of Terrorist Innovation: The Case of Hijacking," Paper presented at the annual meeting of the International Studies Association, San Diego, April 1–4, 2012.

21. Ami Pedahzur, *Suicide Terrorism* (Cambridge, UK: Polity Press, 2005), 22–42.

22. Robert Pape, *Dying to Win: The Strategic Logic of Suicide Terrorism* (New York: Random House, 2005).

23. Navin Bapat, "The Internationalization of Terrorist Campaigns," *Conflict Management and Peace Science* 24 (2007), 280–285.

24. Abrahms, "What Terrorists Really Want," 78–105.

25. Martha Crenshaw, "The Effectiveness of Terrorism in the Algerian War," in Martha Crenshaw (Ed.), *Terrorism in Context* (University Park: Pennsylvania State University Press, 1995), 474–514;

26. Victor Asal and R. Karl Rethemeyer, "The Nature of the Beast: Organizational Structures and the Lethality of Terrorist Attacks," *Journal of Politics* 70:2 (April 2008), 440–446.

27. Byman, "Buddies or Burden," 441.

28. Ibid., 444.

29. Crenshaw, "An Organizational Approach to the Analysis of Political Terrorism," 470. See also Audrey Kurth Cronin, "How al-Qaida Ends: The Decline and Demise of Terrorist Groups," *International Security* 31:1 (Summer 2006), 23.

30. Abrahms, "What Terrorists Really Want."

31. Jessica Stern, "The Protean Enemy," *Foreign Affairs* 82:4 (July–August 2003), 27–40.

32. Jessica Stern and Amit Modi, "Producing Terror: Organizational Dynamics of Survival," in Thomas J. Biersteker and Sue E. Eckert (Eds.), *Countering the Financing of Terrorism* (London: Routledge, 2007), 31–32.

33. Byman, "Buddies or Burden," 439.

34. Barak Mendelsohn, "Al Qaeda and Global Governance: The Constraining Impact of Rigid Ideology," *Terrorism and Political Violence* 26:3 (2014), 470–487.

35. Mendelsohn, "Al Qaeda's Palestinian Problem."

36. Ayman al-Zawahiri, "Knights under the Banner of the Prophet," serialized in *Al-Sharq al-Awsat*, December 2001.

37. Thomas Hegghammer, "The Ideological Hybridization of Jihadi Groups," *Current Trends in Islamic Ideology*, Vol. 9 (Washington, DC: The Hudson Institute, 2009), 26–45.

38. Allan Cullison, "Inside al-Qaeda's Hard Drive," *The Atlantic Monthly* (September 2004), 55–70.

39. Stern, "The Protean Enemy," 1; Abrahms, "What Terrorists Really Want," 88.

40. Lahoud, *Beware of Imitators*, 46.

41. Crenshaw, "Theories of Terrorism," 19.

42. Stern and Modi, "Producing Terror," 19–46.

43. Bloom, *Dying to Kill*, 89.

44. Crenshaw, "Theories of Terrorism," 20.

45. Abrahms, "What Terrorists Really Want."

46. Byman, "Buddies or Burden," 440–441.

47. Bruce Hoffman, "The Myth of Grass-Roots Terrorism: Why Osama bin Laden Still Matters," *Foreign Affairs* 87:3 (May–June 2008), 133–138.

48. Hoffman, "Combating Al Qaeda and the Militant Islamic Threat."

49. Stern and Modi, "Producing Terror," 31. Lia makes the same argument in his attempt to explain the establishment of Islamic emirates. See Lia, "Jihadi Insurgents and the Perils of Territorialisation," Paper presented at the International Studies Association's 52nd Annual Convention. Montreal, Canada, March 16–19, 2011.

50. See Crenshaw, "Theories of Terrorism," 16.

51. Ibid., 24; Bloom, *Dying to Kill*.

52. Crenshaw, "Theories of Terrorism," 9–20.

53. Crenshaw, "An Organizational Approach to the Analysis of Political Terrorism," 473–480.

54. Jones, "Think Again: Al Qaeda," *Foreign Policy* (May–June 2012), 47–51.

55. Al-Zawahiri, "Letter from al-Zawahiri to al-Zarqawi."

56. For example, Tony Badran, "Intercepted Letters from al-Qaeda Leaders Shed Light." Foundation for Defense of Democracies, September 11, 2008.

57. Al-Zawahiri, "Letter from al-Zawahiri to al-Zarqawi"; Atiyatallah, "Letter to Zarqawi from Senior al Qaeda Leader, 'Atiya (December 2005)," Combating Terrorism Center at West Point.
58. Jones, "Think Again."

CHAPTER 4

1. This chapter is based in part on my article "Al Qaeda's Franchising Strategy," *Survival* 53:3 (2011), 29–49.
2. Sageman, *Leaderless Jihad*.
3. For examples of such observations, see Jason Burke, "Think Again: Al-Qaeda," *Foreign Policy*, October 27, 2009; Audrey Cronin, *How Terrorism Ends: Understanding the Decline and Demise of Terrorist Campaigns* (Princeton, NJ: Princeton University Press 2009), 168–171.
4. Leah Farrall, "The Evolution of Command," in *Al-Qaeda's Senior Leadership* (Alexandria, VA: Jane's Strategic Advisory Services, November 2009), 16–20; The Abbottabad Documents; *U.S. v. Abid Naseer*, Case #415A-NY-302248.
5. As such it is distinct from cases of groups who took al-Qaeda's name unilaterally. Such groups may share its ideology, but without the consent of AQC they cannot be viewed as part of the organization. One example for such a group is Noordin Top's al-Qaeda for the Malay Archipelago. The group splintered from the Southeast Asian Jema'a Islamiya. See International Crisis Group, *Terrorism in Indonesia: Noordin's Networks*, Asia Report No. 114, May 5, 2006.
6. Leah Farrall, "How al Qaeda Works: What the Organization's Subsidiaries Say about Its Strength," *Foreign Affairs* 90:2 (2011), 128–138.
7. See, for example, Peter Bergen, *The Longest War* (New York: Free Press, 2011), 86–94.
8. Saif al-'Adl, "Al-'Adl Letter," CTC Harmony Project.
9. For example, see Bruce Riedel, "The Return of the Knights: al-Qaeda and the Fruits of Middle East Disorder," *Survival* 49:3 (2007), 107–120.
10. Fawaz Gerges, *The Rise and Fall of Al-Qaeda* (New York: Oxford University Press, 2011), 59.
11. Cullison, "Inside Al-Qaeda's Hard Drive."
12. Camille Tawil, "The 'Other Face' of al-Qa'idah, parts 1–2, *Al-Hayat*, September 25–26, 2010; Vernie Liebl, "Al Qaida on the US Invasion of Afghanistan in Their Own Words," *Small Wars & Insurgencies* 23:3 (2012), 542–568.
13. Abu Yahya al-Libi, *Moderation of Islam ... Moderation of Defeat*, OSC, May 22, 2008. Note that most scholars avoid discussing such long-term objectives, probably because they are so ambitious that their attainment appears unrealistic and their articulation disingenuous or simply delusional. For one exception, see David Kilcullen, "Countering Global Insurgency," *Journal of Strategic Studies* 28:4 (2005), 604.

14. Perhaps the clearest articulation of that strategy appeared in a 2013 document authored by al-Zawahiri. This document, titled "general guidelines for jihad," was written in response to mounting evidence that excesses committed by al-Qaeda's franchises badly hurt the organization's image and its ability to operate. These self-inflicted wounds led bin Laden to order the preparation of a document that would publicly set guidelines for actions, thus instructing the franchises what kind of actions are appropriate, while clearly identifying which activities would be considered unsanctioned transgressions. It is not clear why it took so long to release the document, over two years after bin Laden's death. Communication problems between the group's leadership and the franchises may have slowed the process of consultation that bin Laden ordered before the document was to become public. It is also possible that al-Zawahiri, who inherited the task from bin Laden, needed to be convinced of its importance and that it is wise to admit that al-Qaeda's affiliates often drifted from the path charted by the central command. Ayman al-Zawahiri, "General Guidelines for Jihad," Site Intelligence Group, September 13, 2013; The Abbottabad Documents, SOCOM-2012-0000017, and SOCOM-2012-0000019.

15. The Abbottabad Documents, SOCOM-2012-0000019.

16. Al-Zawahiri, "General Guidelines for Jihad."

17. Ibid.

18. Muhammad al-Obaidi, Nassir Abdullah, and Scott Helfstein, *Deadly Vanguards: A Study of al-Qa'ida's Violence against Muslims* (West Point, NY: Combating Terrorism Center, 2009).

19. The Abbottabad Documents, SOCOM-2012-0000019.

20. For example, see al-Sahab, "The Will of the Martyr Uthman Who Carried Out a Suicide Operation," OSC, March 5, 2007; Abu Yahya al-Libi, "Yemeni Government to America: I Sacrifice Myself for Your Sake," OSC, February 22, 2010.

21. Al-Zawahiri, "General Guidelines for Jihad."

22. Osama bin Laden, "Declaration of War," *al-Quds al-Arabi*, August 23, 1996.

23. For example, see Osama Bin Laden, "Bin Ladin Praises, Introduces Will of Sep 11 Hijacker in New Video," OSC, September 11, 2007.

24. Al-Zawahiri, "Letter to Abu-Musab al-Zarqawi."

25. Sulayman Abu Ghayth, "Al-Qa'ida Spokesman Abu-Ghayth Confirms Mombasa, Other Operations," Jihadunspun, December 7, 2002.

26. For a recent example, see Ayman al-Zawahiri, "Zawahiri Speaks on the 12th Anniversary of 9/11, Calls for Attack on US," Site Intelligence Group, September 12, 2013.

27. World Islamic Front Against Crusaders and Jews, "Jihad Against Jews and Crusaders," February 23, 1998.

28. Abu Bakr Naji, *The Management of Savagery: The Most Critical Stage Through Which the Umma Will Pass*, translated by William McCants (Boston: John M. Olin Institute for Strategic Studies at Harvard University, May 2006), 76.

29. Mendelsohn, *Combating Jihadism*, 37–62.

30. Michael Scheuer, "Coalition Warfare: How al-Qaeda Uses the World Islamic Front Against Crusaders and Jews, Part 1" *Terrorism Focus* 2:7 (March 31, 2005).

31. Steven Brooks, "The Near and Far Enemy Debate," in Assaf Moghadam and Brian Fishman (Eds.), *Fault Lines in Global Jihad: Organizational, Strategic, and Ideological Fissures* (London: Routledge, 2011), 51; Yotam Feldner, Yigal Carmon, and Daniel Lev, "The Al-Gama'a Al-Islamiyya Cessation of Violence: An Ideological Reversal," *MEMRI, Inquiry and Analysis Series—No. 309*, December 21, 2006; Gerges, *The Rise and Fall of Al-Qaeda*, 35–36, 64–65.

32. Vahid Brown, "Classical and Global Jihad: Al-Qa'ida's Franchising Frustrations," in Assaf Moghadam and Brian Fishman (Eds.), *Fault Lines in Global Jihad: Organizational, Strategic, and Ideological Fissures* (London: Routledge, 2011), 103.

33. Andrew Higgins and Alan Cullison, "Saga of Dr. Zawahri Sheds Light on the Roots of al Qaeda," *Wall Street Journal*, July 2, 2002; Muhammad al-Shafi'i, "Al-Zawahiri's Secret Papers, Part 4," *Al-Sharq al-*Awsat, December 16, 2002; Gerges, *The Rise and Fall of Al-Qaeda*, 35–37.

34. Muhammad al-Shafi'i, "Al-Zawahiri's Secret Papers, part 1," *Al-Sharq al-*Awsat, December 13, 2002.

35. For example, see Montasser al-Zayyat, *The Road to Al Qaeda: The Story of bin Laden's Right-Hand Man* (London: Pluto Press, 2004), 97; "Part Three of Dr Fadl's Book on Future of Conflict in Afghanistan," *Al-Sharq al-Awsat*, March 1, 2010.

36. "Unity and 9/11," *Vanguards of Khorasan* 12, Site Intelligence Group, October 10, 2008.

37. Brian Fishman, *Dysfunction and Decline: Lessons Learned from Inside al Qa'ida in Iraq* (West Point, NY: Combating Terrorism Center, 2009).

38. Al-Zawahiri, "Zawahiri Speaks on the 12th Anniversary of 9/11."

39. Jabhat al-Nusra, "Nusra Rejects Trials for Regime Figures, Demands 'Death by Sword," *Syria Direct*, May 21, 2014, http://syriadirect.org/news/nusra-rejects-trials-for-regime-figures-demands-death-by-sword/.

40. Naji, *The Management of Savagery*, 47–53.

41. Osama Bin Laden, "A Message to Our People in Iraq," October 23, 2007.

42. Sayd Saleem Shahzad, "Broadside Fired at al-Qaeda Leaders," *Asia Times*, December 10, 2010; Vahid Brown, "Al-Qa'ida Revisions: The Five Letters of Sayf al-'Adl," *Jihadica*, February 10, 2011; Al-'Adl, "Al-'Adl Letter."

43. "Part One of Dr Fadl's Book on Future of Conflict in Afghanistan," *Al-Sharq al-Awsat*, February 25, 2010.

44. Mendelsohn, "Al Qaeda's Palestinian Problem"; Fishman, *Dysfunction and Decline*.

45. Abu-Yahya al-Libi, *Refuting the Falsehood of the Rationalization Document*, OSC, December 13, 2008; Ayman al-Zawahiri, *The Exoneration*, OSC, March 5, 2008.

46. The Abbottabad Documents, SOCOM-2012-0000004.

47. Bill Roggio, "Senior Al-Qaeda Operative Abd al-Hadi al-Iraqi Captured," *The Long War Journal*, April 27, 2007, http://www.longwarjournal.org/archives/2007/04/senior_al_qaeda_oper.php.

48. The Abbottabad Documents, SOCOM-2012-0000010.

49. Jason Burke, "Perceptions of Leaders: Examining Extremist Views of Al-Qaeda," in *Al-Qaeda's Senior Leadership* (Alexandria, VA: Jane's Strategic Advisory Services, November 2009), 2–6. Brachman, too, underscores AQC's problem to remain relevant, although he focuses on its difficulty to appeal to a new generation of youth. Jarret Brachman, "Retaining Relevance: Assessing Al-Qaeda's Generational Evolution," in *Al-Qaeda's Senior Leadership*, 26.

50. For example, see Vahid Brown, *Cracks in the Foundation: Leadership Schisms in al-Qa'ida from* 1989–2006 (West Point, NY: Combating Terrorism Center, September 2007); Mustafa Hamid, "The Afghan-Arabs," serialized in *Al-Sharq al-Awsat*, June-July, 2005; and Al-'Adl, "Al Adl Letter."

51. Hamid, "The Afghan-Arabs."

52. For example, see Raffaello Pantucci, "Manchester, New York and Oslo: Three Centrally Directed Al-Qa'ida Plots," *CTC Sentinel* 3:8 (August 2010), 10–13; Petter Nesser and Brynjar Lia, "Lessons Learned from the July 2010 Norwegian Terrorist Plot," *CTC Sentinel* 3:8 (August 2010), 13–17.

53. Rohan Gunaratna and Andres Nielsen, "Al Qaeda in the Tribal Areas of Pakistan and Beyond," *Studies in Conflict and Terrorism* 31 (2008), 798.

54. "Al Qa'ida's Five Aspects of Power," 4.

55. Kilcullen, "Countering Global Insurgency," 602.

56. Osama bin Laden, "Osama bin Laden's Address to Americans," Intelcenter, October 29, 2004.

57. For example, see Badran, "Intercepted Letters from al-Qaeda Leaders."

58. For example, ibid.

59. "Al Qa'ida's Five Aspects of Power," 1–4.

60. Farrall, "The Evolution of Command," 20.

61. Brachman, "Retaining Relevance: Assessing Al-Qaeda's Generational Evolution," 28.

62. Although the prominent role the American imam Anwar al-Awlaki plays in AQAP is also a prime reason for its more direct challenge to the US.

63. Thomas Joscelyn and Bill Roggio, "AQAP's Emir Also Serves as al-Qaeda's General Manager," *The Long War Journal*, August 6, 2013, http://www.longwarjournal.org/archives/2013/08/aqap_emir_also_serve.php.

64. Abu-Yahya al-Libi, "Yemeni Government to America: I Sacrifice Myself for Your Sake."

65. Ibid.

66. Abu Muhammad al-Adnani, "ISIL Spokesman Criticizes Zawahiri Letter," Site Intelligence Group, June 19, 2013; Abu Muhammad al-Adnani, "ISIL Spokesman Denounces General Command of al-Qaeda," Site Intelligence Group, April 18, 2014; Abu Muhammad al-Adnani, "ISIL Refuses Zawahiri Order to Withdraw from Syria, Responses to Message," Site Intelligence Group, May 12, 2014.

CHAPTER 5

1. Mendelsohn, "Al Qaeda's Palestinian Problem."
2. Bin Laden, *Declaration of War*; Bernard Lewis, "License to Kill," Foreign Affairs 77:6 (1998), 14–19.
3. Cook, *Understanding Jihad*.
4. Mendelsohn, *Combating Jihadism*, 63–88.
5. The Abbottabad Documents, SOCOM-2012-0000019.
6. Ali H. Soufan with Daniel Freedman, *The Black Banners: The Inside Story of 9/11 and the War against al-Qaeda* (New York: W. W. Norton, 2011), xvii–xviii.
7. AQIS, *Resurgence*, issue 1 (2014), 39; The Islamic State, *Dabiq*, issue 1 (2014), 4–5; The Islamic State, *Dabiq*, issue 3 (2014), 15; The Islamic State, *Dabiq*, issue 4 (2014), 32–35.
8. Naji, *The Management of Savagery*.
9. Thomas Hegghammer, "Syria's Foreign Fighters," *Foreign Policy*, December 9, 2013. http://foreignpolicy.com/2013/12/09/syrias-foreign-fighters/.
10. Al-Zawahiri, "Knights under the Banner of the Prophet."
11. Peter Bergen and Paul Cruickshank, "Revisiting the Early Al Qaeda: An Updated Account of Its Formative Years," *Studies in Conflict & Terrorism* 35:1 (2012), 17–23.
12. Naji, *The Management of Savagery*.
13. Ibid.
14. Fu'ad Husayn, "Al Zarqawi, The Second Generation of al Qa'ida," Serialized in *al Quds al Arabi*, June–July 2005.
15. Atiyatallah, "Letter to Zarqawi from Senior al Qaeda Leader, 'Atiya."
16. Husayn, "Al Zarqawi, The Second Generation of al Qa'ida."
17. Abu Umar al-Baghdadi, "The Religion Is the Advice," OSC, February 14, 2008.
18. Thomas Hegghammer, *The Failure of Jihad in Saudi Arabia* (West Point, NY: Combating Terrorism Center, 2010).
19. Al-Zawahiri, "Knights under the Banner of the Prophet."
20. Robert I. Rotberg, "Failed States in a World of Terror," *Foreign Affairs* 81:4 (July–August 2002), 127–140.
21. On the hostility and differences between the two movements, see Marc Lynch, "Jihadis and the Ikhwan," in Assaf Moghadam and Brian Fishman (Eds.), *Fault Lines in Global Jihad: Organizational, Strategic, and Ideological Fissures* (London: Routledge, 2011), 161–183.
22. "Leader in al Qassam Brigades Denounces Abu Umar al Baghdadi for Criticizing Hamas," OSC, February 19, 2008.
23. Robert Jervis, Richard Ned Lebow, and Janice Gross Stein (Eds.), *Psychology and Deterrence* (Baltimore, MD: Johns Hopkins University Press, 1985).
24. Neta Crawford, "The Passion of World Politics: Propositions on Emotion and Emotional Relationships," *International Security* 24:4 (2000), 116–156.

25. Irving Janis, *Victims of Groupthink: Psychological Studies of Policy Decisions and Fiascoes* (Oxford, UK: Houghton Mifflin, 1972).

26. Lee Ross and Richard E. Nisbett, *The Person and the Situation: Essential Contributions of Social Psychology* (New York: McGraw Hill, 1991).

27. George A. Quattrone, and Amos Tversky, "Contrasting Rational and Psychological Analysis of Political Choice," *American Political Science Review* 82:3 (1988), 721.

28. Rose McDermott, *Risk Taking in International Relations: Prospect Theory in American Foreign Policy* (Ann Arbor: University of Michigan Press, 1998).

29. Arjen Boin, Paul Hart, Eric Stern, and Bengt Sundelius, *The Politics of Crisis Management: Political Leadership under Pressure* (Cambridge, UK: Cambridge University Press, 2005), 29–30.

30. Margaret Hermann, "Indicators of Stress in Policymakers during Foreign Policy Crises," *Political Psychology* 1:1 (1979), 27–46.

31. Richard Ned Lebow, *Between Peace and War: The Nature of International Crisis* (Baltimore, MD: Johns Hopkins University Press, 1984); Richard Ned Lebow, "Transitions and Transformations: Building International Cooperation," *Security Studies* 6:3 (1997), 154–179.

CHAPTER 6

1. Anthony Cordesman and Nawaf Obaid, *National Security in Saudi Arabia: Threats, Responses, and Challenges* (Westport, CT: Praeger Security International, 2005), 113; Craig Whitlock, "Al Qaeda Shifts Its Strategy in Saudi Arabia," *Washington Post*, December 28, 2004, A28.

2. According to one study, at its peak AQAP had between 500 and 600 members. See Cordesman and Obaid, *National Security in Saudi Arabia*, 133.

3. Thomas Hegghammer, *Jihad in Saudi Arabia: Violence and Pan-Islamism since 1979* (Cambridge, UK: Cambridge University Press, 2010), 166–185, and 202–217.

4. Bin Laden, "Declaration of War."

5. Osama bin Laden, Interview by Peter Arentt, conducted on March 22, 1997, aired on CNN, May 10, 1997.

6. Lewis, "License to Kill."

7. Center for Islamic Studies and Research, *The Operation of 11 Rabi Al-Awaal: The East Riyadh Operation and Our War with the United States and Its Agents*, OSC, August 1, 2003.

8. Steve Coll, *The Bin Ladens: An Arabia Family in the American Century* (New York: Penguin Press, 2008).

9. Fawaz Gerges, *The Far Enemy: Why Jihad Went Global* (Cambridge, UK: Cambridge University Press, 2005), 76.

10. Khaled al-Hammadi, "Bin Laden's Former 'Bodyguard' Interviewed on al Qaeda Strategies, Part 7," *Al-Quds al-Arabi*, April 2, 2005.

11. Naji, *The Management of Savagery*.

12. Hegghammer, *Jihad in Saudi Arabia*, 112–142.

13. Ibid., 144.

14. Cordesman and Obaid, *National Security in Saudi Arabia*, 113–114.

15. Mendelsohn, *Combating Jihadism*, 113–134, and 161–184.

16. Hegghammer, *Jihad in Saudi Arabia*, 163–165.

17. According to Hegghammer, in the aftermath of the US invasion, between 300 and 1,000 jihadis returned to Saudi Arabia from Afghanistan. Hegghammer, *Jihad in Saudi Arabia*, 165.

18. Ron Suskind, *The One Percent Doctrine* (New York: Simon & Schuster, 2006), 146–147; Hegghammer, *Jihad in Saudi Arabia*, 184.

19. Hegghammer, *The Failure of Jihad in Saudi Arabia*.

20. Hegghammer, *Jihad in Saudi Arabia*, 174–175.

21. Whitlock, "Al Qaeda Shifts Its Strategy in Saudi Arabia."

22. "Zarqawi's Pledge of Allegiance to al-Qaeda: From Mu'askar al-Battar, Issue 21," *Terrorism Monitor* 2:24, December 15, 2004.

23. "Osama bin Laden to the Iraqi people: It Is Forbidden to Participate in Iraqi & PA Elections; Jihad in Palestine and Iraq Is Incumbent upon Residents of All Muslim Countries, not Just Iraqis and Palestinians; Zarqawi Is the Commander of Al-Qa'ida in Iraq," MEMRI: Special Dispatch Series, no. 837, December 30, 2004; "Zarqawi's Pledge of Allegiance to al-Qaeda."

24. Sami Yousafzai and Ron Moreau, "Terror Broker," *Newsweek*, April 11, 2005, 56.

25. "Bin Laden Tape: Text," *BBC*, February 12, 2003, http://news.bbc.co.uk/2/hi/middle_east/2751019.stm.

26. Gerges, *The Far Enemy*, 256.

27. "Zarqawi's Pledge of Allegiance to al-Qaeda."

28. Brian Fishman and Joseph Felter, *Al-Qa'ida's Foreign Fighters in Iraq: A First Look at the Sinjar Records* (West Point, NY: Combating Terrorism Center, 2007).

29. "Zarqawi's Pledge of Allegiance to al-Qaeda."

30. This was not al-Zarqawi's first time in Afghanistan. He arrived at the country a decade earlier, stayed there from 1989 to 1993, and participated in some of the battles against the Najibullah regime. See Mary Anne Weaver, "The Short, Violent Life of Abu Musab al-Zarqawi," *The Atlantic* (July/August 2006).

31. Weaver, "The Short, Violent Life of Abu Musab al-Zarqawi"; Peter Bergen, *The Osama bin Laden I Know* (New York: Free Press, 2006), 354.

32. "Saudi Daily Plays Up Differences between Al-Zarqawi, His Mentor," BBC Monitoring Middle East, July 10, 2005.

33. Bergen, *The Osama bin Laden I know*, 361–362.

34. Abu Musab al-Zarqawi, "Zarqawi Letter," February 2004 Coalition Provisional Authority English Translation of Terrorist Musab al Zarqawi Letter Obtained by United States Government in Iraq, 2001–2009, state.gov/p/nea/rls/31694.htm.

35. Ibid.

36. Gerges, *The Far Enemy*, 257.

37. Although not as explicit, a similar claim that AQI must first focus on its primary enemy is also expressed in a letter from Abu Yahya al-Libi to al-Zarqawi, which was posted to jihadi online forums. See Abu Yahya al-Libi, "A Letter to Abu Musab al-Zarqawi from Abu Yehia al-Libi," Site Intelligence Group, December 21, 2005.
38. That is not to suggest that there were no al-Qaeda leaders with very strong anti-Shia positions. For example, see Abu Yahya al-Libi, "We Are Not Huthists, Do Not Focus on the Speck and Ignore the Plank," OSC, February 6, 2010.
39. Al-Zawahiri, "Letter from al-Zawahiri to al-Zarqawi."
40. Ibid.
41. Atiyatallah, "Letter to Zarqawi from Senior al Qaeda Leader, 'Atiya.'"
42. Mujahidin Shura Council, "Statement of Mujahidin Shura Council on Establishment of 'Islamic State of Iraq,'" OSC, October 15, 2006.
43. This view of al-Qaeda's position toward the ISI stands in contradiction to Brian Fishman's argument that al-Qaeda encouraged its founding. Although I agree with Fishman that al-Qaeda contemplated experimenting with Islamic governance in Iraq and considered it important to convert operational success to political effects, I argue that al-Qaeda was waiting for the right conditions. It did not accept its branch's focus on coercion in dealing with fellow Sunni groups and would have probably been willing to wait until the Sunni insurgent groups achieved unity. This interpretation is supported by evidence that was not available at the time Fishman wrote his report, which reveals that AQC was not involved in the decision to establish the ISI. Brian Fishman, *Redefining the Islamic State: The Fall and Rise of Al-Qaeda in Iraq* (Washington, DC: New America Foundation, 2011).
44. Al-Zawahiri, "Letter from al-Zawahiri to al-Zarqawi."
45. Ayman al-Zawahiri, "Dr. Ayman al-Zawahiri Elegizes Abu Musab al-Zarqawi in a Video Speech," Site Intelligence Group, June 23, 2006.
46. Ayman al-Zawahiri, "Zawahiri Details Relationship with ISIL, Repeats Call to Return to Iraq," Site Intelligence Group, May 2, 2014.
47. Badran, "Intercepted Letters from al-Qaeda Leaders."
48. For example, "Kuwaiti Cleric Hamid al-Ali Cautions Muslims of Difference between Jihad, Imamate," OSC, October 23, 2006; "Hamid al-Ali Makes Recommendation To 'Retract the Establishment of the Islamic State,'" OSC, April 9, 2007.
49. The Islamic State of Iraq, "Notifying Mankind of the Birth of the Islamic State—A Study from the Ministry of Shari'a Councils of the Islamic State of Iraq Regarding the State's Establishment and Purpose," Site Intelligence Group, January 29, 2007.
50. "Pressure Grows on al Qaeda in Iraq," *ABC News*, January 30, 2006, http://abcnews.go.com/International/story?id=1557349; Fishman, *Redefining the Islamic State*.
51. The Islamic State of Iraq, "Notifying Mankind of the Birth of the Islamic State."
52. Bin Laden, "A Message to Our People in Iraq"; Abu Yahya al-Libi, "Iraq between Victory, Conspiratorial Intrigues," OSC, March 22, 2007.
53. Al-Adnani, "ISIL Refuses Zawahiri Order to Withdraw from Syria, Responses to Message."

54. Atiyahallah, "Letter to Zarqawi from Senior al Qaeda Leader, 'Atiya."

55. Fishman, *Dysfunction and Decline*, 2–3.

56. "Statement of Mujahidin Shura Council on Establishment of 'Islamic State of Iraq.'"

CHAPTER 7

1. Jean-Pierre Filiu, "The Local and Global Jihad of al-Qa'ida in the Islamic Maghrib," *Middle East Journal* 63:2 (Spring 2009), 217–220; Camille Tawil, *Brothers in Arms: The Story of Al-Qa'ida and the Arab Jihadists* (London, UK: SAQI, 2010), 119–124.

2. Al-Sahab, "Hot Issues Interview with Shaykh Ayman al-Zawahiri," OSC, September 10, 2006.

3. AQIM, "Salafist Group for Call and Combat Announces Its New Name as al-Qaeda Organization in the Islamic Maghreb," Site Intelligence Group, January 26, 2007.

4. "Salafist Group for Call and Combat (GSPC) Claims Responsibility for Bombing of Halliburton-Subsidiary Employees in Bouchaoui, Near Algiers," Site Intelligence Group, December 11, 2006.

5. Craig Whitlock, "Al-Qaeda's Far Reaching New Partner," *Washington Post*, October 5, 2006, A1.

6. Filiu, "The Local and Global Jihad of al-Qa'ida in the Islamic Maghrib," 221.

7. Andrew Black, "The Reconstituted Al-Qaeda Threat in the Maghreb," *Terrorism Monitor* 5:2 (February 2007).

8. Guido Steinberg and Isabelle Werenfels, "Between the 'Near' and the 'Far' Enemy: Al-Qaeda in the Islamic Maghreb," *Mediterranean Politics* 12:3 (2007), 407–409.

9. "An Interview with Abdelmalek Droukdal," *New York Times*, July 1, 2008, http://www.nytimes.com/2008/07/01/world/africa/01transcript-droukdal.html?pagewanted=all; "Interview with Mokhtar bin Muhammad Belmokhtar, "Khalid Abu'l 'Abbas," Al-Qa'ida in the Islamic Maghreb Field Commander," View from the Occident Blog, http://occident2.blogspot.com/2011/11/interview-with-mukhtar-bin-muhammad.html, November 19, 2011; Andrew Lebovich, "AQIM's Mokhtar Belmokhtar Speaks Out," *al-Wasat Blog*, November 21, 2011, http://thewasat.wordpress.com/2011/11/21/aqims-mokhtar-belmokhtar-speaks-out; Souad Mekhennet, Michael Moss, Eric Shmitt, Elaine Sciolino, and Margot Williams, "Ragtag Insurgency Gains a Lifeline From Al Qaeda," *New York Times*, July 1, 2008, A1.

10. Christopher Chivvis and Andrew Liepman, "North Africa's Menace: AQIM's Evolution and the U.S. Policy Response," RAND Corporation (September 2013), 3.

11. Assaf Moghadam, *The Globalization of Martyrdom: Al Qaeda, Salafi Jihad, and the Diffusion of Suicide Attacks* (Baltimore, MD: John Hopkins University Press, 2008), 61–62.

12. J. Peter Pham, "Foreign Influences and Shifting Horizons: The Ongoing Evolution of al Qaeda in the Islamic Maghreb," *Orbis* 55:2 (Spring 2011), 247–249; Mathieu Guidere, "The Timbuktu Letters: New Insights about AQIM," *Res Militaris* 4:1 (2014), 5.

13. Rukmini Callimachi, "Paying Ransoms, Europe Bankrolls Qaeda Terror," *New York Times*, July 29, 2014.

14. "An Interview with Abdelmalek Droukdal."

15. Stephen Harmon, "From GSPC to AQIM: The Evolution of an Algerian Islamist Terrorist Group Into an Al-Qa'ida Affiliate and Its Implications for the Sahara-Sahel Region," *Concerned Africa Scholars*, Bulletin no. 85 (Spring 2010), 12–29.

16. International Crisis Group, "Islamism, Violence and Reform in Algeria: Turning the Page," *Middle East Report* no. 29 (July 2004), 2.

17. Stephen Ulph, "Disarray in the Algerian GSPC," *Terrorism Focus* 1:7, October 29, 2004; Stephen Ulph, "Declining in Algeria, GSPC Enters International Theater," *Terrorism Focus* 3:1, January 9, 2006.

18. Whitlock, "Al-Qaeda's Far Reaching New Partner."

19. Tawil, *Brothers in Arms*, 195.

20. Jason Burke, *The 9/11 Wars* (London: Penguin Books, 2011), 416–417.

21. Filiu, "The Local and Global Jihad of al-Qa'ida in the Islamic Maghrib," 222.

22. Black, "The Reconstituted Al-Qaeda Threat in the Maghreb"; Filiu, "The Local and Global Jihad of al-Qa'ida in the Islamic Maghrib," 221.

23. Camille Tawil, "New Strategies in Al-Qaeda's Battle for Algeria," *Terrorism Monitor* 7:22, July 27, 2009.

24. Chivvis and Liepman, "North Africa's Menace," 4.

25. Lebovich, "AQIM's Mokhtar Belmokhtar Speaks Out."

26. Pham, "Foreign Influences and Shifting Horizons," 244–245.

27. Abu Musab Abdul Wadud, "'We Are Coming'—A Video Speech from Abu Musab Abdul Wadud, emir of the Salafist Group for Call and Combat (GSPC) in Algeria," Site Intelligence Group, January 8, 2007.

28. Jean-Luc Marret, "Al-Qaeda in Islamic Maghreb: A 'Glocal' Organization," *Studies in Conflict & Terrorism* 31 (2008), 543; Steinberg and Werenfels, "Between the 'Near' and the 'Far' Enemy," 409–411; Geoff Porter, "Splits Revealed Inside Al-Qaeda in the Islamic Maghreb," *Terrorism Monitor*, September 14, 2007.

29. Chivvis and Liepman, "North Africa's Menace," 4.

30. Burke, *The 9/11 Wars*, 416–417.

31. AQIM, "AQIM Audio Interview with Political Committee Head," Site Intelligence Group, May 4, 2009.

32. Andrew Black, "AQIM's Expanding International Agenda," *CTC Sentinel* 1:5 (April 2008), 12–14.

33. Caitriona Dowd and Cliondah Raleigh, "The Myth of Global Islamic Terrorism and Local Conflict in Mali and the Sahel," *African Affairs* 112:448 (2013), 504.

34. Burke, *The 9/11 Wars*, 417–418.

35. Jean-Pierre Filiu, "al-Qa'ida in the Islamic Maghreb: A Case Study in the Opportunism of Global Jihad," *CTC Sentinel* 3:4 (April 2010), 14–15; Chivvis and Liepman, "North Africa's Menace," 5.
36. On AQIM's internal infighting, see Guidere, "The Timbuktu Letters."
37. "Al-Qaida Papers: Mali–Al-Qaeda's Sahara Playbook," *Associated Press*, February 14, 2013, hosted.ap.org/specials/interactives/_international/_pdfs/al-qaida-manifesto.pdf; Rukmini Callimachi, "In Timbuktu, Al-Qaida Left Behind a Manifesto," *Associated Press*, February 14, 2013.
38. The Abbottabad Documents, SOCOM-2012-0000010.
39. "Al-Qaida Paper: The Yemen Letters," *Associated Press*, August 9, 2013, hosted.ap.org/specials/interactives/_international/_pdfs/al-qaida-papers-how-to-run-a-state.pdf; Rukmini Callimachi, "Yemen Terror Boss Left Blueprint for Waging Jihad," *Associated Press*, August 9, 2013.
40. Aaron Zelin, Daveed Gartenstein-Ross, and Andrew Lebovich, "Al-Qa'ida in the Islamic Maghreb's Tunisia Strategy," *CTC Sentinel* 6:7 (July 2013), 24–25.
41. Carla Humud, Alexis Arieff, Lauren Ploch Blanchard, Christopher Blanchard, Jeremy Sharp, and Kenneth Katzman, *Al Qaeda-Affiliated Groups: Middle East and Africa* (Washington, DC: Congressional Research Service, October 2014), 19–20; Guidere, "The Timbuktu Letters," 13–14.
42. "Al-Qa'ida in Yemen Vows to Continue Jihad, Identifies Group's Leader in Yemen," OSC, June 21, 2007.
43. Michael Knights, "Jihadist Paradise: Yemen's Terrorist Threat Re-emerges," *Jane's Intelligence Review* (June 2008), 22–24.
44. AQAP, "We Start from Here and We Will Meet at al-Aqsa," OSC, January 24, 2009.
45. Joscelyin and Roggio, "AQAP Emir Also Serves as al Qaeda's General Manager."
46. Johnsen, *The Last Refuge*, 17–34.
47. Abdulelah Shaye, "Interview with Abu Baseer al-Wuhayshi," *Al-Jazeera*, January 26, 2009.
48. Ibid.
49. Bryce Loidolt, "Managing the Global and Local: The Dual Agendas of Al Qaeda in the Arabian Peninsula," *Studies in Conflict & Terrorism* 34 (2011), 105–107.
50. Shaye, "Interview with Abu Baseer al-Wuhayshi."
51. Barak Barfi, *Yemen on The Brink? The Resurgence of al Qaeda in Yemen* (Washington, DC: New America Foundation, January 2010), 2–6.
52. On jihadis' appreciation of Yemen's terrain and arms' accessibility, see Loidoit, "Managing the Global and Local," 105–106.
53. Barfi, *Yemen on the Brink?*, 12–13.
54. Hegghammer, *The Failure of Jihad in Saudi Arabia*, 27.
55. The Abbottabad Documents, SOCOM-2012-0000019 and SOCOM-2012-0000016.
56. The Abbottabad Documents, SOCOM-2012-0000016.
57. The Abbottabad Documents, SOCOM-2012-0000017.

58. The Abbottabad Documents, SOCOM-2012-0000016.

59. Nelly Lahoud, Stuart Caudill, Liam Collins, Gabrield Koehler-Derric, Don Rassler, and Muhammad al-'Ubaydi, *Letters from Abbottabad: Bin Laden Sidelined?* (West Point, NY: The Combating Terrorism Center, May 2012), 33–34.

60. Ibid., 35.

61. Sudarsan Raghavan, "In Yemen, Tribal Militias in a Fierce Battle with al-Qaeda Wing," *Washington Post*, September 10, 2012, https://www.washingtonpost.com/world/middle_east/in-yemen-tribal-militias-in-a-fierce-battle-with-al-qaeda-wing/2012/09/10/0cce6f1e-f2b2-11e1-b74c-84ed55e0300b_story.html.

62. "Al-Qaida Paper: The Yemen Letters."

63. Loidolt, "Managing the Global and Local," 103.

64. Bill Roggio, "Yemeni Jihadi Claims Anwar al Awlaki, Samir Khar Killed in Airstrike," *The Long War Journal*, September 30, 2011, http://www.longwarjournal.org/archives/2011/09/yemeni_jihadi_claims_anwar_al.php.

65. Scott Shane and Eric Schmitt, "Qaeda Plot to Attack Plane Foiled, U.S. Officials Say," *New York Times*, May 7, 2012, A12.

66. Jason Linkins, "Al Qaeda's Inspire Magazine Returns, Recommends Forest Fires as Next Great Terror Innovation," *Huffington Post*, May 3, 2012.

67. Al-Sahab, "Zawahiri Announces Joining Shabaab to al-Qaeda," Site Intelligence Group, February 9, 2012.

68. *U.S. v. Abid Naseer*, Government Exhibits 425 and 427.

69. Stig Jarle Hansen, *Al-Shabaab in Somalia: The History and Ideology of a Militant Islamist Group, 2005–2012* (London: Hurst, 2013), 26–47.

70. Ibid., 49–102.

71. "Somalia's al-Shabab Rebels Leave Mogadishu," *BBC News*, August 6, 2011, http://www.bbc.com/news/world-africa-14430283.

72. Hansen, *Al-Shabaab in Somalia*, 24, 45–46.

73. Ahmed Abdi Godane, "Emir of Shabaab Places Group within Global Jihad," Site Intelligence Group, June 2, 2008.

74. Nelly Lahoud, "The Merger of Al-Shabab and Qa'idat al-Jihad," *CTC Sentinel* 5:2 (February 2012), 1–5; Lahoud, *Beware of Imitators*, 94–98.

75. Al-Shabab, "At Your Service, O Usama," Site Intelligence Group, September 20, 2009.

76. The Abbottabad Documents, Combating Terrorism Center, SOCOM-2012-000005.

77. For example, Abu Yahya al-Libi, "Somalia . . . Victory Comes with Patience," OSC, February 13, 2009.

78. Christopher Anzalone, "The Formalizing of an Affiliation: Somalia's Harakat al-Shabab al-Mujahideed & Al-Qa'ida Central," *al-Wasat blog*, February 10, 2012, https://thewasat.wordpress.com/2012/02/10/the-formalizing-of-an-affiliation-somalias-harakat-al-shabab-al-mujahideen-al-qaida-central/.

79. Lahoud, "The Merger of Al-Shabab and Qa'idat al-Jihad," 2–3.

80. Lahoud, "The Merger of Al-Shabab and Qa'idat al-Jihad." Documents written by the American jihadi Ommar Hammami lend further support to this interpretation. See Clint Watts, "Hammami's Latest Call Reveals Deceit, Dissention and Death in Shabaab & al Qaeda," *Selected Wisdom*, January 8, 2013, http://selectedwisdom.com/?p=901.

81. The Abbottabad Documents, Combating Terrorism Center, SOCOM-2012-000005.

82. Anzalone, "The Formalizing of an Affiliation."

83. *U.S. v. Abid Naseer*, Government Exhibit 425.

84. Al-Shabab, "Shabaab Announces Death of al-Qaeda Official in Drone Strike," Site Intelligence Group, January 21, 2012.

85. Lahoud, "The Merger of Al-Shabab and Qa'idat al-Jihad."

86. Abdi Aynte, "Understanding the al-Shabaab/al-Qaeda 'Merger,'" *African Arguments*, March 19, 2012, http://africanarguments.org/2012/03/19/understanding-the-al-shabaabl-qaeda-%E2%80%98merger%E2%80%99-by-abdi-aynte/.

87. Clint Watts, Jacob Shapiro, Vahid Brown, *Al-Qa'ida's (Mis)Adventures in the Horn of Africa* (West Point, NY: Combating Terrorism Center, July 2007).

88. Clint Watts, "Deciphering Hammami Scenarios & Shabaab Splits," *Selected Wisdom*, March 29, 2012, http://selectedwisdom.com/?p=589; Clint Watts, "Al Qaeda & al Shabaab Merger: Why Now?" *Selected Wisdom*, February 18, 2012, http://selectedwisdom.com/?p=548.

89. For example, see Omar Hammami, "Hammami Exposes Inner Workings of Shabaab, Details Conflict (Part 1)," Site Intelligence Group, January 5, 2013; Omar Hammami, "Hammami Exposes Inner Workings of Shabaab, Details Conflict (Part 2)," Site Intelligence Group, January 10, 2013; Omar Hammami, "Hammami Exposes Inner Workings of Shabaab, Details Conflict (Part 3)," Site Intelligence Group, January 14, 2013; Al-Shabab, "Shabaab Responds to Abu Mansour al-Amriki's Allegations," Site Intelligence Group, December 17, 2012; J. M. Berger, "Omar and Me: My Strange, Frustrating Relationship with an American Terrorist," *Foreign Policy*, September 17, 2013, http://foreignpolicy.com/2013/09/17/omar-and-me/.

90. For example, see Ibrahim al-Afghani "Shabaab Official Speaks Out against Leader, Appeals to Zawahiri for Help (Document)," Site Intelligence Group, April 10, 2013; Zubeir al-Muhajir, "Iko Matata—Yes, There Are Problems," Site Intelligence Group, April 24, 2013.

91. A position shared by Watts, "Al Qaeda & al Shabaab Merger."

92. Al-Sahab, "Zawahiri Announces Joining Shabaab to al-Qaeda."

93. "Al-Qaeda Participates in Aid Distribution to Somali Drought Victims," Site Institute, October 13, 2011. More extensive details of the various links between al-Qaeda and al-Shabab can be found in Anzalone, "The Formalizing of an Affiliation."

94. Anzalone, "The Formalizing of an Affiliation"; Christopher Anzalone, "al-Shabab's Setbacks in Somalia," *CTC Sentinel* 4:10 (October 2011), 22–25.

95. Watts, "Al Qaeda & al Shabaab Merger."
96. Christopher Harnish, *The Terror Threat from Somalia: The Internationalization of al Shabaab* (Washington, DC: The American Enterprise Institute, February 2010), 27–29.
97. The Abbottabad Documents, SOCOM-2012-0000010.
98. Aynte, "Understanding the al-Shabaab/al-Qaeda 'Merger.'"
99. Al-Shabab, "Shabaab Leadership Forbids Establishment of New Groups," Site Intelligence Group, April 3, 2012.
100. "Interview with Shabaab Official Highlights Shabaab's Internal Divisions," *Flashpoint Partners*, March 31, 2012.
101. Hassan Abukar, "Somalia: The Godane Coup and the Unravelling of Al-Shabaab," *African Arguments*, July 2, 2013, http://africanarguments.org/2013/07/02/somalia-the-godane-coup-and-the-unraveling-of-al-shabaab-%E2%80%93-by-hassan-m-abukar/.
102. Al-Afghani, "Shabaab Official Speaks Out against Leader, Appeals to Zawahiri for Help (Document)."
103. Al-Shabab, "Shabaab Appoints New Leader after Death of Godane, Renews Pledge to Zawahiri," Site Intelligence Group, September 6, 2014.

CHAPTER 8

1. "Jihadist Website Posts 'Communique' on Egyptian Islamic Group Joining al-Qa'ida," OSC, August 8, 2006.
2. Gilles Kepel, *Jihad: The Trail of Political Islam* (Cambridge, MA: Harvard University Press, 2003), 276–298.
3. Tawil, *Brothers in Arms*, 103–107.
4. Muhammad al-Shafi'I, "Al-Zawahiri's Secret Papers, Part 3," *Al-Sharq al-Awsat*, December 15, 2002; Muhammad al-Shafi'I, "Al-Zawahiri's Secret Papers, Part 5," *Al-Sharq al-Awsat*, December 17, 2002.
5. Gerges, *The Rise and Fall of Al-Qaeda*, 65.
6. Omar Ashour, "Lions Tamed? An Inquiry into the Causes of De-Radicalization of Armed Islamist Movements: The Case of the Egyptian Islamic Group," *Middle East Journal* 61:4 (Autumn, 2007), 596–625.
7. Al-Gama'a al-Islamiya, "The Strategy and Bombings of Al-Qa'ida: Errors and Perils," serialized in *Al-Sharq al-Awsat*, January 2004.
8. Al-Gama'a al-Islamiya, "The Strategy and Bombings of Al-Qa'ida"; Feldner, Carmon, and Lev, "The Al-Gama'a Al-Islamiyya Cessation of Violence."
9. Montasser al-Zayyat, *The Road to al-Qaeda: The Story of Bin Laden's Right-Hand Man* (London: Pluto Press, 2004).
10. See the al-Qaeda Statement Index, gtrp.haverford.edu/aqsi/aqsi-home.
11. "Jihadist Website Posts 'Communique' on Egyptian Islamic Group Joining al-Qa'ida."

12. "Egyptian Al-Jama'ah al-Islamiyah Denies Joining Al-Qa'ida," OSC, August 7, 2006; "Interview with Dr. Najih Ibrahim, theoretician of the Egyptian Al-Jama'ah Al-Islamiyah," *Al-Sharq al-Awast*, August 13, 2006; Abduh Zaynah, "Egyptian Islamic Group: Al-Zawahiri Wanted to Implicate Us before London Plot Was Uncovered. Said Iran Has Its Own Agenda But Cards in Lebanon Should Not Be Mixed Up," *Al-Sharq al-Awsat*, August 14, 2006.

13. "Egypt's Muhammad Khalil al-Hakaymah Calls for 'Unity' of Islamic Groups," OSC, November 3, 2006; "Al-Hakaymah Responds to Sayyid Imam Document 'Rationalization of Jihad Operations,'" OSC, November 28, 2007; Chris Zambelis, "EIG's Muhammed al-Hakaima Continues to Incite Jihad," *Terrorism Focus* 3:39 (October 2006); Chris Zambelis, "Al-Hakaima Positions Himself for Key Role in the Global Salafi-Jihad," *Terrorism Focus* 3:41 (October 2006).

14. Roggio, "Senior al Qaeda leader Thought Killed in North Waziristan Strike."

15. Al-Zawahiri, "Knights under the Banner of the Prophet."

16. Tawil, *Brothers in Arms*.

17. Camile Tawil, "The Changing Face of the Jihadist Movement in Libya," *Terrorism Monitor*, 7:1, January 9, 2009; Alison Pargeter, "LIFG Revisions Unlikely to Reduce Jihadist Violence," *CTC Sentinel* 2:10 (October 2009), 7–9; Cruickshank, "LIFG Revisions Posing Critical Challenge to al-Qa'ida." *CTC Sentinel* 2:10 (December 2009), 5–8.

18. Noman Benotman, "Al-Qaeda: Your Armed Struggle Is Over—An Open Letter to bin Laden," September 10, 2010.

19. Alison Pargeter, "LIFG: An Organization in Eclipse," *Terrorism Monitor* 3:21, November 3, 2005; Pargeter, "LIFG Revisions Unlikely to Reduce Jihadist Violence."

20. Al-Sahab, "Al-Zawahiri, Al-Libi: Libyan Islamic Fighting Group Joins Al-Qa'ida," OSC, November 3, 2007.

21. Ibid.

22. Cruickshank, "LIFG Revisions Posing Critical Challenge to al-Qa'ida."

23. Al-Sahab, "Al-Zawahiri, Al-Libi: Libyan Islamic Fighting Group Joins Al-Qa'ida."

24. Camille Tawil, "Islamic Fighting Group Wants Its Leaders in Afghanistan, Iran to Participate in Dialogue with Libyan Security Agencies," *Al-Hayat*, January 28, 2007.

25. Ibid.

26. Kevin Jackson, "Abu al-Layth al-Libi," Jihadi Bios Project (West Point, NY: Combatting Terrorism Center, 2015); Tawil, *Brothers in Arms*, 179–181.

27. Alison Pargeter, "The LIFG's Current Role in the Global Jihad," *CTC Sentinel* 1:5 (April 2008), 5–6.

28. *U.S. v. Abid Naseer*, document 427.

29. Fishman and Felter, *Al-Qa'ida's Foreign Fighters in Iraq*, 10; Abu Yahya al-Libi, "Iraq between Stages, Conspiratorial Intrigue," OSC, March 22, 2007.

30. Camille Tawil, "Libyan Islamists Back Away from al-Qaeda Merger in Reconciliation with Qaddafi Regime," *Terrorism Monitor* 7:17, June 18, 2009; Pargeter, "LIFG Revisions Unlikely to Reduce Jihadist Violence."

31. ICT's Jihadi Websites Monitoring Group, "The De-Radicalization Process of Terrorist Organizations: The Libyan Case," Interdisciplinary Center, Hertzeliya, August 2010; Cruickshank, "LIFG Revisions Posing Critical Challenge to al-Qa'ida." Interestingly, the LIFG chose not to mention al-Qaeda in the name of the book, although al-Qaeda's actions were a primary target of the work.

32. Peter Neumann, "Foreign Fighter Total in Syria/Iraq Now Exceeds 20,000; Surpasses Afghanistan Conflict in the 1980s," International Centre for the Study of Radicalization, January 26, 2015; Fishman and Felter, *Al-Qa'ida's Foreign Fighters in Iraq*.

33. *U.S. v. Abid Naseer*, document 427.

34. Al-Zawahiri, "Knights under the Banner of the Prophet."

35. Bin Laden, "Declaration of War"; World Islamic Front, "Jihad Against Jews and Crusaders."

36. "The Al-Qaeda Statement Index," Haverford College.

37. Hussein, "Al-Zarqawi."

38. Asad al-Jihad2, "The Timing of the Entrance of the Al-Qa'ida Organization to Palestine," OSC, January 28, 2008.

39. Al-Sahab, "Interview with Shaykh Ayman al-Zawahiri," OSC, May 5, 2007.

40. Ayman al-Zawahiri, "Spiteful Britain and Its Indian Slaves," July 10, 2007.

41. Al-Libi, "Palestine, Warning Call and Cautioning Cry," OSC, April 29, 2007; Al-Zawahiri, "Realities of the Conflict Between Islam and Unbelief," OSC, December 21, 2006.

42. Abu Yahya al-Libi, "Palestine, Warning Call and Cautioning Cry."

43. Al-Zawahiri, "Realities of the Conflict between Islam and Unbelief," in Laura Mansfield, *His Own Words: Translation and Analysis of the Writings of Dr. Ayman Al-Zawahiri* (Old Tappan, NJ: TLG Publications, 2006), 319–320.

44. Al-Sahab, "Interview with Shaykh Ayman al-Zawahiri."

45. Ayman al-Zawahiri, "Open Interview—Part One," OSC, April 3, 2008.

46. Al-Baghdadi, "The Religion Is the Advice."

47. Hamas, "'Leader in Al-Qassam Brigades Denounces Abu Umar al-Baghdadi for Criticizing Hamas," February 19, 2008.

48. "Hamas: We Are No Al Qaeda," NEFA Foundation, April 24, 2006.

49. Clancy Chassay, "The Gun or the Ballot Box? Hamas or al Qaeda?" Ikhwanweb, April 1, 2006, http://www.ikhwanweb.com/article.php?id=4507.

50. Barak Mendelsohn, "Islamists Infighting: Understanding al Qaeda's Critique of Hamas," Annual meeting of the International Studies Association, New York, February 15–18, 2009.

51. Ashraf al-Hawar, "The Hard-Liners Accuse Hamas of Launching a War on Salafism," *al-Quds al-Arabi*, September 19, 2008.

52. Barak Mendelsohn, "Hamas and Its Discontents: The Battle over Islamic Rule in Gaza," *Foreign Affairs*, September 9, 2009.

53. Asmaa al-Ghoul, "Islamic State Rejected Gaza Jihadists' Offer of Allegiance," *Al-Monitor*, January 7, 2015, http://www.al-monitor.com/pulse/originals/2015/01/islamic-state-presence-in-gaza.html.

54. Al-Zawahiri, "Open Interview—Part One."

55. Osama bin Laden, "The Way to Foil Plots," OSC, December 29, 2007; Bin Laden, "The Way for the Salvation of Palestine," OSC, March 21, 2008; Al-Baghdadi, "The Religion Is the Advice."

56. Bin Laden, "The Way to Foil Plots."

CHAPTER 9

1. Abouzeid, "The Jihad Next Door."

2. Ibid.

3. The Islamic State, *Dabiq*, issue 1 (1914), 4–5.

4. "Syria's Al-Nusra Front Leader Interviewed on Conflict, Political Vision," BBC Monitoring Middle East, December 22, 2013.

5. Jabhat al-Nusra, "New Jihadist Group Declares Presence in Levant, Calls for Action," Site Intelligence Group, January 23, 2012.

6. Abouzeid, "The Jihad Next Door."

7. Rania Abouzeid, "Interview with Official of Jabhat al-Nusra, Syria's Islamist Militia Group," *Time*, December 25, 2012, http://world.time.com/2012/12/25/interview-with-a-newly-designated-syrias-jabhat-al-nusra/; Elizabeth O'Bagy, *Jihad in Syria*, Middle East Security Report 6 (Washington DC: Institute for the Study of War, September 2012), 32.

8. There are reports that by April 2013, JN had lost some of that trust—although given later developments it likely reflected belligerent behavior by the ISI, seeking to assert a more prominent role in Syria. Elizabeth O'Bagy, "Syria Update 13–05: Jabhat Nusra Aligns with al-Qaeda," Institute for the Study of War, April 15, 2013.

9. "Syria's Al-Nusra Front Leader Interviewed on Conflict, Political Vision."

10. Charles Lister, *Dynamic Stalemate: Surveying Syria's Military Landscape* (Doha, Qatar: Brooking Doha Center, 2014), 7.

11. "Syria's Al-Nusra Front Leader Interviewed on Conflict, Political Vision."

12. For an elaborate discussion of JN's governance, see Jennifer Cafarella, *Jabhat al-Nusra in Syria: An Islamic Emirate for al-Qaeda* (Washington, DC: Institute for the Study of War, December 2014).

13. According to Hassan Hassan and Michael Weiss, Abu Bakr gave secret *bay'a* to al-Zawahiri. See Michael Weiss and Hassan Hassan, *ISIS: Inside the Army of Terror* (New York: Regan Arts, 2015), 171.

14. Seth Jones, *A Persistent Threat: The Evolution of al Qa'ida and Other Salafi Jihadists* (Washington DC: RAND, 2014), 7.

15. "The Pen and the Sword—Al-Qaeda's Attempts to Mediate Jihadist Dispute," *Jane's Terrorism and Security Monitor*, July 1, 2013.

16. Abu Bakr al-Baghdadi, "ISI Leader Rebrands ISI and al-Nusra Front as 'Islamic State in Iraq and the Levant,'" Site Intelligence Group, April 8, 2013.

17. Note, though, that if al-Baghdadi did not see the ISI as a part of al-Qaeda at that time, as he would later claim, then he would not have needed to distance himself from AQC.

18. Abu Muhammad al-Joulani, "Al-Nusra Front Confirms Link to ISI, Pledges to Zawahiri," Site Intelligence Group, April 10, 2013.

19. Basma Atassi, "Qaeda Chief Annuls Syrian-Iraqi Jihad Merger," *Al-Jazeera*, June 9, 2013, http://www.aljazeera.com/news/middleeast/2013/06/2013699425657882.html.

20. Al-Joulani, "Al-Nusra Front Confirms Link to ISI, Pledges to Zawahiri."

21. O'Bagy, "Syria Update 13-05"; Aymenn Jawad al-Tamimi, "Jabhat al-Nusra's Relations with Other Rebels after the Bay'ah to Zawahiri," *Jihadology*, May 14, 2013, http://jihadology.net/2013/05/14/guest-post-jabhat-al-nusras-relations-with-other-rebels-after-the-bayah-to-zawahiri/.

22. Rita Katz and Adam Raisman, "Special Report on the Power Struggle between al-Qaeda Branches and Leadership," Site Intelligence Group, June 24, 2013.

23. Ahrar al-Sham, "Ahrar al-Sham Criticizes ISI Leader's Declared Islamic State in Iraq and Syria."

24. Al-Tamimi, "Jabhat al-Nusra's Relations with Other Rebels."

25. Al-Zawahiri, "Zawahiri Reportedly Settles Dispute between ISI, al-Nusra Front."

26. Abu Bakr al-Baghdadi, "ISI Leader Takes Issue with Zawahiri Letter in Alleged Audio Speech," Site Intelligence Group, June 15, 2013.

27. Al-Adnani, "ISIL Spokesman Criticizes Zawahiri Letter."

28. Ibid.

29. Ibid.

30. Ayman al-Zawahiri, "Zawahiri Details Relationship with ISIL, Repeats Call to Return to Iraq," Site Intelligence Group, May 2, 2014.

31. Al-Adnani, "ISIL Spokesman Criticizes Zawahiri Letter."

32. See Mendelsohn, *Combating Jihadism*; Mendelsohn, "God versus Westphalia."

33. Al-Adnani, "ISIL Spokesman Criticizes Zawahiri Letter."

34. For example, see Ayman al-Zawahiri, "Zawahiri Calls for Unity in Creed, Attacks Egyptian Constitution," Site Intelligence Group, April 6, 2013.

35. For example, Al-Zawahiri, "General Guidelines for Jihad."

36. Charles C. Caris and Samuel Reynolds, *Middle Eastern Security Report 22: ISIS Governance in Syria* (Washington, DC: Institute for the Study of War, July 2014), 10–14.

37. Charles Lister, "Syria's New Rebel Front," *Foreign Policy*, January 8, 2014, http://foreignpolicy.com/2014/01/08/syrias-new-rebel-front/.

38. Abu Muhammad al-Joulani, "Al-Nusra Front Leader Gives Update on Syrian Jihad, Touts Success," Site Intelligence Group, July 22, 2013.

39. Aymenn Jawad al-Tamini, "The Dawn of the Islamic State of Iraq and Ash-Sham," in Hillel Fradkin, Husain Haqqani, Eric Brown, and Hassan Mneimneh (Eds.), *Current Trends in Islamist Ideology*, vol. 16 (Washington DC: Hudson Institute, 2014), 9–12.

40. Valerie Szybaia, "Al-Qaeda Shows Its True Colors in Syria," Institute for the Study of War, August 1, 2013.

41. Jabhat al-Nusra, "Al-Nusra Front Announces Compliance with Zawahiri's Order Regarding ISIL," Site Intelligence Group, May 4, 2014.

42. Abu Muhammad al-Joulani, "Al-Nusra Front Leader Julani Offers Initiative to Settle Factional Conflict," Site Intelligence Group, January 7, 2014.

43. Abu Khalid al-Suri, "Message Attributed to Zawahiri's Arbiter in Syria Gives Advice to ISIL," Site Intelligence Group, January 17, 2014; Joshua Landis, "The Battle between ISIS and Syria's Rebel Militias," *Syria Comment*, January 4, 2014, http://www.joshualandis.com/blog/battle-isis-syrias-rebel-militias/.

44. Al-Zawahiri, "Zawahiri Urges Jihadi Groups in Syria to End Factional conflict," Site Intelligence Group, January 24, 2014.

45. Barak Mendelsohn and Ariel I. Ahram, "Al Qaeda's Syria Problem," *Foreign Policy*, January 23, 2014, http://foreignpolicy.com/2014/01/23/al-qaedas-syria-problem/.

46. Thomas Joscelyn, "Saudi Cleric's Reconciliation Initiative for Jihadists Draws Wide Support, Then a Rejection," *The Long War Journal*, January 27, 2014, http://www.longwarjournal.org/archives/2014/01/saudi_clerics_reconc.php.

47. Thomas Joscelyn, "Pro-al Qaeda Saudi Cleric Calls on ISIS Members to Defect," *The Long War Journal*, February 3, 2014, http://www.longwarjournal.org/archives/2014/02/pro-al_qaeda_saudi_c.php.

48. The statement is dated January 22. It is likely that its release was delayed for a few days in the hope that the intensive mediation efforts would bear fruit.

49. Qaedat al-Jihad—The General Command, "Al-Qaeda Disassociates from ISIL," Site Intelligence Group, February 3, 2014.

50. Nelly Lahoud and Muhammad al-'Baydi, "The War of Jihadists in Syria," *CTC Sentinel* 7:3 (March 2014), 2.

51. Abu Qatada al-Filistini, "Radical Cleric Abu Qatada Advises Fighters in Syria to Reconcile," *Site Intelligence Group*, November 5, 2013; Tamer al-Samadi, "Rift Grows between Jabhat al-Nusra and ISIS," *Al-Hayat*, November 15, 2013.

52. Ayman al-Zawahiri, "Zawahiri Denies Changing His Ideology, Speaks in Interview on Syrian Conflict, Egypt, War with the U.S.," Site Intelligence Group, April 18, 2014.

53. Ibid.

54. Ibid. See also "Syria's Al-Nusra Front Leader Interviewed on Conflict, Political Vision."

55. Ayman al-Zawahiri, "Zawahiri Details Relationship with ISIL, Repeats Call to Return to Iraq," Site Intelligence Group, May 2, 2014.

56. Ibid. For testimonial from a senior JN official confirming that there had been authority relations between al-Zawahiri and al-Baghdadi until the latter reneged, see "Jabhat al-Nusra Reacts on ISIS Spokesman al-Adnani (Part I)," *Pietervanostaeyen Blog*, March 27, 2013, https://pietervanostaeyen.wordpress.com/2014/03/27/jabhat-an-nusra-reacts-on-isis-spokesman-al-adnani-part-i/.

57. Al-Adnani, "ISIL Refuses Zawahiri Order to Withdraw from Syria, Responses to Message."

58. Al-Zawahiri, "Zawahiri Details Relationship with ISIL."

59. Ibid.

60. Al-Adnani, "ISIL Spokesman Denounces General Command of al-Qaeda."

61. Al-Adnani, "ISIL Refuses Zawahiri Order to Withdraw from Syria, Responses to Message."

62. Ibid.

63. Ibid.

64. Brian Fishman, "Fourth Generation Governance: Sheikh Tamimi defends the Islamic State of Iraq," Combating Terrorism Center, March 23, 2007.

65. Al-Maqdisi strongly rejects the notion that ISIS is an Islamic state. When referring to ISIS he adds the word "organization" so as not to lend any legitimacy to what he sees as ISIS's faulty claims. For example, see Abu Muhammad al-Maqdisi, "A Call to the Umma and Mujahideen," May 2014. Available at Jihadology.com.

66. Al-Adnani, "ISIL Spokesman Denounces General Command of al-Qaeda."

67. Al-Adnani, "ISIL Refuses Zawahiri Order to Withdraw from Syria."

68. Ibid.

69. Al-Adnani, "ISIL Spokesman Denounces General Command of al-Qaeda"; "ISIL Refuses Zawahiri Order to Withdraw from Syria, Responses to Message."

70. Al-Adnani, "ISIL Refuses Zawahiri Order to Withdraw from Syria."

71. Al-Adnani, "ISIL Spokesman Denounces General Command of al-Qaeda."

72. Ibid.

73. Ibid.

74. Al-Adnani, "ISIL Refuses Zawahiri Order to Withdraw from Syria."

75. Al-Adnani, "ISIL Spokesman Denounces General Command of al-Qaeda."

76. Al-Adnani, "ISIS Spokesman Declares Caliphate, Rebrands Group as "Islamic State," Site Intelligence Group, June 29, 2014.

77. Abu Bakr al-Baghdadi, "A Message to the Mujahidin and the Muslim Umma in the Month of Ramadan," Al-Hayat Media Center, July 1, 2014.

78. The Islamic State, "The Biography of Khalifa Abu Bakr Al-Baghdadi, Amir Ul Mu'minin (Commander of the Believers)," July 2, 2014.

79. "Islamic State Video Promotes Destruction of Iraq-Syria Border Crossing," Site Intelligence Group, June 30, 2014.

80. Al-Baghdadi, "A Message to the Mujahidin and the Muslim Ummah."

81. Thomas Hegghammer, "Calculated Caliphate," *Lawfare*, July 6, 2014, http://www.lawfareblog.com/foreign-policy-essay-calculated-caliphate.

82. J. M. Berger, "The State of the 'Caliphate' Is . . . Meh," *Intelwire*, July 2, 2014, http://news.intelwire.com/2014/07/the-caliphate-so-far-flatlining.html.

83. Cafarella, *Jabhat al-Nusra in Syria*.

84. Aaron Lund, "What Is the Khorasan Group and Why Is the U.S. Bombing It in Syria," Carnagie Endowment for International Peace, September 23, 2014.

CHAPTER 10

1. Al-Sahab, "Al-Qaeda Announces the Establishment of "Qaedat al-Jihad in the Indian Subcontinent," Site Intelligence Group, September 3, 2014.

2. Ibid.

3. Al-Adnani, "ISIL Refuses Zawahiri Order to Withdraw from Syria, Responses to Message."

4. J. M. Berger, "Zawahiri Falls Off the Map, Is Rebuked by Top al Nusra Figure," *Intelwire*, August 18, 2014, http://news.intelwire.com/2014/08/zawahiri-falls-off-map-gets-rebuked-by.html; Thomas Joscelyn, "Jihadist Ideologues Call on Zawahiri to Detail Problems with Former al Qaeda Affiliate," *The Long War Journal*, April 11, 2014, http://www.longwarjournal.org/archives/2014/04/jihadist_ideologues.php; Ibrahim Al-Afghani, "Shabaab Official Speaks Out Against Leader"; Al-Muhajir, "Iko Matata—Yes, There are Problems."

5. An example of such a bland statement: AQAP, "AQAP Officially Releases Message of Advice to Jihadi Factions in Syria to End Hostilities," Site Intelligence Group, March 3, 2014.

6. Abu Bakr al-Baghdadi, "IS Leader Abu Bakr al-Baghdadi Rallies Fighters, Welcomes New Pledges," Site Intelligence Group, November 13, 2014; AQAP, "AQAP Rebukes Abu Bakr al-Baghdadi, Rejects IS' "Caliphate," Site Intelligence Group, November 21, 2014.

7. Al-Zawahiri, "Zawahiri Details Relationship with ISIL, Repeats Call to Return to Iraq."

8. The Abbottabad Documents SOCOM-2012-0000019 and SOCOM-2012-0000005.

9. Anne Stenersen and Philipp Holtman, "The Three Functions of UBL's 'Greater Pledge' to Mullah Omar (2001–2006–2014)," *Jihadology*, January 8, 2015, http://jihadology.net/2015/01/08/guest-post-the-three-functions-of-ubls-greater-pledge-to-mullah-omar-2001-2006-2014/; Vahid Brown, "The Façade of Allegiance: Bin Laden's Dubious Pledge to Mullah Omar," *CTC Sentinel* 3:1 (2010), 1–6.

10. Lia, "Jihadi Insurgents and the Perils of Territorialisation."

11. AQAP, "AQAP Rebukes Abu Bakr al-Baghdadi, Rejects IS' 'Caliphate.'"

12. Qaedat al-Jihad, "Al-Qaeda Disassociates from ISIL."

13. Abu Muhammad Al-Maqdisi, "And Be Not Like Her Who Undoes the Thread Which She Has Spun, After It Has Become Strong," *Pietervanostaeyen Blog*, July 14, 2014, https://pietervanostaeyen.wordpress.com/2014/07/14/and-be-not-like-her-who-undoes-the-thread-which-she-has-spun-after-it-has-become-strong-by-shaykh-abu-muhammad-al-maqdisi/.

14. Majid bin Muhammad Al-Majid, "Brigades of Abdullah Azzam Leader Expresses Concerns to Zawahiri about ISIL in Posthumous Message," Site Intelligence Group, May 23, 2014.

15. Al-Sahab, "The West and the Dark Tunnel," OSC, September 22, 2009.

16. Rita Katz and Adam, Raisman, "Syrian Jihad: The Weakening of al-Qaeda's Leadership," Site Intelligence Group, April 8, 2014.

17. Al-Maqdisi, "A Call to the Ummah and Mujahideen."

18. For example, Abu Qatada Al-Filistini, "A Message to the People of Jihad and Those Who Love Jihad," *Pietervanostaeyen Blog*, April 28, 2014, https://pietervanostaeyen.wordpress.com/2014/04/28/a-message-of-shaykh-abu-qatadat-al-filistini-a-letter-to-the-people-of-jihad/; Al-Maqdisi, "And Be Not Like Her Who Undoes the Thread Which She Has Spun, After It Has Become Strong; Cole Bunzel, "The Islamic State of Disunity: Jihadism Divided," *Jihadica*, January 30, 2014, http://www.jihadica.com/the-islamic-state-of-disunity-jihadism-divided/.

19. Al-Filistini, "A Message to the People of Jihad."

20. Abu Qatada al-Filistini, "Radical Cleric Abu Qatada Advises Fighters in Syria to Reconicle."

21. Cole Bunzel, "A Jihadi Civil War of Words: The Ghuraba' Media Foundation and Minbar al-Tawhid wa'l-Jihad," *Jihadica*, October 21, 2014, http://www.jihadica.com/a-jihadi-civil-war/; Joas Wagemakers, "Al-Qaida Advises the Arab Spring," *Jihadica*, September 21, 2013, http://www.jihadica.com/al-qaida-advises-the-arab-spring-yemen/; Cole Bunzel, "The Islamic State of Disunity: Jihadism Divided," *Jihadica*, January 30, 2014, http://www.jihadica.com/the-islamic-state-of-disunity-jihadism-divided/; "Shumukh al-Islam Network Announces Support for ISIL," Site Intelligence Group, March 11, 2014.

22. Bunzel, "A Jihadi Civil War of Words."

23. AQIM, "AQIM Rejects IS' Declared Caliphate, Calls Jihadi Leaders to Rectify Issues," Site Intelligence Group, July 14, 2014; AQAP, "AQAP Rebukes Abu Bakr al-Baghdadi, Rejects IS' Caliphate."

24. Al-Shabab, "Shabaab Appoints New Leader after Death of Godane, Renews Pledge to Zawahiri," Site Intelligence Group, September 6, 2014.

25. J. M. Berger, "The Islamic State vs. al-Qaeda: Who's Winning the War to Become the Jihadi Superpower?," *Foreign Policy*, September 2, 2014, http://foreignpolicy.com/2014/09/02/the-islamic-state-vs-al-qaeda/.

26. "Message Attributed to AQIM in the 'Central Region' Gives Advice to ISIL," SITE Intelligence Group, March 24, 2014.

27. Omar Shabbi, "AQIM Defectors Raise Fears of IS Branch in North Africa," *Al-Monitor*, September 9, 2014, http://www.al-monitor.com/pulse/originals/2014/09/north-africa-algeria-aqim-establish-islamic-state.html.

28. Katz and Raisman, "Syrian Jihad: The Weakening of al-Qaeda's Leadership," Site Intelligence Group, April 8, 2014.

29. Al-Zawahiri, "General Guidelines for Jihad."

30. AQAP, "AQAP Says Disobedient Fighter Responsible for Hospital Attack in Sana'a," Site Intelligence Group, December 21, 2013.

31. For example, Usama Mahmoud, "AQIS Condemns Peshawar School Attack, Clarifies Purpose and Legitimate Targets of Jihad," Site Intelligence Group, December 20, 2014.

32. Atiyatallah, "The People's Revolt . . . the Fall of the Corrupt Arab Regime . . . the Demolishment of the Idol of Stability . . . and the New Beginning," *The Global Islamic Media Front*, February 16, 2011, http://worldanalysis.net/modules/smartsection/item.php?itemid=25; Al-Sahab, "As-Sahab Video Focuses on Current State of Conflict (Part One)," Site Intelligence Group, September 13, 2012.

33. For example, AQAP, "AQAP Expresses Solidarity with IS Amidst U.S. Airstrikes, Threatens U.S.," Site Intelligence Group, August 14, 2014.

34. Barack Obama, "Transcript: President Obama's Speech Outlining Strategy to Defeat Islamic State," *Washington Post*, September 10, 2014, http://www.washingtonpost.com/politics/full-text-of-president-obamas-speech-outlining-strategy-to-defeat-islamic-state/2014/09/10/af69dec8-3943-11e4-9c9f-ebb47272e40e_story.html.

Bibliography

ARCHIVES

- The Abbottabad Documents, Combating Terrorism Center, West Point, NY.
- The Harmony Project, Combating Terrorism Center, West Point, NY.
- The al-Qaeda Statement Index, Haverford College, Haverford, PA.
- Site Intelligence Group, Washington, DC.
- Open Source Center (OSC), Reston, VA.

SOURCES

Abouzeid, Rania, "Interview with Official of Jabhat al-Nusra, Syria's Islamist Militia Group," *Time*, December 25, 2012.

Abouzeid, Rania, "The Jihad Next Door: The Syrian Roots of Iraq's Newest Civil War," *Politico*, June 23, 2014.

Abrahms, Max, "What Terrorists Really Want: Terrorist Motives and Counterterrorism Strategies," *International Security* 32:4 (Spring 2008), 78–105.

Abu Ghayth, Sulayman, "Al-Qa'ida Spokesman Abu-Ghayth Confirms Mombasa, Other Operations," www.jihadunspun.com/BinLadensNetwork/statements/agok.html, December 7, 2002.

Abu Musab Abdul Wadud, "'We are Coming'—A Video Speech from Abu Musab Abdul Wadud, Emir of the Salafist Group for Call and Combat (GSPC) in Algeria," Site Intelligence Group, January 8, 2007.

Abukar, Hassan, "Somalia: The Godane Coup and the Unravelling of Al-Shabaab," *African Arguments*, July 2, 2013.

Ahrar al-Sham, "Ahrar al-Sham Criticizes ISI Leader's Declared Islamic State in Iraq and Syria," Site Intelligence Group, May 6, 2013.

Al-'Adl, Saif, "Al-'Adl Letter," CTC Harmony Project, https://www.ctc.usma.edu/v2/wp-content/uploads/2013/10/Al-Adl-Letter-Translation1.pdf.

Al-Adnani, Abu Muhammad, "ISIL Refuses Zawahiri Order to Withdraw from Syria, Responses to Message," Site Intelligence Group, May 12, 2014.

Al-Adnani, Abu Muhammad, "ISIL Spokesman Declares Caliphate, Rebrands Group as "Islamic State," Site Intelligence Group, June 29, 2014.

Al-Adnani, Abu Muhammad, "ISIL Spokesman Denounces General Command of al-Qaeda," Site Intelligence Group, April 18, 2014.

Al-Afghani, Ibrahim, "Shabaab Official Speaks Out against Leader, Appeals to Zawahiri for Help (Document)," Site Intelligence Group, April 10, 2013.

Al-Baghdadi, Abu Bakr, "A Message to the Mujahidin and the Muslim Umma in the Month of Ramadan," Al-Hayat Media Center, July 1, 2014.

Al-Baghdadi, Abu Bakr, "IS Leader Abu Bakr al-Baghdadi Rallies Fighters, Welcomes New Pledges," Site Intelligence Group, November 13, 2014.

Al-Baghdadi, Abu Bakr, "ISI Leader Rebrands ISI and al-Nusra Front as 'Islamic State in Iraq and the Levant,'" Site Intelligence Group, April 8, 2013.

Al-Baghdadi, Abu Bakr, "ISI Leader Takes Issue with Zawahiri Letter in Alleged Audio Speech," Site Intelligence Group, June 15, 2013.

Al-Baghdadi, Abu Umar, "The Religion Is the Advice," OSC, February 14, 2008.

Al-Filistini, Abu Qatada, "A Message to the People of Jihad and Those Who Love Jihad," *Pietervanostaeyen Blog*, April 28, 2014, https://pietervanostaeyen.word-press.com/2014/04/28/a-message-of-shaykh-abu-qatadat-al-filistini-a-letter-to-the-people-of-jihad.

Al-Filistini, Abu Qatada, "Radical Cleric Abu Qatada Advises Fighters in Syria to Reconcile," Site Intelligence Group, November 5, 2013.

Al-Gama'a al-Islamiya, "The Strategy and Bombings of Al-Qa'ida: Errors and Perils," serialized in *al-Shark al-Awsat*, January 2004.

Al-Ghoul, Asmaa, "Islamic State Rejected Gaza Jihadists' Offer of Allegiance," *Al-Monitor*, January 7, 2015.

Al-Hakaymah, Khalil, "Al-Hakaymah Responds to Sayyid Imam Document 'Rationalization of Jihad Operations,'" OSC, November 28, 2007.

Al-Hakaymah, Khalil, "Egypt's Muhammad Khalil al-Hakaymah Calls for 'Unity' of Islamic Groups," OSC, November 3, 2006.

Al-Hammadi, Khaled, "Bin Laden's Former 'Bodyguard' Interviewed on al Qaeda Strategies," serialized in *Al-Quds al-Arabi*, March-April 2005.

Al-Hawar, Ashraf, "The Hard-Liners Accuse Hamas of Launching a War on Salafism," *al-Quds al-Arabi*, September 19, 2008.

Al-Joulani, Abu Muhammad, "Al-Nusra Front Confirms Link to ISI, Pledges to Zawahiri," Site Intelligence Group, April 10, 2013.

Al-Joulani, Abu Muhammad, "Al-Nusra Front Leader Gives Update on Syrian Jihad, Touts Success," Site Intelligence Group, July 22, 2013.

Al-Joulani, Abu Muhammad, "Al-Nusra Front Leader Julani Offers Initiative to Settle Factional Conflict," Site Intelligence Group, January 7, 2014.

Al-Libi, Abu Yahya, "A Letter to Abu Musab al-Zarqawi from Abu Yehia al-Libi," Site Intelligence Group, December 21, 2005.

Al-Libi, Abu Yahya, "Iraq between Victory, Conspiratorial Intrigues," OSC, March 22, 2007.

Al-Libi, Abu Yahya, "Moderation of Islam ... Moderation of Defeat," OSC, May 22, 2008.

Al-Libi, Abu Yahya, "Palestine, Warning Call and Cautioning Cry," OSC, April 29, 2007.

Al-Libi, Abu-Yahya, "Refuting the Falsehood of the Rationalization Document," OSC, December 13, 2008.

Al-Libi, Abu Yahya, "Somalia ... Victory Comes with Patience," OSC, February 13, 2009.

Al-Libi, Abu Yahya, "We Are Not Huthists, Do Not Focus on the Speck and Ignore the Plank," OSC, February 6, 2010.

Al-Libi, Abu Yahya, "Yemeni Government to America: I Sacrifice Myself for Your Sake," OSC, February 22, 2010.

Al-Majid, Majid bin Muhammad, "Brigades of Abdullah Azzam Leader Expresses Concerns to Zawahiri about ISIL in Posthumous Message," Site Intelligence Group, May 23, 2014.

Al-Maqdisi, Abu Muhammad, "A Call to the Ummah and Mujahideen," *Jihadology*, May 2014.

Al-Maqdisi, Abu Muhammad, "And Be Not Like Her Who Undoes the Thread Which She Has Spun, After It Has Become Strong," *Pietervanostaeyen Blog*, July 14, 2014, https://pietervanostaeyen.wordpress.com/2014/07/14/and-be-not-like-her-who-undoes-the-thread-which-she-has-spun-after-it-has-become-strong-by-shaykh-abu-muhammad-al-maqdisi/

Al-Muhajir, Zubeir, "Iko Matata—Yes, There Are Problems," Site Intelligence Group, April 24, 2013.

Al-Obaidi, Muhammad, Nassir Abdullah, and Scott Helfstein, *Deadly Vanguards: A Study of al-Qa'ida's Violence Against Muslims* (West Point, NY: Combating Terrorism Center, 2009).

Al-Shabab, "At Your Service, O Usama," Site Intelligence Group, September 20, 2009.

Al-Shabab, "Shabaab Announces Death of al-Qaeda Official in Drone Strike," Site Intelligence Group, January 21, 2012.

Al-Shabab, "Shabaab Appoints New Leader after Death of Godane, Renews Pledge to Zawahiri," Site Intelligence Group, September 6, 2014.

Al-Shabab, "Shabaab Leadership Forbids Establishment of New Groups," Site Intelligence Group, April 3, 2012.

Al-Shabab, "Shabaab Responds to Abu Mansour al-Amriki's Allegations," Site Intelligence Group, December 17, 2012.

Al-Sahab, "Al-Qaeda Announces the Establishment of "Qaedat al-Jihad in the Indian Subcontinent," Site Intelligence Group, September 3, 2014.

Al-Sahab, "Al-Qaeda Releases Video for 13th Anniversary of 9/11, Denies Reports of Waning Influence," Site Intelligence Group, September 14, 2014.

Al-Sahab, "Al-Zawahiri, Al-Libi: Libyan Islamic Fighting Group Joins Al-Qa'ida," OSC, November 3, 2007.

Al-Sahab, "As-Sahab Video Focuses on Current State of Conflict (Part One)," Site Intelligence Group, September 13, 2012.

Al-Sahab, "Hot Issues Interview with Shaykh Ayman al-Zawahiri," OSC, September 10, 2006.

Al-Sahab, "Interview with Shaykh Ayman al-Zawahiri," OSC, May 5, 2007.

Al-Sahab, "The West and the Dark Tunnel," OSC, September 22, 2009.

Al-Sahab, "The Will of the Martyr Uthman Who Carried Out a Suicide Operation," OSC, March 5, 2007.

Al-Sahab, "Zawahiri Announces Joining Shabaab to al-Qaeda," Site Intelligence Group, February 9, 2012.

Al-Samadi, Tamer, "Rift Grows between Jabhat al-Nusra and ISIS," *Al-Hayat*, November 15, 2013.

Al-Shafi'i, Muhammad, "Al-Zawahiri's Secret Papers," serialized in *Al-Sharq Al-Awsat*, December 2002.

Al-Suri, Abu Khalid, "Message Attributed to Zawahiri's Arbiter in Syria Gives Advice to ISIL," Site Intelligence Group, January 17, 2014.

Al-Tamimi, Aymenn Jawad, "Jabhat al-Nusra's Relations with Other Rebels after the Bay'ah to Zawahiri," Jihadology, May 14, 2013.

Al-Tamini, Aymenn Jawad, "The Dawn of the Islamic State of Iraq and Ash-Sham," in Hillel Fradkin, Husain Haqqani, Eric Brown, and Hassan Mneimneh (eds.), *Current Trends in Islamist Ideology*, Vol. 16 (Washington, DC: Hudson Institute, 2014).

Al-Zarqawi, Abu Musab, "February 2004 Coalition Provisional Authority English Translation of Terrorist Musab al Zarqawi Letter Obtained by United States Government in Iraq, 2001–2009." US Department of State, http://2001-2009. state.gov/p/nea/rls/31694.htm.

Al-Zawahiri, Ayman, "Dr. Ayman al-Zawahiri Elegizes Abu Musab al-Zarqawi in a Video Speech," Site Intelligence Group, June 23, 2006.

Al-Zawahiri, Ayman, "General Guidelines for Jihad," Site Intelligence Group, September 13, 2013.

Al-Zawahiri, Ayman, "Knights under the Banner of the Prophet," serialized in *Al-Sharq al-Awsat*, December 2001.

Al-Zawahiri, Ayman, "Letter from al-Zawahiri to al-Zarqawi, 9 July 2005," DNI.gov, October 11, 2005.

Al-Zawahiri, Ayman, "Open Interview—Part One," OSC, April 3, 2008.

Al-Zawahiri, Ayman, "Realities of the Conflict between Islam and Unbelief," OSC, December 21, 2006.

Al-Zawahiri, Ayman, "Spiteful Britain and its Indian Slaves," July 10, 2007.

Al-Zawahiri, Ayman, *The Exoneration*, OSC, March 5, 2008.

Al-Zawahiri, Ayman, "Zawahiri Calls for Unity in Creed, Attacks Egyptian Constitution," Site Intelligence Group, April 6, 2013.

Al-Zawahiri, Ayman, "Zawahiri Denies Changing His Ideology, Speaks in Interview on Syrian Conflict, Egypt, War with the U.S.," Site Intelligence Group, April 18, 2014.

Al-Zawahiri, Ayman, "Zawahiri Details Relationship with ISIL, Repeats Call to Return to Iraq," Site Intelligence Group, May 2, 2014.

Al-Zawahiri, Ayman, "Zawahiri Gives General Guidelines for Jihad Regarding Military, Propaganda," Site Intelligence Group, September 13, 2013.

Al-Zawahiri, Ayman, "Zawahiri Urges Jihadi Groups in Syria to End Factional Conflict," Site Intelligence Group, January 24, 2014.

Al-Zayyat, Montasser, *The Road to Al Qaeda: The Story of bin Laden's Right-Hand Man* (London: Pluto Press, 2004).

Anzalone, Christopher, "Al-Shabab's Setbacks in Somalia," *CTC Sentinel* 4:10 (October 2011), 22–25.

Anzalone, Christopher, "The Formalizing of an Affiliation: Somalia's Harakat al-Shabab al-Mujahideed & Al-Qa'ida Central," *al-Wasat Blog*, February 10, 2012, https://thewasat.wordpress.com/2012/02/10/the-formalizing-of-an-affiliation-so malias-harakat-al-shabab-al-mujahideen-al-qaida-central/

AQAP, "AQAP Expresses Solidarity with IS Amidst U.S. Airstrikes, Threatens U.S.," Site Intelligence Group, August 14, 2014.

AQAP, "AQAP Officially Releases Message of Advice to Jihadi Factions in Syria to End Hostilities," Site Intelligence Group, March 3, 2014.

AQAP, "AQAP Rebukes Abu Bakr al-Baghdadi, Rejects IS' 'Caliphate,'" Site Intelligence Group, November 21, 2014.

AQAP, "AQAP Says Disobedient Fighter Responsible for Hospital Attack in Sana'a," Site Intelligence Group, December 21, 2013.

AQAP, "We Start from Here and Will Meet at al-Aqsa," OSC, January 24, 2009.

AQIM, "AQIM Audio Interview with Political Committee Head," Site Intelligence Group, May 4, 2009.

AQIM, "Salafist Group for Call and Combat Announces Its New Name as al-Qaeda Organization in the Islamic Maghreb," Site Intelligence Group, January 26, 2007.

AQIS, *Resurgence*, issue 1 (2014).

Arquilla, John, and David Ronfeldt (eds.), *Networks and Netwars: The Future of Terror, Crime, and Militancy* (Santa Monica, CA: RAND, 2001).

Asad al-Jihad2, "The Timing of the Entrance of the Al-Qa'ida Organization to Palestine," OSC, January 28, 2008.

Asal, Victor, and R. Karl Rethemeyer, "The Nature of the Beast: Organizational Structures and the Lethality of Terrorist Attacks," *The Journal of Politics* 70:2 (April 2008), 437–449.

Ashour, Omar, "Lions Tamed? An Inquiry into the Causes of De-Radicalization of Armed Islamist Movements: The Case of the Egyptian Islamic Group," *Middle East Journal* 61:4 (Autumn, 2007), 596–625.

Associated Press, "Al-Qaida Papers: Mali–Al-Qaeda's Sahara Playbook," February 14, 2013. hosted.ap.org/specials/interactives/_international/_pdfs/al-qaida-manifesto.pdf.

Associated Press, "Al-Qaida Papers: The Yemen Letters," August 9, 2013. hosted.ap.org/specials/interactives/_international/_pdfs/al-qaida-papers-how-to-run-a-state.pdf.

Atassi, Basma, "Qaeda Chief Annuls Syrian-Iraqi Jihad Merger," *Al-Jazeera*, June 9, 2013.

Atiyatallah, "Letter to Zarqawi from Senior al Qaeda Leader, 'Atiya," Combating Terrorism Center at West Point, https://www.ctc.usma.edu/v2/wp-content/uploads/2013/10/Atiyahs-Letter-to-Zarqawi-Translation.pdf.

Atiyatallah, "The People's Revolt … the Fall of the Corrupt Arab Regime … the Demolishment of the Idol of Stability … and the New Beginning," *The Global Islamic Media Front*, February 16, 2011.

Aynte, Abdi, "Understanding the al-Shabaab/al-Qaeda 'Merger,'" *African Arguments*, March 19, 2012.

Bacon, Tricia, *Strange Bedfellows or Brothers-in-Arms: Why Terrorist Groups Ally*, Ph.D. Dissertation, Georgetown University (2013).

Badran, Tony, "Intercepted Letters from al-Qaeda Leaders Shed Light." Foundation for Defense of Democracies, September 11, 2008.

Bakke, Kristin, Kathleen Gallagher Cunningham, and Lee Seymour, "A Plague of Initials: Fragmentation, Cohesion, and Infighting in Civil Wars," *Perspectives on Politics* 10:2 (2012), 265–283.

Bapat, Navin, "The Internationalization of Terrorist Campaigns," *Conflict Management and Peace Science* 24 (2007), 265–280.

Bapat, Navin, and Kanisha Bond, "Alliances between Militant Groups," *British Journal of Political Science* 42:4 (2012), 793–824.

Barfi, Barak, *Yemen on The Brink? The Resurgence of al Qaeda in Yemen* (Washington, DC: New America Foundation, January 2010).

BBC Monitoring Middle East, "Syria's Al-Nusra Front Leader Interviewed on Conflict, Political Vision," December 22, 2013.

Bennett, Brian, "Al Qaeda's Yemen Branch Has Aided Somalia's Militants," *Los Angeles Times*, July 18, 2011.

Benotman, Noman, "Al-Qaeda: Your Armed Struggle Is Over—An Open Letter to bin Laden," September 10, 2010.

Berger, J. M., "Omar and Me: My Strange, Frustrating Relationship with an American Terrorist," *Foreign Policy*, September 17, 2013, http://foreignpolicy.com/2013/09/17/omar-and-me/

Berger, J. M., "The Islamic State vs. al-Qaeda: Who's Winning the War to Become the Jihadi Superpower?" *Foreign Policy*, September 2, 2014, http://foreignpolicy.com/2014/09/02/the-islamic-state-vs-al-qaeda/

Berger, J. M., "The State of the 'Caliphate' Is . . . Meh," *Intelwire*, July 2, 2014, http://news.intelwire.com/2014/07/the-caliphate-so-far-flatlining.html.

Berger, J. M., "Zawahiri Falls Off the Map, Is Rebuked by Top al Nusra Figure," *Intelwire*, August 18, 2014, http://news.intelwire.com/2014/08/zawahiri-falls-off-map-gets-rebuked-by.html.

Bergen, Peter, *Holy War, Inc.: Inside the Secret World of Osama bin Laden* (St. Ives: Clays, 2001).

Bergen, Peter, *The Longest War* (New York: Free Press, 2011).

Bergen, Peter, *The Osama bin Laden I Know* (New York: Free Press, 2006).

Bergen, Peter, and Paul Cruickshank, "Revisiting the Early Al Qaeda: An Updated Account of Its Formative Years," *Studies in Conflict & Terrorism* 35:1 (2012), 1–36.

Bin Laden, Osama, "A Message to Our People in Iraq," October 23, 2007.

Bin Laden, Osama, "Bin Ladin Praises, Introduces Will of Sep 11 Hijacker in New Video," OSC, September 11, 2007.

Bin Laden, Osama, "Declaration of War," *al-Quds al-Arabi*, August 23, 1996.

Bin Laden, Osama, "Interview by Peter Arentt, Conducted on March 22, 1997," aired on CNN, May 10, 1997.

Bin Laden, Osama, "Osama bin Laden's Address to Americans," IntelCenter, October 29, 2004.

Bin Laden, Osama, "The Way for the Salvation of Palestine," OSC, March 21, 2008.

Bin Laden, Osama, "The Way to Foil Plots," OSC, December 29, 2007.

Black, Andrew, "AQIM's Expanding International Agenda," *CTC Sentinel* 1:5 (April 2008), 12–14.

Black, Andrew, "The Reconstituted Al-Qaeda Threat in the Maghreb," *Terrorism Monitor* 5:2 (February 2007).

Bloom, Mia, *Dying to Kill: The Allure of Suicide Terror* (New York: Columbia University Press, 2005).

Boin, Arjen, Paul Hart, Eric Stern, and Bengt Sundelius, *The Politics of Crisis Management: Political Leadership under Pressure* (Cambridge, UK: Cambridge University Press, 2005).

Brachman, Jarret, "Retaining Relevance: Assessing Al-Qaeda's Generational Evolution," in *Al-Qaeda's Senior Leadership* (Alexandria, VA: Jane's Strategic Advisory Services, November 2009).

Brooke, Steven, "The Near and Far Enemy Debate," in Assaf Moghadam and Brian Fishman (eds.), *Fault Lines in Global Jihad: Organizational, Strategic, and Ideological Fissures* (London: Routledge, 2011), 47–68.

Brown, Vahid, "Al-Qa'ida Revisions: The Five Letters of Sayf al-'Adl," *Jihadica*, February 10, 2011.

Brown, Vahid, "Classical and Global Jihad: Al-Qa'ida's Franchising Frustrations," in Assaf Moghadam and Brian Fishman (eds.), *Fault Lines in Global Jihad: Organizational, Strategic, and Ideological Fissures* (London: Routledge, 2011).

Brown, Vahid, *Cracks in the Foundation: Leadership Schisms in al-Qa'ida from 1989–2006* (West Point, NY: Combating Terrorism Center, September 2007).

Brown, Vahid, "The Façade of Allegience: Bin Laden's Dubious Pledge to Mullah Omar," *CTC Sentinel* 3:1 (2010), 1–6.

Bunzel, Cole, "A Jihadi Civil War of Words: The Ghuraba' Media Foundation and Minbar al-Tawhid wa'l-Jihad," *Jihadica*, October 21, 2014.

Bunzel, Cole, "The Islamic State of Disunity: Jihadism Divided," *Jihadica*, January 30, 2014.

Burke, Jason, "Perceptions of Leaders: Examining Extremist Views of Al-Qaeda," in *Al-Qaeda's Senior Leadership* (Alexandria, VA: Jane's Strategic Advisory Services, November 2009).

Burke, Jason, *The 9/11 Wars* (London: Penguin Books, 2011).

Burke, Jason, "Think Again: Al-Qaeda," *Foreign Policy*, October 27, 2009, http://foreignpolicy.com/2009/10/27/think-again-al-qaeda-4/

Byman, Daniel, *Breaking the Bonds between Al-Qa'ida and Its Affiliate Organizations*, Analysis Paper Number 27 (Washington DC: The Brookings Institution, August 2012).

Byman, Daniel, "Buddies or Burdens? Understanding the Al Qaeda Relationship with Its Affiliate Organizations," *Security Studies* 23 (2014), 431–470.

Cafarella, Jennifer, *Jabhat al-Nusra in Syria: An Islamic Emirate for al-Qaeda* (Washington, DC: Institute for the Study of War, December 2014).

Callimachi, Rukmini, "In Timbuktu, Al-Qaida Left Behind a Manifesto," *Associated Press*, February 14, 2013.

Callimachi, Rukmini, "Paying Ransoms, Europe Bankrolls Qaeda Terror," *New York Times*, July 29, 2014.

Callimachi, Rukmini, "Yemen Terror Boss Left Blueprint for Waging Jihad," *Associated Press*, August 9, 2013.

Caris, Charles C., and Samuel Reynolds, *Middle Eastern Security Report 22: ISIS Governance in Syria* (Washington, DC: Institute for the Study of War, July 2014).

Center for Islamic Studies and Research, *The Operation of 11 Rabi Al-Awaal: The East Riyadh Operation and Our War with the United States and Its Agents*, OSC, August 1, 2003.

Chassay, Clancy, "The Gun or the Ballot Box? Hamas or al Qaeda?," *Ikhwanweb*, April 1, 2006, http://www.ikhwanweb.com/article.php?id=4507.

Chivvis, Christopher, and Andrew Liepman, "North Africa's Menace: AQIM's Evolution and the U.S. Policy Response," RAND Corporation (September 2013).

Christia, Fotini, *Alliance Formation in Civil Wars* (Cambridge, UK: Cambridge University Press, 2012).

Coll, Steve, *The Bin Ladens: An Arabia Family in the American Century* (New York: Penguin Press, 2008).

Combating Terrorism Center, "Al Qa'ida's Five Aspects of Power," *CTC Sentinel* 2:1 (January 2009), 1–4.

Cook, David, *Understanding Jihad* (Berkeley: University of California Press, 2005).

Cordesman, Anthony, and Nawaf Obaid, *National Security in Saudi Arabia: Threats, Responses, and Challenges* (Westport, CT: Praeger Security International, 2005).

Crawford, Neta, "The Passion of World Politics: Propositions on Emotion and Emotional Relationships," *International Security* 24:4 (2000), 116–156.

Crenshaw, Martha, "An Organizational Approach to the Analysis of Political Terrorism," *Orbis* 29:3 (Fall 1985), 465–489.

Crenshaw, Martha, "The Effectiveness of Terrorism in the Algerian War," in Martha Crenshaw (ed.), *Terrorism in Context* (University Park: Pennsylvania State University Press, 1995), 474–514.

Crenshaw, Martha, "Theories of Terrorism: Instrumental and Organizational Approaches," in David C. Rapoport (ed.), *Inside Terrorist Organizations* (London: Frank Cass, 2001), 13–31.

Cronin, Audrey Kurth, *Ending Terrorism: Lessons for Defeating al-Qaeda* (London: Routledge, 2008).

Cronin, Audrey Kurth, "How al-Qaida Ends: The Decline and Demise of Terrorist Groups," *International Security* 31:1 (Summer 2006), 7–48.

Cronin, Audrey Kurth, *How Terrorism Ends: Understanding the Decline and Demise of Terrorist Campaigns* (Princeton, NJ: Princeton University Press 2009).

Cruickshank, Paul, "LIFG rRevisions Posing Critical Challenge to al-Qa'ida," *CTC Sentinel* 2:10 (December 2009), 5–8.

Cullison, Allan, "Inside al-Qaeda's Hard Drive," *The Atlantic Monthly* (September 2004).

Cunningham, Kathleen Gallagher, Kristin Bakke and Lee Seymour, "Shirts Today, Skins Tomorrow: Dual Contests and the Effects of Fragmentation in Self-Determinations Disputes," *Journal of Conflict Resolution* 56:1 (2012), 67–93.

Dowd, Caitriona, and Cliondah Raleigh, "The Myth of Global Islamic Terrorism and Local Conflict in Mali and the Sahel," *African Affairs* 112:448 (2013), 498–509.

Farrall, Leah, "How al Qaeda Works: What the Organization's Subsidiaries Say about Its Strength," *Foreign Affairs* 90:2 (2011), 128–138.

Farrall, Leah, "The Evolution of Command," in *Al-Qaeda's Senior Leadership* (Alexandria, VA: Jane's Strategic Advisory Services, November 2009).

Farrall, Leah, "Will Al-Qa'ida and Al-Shabab Formally Merge?," *CTC Sentinel* 4:7 (July 2011), 94–98.

Fearon, James D., "Domestic Political Audiences and the Escalation of International Disputes," *The American Political Science Review* 88: 3 (1994), 577–592.

Feldner, Yotam, Yigal Carmon, and Daniel Lev, "The Al-Gama'a Al-Islamiyya Cessation of Violence: An Ideological Reversal," *MEMRI, Inquiry and Analysis Series— No. 309*, December 21, 2006.

Filiu, Jean-Pierre, "al-Qa'ida in the Islamic Maghreb: A Case Study in the Opportunism of Global Jihad," *CTC Sentinel* 3:4 (April 2010), 14–15.

Filiu, Jean-Pierre, "The Local and Global Jihad of al-Qa'ida in the Islamic Maghrib," *Middle East Journal* 63:2 (Spring 2009), 213–226.

Fishman, Brian, *Dysfunction and Decline: Lessons Learned from Inside al Qa'ida in Iraq* (West Point, NY: Combating Terrorism Center, 2009).

Fishman, Brian, "Fourth Generation Governance: Sheikh Tamimi Defends the Islamic State of Iraq," Combating Terrorism Center, March 23, 2007.

Fishman, Brian, *Redefining the Islamic State: The Fall and Rise of Al-Qaeda in Iraq* (Washington, DC: New America Foundation, 2011).

Fishman, Brian, and Joseph Felter, *Al-Qa'ida's Foreign Fighters in Iraq: A First Look at the Sinjar Records* (West Point, NY: Combating Terrorism Center, 2007).

Gerges, Fawaz, *The Far Enemy: Why Jihad Went Global* (Cambridge, UK: Cambridge University Press, 2005).

Gerges, Fawaz, *The Rise and Fall of Al-Qaeda* (New York: Oxford University Press, 2011).

Godane, Ahmed Abdi, "Emir of Shabaab Places Group within Global Jihad," Site Intelligence Group, June 2, 2008.

Grant, Robert, and Charles Baden-Fuller, "A Knowledge Accessing Theory of Strategic Alliances," *Journal of Management Studies* 41:1 (January 2004), 61–84.

Guidere, Mathieu, "The Timbuktu Letters: New Insights about AQIM," *Res Militaris* 4:1 (2014).

Gunaratna, Rohan, and Andres Nielsen, "Al Qaeda in the Tribal Areas of Pakistan and Beyond," *Studies in Conflict & Terrorism* 31 (2008), 775–807.

Hamid, Mustafa, "The Afghan-Arabs," serialized in *Al-Sharq al-Awsat*, June–July, 2005.

Hammami, Omar, "Hammami Exposes Inner Workings of Shabaab, Details Conflict (Part 1)," Site Intelligence Group, January 5, 2013.

Hammami, Omar, "Hammami Exposes Inner Workings of Shabaab, Details Conflict (Part 2)," Site Intelligence Group, January 10, 2013.

Hammami, Omar, "Hammami Exposes Inner Workings of Shabaab, Details Conflict (Part 3)," Site Intelligence Group, January 14, 2013.

Hansen, Stig Jarle, *Al-Shabaab in Somalia: The History and Ideology of a Militant Islamist Group, 2005–2012* (London: Hurst, 2013).

Harmon, Stephen, "From GSPC to AQIM: The Evolution of an Algerian Islamist Terrorist Group into an Al-Qa'ida Affiliate and Its Implications for the Sahara-Sahel Region," *Concerned Africa Scholars*, Bulletin no. 85 (Spring 2010), 12–29.

Harnish, Christopher, *The Terror Threat from Somalia: The Internationalization of al Shabaab* (Washington, DC: The American Enterprise Institute, February 2010).

Hegghammer, Thomas, "Calculated Caliphate," *Lawfare*, July 6, 2014, http://www.lawfareblog.com/foreign-policy-essay-calculated-caliphate.

Hegghammer, Thomas, *Jihad in Saudi Arabia: Violence and Pan-Islamism since 1979* (Cambridge, UK: Cambridge University Press, 2010).

Hegghammer, Thomas, "Syria's Foreign Fighters," *Foreign Policy*, December 9, 2013, http://foreignpolicy.com/2013/12/09/syrias-foreign-fighters/

Hegghammer, Thomas, *The Failure of Jihad in Saudi Arabia* (West Point, NY: Combating Terrorism Center, 2010).

Hegghammer, Thomas, "The Ideological Hybridization of Jihadi Groups," *Current Trends in Islamic Ideology*, Vol. 9 (Washington, DC: The Hudson Institute, 2009), 26–45.

Hermann, Margaret, "Indicators of Stress in Policymakers during Foreign Policy Crises," *Political Psychology* 1:1 (1979), 27–46.

Higgins, Andrew, and Alan Cullison, "Saga of Dr. Zawahri Sheds Light on the Roots of al Qaeda," *Wall Street Journal*, July 2, 2002.

Hoffman, Bruce, "Combating Al Qaeda and the Militant Islamic Threat," Testimony presented to the House Armed Services Committee, Subcommittee on Terrorism, Unconventional Threats and Capabilities (February 16, 2006).

Hofmann, Bruce, *Inside Terrorism* (New York: Columbia University Press, 2006).

Hoffman, Bruce, "The Myth of Grass-Roots Terrorism: Why Osama bin Laden Still Matters," *Foreign Affairs* 87:3 (May–June 2008), 133–138.

Horowitz, Michael, and Phillip Potter, "Allying to Kill: Terrorist Intergroup Cooperation and the Consequences for Lethality," *Journal of Conflict Resolution* 58:2 (2014), 199–225.

Horowitz, Michael, and Phillip Potter, "The Life-Cycle of Terrorist Innovation: The Case of Hijacking," Paper presented at the annual meeting of the International Studies Association, San Diego, April 1–4, 2012.

Humud, Carla, Alexis Arieff, Lauren Ploch Blanchard, Christopher Blanchard, Jeremy Sharp, and Kenneth Katzman, *Al Qaeda-Affiliated Groups: Middle East and Africa* (Washington, DC: Congressional Research Service, October 2014).

Husayn, Fu'ad, "Al Zarqawi, The Second Generation of al Qa'ida," Serialized in *al Quds al Arabi*, June–July 2005.

ICT's Jihadi Websites Monitoring Group, "The De-Radicalization Process of Terrorist Organizations: The Libyan Case," Interdisciplinary Center, Hertzeliya, August 2010.

International Crisis Group, *Indonesia Backgrounder: How the Jemaah Islamiyah Terrorist Network Operates*, Asia Report No. 43, December 2002.

International Crisis Group, *Islamism, Violence and Reform in Algeria: Turning the Page*, Middle East Report no. 29, July 2004.

International Crisis Group, *Jemaah Islamiyah in South East Asia: Damaged But Still Dangerous*, Asia Report No. 63, August 2003.

International Crisis Group, *Terrorism in Indonesia: Noordin's Networks*, Asia Report No. 114, May 2006.

Ikenberry, G. John, *After Victory: Institutions, Strategic Restraint, and the Rebuilding of Public Order after Major Wars* (Princeton, NJ: Princeton University Press, 2001).

Jabhat al-Nusra, "Al-Nusra Front Announces Compliance with Zawahiri's Order Regarding ISIL," Site Intelligence Group, May 4, 2014.

Jabhat al-Nusra, "Jabhat al-Nusra Reacts on ISIS Spokesman al-Adnani (Part I)," *Pietervanostaeyen Blog*, March 27, 2013, https://pietervanostaeyen.wordpress.com/2014/03/27/jabhat-an-nusra-reacts-on-isis-spokesman-al-adnani-part-i/

Jabhat al-Nusra, "New Jihadist Group Declares Presence in Levant, Calls for Action," Site Intelligence Group, January 23, 2012.

Jabhat al-Nusra, "Nusra Rejects Trials for Regime Figures, Demands 'Death by Sword," *Syria Direct*, May 21, 2014.

Jackson, Kevin. "Abu al-Layth al-Libi," Jihadi Bios Project (West Point, NY: Combatting Terrorism Center, 2015).

Jane's Terrorism and Security Monitor, "The Pen and the Sword—Al-Qaeda's Attempts to Mediate Jihadist Dispute," July 1, 2013.

Janis, Irving, *Victims of Groupthink: Psychological Studies of Policy Decisions and Fiascoes* (Oxford, UK: Houghton Mifflin, 1972).

Jervis, Robert, Richard Ned Lebow, and Janice Gross Stein (eds.), *Psychology and Deterrence* (Baltimore, MD: Johns Hopkins University Press, 1985).

Johnsen, Gregory, *The Last Refuge: Yemen, Al-Qaeda, and America's War in Arabia* (New York, NY: W.W. Norton, 2013).

Jones, Seth, *A Persistent Threat: The Evolution of al Qa'ida and Other Salafi Jihadists* (Washington, DC: RAND, 2014).

Jones, Seth, "Think Again: Al Qaeda," *Foreign Policy* (May–June 2012), 47–51.

Jones, Sidney, "The Changing Nature of Jemaah Islamiyah," *Australian Journal of International Affairs* 59:2 (2005), 169–178.

Joscelyn, Thomas, "Jihadist Ideologues Call on Zawahiri to Detail Problems with Former al Qaeda Affiliate," *The Long War Journal*, April 11, 2014, http://www.longwarjournal.org/archives/2014/04/jihadist_ideologues.php.

Joscelyn, Thomas, "Pro-al Qaeda Saudi Cleric Calls on ISIS Members to Defect," *The Long War Journal*, February 3, 2014, http://www.longwarjournal.org/archives/2014/02/pro-al_qaeda_saudi_c.php.

Joscelyn, Thomas, "Saudi Cleric's Reconciliation Initiative for Jihadists Draws Wide Support, Then a Rejection," *The Long War Journal*, January 27, 2014, http://www.longwarjournal.org/archives/2014/01/saudi_clerics_reconc.php.

Joscelyn, Thomas, and Bill, Roggio, "AQAP's Emir Also Serves as al-Qaeda's General Manager," *The Long War Journal*, August 6, 2013, http://www.longwarjournal.org/archives/2013/08/aqap_emir_also_serve.php.

Karmon, Ely, *Coalitions between Terrorist Organizations: Revolutionaries, Nationalists, and Islamists* (Leiden: Martinus Nijhoff Publishers, 2005).

Katz, Rita, and Adam Raisman, "Syrian Jihad: The Weakening of al-Qaeda's Leadership," Site Intelligence Group, April 8, 2014.

Katz, Rita, and Adam Raisman, "Special Report on the Power Struggle Between al-Qaeda Branches and Leadership," Site Intelligence Group, June 24, 2013.

Keohane, Robert, *After Hegemony: Cooperation and Discord in the World Political Economy* (Princeton, NJ: Princeton University Press, 1984).

Kepel, Gilles, *Jihad: The Trail of Political Islam* (Cambridge, MA: Harvard University Press, 2003).

Kilcullen, David, "Countering Global Insurgency," *Journal of Strategic Studies* 28:4 (2005), 597–617.

Knights, Michael, "Jihadist Paradise: Yemen's Terrorist Threat Re-emerges," *Jane's Intelligence Review* (June 2008), 22–24.

Krause, Peter, "The Structure of Success: How the Internal Distribution of Power Drives Armed Group Behavior and National Movement Effectiveness," *International Security* 38:3 (Winter 2013–2014), 72–116.

Kydd, Andrew, and Barbara Walter, "The Strategies of Terrorism," *International Security* 31 (2006), 49–80.

Lahoud, Nelly, *Beware of Imitators: Al-Qa'ida Through the Lens of its Confidential Secretary* (West Point, NY: Combating Terrorism Center, June 2012).

Lahoud, Nelly, "The Merger of Al-Shabab and Qa'idat al-Jihad," *CTC Sentinel* 5:2 (February 2012), 1–5.

Lahoud, Nelly, and Muhammad al-'Baydi, "The War of Jihadists in Syria," *CTC Sentinel* 7:3 (March 2014), 1–6.

Lahoud, Nelly, Stuart Caudill, Liam Collins, Gabrield Koehler-Derric, Don Rassler, and Muhammad al-'Ubaydi, *Letters from Abbottabad: Bin Laden Sidelined?* (West Point, NY: The Combating Terrorism Center, May 2012).

Lake, Eli, and Josh Rogin, "Al Qaeda Conference Call Intercepted by U.S. Officials Sparks Alerts," *The Daily Beast*, August 7, 2013, http://www.thedailybeast.com/articles/2013/08/07/al-qaeda-conference-call-intercepted-by-u-s-officials-sparked-alerts.html.

Landis, Joshua, "The Battle between ISIS and Syria's Rebel Militias," *Syria Comment*, January 4, 2014, http://www.joshualandis.com/blog/battle-isis-syrias-rebel-militias/

Lebovich, Andrew, "AQIM's Mokhtar Belmokhtar Speaks Out," *al-Wasat Blog*, November 21, 2011, http://thewasat.wordpress.com/2011/11/21/aqims-mokhtar-belmokhtar-speaks-out.

Lebow, Richard Ned, *Between Peace and War: The Nature of International Crisis* (Baltimore, MD: Johns Hopkins University Press, 1984).

Lebow, Richard Ned, "Transitions and transformations: Building International Cooperation," *Security Studies* 6:3 (1997), 154–179.

Lewis, Bernard, "License to Kill," *Foreign Affairs* 77:6 (1998), 14–19.

Lia, Brynjar, "Jihadi Insurgents and the Perils of Territorialisation," Paper presented at the International Studies Association's 52nd Annual Convention, Montreal, Canada, March 16–19, 2011.

Liebl, Vernie, "Al Qaida on the US Invasion of Afghanistan in Their Own Words," *Small Wars & Insurgencies* 23:3 (2012), 542–568.

Linkins, Jason, "Al Qaeda's Inspire Magazine Returns, Recommends Forest Fires as Next Great Terror Innovation," *Huffington Post*, May 3, 2012.

Lister, Charles, *Dynamic Stalemate: Surveying Syria's Military Landscape* (Doha, Qatar: Brooking Doha Center, 2014).

Lister, Charles, "Syria's New Rebel Group," *Foreign Policy*, January 8, 2014, http://for-eignpolicy.com/2014/01/08/syrias-new-rebel-front/

Loidolt, Bryce, "Managing the Global and Local: The Dual Agendas of Al Qaeda in the Arabian Peninsula," *Studies in Conflict & Terrorism* 34 (2011), 102–123.

Lund, Aron, "The Politics of the Islamic Front, Part 2: An Umbrella Organization," Carnegie Endowment for International Peace, January 15, 2014.

Lund, Aaron, "What Is the Khorasan Group and Why Is the U.S. Bombing It in Syria," Carnegie Endowment for International Peace, September 23, 2014.

Lynch, Marc, "Jihadis and the Ikhwan," in Assaf Moghadam and Brian Fishman (eds.), *Fault Lines in Global Jihad: Organizational, Strategic, and Ideological Fissures* (London: Routledge, 2011).

Mahmoud, Usama, "AQIS Condemns Peshawar School Attack, Clarifies Purpose and Legitimate Targets of Jihad," Site Intelligence Group, December 20, 2014.

Mansfield, Laura, *His Own Words: Translation and Analysis of the Writings of Dr. Ayman Al-Zawahiri* (Old Tappan, NJ: TLG Publications, 2006).

Marret, Jean-Luc, "Al-Qaeda in Islamic Maghreb: A 'Glocal' Organization," *Studies in Conflict & Terrorism* 31 (2008), 541–552.

McAllister, Brad, "Al Qaeda and the Innovative Firm: Demythologizing the Network," *Studies in Conflict & Terrorism* 27 (2004), 297–319.

McDermott, Rose, *Risk Taking in International Relations: Prospect Theory in American Foreign Policy* (Ann Arbor: University of Michigan Press, 1998).

Mekhennet, Souad, Michael Moss, Eric Shmitt, Elaine Sciolino, and Margot Williams, "Ragtag Insurgency Gains a Lifeline from Al Qaeda," *New York Times*, July 1, 2008.

Mendelsohn, Barak, "Al Qaeda and Global Governance: The Constraining Impact of Rigid Ideology," *Terrorism and Political Violence* 26:3 (2014), 470–487.

Mendelsohn, Barak, "Al Qaeda's Franchising Strategy," *Survival* 53:3 (2011), 29–49.

Mendelsohn, Barak, "Al Qaeda's Palestinian Problem," *Survival* 51:4 (August–September 2009), 71–86.

Mendelsohn, Barak, *Combating Jihadism: American Hegemony and Interstate Cooperation in the War on Terrorism* (Chicago: University of Chicago Press, 2009).

Mendelsohn, Barak, "Dominant Violent Non-State Groups in a Competitive Environment: Insights from Israeli and Palestinian experience," Paper presented at the annual meeting of the American Political Science Association, Chicago, August 29–September 1, 2013.

Mendelsohn, Barak, "God vs. Westphalia: Radical Islamist Movements and the Battle for Organizing the World," *Review of International Studies* 38 (2012), 589–613.

Mendelsohn, Barak, "Hamas and Its Discontents: The Battle over Islamic Rule in Gaza," *Foreign Affairs*, September 9, 2009, https://www.foreignaffairs.com/articles/middle-east/2009-09-09/hamas-and-its-discontents.

Mendelsohn, Barak, "Islamists Infighting: Understanding al Qaeda's Critique of Hamas," Paper presented at the annual meeting of the International Studies Association, New York, February 15–18, 2009.

Mendelsohn, Barak, "The Battle for Algeria: Explaining Fratricidal Violence Among Violent Non-State Actors," Paper presented at the annual meeting of the American Political Science Association, San Francisco, September 3–6, 2015.

Mendelsohn, Barak, and Ariel I. Ahram, "Al Qaeda's Syria Problem," *Foreign Policy*, January 23, 2014, http://foreignpolicy.com/2014/01/23/al-qaedas-syria-problem.

Moghadam, Assaf, "Cooperation between Terrorist Organizations," Paper presented at the annual convention of the International Studies Association, San Diego, April 1–4, 2012.

Moghadam, Assaf, *The Globalization of Martyrdom: Al Qaeda, Salafi Jihad, and the Diffusion of Suicide Attacks* (Baltimore, MD: John Hopkins University Press, 2008).

Mueller, John, *Overblown: How Politicians and Terrorism Industry Inflate National Security Threats, and Why We Believe Them* (New York: Free Press, 2006).

Mujahideen Shura Council, "Statement of Mujahidin Shura Council on Establishment of 'Islamic State of Iraq,' " OSC, October 15, 2006.

Naji, Abu Bakr, *The Management of Savagery: The Most Critical Stage Through Which the Umma Will Pass*, translated by William McCants (Boston: John M. Olin Institute for Strategic Studies at Harvard University, May 2006).

Nesser, Petter, and Brynjar, Lia, "Lessons Learned from the July 2010 Norwegian Terrorist Plot," *CTC Sentinel* 3:8 (August 2010), 13–17.

Neumann, Peter, "Foreign Fighter Total in Syria/Iraq Now Exceeds 20,000; Surpasses Afghanistan Conflict in the 1980s," International Centre for the Study of Radicalization, January 26, 2015.

New York Times, "An Interview with Abdelmalek Droukdal," July 1, 2008.

O'Bagy, Elizabeth, *Jihad in Syria*, Middle East Security Report 6 (Washington, DC: Institute for the Study of War, September 2012).

O'Bagy, Elizabeth, "Syria Update 13–05: Jabhat Nusra Aligns with al-Qaeda," Institute for the Study of War, April 15, 2013.

Obama, Barack, "Transcript: President Obama's Speech Outlining Strategy to Defeat Islamic State," *Washington Post*, September 10, 2014.

Oots, Kent Layne, *A Political Organization Approach to Transnational Terrorism* (New York: Greenwood Press, 1986).

Pantucci, Raffaello, "Manchester, New York and Oslo: Three Centrally Directed Al-Qa`ida Plots," *CTC Sentinel* 3:8 (August 2010), 10–13.

Pape, Robert, *Dying to Win: The Strategic Logic of Suicide Terrorism* (New York: Random House, 2005).

Pearlman, Wendy, and Kathleen Gallagher Cunningham, "Nonstate Actors Fragmentation, and Conflict Processes," *Journal of Conflict Resolution* 56:1 (2012), 3–15.

Pedahzur, Ami, *Suicide Terrorism* (Cambridge, UK: Polity Press, 2005).

Pham, J. Peter, "Foreign Influences and Shifting Horizons: The Ongoing Evolution of al Qaeda in the Islamic Maghreb," *Orbis* 55:2 (Spring 2011), 240–254.

Phillips, Brian, "Terrorist Group Cooperation and Longevity," *International Studies Quarterly* 58:2 (2013), 336–447.

Porter, Geoff, "Splits Revealed Inside Al-Qaeda in the Islamic Maghreb," *Terrorism Monitor* 5:17, September 14, 2007.

Pargeter, Alison, "LIFG: An Organization in Eclipse," *Terrorism Monitor* 3:21, November 3, 2005.

Pargeter, Alison, "LIFG Revisions Unlikely to Reduce Jihadist Violence," *CTC Sentinel* 2:10 (December 2009), 7–9.

Pargeter, Alison, "The LIFG's Current Role in the Global Jihad," *CTC Sentinel* 1:5 (April 2008), 5–6.

Qaedat al-Jihad Organization—General Command, "Al-Qaeda Disassociates from ISIL," Site Intelligence Group, February 3, 2014.

Quattrone, George A., and Amos Tversky, "Contrasting Rational and Psychological Analysis of Political Choice," *American Political Science Review* 82:3 (1988), 719–736.

Raghavan, Sudarsan, "In Yemen, Tribal Militias in a Fierce Battle with al-Qaeda Wing," *Washington Post*, September 10, 2012.

Rashid, Ahmed, *Pakistan on the Brink: The Future of America, Pakistan, and Afghanistan* (New York: Viking, 2012).

Reinares, Fernando, "Who Are the Terrorists? Analyzing Changes in Sociological Profile among Members of ETA," *Studies in Conflict & Terrorism* 27: 6 (November 2004), 465–488.

Riedel, Bruce, "The Return of the Knights: al-Qaeda and the Fruits of Middle East Disorder," *Survival 49:3* (2007), 107–120.

Roggio, Bill, "Senior Al-Qaeda Operative Abd al-Hadi al-Iraqi Captured," *The Long War Journal*, April 27, 2007, http://www.longwarjournal.org/archives/2007/04/senior_al_qaeda_oper.php.

Roggio, Bill, "Yemeni Jihadi Claims Anwar al Awlaki, Samir Khar Killed in Airstrike," *The Long War Journal*, September 30, 2011.

Ross, Lee, and Richard E. Nisbett, *The Person and the Situation: Essential Contributions of Social Psychology* (New York: McGraw Hill, 1991).

Rotberg, Robert I., "Failed States in a World of Terror," *Foreign Affairs* 81:4 (July–August 2002), 127–140.

Ruggie, John G., "Territoriality and Beyond: Problematizing Modernity in International Relations," *International Organization* 47:1 (1993), 139–174.

Sageman, Marc, *Leaderless Jihad: Terror Networks in the Twenty-First Century* (Philadelphia: University of Pennsylvania Press, 2008).

Scheuer, Michael, "Al-Qaeda's Waiting Game," *The American Conservative*, May 21, 2007, http://www.theamericanconservative.com/articles/al-qaedas-waiting-game/

Scheuer, Michael, "Coalition Warfare: How al-Qaeda Uses the World Islamic Front Against Crusaders and Jews, Part 1" *Terrorism Focus* 2: 7, March 31, 2005.

Shabbi, Omar, "AQIM Defectors Raise Fears of IS Branch in North Africa," *Al-Monitor*, September 9, 2014, http://www.al-monitor.com/pulse/originals/2014/09/north-africa-algeria-aqim-establish-islamic-state.html.

Shahzad, Sayd Saleem, "Broadside Fired at al-Qaeda Leaders," *Asia Times*, December 10, 2010, http://www.atimes.com/atimes/South_Asia/LL10Df04.html.

Shane, Scott and Eric Schmitt, "Qaeda Plot to Attack Plane Foiled, U.S. Officials Say," *New York Times*, May 7, 2012.

Shapiro, Jacob N., "Organizing Terror: Hierarchy and Networks in Covert Organizations," Manuscript, Department of Political Science, Stanford University, August 2005.

Shapiro, Jacob N., *The Terrorist's Dilemma: Managing Violent Covert Organizations* (Princeton, NJ: Princeton University Press, 2013).

Shaye, Abdulelah, "Interview with Abu Baseer al-Wuhayshi," *Al-Jazeera*, January 26, 2009.

Sinno, Abdulkader H., *Organizations at War in Afghanistan and Beyond* (Ithaca, NY: Cornell University Press, 2009).

Soufan, Ali H. with Daniel Freedman, *The Black Banners: The Inside Story of 9/11 and the War against al-Qaeda* (New York: W. W. Norton, 2011).

Staniland, Paul, *Networks of Rebellion: Explaining Insurgent Cohesion and Collapse* (Ithaca, NY: Cornell University Press, 2014).

Steinberg, Guido, and Isabelle Werenfels, "Between the 'Near' and the 'Far' Enemy: Al-Qaeda in the Islamic Maghreb," *Mediterranean Politics* 12:3 (2007), 407–413.

Stenersen, Anne, and Philipp Holtman, "The Three Functions of UBL's 'Greater Pledge' to Mullah Omar (2001–2006–2014)," *Jihadology*, January 8, 2015.

Stern, Jessica, "The Protean Enemy," *Foreign Affairs* 82:4 (July–August 2003), 27–40.

Stern, Jessica, and Amit, Modi, "Producing Terror: Organizational Dynamics of Survival," in Thomas J. Biersteker, and Sue E., Eckert (eds.), *Countering the Financing of Terrorism* (London: Routledge, 2007), 19–46.

Suskind, Ron, *The One Percent Doctrine* (New York: Simon & Schuster, 2006).

Szybaia, Valerie, "Al-Qaeda Shows Its True Colors in Syria," Institute for the Study of War, August 1, 2013.

Tankel, Stephen, *Storming the World Stage: The Story of Lashkar-e-Taiba* (Oxford, UK: Oxford University Press, 2011).

Tawil, Camille, *Brothers in Arms: The Story of Al-Qa'ida and the Arab Jihadists* (London: SAQI, 2010).

Tawil, Camille, "Islamic Fighting Group Wants Its Leaders in Afghanistan, Iran to Participate in Dialogue with Libyan Security Agencies," *Al-Hayat*, January 28, 2007.

Tawil, Camille, "Libyan Islamists Back Away from al-Qaeda Merger in Reconciliation with Qaddafi Regime," *Terrorism Monitor* 7:17 (June 18, 2009), 5–6.

Tawil, Camille, "New Strategies in Al-Qaeda's Battle for Algeria," *Terrorism Monitor* 7:22 (July 27, 2009), 5–7.

Tawil, Camile, "The Changing Face of the Jihadist Movement in Libya," *Terrorism Monitor*, 7:1, January 9, 2009.

Tawil, Camille, "The 'Other Face' of al-Qa'idah," serialized in *Al-Hayat*, September 2010.

The Islamic State, *Dabiq*, issue 1 (2014).

The Islamic State, *Dabiq*, issue 3 (2014).

The Islamic State, *Dabiq*, issue 4 (2014).

The Islamic State, "The Biography of Khalifa Abu Bakr Al-Baghdadi, Amir Ul Mu'minin (Commander of the Believers)," July 2, 2014.

The Islamic State of Iraq, "Notifying Mankind of the Birth of the Islamic State—A Study from the Ministry of Shari'a Councils of the Islamic State of Iraq Regarding the State's Establishment and Purpose," Site Intelligence Group, January 29, 2007.

Ulph, Stephen, "Declining in Algeria, GSPC Enters International Theater," *Terrorism Focus* 3:1, January 9, 2006.

Ulph, Stephen, "Disarray in the Algerian GSPC," *Terrorism Focus* 1:7, October 29, 2004.

Wagemakers, Joas, *A Quietist Jihadi: The Ideology and Influence of Abu Muhammad al-Maqdisi* (Cambridge, UK: Cambridge University Press, 2012).

Wagemakers, Joas, "Al-Qaida Advises the Arab Spring," *Jihadica*, September 21, 2013.

Walt, Stephen, *Origins of Alliances* (Ithaca, NY: Cornell University Press, 1987).

Watts, Clint, "Al Qaeda & al Shabaab Merger: Why Now?" *Selected Wisdom*, February 18, 2012, http://selectedwisdom.com/?p=548.

Watts, Clint, "Deciphering Hammami Scenarios & Shabaab Splits," *Selected Wisdom*, March 29, 2012, http://selectedwisdom.com/?p=589.

Watts, Clint, "Hammami's Latest Call Reveals Deceit, Dissention and Death in Shabaab & al Qaeda," *Selected Wisdom*, January 8, 2013, http://selectedwisdom.com/?p=901.

Watts, Clint, Jacob Shapiro, Vahid Brown, *Al-Qa'ida's (Mis)Adventures in the Horn of Africa* (West Point, NY: Combating Terrorism Center, July 2007).

Weaver, Mary Anne, "The Short, Violent Life of Abu Musab al-Zarqawi," *The Atlantic* (July/August 2006).

Weiss, Michael, and Hassan Hassan, *ISIS: Inside the Army of Terror* (New York: Regan Arts, 2015).

View from the Occident Blog, "Interview with Mokhtar bin Muhammad Belmokhtar (Khalid Abu'l 'Abbas), Al-Qa'ida in the Islamic Maghreb Field Commander," November 19, 2011, http://occident2.blogspot.com/2011/11/interview-with-mukhtar-bin-muhammad.html.

Wiktorowicz, Quintan, "Anatomy of the Salafi Movement," *Studies in Conflict & Terrorism* 29 (2006), 207–239.

Whitlock, Craig, "Al Qaeda Shifts Its Strategy in Saudi Arabia," *Washington Post*, December 28, 2004.

Whitlock, Craig, "Al-Qaeda's Far Reaching New Partner," *Washington Post*, October 5, 2006.

World Islamic Front Against Crusaders and Jews, "Jihad Against Jews and Crusaders," February 23, 1998.

Yousafzai, Sami, and Ron Moreau, "Terror Broker," *Newsweek*, April 11, 2005.

Zambelis, Chris, "Al-Hakaima Positions Himself for Key Role in the Global Salafi-Jihad," *Terrorism Focus* 3:41 (October 2006).

Zambelis, Chris, "EIG's Muhammed al-Hakaima Continues to Incite Jihad," *Terrorism Focus* 3:39 (October 2006).

Zaynah, Abduh, "Egyptian Islamic Group: Al-Zawahiri Wanted to Implicate Us before London Plot Was Uncovered. Said Iran Has Its Own Agenda But Cards in Lebanon Should Not Be Mixed Up," *Al-Sharq al-Awsat*, August 14, 2006.

Zelin Aaron, Daveed Gartenstein-Ross, and Andrew, Lebovich, "Al-Qa'ida in the Islamic Maghreb's Tunisia Strategy," *CTC Sentinel* 6:7 (July 2013), 21–25.

Index

Notes and tables are indicated by f and t following the page number.
Surnames starting with al- are alphabetized by remaining portion of name.

274

Index